Roads
from
Past to Future

LEGACIES OF SOCIAL THOUGHT

Charles Lemert, Series Editor

Roads from Past to Future (1997), by Charles Tilly

The Voice of Anna Julia Cooper, including "A Voice from the South" and other essays, papers, and letters (1998), edited by Charles Lemert and Esme Bhan

ROADS
FROM
PAST TO FUTURE

· Charles Tilly ·

Review Essay by
Arthur L. Stinchcombe

ROWMAN & LITTLEFIELD PUBLISHERS, INC.
Lanham • Boulder • New York • Oxford

ROWMAN & LITTLEFIELD PUBLISHERS, INC.

Published in the United States of America
by Rowman & Littlefield Publishers, Inc.
4720 Boston Way, Lanham, Maryland 20706

12 Hid's Copse Road
Cummor Hill, Oxford OX2 9JJ, England

British Library Cataloguing in Publication Information Available

Library of Congress Cataloging-in-Publication Data

Tilly, Charles.
    Roads from past to future / Charles Tilly : review essay by Arthur
L. Stinchcombe.
        p.   cm.—(Legacies of social thought)
    Includes bibliographical references and index.
    ISBN 0-8476-8409-1 (cloth : alk. paper).—ISBN 0-8476-8410-5
(pbk. : alk. paper)
    1. Historical sociology.   2. Social history.   3. Europe—
History—1492–   I. Stinchcombe, Arthur L.   II. Title.
III. Series.
HM104.T52   1997
306'.09—dc21   97-21729
                                                                          CIP

ISBN 0-8476-8409-1 (cloth : alk. paper)
ISBN 0-8476-8410-5 (pbk. : alk. paper)

Printed in the United States of America

 ∞ ™ The paper used in this publication meets the minimum requirements of
American National Standard for Information Sciences—Permanence of Paper for
Printed Library Materials, ANSI Z39.48–1984.

CONTENTS

Series Editor's Foreword

Charles Tilly's *Roads From Past to Future* inaugurates a new book series, *Legacies of Social Thought*. It would be hard to imagine an author and a book that might better represent the high purposes of the series.

Strictly speaking (that is, speaking according to the Oxford English Dictionary), a *legacy* is, first, "the function or office of a delegate or deputy" and, second, "the action or act of bequeathing." I suppose that most moderns would be more familiar with the second definition. In the absence of first-hand, or historical, familiarity with the workings of royal, diplomatic, or papal courts, most who today use the word "legacy" would imagine that the act of bequeathing has little to do with officially delegated responsibilities. Tilly, being famously familiar with these histories, would, no doubt, understand the necessary by-play between the two meanings—and of their proper association with the legacies of social thinkers.

Social thought is indeed an action the function of which is to bequeath knowledge and wisdom about, and on behalf of, the long enduring, sometimes accidental, often baffling social processes with which those ill-equipped or otherwise unable to speak must live. Social thought is always therefore delegated thought—thinking done on behalf of social realities that would otherwise remain mute while working their ways in organizing the intricacies of daily life.

This delegate-function may well be the one office common to all the many varieties of social thinkers. On one side of the field of opinions, social scientists feel themselves called to speak clearly, cumulatively, and with explanatory power of the positive facts of social process. Unlike many of a generation younger than his, Tilly finds nothing embarrassing about this kind of delegated thought. But also unlike some of his own or earlier generations, Tilly goes out of his way (particularly in the early chapters of the book) to reach out to social thinkers of contrary opinion—to those social critics who are more inclined to dismiss the scientific foundations of social thought in favor of, in his word, a narrative approach. The movement to transform social thought into a self-conscious retelling of the local stories of hitherto silent voices in social history is specifically annoying to many who consider themselves delegated to speak the scientific truth of these things. Though Tilly clearly owes allegiance to the scientific ideal, he is generously able to appreciate many of the values of the (usually younger) narrativist group.

Anyone who has known Chuck Tilly for any length of time, even in the most passing of relations, will not be surprised by this generosity of spirit. He is, to be sure, one of the most disciplined craftsmen of his trade. Still, on the few visits I have paid to his former workshop at the New School for Social Research, I was most impressed by his conference room, the considerable length of which was mostly lined, floor to ceiling, with bound copies of the many, many doctoral dissertations whose authors have benefitted from Tilly's hardworking help. Those who have done any sort of scholarly business with Charles Tilly know that one dare not request something of him without being prepared for the quickest of reasonable replies, usually with more attention paid to the task at hand than would seem possible amid all the other work he does. Would that the rest of us could apply so generous a spirit to no less hard work. The worries of some about the future of sociology among the social sciences would be soon calmed.

Those social thinkers who use their good offices to create and bequeath an intellectual legacy are always the hope of the future—the future of social science, yes; but also the future of any and all well-disciplined reflections on social process. I hardly need say in preface to the papers here collected that Tilly has been at the fore of those social thinkers who have led the way in transforming many of the social sciences since the 1970s when his now classic *From Mobilization to Revolution* (1978) was among those works that recalled social thought to sensible structural thinking based on precisely informed historical judgments. With so much moaning and groaning about how sociology, among other social sciences, has failed to produce cumulative knowledge, people have forgotten just how much the more scientific forms of social thought depend, now necessarily, almost spontaneously, on social history. This had not been so much the case since the days of Durkheim and Weber, until Tilly and a few others showed the rest of us the way back *and* ahead—that is, the road from past to future. That the thought of social science is not always in the form of finely articulated propositions should not, as it too often does, distract doubters and critics from the important degree to which its assumptions, categories, references, and findings have advanced in the last quarter century. Tilly has played no small role in this progress.

These, then, are among the reasons why Tilly's *Roads from Past to Future* is the near ideal first volume in a series devoted to the legacies of social thought. In developing the series list I will pursue books written by thinking delegates of an earlier time. There will soon follow a collection of the writings of the great turn-of-the century black feminist, Anna Julia Cooper; and I am developing similar works that will refresh our understanding of other such classic thinkers as Weber and Durkheim. But *Legacies of Social Thought* will always be equally devoted to the presentation of the work of thinkers very much with us. Hence, the justification for the plural, lega*cies*. Social thought today takes different forms, many of which stand well alongside the classic traditions, while others depart rather intentionally.

Charles Tilly's legacy is already considerable; and there is much more to come—a promise that is assured by the very recent (and already widely admired) "Invisible Elbow" which is so appreciatively reviewed below in Arthur Stinchcombe's concluding assay of the Tilly legacy. Tilly is, as I said, both a model of scholarly virtues to which all might well aspire, and a leader in transforming social thought itself. This is why I take such pleasure in the launching of this new series with a book so suited to its purposes— and one so easy, in its own right, to recommend to the reader.

—*Charles Lemert*

· 1 ·

SOCIAL ITINERARIES

How do we get from past to future? If we are examining complex social processes such as industrialization, state formation, or secularization, we follow roads defined by changing configurations of social interaction. Effective social analysis identifies those roads, describes them in detail, specifies what other itineraries they could have taken, then provides explanations for the itineraries they actually followed. Before mapping the particular roads taken by the articles in this book, let us think through some general principles of social cartography.

Social interactions vary in the extent to which they follow explicit models known to the parties; we call this aspect *scripting*. They also vary in the extent to which the parties deploy shared *local knowledge* of the particular circumstances in which they are operating. We can therefore locate any social interaction in the two-dimensional space shown in Figure 1.1. In the lower left-hand corner, where the parties have neither scripts nor substantial local knowledge to guide them, they ordinarily *avoid* social interaction. Nearby, but still a little farther into the territories of scripts and local knowledge, we find the *shallow improvisations*—incorporating a bit of script, a bit more of shared local knowledge—that allow people to eye one another on the street, occupy adjacent seats on subways, or exchange money for a newspaper.

Where scripts are extensive and local knowledge sparse, we can speak of *thin ritual,* for example, in ceremonies awarding honors to outsiders. *Intense ritual* designates those combinations of extensive scripting with abundant shared local knowledge one observes at weddings and funerals; intense ritual gives participants plenty of opportunity for nudges, touches, instructions, and whispered comments within its sacred forms. *Deep improvisation* differs from intense ritual in that it departs from any known script— although, paradoxically, the local knowledge it deploys often includes recollections of shared scripts, as when an avant-garde poet incorporates echoes of well-known verses into an unfamiliar stream of words or when two conversationalists adopt stereotyped ethnic, regional, or class accents

1

to make a point. Finally, *routine social interaction* takes place in the diagram's middle regions, always relying on scripts but tempering them with considerable improvisation; in routine interaction, anyone who stays too close to available scripts comes across as an automaton, an impostor, or a prig.

The scripting/local knowledge diagram projects merely a single still frame from an ongoing motion picture. In real life, persons, social relations, and cultural materials move incessantly from place to place within its territory. A couple passes from slight acquaintance (lower left-hand corner) to dating (somewhere in the triangle among thin ritual, intense ritual, and routine interaction), thence at times to intimacy (closer to deep improvisation). Through repetition and emulation, some improvisations become scripts, for example, when a salesman's successful ploy gets written into the company sales manual. As someone learns a new language, vigilant imitation vindicates itself by facilitating improvisation in that tongue. Collectively, whole populations create new technologies by criticizing established scripts for production or interaction, improvising alternative ways of accomplishing similar work, solidifying them provisionally into new scripts,

Figure 1.1. Scripting and Local Knowledge in Social Interaction

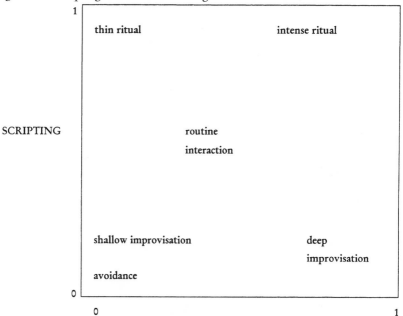

then adapting those scripts as improvising experience identifies difficulties or opportunities for improvement.

These distinctions work just as well at the large scale as at the small. Whole populations that have previously established few mutual commitments frequently practice avoidance or shallow improvisations as they first find themselves entering common territory. Intense ritual sometimes engages a large share of a national citizenry in a coronation, a holiday, or an election. The boundaries of shared local knowledge can correspond to a corporation, a church, or an ethnic diaspora. Routine social interaction occurs among states as well as among individuals.

Social learning processes commonly follow an arc through the diagram's space, starting near the lower left-hand corner with limited scripts and little shared local knowledge, moving upward with mastery of more complex scripts as interacting parties accumulate local knowledge, finally reaching a point where scripting either levels off or actually declines as participants substitute improvisations based on extensive local knowledge for scripts. Individuals often follow such trajectories, but so do organizations and whole populations. In fact, each individual within an organization or a population need not learn the full complement of scripts and local knowledge, just so long as collective accumulation of new knowledge occurs. Figure 1.2 summarizes the trajectories of two sample learning processes—jazz and science—as stylized arcs.

In jazz, the neophyte or newcomer begins ensemble playing with elementary, standard combinations of melody, harmony, and rhythm, moves on to more complex scripts with more freedom to improvise, but—if successful as a jazz musician—eventually devotes much of her energy to improvising. She improvises within limits set by the basic harmony and rhythm attached to the current script as well as by fellow players' own improvisations. Science, in contrast, continuously extends its scripts, its formal representations of the phenomena to be explained, while moving those representations farther and farther into shared local knowledge. Scientists aim to create very general scripts that, when properly used, yield good approximations to, or explanations for, local knowledge. In either jazz or science, learning often occurs collectively, as a whole band masters scripts and local knowledge without any one member's learning everything and as collaborating scientists come to dispose of scripts and local knowledge no single specialist can hope to master.

I call the two arcs "stylized" for three reasons:

1. they reduce the varieties of each genre to just one, when in fact, some technically competent musicians can produce a nigh-perfect

Figure 1.2. Jazz and Science as Learning Processes

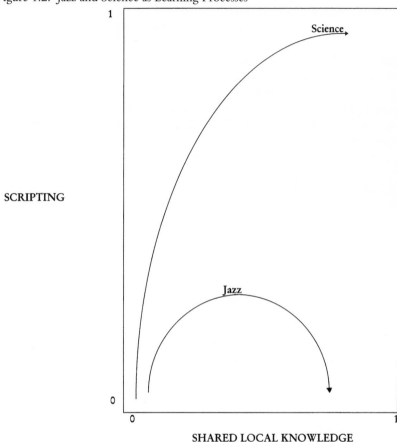

imitation of a 1928 Louis Armstrong record without being able to improvise well together on a simple jazz tune, while some scientists revel in the local knowledge they have acquired of an organism or a geological site rather than in the formalisms that excite their more theoretical brethren;

2. they smooth out the fits, starts, reversals, errors, dead ends, and conflicts that actually mark any such trajectory of collective learning; and

3. seen as collective enterprises rather than individual experiences, no end points mark such social processes; newly acquired local knowl-

edge sometimes disrupts old scripts, pursuit of scripts sometimes generates new local knowledge, and improvisations congeal into new scripts.

Nevertheless, the stylized contrast helps sort out the differences among types of collective learning processes.

Science-style processes typically rest on complex and relatively formal social structures that winnow proposed innovations, select a few, and clip them into place by means of organizational rituals; improvisation occurs widely, but at the edge of these strongly constraining processes. Not only scientific disciplines but also legislatures and bureaucracies follow such trajectories. Jazz-style processes generally rest on more fragmented and variable social structures, establish no explicit procedures for monitoring and selecting innovations, change in an even less unilinear manner, and remain highly open to the diffusion of distinctive new performance styles; not only jazz but also friendly conversation, sexual relations, and shared tastes in art exhibit these characteristics. In between jazz and science lie a number of phenomena that connect large-scale organizational change with the flux of more fragmented social relations, for example, repertoires of contentious claim making, patron-client interactions, and guerrilla warfare.

All these genres are path-dependent in the sense that the previous history of the activity in question strongly limits what can happen next. But the form of path-dependency differs significantly from one end of the range to the other: strongly dependent on organizationally cemented institutions at the science end, more strongly dependent on interlocking personal ties at the jazz end. Conditions for change therefore vary in a parallel fashion: undermining of institutional supports has large impacts at one end, disruption of interpersonal ties makes a big difference at the other.

From one end of the continuum to the other, social interaction operates within limits set by culture, uses culture, and transforms culture. By "culture," I mean shared understandings and their representations. Culture accumulates historically in the process of interaction and locates in social relations. Culture and social relations intertwine to such an extent that one is inconceivable without the other. Only for analytic purposes—for example, to trace alterations in shared understandings of what forms of collective action are possible, desirable, and/or efficacious—dare we separate them.

All this might seem obvious, true by definition. Yet it contradicts a widespread understanding of social life: that individuals and groups (a) internalize scripts in the forms of norms and values, (b) reward and punish one another as a function of how closely their actual behavior conforms to the scripts, and (c) coordinate their performances effectively and satisfyingly precisely to the extent that everyone's behavior *does* conform to shared scripts. In fact, any complex social structure that accomplished the miracle of complete scripting and exact conformity would quickly freeze and crack. Culture does not provide a straitjacket, but a whole wardrobe of possible costumes.

Social interaction wreaks its effects through script-adapting improvisation within limits set by existing social networks and shared understandings. It does so because:

- social interaction consists of incessant error and error correction;
- no one ever has enough information to map the whole web of social relations in which she is operating, much less to calculate the impact of her various possible behaviors throughout the web;
- human beings pour enormous ingenuity into the creation of stories that explain and justify their behavior after the fact;
- those stories, once established, limit people's shared senses of the possibilities and likely consequences of future interaction;
- environmental influences and cumulative effects of other people's interactions continuously alter the likely consequences of established interactional patterns for any particular set of interacting parties.

None of this means, however, that social life lacks order. On the contrary, the secret of social analysis is to follow the outcomes of improvisation within historically accumulated constraints embedded in culture and social ties.

I offer these observations as hard-won yet quite provisional conclusions from forty years of inquiry into a variety of social processes. Since the scripting/local knowledge way of summarizing them has only come to me recently, I can hardly claim that such an understanding has informed my investigations from the start. Nor will I play the game of retrospective teleology, claiming that all my previous work has culminated, and had to culminate, in a dazzling unitary synthesis. I mean only to say that these principles address general questions that have bothered me for many years, but the phrasings and instances of which I have changed repeatedly in response to newly discovered weaknesses of my previous formulations: given the chaos of everyday experience, how and why do orderly social processes seem to occur? Why and how does history matter? What limits and weaknesses do conventional narratives and models of deliberative choice exhibit as bases for our fundamental explanations of social processes? What connections exist between small-scale social life and the processes to which people give such grand names as "industrialization" and "democratization"? How can we reconcile the recurrence, persistence, and apparently orderly change of recognizable patterns in social life—idioms, networks, institutions, shared beliefs—with the tinkering, testing, and tergiversation that goes on all the time?

As Chapters 2 and 3, "Future Social Science" and "Invisible Elbow," in this collection say most explicitly, the necessary reconciliation has a negative and a positive side. Negatively, we must recognize that conventional narratives of social life do indispensable work for interpersonal relations but represent the actual causal structure of social processes very badly; narrative is the friend of communication, the enemy of explanation. We must see that the common conception of social processes as the intended consequences of motivated choices by self-contained, self-motivated actors—individuals, groups, or societies—misconstrues the great bulk of human experience. We must learn that culture does not constitute an autonomous, self-driving realm but intertwines inseparably with social relations. We must understand, finally, that minute description, sympathetic interpretation of actors' experiences, and identification of covariation among a social phenomenon's characteristics, properly pursued, contribute to specifications of what we must explain, but none of them constitutes an *explanation* of social processes.

On the positive side, a neglected explanatory strategy—relational analysis—holds great promise for the understanding of social processes. Relational analysis takes social relations, transactions, or ties as the starting points of description and explanation. It claims that recurrent patterns of interaction among occupants of social sites (rather than, say, mentally lodged models of social structures or processes) constitute the subject matter of social science. In relational analysis, social causation operates within the realm of interaction: conversation transforms language, struggle transforms power structures, daily interchanges in the course of production transforms the character of work. Nineteenth-century predecessors of contemporary social science such as Karl Marx and Georg Simmel took strongly relational views of their subject matters, with Marx building much of his theory around relations of production and Simmel attaching great importance to relational configurations such as the dyad and the triad. During the twentieth century, however, three other approaches competed for dominance in the social sciences: *methodological individualism, phenomenological individualism,* and *systems theories.*

Methodological individualism takes the calculating individual as its fundamental unit, seeking to derive all social processes from the cumulative effects of individual choices within specified constraints; even outside of economics, neoclassical microeconomics often serves as its exemplar. Phenomenological individualism starts from human consciousness and, in extreme cases, ends there as well: in the extreme version that we call solipsism, phenomenological individual denies the possibility of knowledge surpassing an individual's private awareness, while in the equally extreme version that we call constructivism, all knowable social life that takes place in the zone of beliefs and language. Systems theories posit groups, societies, or other self-sustaining social units that have laws of their own and that constrain the individuals within them. Many analysts have, of course, attempted syntheses of these approaches, for example, by treating individuals as systems within systems.

Standard criticisms of methodological individualism, including its rational-choice variant, complain about its unrealistic portrayal of human decision making. While valid, that complaint misses the major difficulty: methodological individualism lacks a theory of consequences and connections to link one decision-making circumstance to the next. How do decisions, as mental events, wreak their consequences? How do they connect with adjacent decisions by related actors? How do they change the world, create different conditions for the next round of decisions?

Microeconomic theorists, from whom methodological individualists frequently draw their inspiration, ordinarily answer such questions by invoking operations of an implacable, impersonal, selective market. Even on economic ground, such a reply leaps past great difficulties in showing how markets actually accomplish such feats as setting prices, transmitting information about product quality, and connecting producers with their customers. Outside of the market world, in any case, no plausible equivalent set of mechanisms exists. The same difficulty besets phenomenological individualism; it, too, lacks a credible theory of consequences and connections, specifying the causal mechanisms that link one state of consciousness to the next. In fact, all three of the standard approaches—methodological individualism, phenomenological individualism, and systems theories—lack a credible account of social causation.

The two individualisms have nevertheless enjoyed a great intuitive advantage: as "Future Social Science" suggests, they correspond more closely than systems theories or relational analyses to the narratives in which human beings ordinarily package their accounts of human affairs. Narrative presents stories observing classic unities of time and place in which limited numbers of self-motivated individuals act in response to deliberation and/or impulse, thus producing all the events worth mentioning, in the manner of a well-crafted play. Narrative lends itself readily to a moral reading of social life, since it makes each individual responsible for her own actions and their consequences.

Our two individualisms offer competing accounts of how narrative works; methodological individualism generates stories from motivated individual decisions within contraints given a priori, while phenomenological individualism creates stories that either result from individual consciousness or take place entirely within individual consciousness. The most strenuous arguments against methodological individualism come from phenomenological individualists who accept the narrative structure, but think their methodological cousins have gotten individual experience wrong. The two schools compete for control of narrative.

Even systems theories, however, have sometimes proceeded in an essentially narrative mode, attributing self-sufficient intention (or at least direction) to social classes, social movements, societies, even to processes such as revolution. "Natural histories" of social processes tell just such stories. Still, thoroughgoing systems theories and relational analyses characteristically reject narrative as an adequate representation of social causation, turning instead to nonnarrative metaphors or full-fledged formal models of causal processes. Metaphors of social complexes as organisms, machines, clouds, networks, or musical repertoires have the advantages of evoking interdependence without intention in quickly recognizable analogies. Formal models sacrifice the advantage of familiarity for the greater advantage of precision.

Relational analysis meshes badly with narrative, since it necessarily attends to simultaneous, indirect, incremental, and unnoticed cause-effect connections. (Take the simplest possible example: if changing relations of A and B to C significantly influence the relation *between* A and B, a narrative of actions by self-motivated actors A and B alone will misrepresent the relevant causal processes.) Relational analysis can, however, proceed quite effectively by means of metaphors or formal models. Metaphors of fluids, networks, and ecosystems, or models presenting similar dynamic structures more abstractly, serve relational analysis well.

In contrast to its competitors, relational analysis treats social transactions as (a) exhibiting considerable regularities, (b) impinging strongly on the attributes, behaviors, identities, and consciousness of human beings, and (c) constituting through concatenation and regularization the larger structures that other analysts portray as groups, organizations, and societies. Relational analysts often recognize the central importance of narrative, not as an adequate representation of causal processes, but as an interactive device, a means by which humans create, sustain, and transform their social relations.

Network analysis offers a simplified version of relational thinking, one that has made enormous contributions to our understanding of how actors who are not communicating directly nevertheless influence one another's actions. But (as Arthur Stinchcombe indicates in Chapter 13) standard network analysis lacks two crucial elements of a valid social theory: a clear account of what passes through its connections and a compelling specification of its causal mechanisms. The essays that follow chronicle a long encounter with network thinking and an earnest effort to specify relational content and causal mechanisms. The effort remains woefully incomplete, but such chapters as "Parliamentarization of Popular Contention in Great Britain" at least show in what direction it runs.

One strand of the fabric in "Parliamentarization" illustrates the error-filled process by which I have arrived at its ideas. Much influenced by the Marxist popular histories of Eric Hobsbawm, George Rudé, and their colleagues, but dubious about the simple distinction between "prepolitical" and "political" forms of popular collective action they often employed, I long experimented with typologies of contentious action that would help sort out the catalogs of events I was collecting for France and other countries. One ancient specimen appears in "The Modernization of Political Conflict in France" (Chapter 4), an essay that distances itself nervously from modernization theories yet argues that structural change deeply altered the character of collective violence in France during the nineteenth century. It adopts the calamitous typology "primitive," "reactionary," and "modern," thus reinstating the progressive, evaluative teleology it has just rejected.

The three-part scheme does not get everything wrong. Its typology rightly separates instances of conflict in which (a) established parties are competing for position within a well-defined local structure, as in many intervillage fights; (b) members of some population threatened by massive demands upon them—notably, in this case, by capitalists or agents of the expanding French state—resist those demands forcefully; or (c) groups that lack power bid for recognition or new advantages. But the taxonomy mistakenly identifies those three circumstances with concrete forms of action (as if, for example, strikes and demonstrations could not embody either defensive, offensive, or competitive claims). It also places them in a progressive temporal sequence, thus inviting other analysts to apply the same typology elsewhere and thereby judge the maturity of populations or movements they are examining. To my retrospective chagrin, many other analysts did precisely that. Result: a muddle.

Four or five years after publishing "Modernization," I began using the idea of *repertoires* to describe the forms of popular collective action. I argued that

1. any population has at its disposal a limited number of known sequences for acting together—shaming ceremonies, forcible expul-
   sions, and petitioning assemblies for one population, formal public
   meetings and demonstrations for another;
2. those established forms change as a result of collective learning and
   of changes in the supporting social structure, but they tend to
   change together as a bloc;
3. times of rapid structural change and/or intense conflict produce
   more rapid and decisive shifts in repertoires than the incremental
   alterations of other times;
4. within the same polity, similar populations operated with similar
   repertoires.

I then historicized the repertoires in my catalogs of events by labeling the
periods, places, and populations that sustained them—for example, "eighteenth-century" versus "nineteenth-century" repertoires for France and
Great Britain or for particular populations within those time-place categories—but abandoned the earlier progressive typologies.

So far, so good . . . but not good enough! Another five years or so of
research and writing on contentious politics (as well as challenges from
students and critics) forced me to recognize three deep flaws of that characterization: (1) it took a narrowly instrumental view of repertoires, implicitly
analogizing them to firearms or bureaucratic procedures; (2) it assumed that
one party at a time learned, used, and altered a repertoire; and (3) it offered
no coherent causal account of changes in repertoires.

The solution for all three flaws was to notice that repertoires rested on
extensive shared understandings concerning possible forms of action and
their links to possible outcomes, that they consisted of well-defined im-
provisatory performances within broadly defined scripts, that each performance linked at least two parties of mutual claim makers, and that
changes in performances occurred as a consequence of strategic interactions
between and among the parties, both within and outside open moments of
contention. The resulting conception gave a much larger place to culture—
shared understandings and their representations—than had my previous
formulations.

This sort of rethinking led easily to the sort of analysis reported in
"Parliamentarization of Popular Contention in Great Britain." That essay
centers on changing contentious claims linking different sets of parties
within Great Britain between 1758 and 1834. It employs formal methods
borrowed directly from conventional network analysis. "Parliamentarization" embodies a significant conceptual-methodological insight: that rela-

tions between claimants and objects of claims form not isolated pairs, but whole webs of relationship the configurations of which (a) vary from one kind of claim to another, and (b) alter systematically as a consequence of interaction between broad structural changes and the course of struggle itself. The essay also identifies dramatic increases in the centrality of parliamentary institutions not only to politics as usual, but also to a wide range of popular mobilization. It offers the most explicit and thoroughgoing relational analysis of all the pieces I have selected for this book.

Surely this formulation will, like arlier efforts, turn out to have serious obscurities and weaknesses. It looks better than its predecessors and seems to fit the evidence at hand reasonably well. But its extension to other cases and its extrapolation to other features of British political life in the same periood will inevitably reveal it to be, at best, an interesting approximation. The most I can hope is that the approximation moves the investigation of popular contention in a fruitful direction rather than into the dead end represented by such typologies as primitive, reactionary, and modern.

We could trace other long-term subjects of my work through similar sequences of trial, error, critique, correction, and reformulation. From my earliest work, I have puzzled over regularities in revolutionary processes, relations between state formation and the organization of coercion, differences between indirect and direct rule, network settings of collective interaction, and a few other problems readers may enjoy identifying as they recur from paper to paper. I have made many mistakes and entered many culs-de-sac with regard to each of them. Yet many of my exits from blind alleys, and a number of my other wanderings along the roads of social processes, have followed similar strategies. Arthur Stinchcombe's concluding essay has it right: just as these analyses repeatedly ask how historical accumulations of experience crystallize in shared understandings about future possibilities that then guide current social interaction, the collection as a whole traverses roads from past to future, then returns repeatedly to the location of present social life along those roads.

The chapters that follow fall far short of a complete inventory of my erratic itinerary. They exclude almost all of my many efforts to understand contemporary cities and urbanization, work and labor markets, social movements, economic inequality, and historiography. Within each of four areas that have preoccupied me since early in my career—ways of knowing, contention and social change, power and inequality, and population processes—I have chosen two or three papers that seem worth reprinting for their approaches to the problems they address. Except for minor editorial corrections, they appear here in their original form, with two inevitable consequences: (1) in some regards, they contradict one another; and (2) they present some formulations I would no longer defend. I do not claim, furthermore, that they all conform to the program of theory and research implied by the scripting/local knowledge scheme with which this introduction began. I do claim that the scheme summarizes some of the more valuable lessons one can draw from the whole body of inquiry laid out here.

I also claim that in his concluding essay Arthur Stinchcombe has done it again: he has identified currents in an author's work more effectively than the author had managed alone. Even if you care little about the historical and theoretical issues this book addresses, read Stinchcombe to learn how uncertain representations of the future derived from past experience constrain present social interaction. His essay gives you jazz and science at the same time. I don't know whether to call his work "jazzy science" or "scientific jazz." Maybe it doesn't matter. In real life, after all, smart human beings follow more than one road from past to future.

· *Part One* ·

WAYS OF KNOWING

· 2 ·

FUTURE SOCIAL SCIENCE

HALF-HAPPENINGS

"Pienso en las cosas," wrote Jorge Luis Borges in *Historia de la Noche,* "que pudieron ser y no fueron": I think about things that could have been but never were. His poem mentions the treatise on Saxon mythology that chronicler Bede never wrote, history without Helen of Troy's face, the American Confederacy's victory at Gettysburg, the unicorn's other horn, and more. Without obvious effort, Borges's poetry vivifies anagrams, nursery rhymes, shopping lists, and descriptions of ordinary objects—trivia, one might wrongly say. Wrongly, because things that never happened are profoundly important.

We could add to Borges's list a Mongol empire that conquered the rest of the twelfth-century world, surgeons condemned to their academic cousins' genteel poverty, cities without wheels, households in control of their own armies, fertility decline in the absence of mortality decline, money bereft of commodities. This roster differs from Borges's: all these things have actually half-happened somewhere. The Mongols did conquer, however temporarily, much of their known world; surgeons in Mexico or Cuba occupy economic positions more similar to that of professors than they do in the United States; cities of the Ottoman Empire before 1900 existed in the near-absence of wheeled vehicles; and so on down the list.

The half-happening of these events provides the rationale of social science. Social science is the systematic study of what could happen, what could have happened, what will possibly happen, in human social life, and why. It differs from poetry, science fiction, speculative history, and philoso-

---

This chapter will appear as "Future Social Sciences," in Wolfgang Natter, Ted Schatzki, and John Paul Jones, eds., *Disciplining Boundaries* (New York: Guilford, forthcoming). Reprinted by permission.

17

phy by grounding its thought about the nonexistent in verifiable analyses of what has so far been possible or has even occurred. But it still concerns that which is not, was not, or will not be. Even sociology, for all its orientation to the present (or, given the lag between observation and analysis, the recent past), concerns what might be and might have been.

Is this absurd? Does not sociology deal with facts, social facts? Emile Durkheim, after all, made much of that assertion. Sociology certainly brings us descriptive demography, censuses, other large-scale surveys, and numerous other fact-finding efforts. David Riesman once said in my hearing that sociology deals with whether what people think is so *is* so. As one of American life's most observant analysts, Riesman deserves respectful attention. The attack on shibboleths and shams by means of well-ordered evidence brings honor to social science. Yet to center the enterprise on social criticism is to hamper it thrice: first by organizing it around whatever ideas lay thinkers hold dear, second by making it hostage to shifts in political fashion and public opinion, third by placing boulders in the path of cumulative knowledge. No, social science must deal with potentialities more than actualities. Indeed, it does.

That is why under the headline FUTURE SOCIAL SCIENCE we can speak intelligibly about social science *and* the future, as well as social science *in* the future. Except for its help in clarifying the implications of one argument or another, making unconditional predictions about the future is an idle task; our examination of past and present gives no warrant for assuming that strong trends we now observe will continue indefinitely or that social structures and processes will repeat themselves in the same order as years roll on. But an understanding of social causation allows us to carry on two intellectual tasks that resemble forecasting tomorrow's weather: first, constructing *contingent* predictions in the form "If conditions A, B, and C occur, then outcome X is also likely to occur"; and second, laying out *alternative* social scenarios that various combinations of assumptions, observations, and causal regularities identify as possible, likely, and/or desirable. Either operation involves specifying what will *not* happen under the assumed conditions.

Let me explain and qualify. Social-scientific social criticism proceeds from the assumption, theory, or knowledge that a segment of the world under examination could be different from—and better than—what it is. Without an alternative, criticism loses its point. To complain about ocean tides or the necessity of oxygen to life may give personal satisfaction, but otherwise it forwards no improvement in the human condition. The alternative can come, of course, from an ideal, from existing experiences elsewhere, or from programs that some set of actors are currently advocating.

The peculiar genius of the social scientist, when it exists, concerns principles of change and variation that show nonexistent conditions to be possible—or to *have been* possible: Barrington Moore Jr. titles chapter 11 of his book *Injustice* "The Suppression of Historical Alternatives: Germany 1918–1920." The chapter asks under what conditions a durable democratic revolution could have occurred in Germany. If the notion of suppressed historical alternatives, he says,

> is to be more than a rhetorical device to trigger off suitable moral emotions (e.g., condemnation of all existing social institutions, romantic glorification of any struggle against authority) it ought to be possible to show in some concrete historical situation just what was possible and why. That means marshaling evidence, creating and testing an argument, in the same way one goes about explaining any form of human behavior. (Moore 1979: 376)

Precisely. In a surprisingly similar vein, James Coleman's magnum opus (or omnium-gatherum) on social theory calls for a "new social science" serving the design of now-nonexistent social arrangements that would mitigate the deleterious effects of the last century's drift toward powerful and all-encompassing corporate actors (Coleman 1990: 650–666).

That new social science, like Barrington Moore's historical analysis, has the mission of distilling from the order of existing social life principles permitting the specification of other viable permutations that have not yet existed. Unlike the economist who argues that the market has already generated the least-bad possible solution, unlike the philosopher who compares the miseries of today with a glowing abstract ideal, unlike the poet whose flights will away the constraints of cost and gravity, unlike the historian who wrings his hands about the world he inhabits in memory of some golden age, Coleman's new social scientist discerns and invents possible institutions. Some of the invented institutions are, no doubt, worse than those that already exist. But some, at least, are better and attainable under specified conditions. Thus social science complements moral philosophy by ordering the comparison of what actually exists with what could be and by asking which moral principles could be realized, and how, in the sort of world we know. Whether or not the aspiration to grand design drives them, social scientists who reliably identify the processes generating past or present social life inevitably form propositions, however suppressed, about what could have been, about what can be, about what might happen next.

Many obstacles arise to the realization of that prophetic promise: the prejudices and hidden interests we all-too-human investigators bring to the enterprise of social science, the resistance of other people (including holders of essential resources) to serious inquiry into human affairs, the sheer complexity of social life. This paper concentrates on just three difficulties faced by the next round of social-scientific work: inconsistencies between standard ways of discussing human affairs and the idioms of social science; presence of multiple, partly contradictory agendas among social scientists; and skepticism about the feasibility of the whole undertaking. By identifying these three as difficulties, I do not mean to say they contribute nothing of value, any more than I say we should dry up the Caribbean because it inhibits easy movement from island to island. They simply represent circumstances we must keep in mind, and possibly modify, if we are to create a more general and effective social science.

Narratives and Explanations

Note first a problem of comprehension posed by the sort of counterfactual explanatory activity social scientists properly employ: it clashes with a widely preferred way of doing social analysis, which is to embed both causes and morals in stories about individuals and groups. Most of us love good stories. Validating in vivid illustrations and apt anecdotes the principles they are trying to expound, compelling lecturers typically weave back and forth between story and argument. That was one of my teacher George Homans's outstanding talents: although the stories George told when playing sociologist were most often summaries of systematic research, his lectures and books typically alternated statements of principle with extended, apposite illustrations; even when you did not accept the principle, the well-told stories clarified what was at issue. Yet the intuitively obvious appeal of skillful narrative is actually puzzling. Why should we not prefer elegant, simplifying schemes that neatly place otherwise disorderly elements of social life in relation to one another? In the worlds of music, of visual art, of food, do we not usually prefer orderly arrays to the fragmented equivalent of anecdotes?

In this regard, work by psychologists Gordon Bower and Daniel Morrow contains important lessons for social scientists—indeed for anyone in the business of explaining social life to other people. Bower and Morrow (1990) describe experiments elucidating how readers or listeners construct mental models of situations someone else describes to them. According to this analysis, readers and listeners (1) translate texts into underlying conceptual propositions, (2) use previous knowledge to find referents, in real or hypothetical worlds, for the entities distinguished by the text, (3) employ the propositions and analogies to interpret new elements of the text, but also (4) modify their general representation of the situation as a function of those new elements; that much constitutes their mental model of the situation.

A mental model ordinarily takes the form of a play with motivated actors who cause whatever new events and changes appear as the text unfolds. Mental models are narratives. "The internal representation of a narrative," report Bower and Morrow,

> contains two major parts. First, an internal representation includes descriptions of the cast of characters, their occupations, relationships, and personal traits. These are important because they usually explain the characters' goals, plans, and actions as the plot develops. Second, the representation includes a mental map of the physical settings in which the actions occur. The settings provide enabling (or constraining) conditions for the actions. (Bower and Morrow 1990: 44)

In Bower and Morrow's experiments, subjects memorized maps of complex spaces filled with objects in specific places within them, read stories of events occurring in those spaces, then answered questions about the locations of objects. The results showed convincingly that the flow of motivated actions in the stories—including such matters as how central a given character was—influenced how well subjects recalled where objects were. Subjects, furthermore, appear to have followed the mental processes they or the story imputed to the actor, rather than tracking the actor like a video camera; if the actor thought about some place other than the one in which he or she was currently located, for example, that other place took priority.

These experiments and the larger body of studies on which they build suggest that unless trained to work otherwise, people map what they observe and learn into motivated narratives. (Whether that tendency is peculiar to Western culture or somehow built into the human brain, however, will remain uncertain until someone has conducted rigorous cross-cultural research on the subject.) Such a circumstance has profound implications for any sort of social analysis: to the extent that an analysis deviates from a motivated narrative, untrained readers and auditors will have trouble understanding it.

Unlike much of social science, such narratives assume self-propelled units, the explanation of the behavior of which lies entirely in their conscious confrontation with changing environments. Combined with the observation that many standard ways of doing analyses in history, sociology, economics, and other social sciences deviate greatly from motivated narrative, the principle helps explain a number of puzzling phenomena. For example:

- Beginning students in sociology and psychology actively but confusedly resist the analytical frames their teachers try to teach them.
- Biography, military history, and new accounts of great events remain great favorites among nonspecialist readers (not to mention buyers and televiewers) of history, while the analytic works that often excite specialists draw yawns from the public.
- Romantic movements within the social sciences recurrently feature bringing real people back in and jettisoning the abstractions.
- Analogies with personal experiences make abstract social-scientific concepts much easier to understand.
- Juries and judges, embedded in their own reconstructions of the story at hand, have trouble understanding the expert testimony of social scientists.
- Critics complain that social scientists apply cumbersome names and schemes to phenomena better understood and conveyed by novelists.

If people have built-in preferences, whether genetic or cultural, for motivated narratives, all these circumstances become more comprehensible.

What should we do about it? If our only object as social scientists were to be popular, widely read, and easily understood, the answer would be obvious: embed what we have to say in stories involving readily identifiable people in familiar settings. Social scientists who have reached wide audiences, such as David Riesman, have commonly done just that. The danger is not quite so obvious: that narratives will distort the actual social process and our models of it. To the extent, for example, that social action results from cumulative modification of its constraints (rather than from changes in actors' motives), involves modification of an actor's decision rules or self-identification from situation to situation, consists of rapid *inter*action among multiple actors, depends on relationships extending significantly beyond the immediate setting of any particular actor, or responds to numerous variables simultaneously, internally motivated narratives misrepresent it. The chief alternatives to casting social analysis as narrative are either to teach audiences how to break with narrative or to find some way of binding narrative to other forms of presentation so each strengthens the other.

Social scientists and historians do all three at various times. Some make it their business to tell, explicate, and gloss stories related or experienced by other people, in hopes of making the experience intelligible to outsiders.

In a highly codified form, we call such a program *hermeneutic* (Heller 1989). Others discard narrative entirely in favor of matching systematic observations of variation in social behavior to abstract arguments concerning that behavior. One codified form of that program is the standard sequence of modeling, measurement, estimation, and testing (Abell 1971).

The third program—binding narrative to nonnarrative presentations—entails greater risk and variety than the first two because it is so easy for the narrative part to squirm away from the rest. Charles Ragin's (1987) variant of comparative case studies is an attempt to make the connection firm. Recent essays by William Sewell, Margaret Somers, and George Steinmetz work even harder to integrate narrative and social explanation. In a similar vein, Viviana Zelizer's studies of economic processes provide outstanding models of junction between cultural and causal analyses. Nevertheless, as we shall see, the program needs much more effort.

Even among those who share my confidence in the potentialities of social science, the current multiplicity of viewpoints presents serious obstacles to effective analysis. Precisely because such important questions are at risk, investigators vary in four crucial regards: in factual assumptions, in causal reasoning, in standards of evidence, and in agendas for inquiry. These variations produce, among other things, distinctive national traditions in the social sciences. Contrasts immediately strike the eye: French social science as a whole, for example, stands out for its recurrent use of sweeping formulations and its relative disinterest in formal confrontations of models with data, while Scandinavian social science stresses formal modeling and meticulous measurement.

The degree of nationalism, to be sure, varies by discipline; it has a substantially larger influence, on the whole, in history and political science than in psychology and economics, for reasons that themselves deserve exploration. Even in economics, nevertheless, we can see such differences as the enormous predominance of formal neoclassical models in the United States and the wider adoption of institutional, Marxist, or historical approaches in most of Europe and Latin America. Because factual assumptions, causal reasoning, standards of evidence, and agendas for inquiry vary across disciplines, groups, and countries, conversation among social scientists often resembles a *dialogue de sourds* in which each party is making the wrong sense of the other's sounds.

Variation in social science's national languages causes only part of the difficulty. Social-scientific work takes place at many levels of abstraction and elaboration, with multiple approaches to description, interpretation, and explanation. For the sake of discussion, let us reduce them to four recurrent kinds of analysis:

1. *description,* in which analysts often use *categories* to bring out the similarities to, and differences from, other social phenomena—for example, deciding whether a given economy is "capitalist" or not;
2. search for *recurrences,* in which analysts commonly adopt *invariant models* of the phenomena in question—for example, invariant models of revolution or social movement;
3. search for *principles of variation,* in which analysts commonly adopt *variant models* of the phenomena in question—for example, variant models of organizational change or forms of economic organization;
4. search for *causes,* in which analysts seek to identify general causal mechanisms in sequences that themselves do not conform to invariant or even variant models—for example, tracing the history of the Cuban state since 1898 as a geologist might trace the history of a volcano.

Social scientists vary widely in their preferences among these levels. The most skeptical, as we shall see in a moment, raise doubts whether even systematic description makes sense, which means searches for recurrences, for principles of variation, or, much less, for causes are total wastes of time.

Those who have more confidence in the feasibility of systematic knowledge still vary in their relative emphases on recurrences, variation, and causes. In studies of migration, for example, social scientists have repeatedly treated the phenomenon like stretch socks: one size fits all. They have adopted invariant models to which they suppose all kinds of migration conform. In the study of labor markets, on the other hand, a genuine struggle has occurred between those neoclassical theorists who insist that all systems of employment constitute variants on the same basic mechanisms of selective hiring, payment, and promotion and those institutionalists, Marxists, and historicists who insist on the great variability of labor markets not only between major types of economy, but within the same economy as well.

Social science's most sophisticated and difficult work, however, takes place at the third and fourth levels, at the edge of the searches for causes and for principles of variation. Thus Arthur Stinchcombe's study of labor control systems within the nineteenth-century Caribbean invokes general principles of variation in examining the differences between sugar production and other economic activities, but also seeks to account for the particular histories of Cuba, Haiti, Jamaica, and other places by reconstructing their histories instead of merely placing them in big analytic boxes. That sort of work, in my view, constitutes the future of social science.

In order to carry on that sort of work, however, social scientists will have to clarify their thinking about the elementary units, the starting points, of social analysis. Historically, social theorists have imagined four different starting points. First, they have treated *society* as a global phenomenon with its own rationales and powers, either in the manner of classic social theory or in the more recent style of systems theory. Second, they have taken the *individual* as the fundamental unit in a manner that goes back at least to utilitarian thinking, but these days finds its clearest expression in the program of methodological individualism. Third, they have taken the *individual-society nexus* as the point of departure, imputing an inescapably social nature to every person, but treating society as a coherent whole in the manner of Emile Durkheim or Michel Foucault. Finally, but less often, they have followed the lead of Georg Simmel and John R. Commons in adopting the transaction, social relation, or *interaction* as their chief analytic building block; network analysis offers one thriving example of this fourth choice. But as institutional analyses gain strength in studies of firms and markets, economics is moving toward interaction as well.

You can see where I am heading: toward an advocacy of causal analysis in an interactionist framework. I also advocate historicizing social analysis and informing it with a clearer understanding of culture, in the sense of shared understandings and their objectifications, but those advocacies entail arguments that would take this chapter too far afield. In the long run, I see a general movement in these directions as crucial to the advance of social science. I even claim to see the movement happening.

POSTMODERN SKEPTICISM

In my own social-scientific world, organized, disabling skepticism offers the largest threat to such a promise. In the jungle of social-scientific theory, skepticism serves scholars well, so long as it operates as a machete, not as an entangling vine. If a skeptical young economist or geographer hacks a path through the abstractions her elders have planted, we can only cheer the exploit. If, on the other hand, skepticism about the accessibility and coherence of social science's subject matter coils around a young practitioner to the point of paralysis, it defeats its purpose. In North America and Western Europe, recent social-scientific skepticism has taken right-wing and left-wing forms. On the Right, reactionary governments and intellectuals have reinforced the partly justified suspicion that social scientists concern themselves disproportionately with unmasking power, oppression, and inequality, thereby threatening existing structures of control. On the Left, the failures of many rebellious movements, the disarray of world socialism, and the survival of corrupt states promote a disillusion combining doubt about all great schemes with fear that our very ways of thought and speech imprison us to a degree that renders collective action hopeless.

At a time when literary models of analysis have gained wide popularity among graduate students and junior professors in North American social science, we run the risk of excessive skepticism. Virtuous vilification of cant skids over into careless condemnation of the entire social-scientific enterprise. Criticism that appears to identify weaknesses in particular theories and empirical claims actually embodies profound doubts concerning the existence of coherent social processes (deep ontological skepticism) and concerning the accessibility of social processes to systematic knowledge (deep epistemological skepticism).

Recent brands of skepticism do have their good points. We oldsters should recognize that (1) to an important degree our own generation's social-scientific accomplishments rested on the questioning of conventional wisdom; (2) on the whole, social scientists do a public service by demonstrating the inadequacy of widely believed misstatements concerning social life; and (3) many recent essays in social-scientific skepticism continue the commendable effort to make theories politically relevant as spurs and guides to action, as political tools, as head-clearing analyses, and as inventories of worlds that do not now exist, but could exist.

Alas, the current round of skepticism also has some dangerous features: failure to erect criteria and procedures for the falsification of arguments; unclear criteria for priority among competing analyses; uneasy statement of ontological and epistemological premises; and, hence, abandonment of cumulation as a goal and an actual outcome of social inquiry. Unmasking is satisfying and sometimes useful, especially as training for advanced students; I certainly did it myself as a graduate student. But it is a form of parasitism that depends on the condition of its host. It does not produce a self-sustaining program of inquiry.

Not every social scientist has fallen prey to uncertainty. Hardly a scintilla of self-doubt appears in Ralph Turner's recent characterization of sociology, or among the essays on the discipline's future assembled a few years ago by Edward Borgatta and Karen Cook, or in Neil Smelser's massive handbook of sociology (Turner 1990; Borgatta and Cook 1988; Smelser 1988). Turner, to be sure, speaks of sociology as a discipline worried about its lack of coherence, yet he presents "interpretative" sociology not as a deep challenge to premises, but as a source of findings awaiting integration into general theories of culture and social structure (Turner 1990: 674). Richard Berk explains how applied sociology can "save" basic sociology—

which presumes that the discipline needs, deserves, and lends itself to salvation. Berk portrays the discipline's troubles as flowing from faulty methodology, rather than from defective fundamental presumptions (Berk 1988: 57–58). Smelser writes, indeed, of attacks on "sociological positivism." The attacks turn out, however, to consist of symbolic interactionism, neo-Marxism, microsociology, and various conflict sociologies (Smelser 1988: 11). Although each of these does have its own characteristic ontology and epistemology, sociologists, including Smelser, have generally managed to treat them as alternative approaches to the analysis of a social life presumed to be coherent and knowable, not as deep doubts concerning social life's coherence and knowability.

The recent youngsters' critique, I think, goes farther. It even goes beyond the venerable distinction between natural sciences and human sciences, with its implication that any study of conscious, rationalizing, reactive human beings require a method different from those that deal effectively with natural objects. It draws on deconstruction and other forms of literary theory to define our supposed knowledge of social life as a set of constructed—or even fabricated—texts almost infinitely susceptible to multiple, changing interpretations. The flags that fly do not belong to Wilhelm Dilthey and Herbert Blumer, but to Michel Foucault and Jacques Derrida.

Not everyone who gives serious attention to discourse rallies to the radical skepticism of Foucault or Derrida. In writing of the "social construction" of the medical malpractice crisis, for example, Stephen Fielding (1990) treats shared beliefs as products of contingent social processes, but nevertheless takes for granted that we, as social scientists, can analyze those contingent social processes and the beliefs they generate in a relatively reliable way. Fielding innovates without abandoning the conventional assumption of orderly and knowable social processes.

The next step is crucial. When Joan Scott criticizes Cynthia Fuchs Epstein's *Deceptive Distinctions* for its appeal to an objective judgment of research results, Scott challenges the very possibility of reliable knowledge. In the human sciences, she claims, "as in society as a whole, contests about knowledge are contests for power; labels of good and bad, objective and prejudiced, are but weapons in the contests. Social science is not then about 'truth,' but about knowledge and its relationship—critical or subservient—to power" (Scott 1989: 92). Notice her declaration's enormous NOT . . . BUT; all claims to knowledge become *nothing but* weapons. This second step takes us into the abyss of radical skepticism.

In a challenging review of organizational theory, Joan Acker has endorsed Joan Scott's analysis of gender and criticized such writers as Rosabeth Moss Kanter and Ulla Ressner for prepetuating the "assumption of mainstream organizational theory that organizations are gender-neutral social phenomena" (Acker 1990: 144). Although Acker refers in passing to empirical evidence concerning gender segregation within organizations, she presents organizations not as observable sets of social relations, but as embodiments of a "logic" that simultaneously creates and disguises gender distinctions. "Feminist research and theorizing," she concludes,

> by continuing to puzzle out how gender provides the subtext for arrangements of subordination, can make some contributions to a future in which collective action to do what needs doing—producing goods, caring for people, disposing of the garbage—is organized so that dominance, control, and subordination, particularly the subordination of women, are eradicated, or at least minimized, in our organization life. (Acker 1990: 155)

What action follows? Not a program of empirical investigation, but a recasting of language and practice—a recasting of which I might well approve, but one that severs the connection between restated theory and systematically accumulated evidence. One foot dangles above the abyss of radical skepticism. Over the last decade, this sort of skepticism has gained ground in North American social science and history. Although Joan Scott and Joan Acker are established authorities, versions of their positions reappear constantly among the young people I encounter in social science circles. Many dissertations now in progress—or is it regress?—will, I fear, plunge into the abyss.

The abyss has no bottom. You may remember the fable of the Indian sage who responded to the Westerner's challenge of the belief that the earth rested on the back of a giant turtle: asked on what the turtle stood, he replied, "another turtle," and faced with an endless reiteration of the question, he terminated the inquiry by declaring, "It's turtles all the way down." This stack of turtles is worse, for even in principle it denies that an "all the way down" can exist. If the turtle story illustrates the Old Shell Game of searching for prime movers (or, in this case, prime stayers), we might call this set of literary challenges the "New Shell Game": the argument that our claimed knowledge consists entirely of unverifiable rhetorical gestures, deeply meaningful for their social consequences, but simply impervious to evidence.

Why impervious? First, according to the postmodern view, because the social world does not consist of orderly processes that exist independent of any particular consciousness. Second, because all knowledge of social life passes through—indeed, forms in—the prism of language. Third, because all communication concerning social processes entails exercises of power. That the first assertion denies the possible validation of the third should not deter us from recognizing a profound challenge.

Spelled out completely, the challenge denies the possibility of verifiable, cumulative, reliable social knowledge. It narrows the mission of the social sciences to advocacy and social criticism. It undercuts all interpersonal procedures for assessing the relative validity of competing propositions about social life in general or in particular. It attacks any claim of superior knowledge and thereby removes all justification for the existence of social science as a distinctive enterprise. It makes one wonder, in fact, why anyone who holds such views continues to teach, do research, or claim attention as a specialist in social processes.

Who Cares?

Why, then, should we lesser skeptics care? Won't the critics simply commit intellectual hara-kiri? We have three reasons for caring strongly. The first is that the admixture of cultural determinism, idealism, historicism, and relativism points in an exaggerated way to a general problem in social-scientific analysis: the inadequate junctions we have so far fashioned between phenomenology and causal accounting, between purposive and causal models, between historical embeddedness and patterned recurrence, between culture and social relations, between language and action. In the long run, no banishment of one term or the other, and no reduction of one term to the other, will deal adequately with the complexity, contingency, coherence, and reality of social processes. The confrontation with organized skepticism should challenge us to new syntheses.

Our second reason for caring is that postmodern ideas have a strong political appeal to the hope of social science: graduate students. They provide the means of defining senior scholars' efforts as worthless and deluded, of awarding criticism the privileged position among social-scientific arts, and of rejecting education in both empirical methods and formal analysis as a waste of time. At least in North America and Western Europe, social science runs the risk of squandering the brains of a talented generation.

The third reason for caring is that we have, at last, an opportunity to clarify the philosophical bases of sociological inquiry. For a long time, social scientists have shied away from ontological and epistemological discussions on the intuitions that they led directly to esoteric, ultimately unresolvable, questions of philosophy. As a consequence, most of us have improvised far too long on the basis of dubious, unclear premises; that improvisation has made the whole field vulnerable to the bitter wind of deconstruction. We should welcome and promote the debate in hopes of creating a sounder philosophical foundation for our inquiries.

My point is not to defend scientism, power plays, mystification, or cant; let us agree to persecute them all until they die. At issue is the capacity of the social sciences, now and in any possible form, to generate systematic knowledge. At issue, therefore, is social scientists' mission in life. Systematic knowledge, in this sense, consists of explanations for phenomena that more than one individual can observe, explanations that transfer logically and correctly from one situation to another.

Systematic knowledge often fails, but it fails less often than common sense or conventional wisdom. It permits relatively accurate contingent prediction and retrodiction to observable social situations. It leads to relatively correct and fruitful inferences from one zone of knowledge to another. It helps its holders to anticipate the consequences of various interventions in social life. It lends itself to falsification, revision, and accumulation. It does so by means of close, continuous, critical scrutiny of the outcomes of its central operations: contingent prediction, retrodiction, inference, and intervention. In order to bet on systematic knowledge, we need not dazzle ourselves with images of physics or molecular biology. Indeed, those who deny the possibility of systematic knowledge in the social sciences have the stronger obligation to point out whether they are also claiming that practical knowledge and the findings of natural science are nothing but constructed myths.

The crucial questions are not trivial. They concern the nature of social reality and its accessibility to human knowledge; they concern ontology and epistemology. Although such philosophical issues often cause terminal boredom, here they are vital for several reasons:

1. Most of the challenges to existing social science claims of knowledge actually challenge the *possibility* of knowledge on ontological grounds, epistemological grounds, or both.
2. If social reality is ultimately without order and/or unknowable in any reliable way, the social sciences have no hope of generating even minimally systematic knowledge.
3. Without access to systematic knowledge, social scientists have no valid claim to prior attention, much less to livelihoods.

My job is fairly secure; I am not worried about my own livelihood, but about the futures of young people who invest years in the graduate study of social science. Anyone, including prospective professionals, who denies any possibility of systematic social knowledge ought to answer these questions:

1. In what sense does the challenge extend to all knowledge of any kind? Does it, for example, include practical knowledge: how to get home, when trains will come, where to find a can opener? Or does it only apply to some kinds of knowledge?
2. If the challenge applies only to knowledge of social life, what is the principle that distinguishes social life, and where does the line appear?
3. Does the challenge rule out the possibility of systematic knowledge in biology? Psychology? (If not, shouldn't we simply push biology or psychology as far as they can go?) If not, is that because of a mind/body distinction?
4. Do all claims to systematic knowledge constitute both injustice (Foucault) and fraud (Scott)?
5. How, if at all, should we choose among claims to knowledge: through their political implications and political practicality? Through their rhetorical effectiveness? Through their hermeneutic authenticity? Or have we no criteria for choice?

This discussion arises prior to, and distinct from, the evaluation of current truth claims for particular branches of social science. Nevertheless, we can well ask these questions in conjunction with the sort of inquiry that James Rule (1988) has conducted for questions of social order and civil violence: does the actual practice of investigation in our fields give evidence of cumulation?

For the record, let me join Rule in saying that social science produces *some* systematic knowledge, but not a lot. Reliable knowledge is always provisional, always relative to previous and competing claims to knowledge. It is not absolute and authoritative. I claim, in fact, we are accumulating some systematic knowledge of linguistics, interpersonal networks, demographic processes, ethnicity, political mobilization, and many other areas of social life. But for the moment that is not the point. We must deal with prior questions: the character of social reality, the possibility of knowing it reliably.

Need I spell out the rest? It lies within our power to increase the cumulation and power of social science. To do so, we must build bridges between narrative and effective explanation, create international conversations on topics that currently tend to nationalize, reduce the prevalence of description and invariant models, emphasize the search for causes of variation—including variants that could occur but have not yet done so—in social processes, shift to social interaction rather than society or the individual as the starting point of analysis, and, above all, overcome the deep relativism that now affects so many social analysts. In studies of economic processes, political change, organizational structure, and elsewhere, these improvements are all happening. We can therefore choose: wring our hands about the impossibility of social science, or roll up our sleeves and go back to work.

NOTES

I have adapted parts of this text from my various prefaces to the review-essays section of *Sociological Forum,* vols. 1–6. The international conference on "Las Ciencias Sociales en el Mundo Contemporaneo" (Havana, December 1993) heard an earlier, abbreviated version of the paper.

REFERENCES

Abell, Peter. 1971. *Model Building in Sociology.* New York: Schocken.

Acker, Joan. 1990. "Hierarchies, Jobs, Bodies: A Theory of Gendered Organizations." *Gender and Society* 4: 139–158.

Berk, Richard A. 1988. "How Applied Sociology Can Save Basic Sociology." In Edgar F. Borgatta and Karen S. Cook, eds., *The Future of Sociology.* Newbury Park, CA: Sage.

Borgatta, Edgar F., and Karen S. Cook, eds. 1988. *The Future of Sociology.* Newbury Park, CA: Sage.

Bower, Gordon H., and Daniel G. Morrow. 1990. "Mental Models in Narrative Comprehension." *Science* 247: 44–48.

Coleman, James S. 1990. *Foundations of Social Theory.* Cambridge, MA: Harvard University Press.

Fielding, Stephen L. 1990. "The Social Construction of a Medical Malpractice Crisis: A Case Study of Massachusetts Physicians." *Sociological Forum* 5: 279–295.

Heller, Agnes. 1989. "From Hermeneutics in Social Science toward a Hermeneutics of Social Science." *Theory and Society* 18: 291–322.

Moore, Barrington, Jr. 1979. *Injustice: The Social Bases of Obedience and Revolt.* White Plains, NY: M. E. Sharpe.

Ragin, Charles C. 1987. *The Comparative Method: Moving beyond Qualitative and Quantitative Methods.* Berkeley: University of California Press.

Rule, James B. 1988. *Theories of Civil Violence.* Berkeley: University of California Press.

Scott, Joan Wallach. 1989. "The Pitfalls of 'Scientific' Feminism." *Tikkun* (March–April): 90–92.

Sewell, William H., Jr. 1992. "A Theory of Structure: Duality, Agency, and Transformation." *American Journal of Sociology* 98: 1–29.

Smelser, Neil J., ed. 1988. *Handbook of Sociology.* Newbury Park, CA: Sage.

Somers, Margaret R. 1992. "Narrativity, Narrative Identity, and Social Action: Rethinking English Working-Class Formation." *Social Science History* 16: 591–630.

———. 1993. "Citizenship and the Place of the Public Sphere: Law, Community, and Political Culture in the Transition to Democracy." *American Sociological Review* 58: 587–620.

Steinmetz, George. 1993. "Reflections on the Role of Social Narratives in Working-Class Formation: Narrative Theory in the Social Sciences." *Social Science History* 16: 489–516.

Stinchcombe, Arthur L. 1994. "Freedom and Oppression of Slaves in the Eighteenth-Century Caribbean." *American Sociological Review* 59: 911–929.

Turner, Ralph H. 1990. "The Many Faces of American Sociology: A Discipline in Search of Identity." *American Behavioral Scientist* 33: 662–684.

Zelizer, Viviana. 1985. *Pricing the Priceless Child: The Changing Social Value of Children.* New York: Basic Books.

———. 1988. "Beyond the Polemics on the Market: Establishing a Theoretical and Empirical Agenda." *Sociological Forum* 3: 614–634.

———. 1994. *The Social Meaning of Money.* New York: Basic Books.

· 3 ·

INVISIBLE ELBOW

In 1714, near the end of Louis XIV's long life and reign, the duke of Noailles found that the aging king had burned some of his memoirs. The duke persuaded his sovereign not to destroy the rest, then took charge of ordering the king's papers for posterity. We can be glad he did, for Louis XIV's memoirs make vivid reading. Although they don't contain the probably apocryphal phrase "L'Etat, c'est moi," they do include this similar reflection on the "disorder" he inherited in 1661 when, on Cardinal Mazarin's death, he began to rule France without a prime minister:

> Of all the observations I will make in this review, none touched my mind and heart more than knowledge of all my peoples' exhaustion after the enormous changes they had experienced. . . . We ought to agree that nothing establishes the well-being and calm of the provinces so much as that complete unification of all authority in the single person of the sovereign. (Bibliothèque Nationale [BN], Parish, Fonds Français 6732)

Crowned king as a five-year-old in 1643 (by no coincidence, the year of the vast rebellion in southwestern France), Louis survived the tumultuous civil war of the Fronde from 1648 to 1653. He and Mazarin spent the remainder of the 1650s patching France back together. At Mazarin's death in 1661, twenty-three-year-old Louis assumed command of the ramshackle state's highest levels. Looking back at 1661 more than half a century later, Louis took credit for restoring order, checking the excesses of rapacious, arbitrary military governors, and creating a rational administration for his beloved subjects. Oh, the beneficent power of despots!

With Louis's establishment of personal rule in 1661, Jean-Baptiste Colbert supplanted the newly dispossessed and imprisoned Nicolas Fouquet as the Crown's chief financial officer. Colbert became a legendary state

This chapter was first published as "Invisible Elbow," *Sociological Forum* 11 (1996): 589–601. Reprinted by permission.

builder. Colbert's abundant correspondence from those years, however, does not reveal sure-handed implementation of a foresighted plan. Instead, the letters and reports portray clever, determined, but often desperate improvisation in the face of unexpected reactions—both popular and elite—to royally sanctioned initiatives.

During 1662, Colbert's far-flung correspondents reported almost daily "troubles." Among other events, they complained about municipal officers of Nantes who used an edict of Brittany's Parlement to stop royally requisitioned grains from moving upstream, narrated a "sedition in St. Julien [Poitiers] against royal clerks and guards who on royal orders were trying to set up an office to mark [and thereby tax] paper," described another "sedition" in Montpellier when inhabitants blocked collection of a royally sanctioned toll designed for payment of the city's debts to the Crown, sent a list of "parishes in various Elections of the Generality of Moulins where we must send troops in order to collect the *taille* [France's principal property tax]," and detailed the repression—1 man hanged, 3 broken on the wheel, 365 sent to the galleys—of an antitax insurrection near Boulogne (BN, Mélanges Colberg [MC], 107, 109 bis, 112 bis).

In each of these events, and many more, royal initiatives misfired, then royal agents tried to repair the damage with their all-purpose tool, repression. On 24 October, intendant Saint-Luc wrote from Agen that:

> Having received at my departure the king's order to tell him what I thought would best serve him in Guyenne I think nothing is more important than to rebuild the castle of Ha. The eagerness of Bordeaux's people to destroy it reveals that they believed it to be the ruin of their freedom and the most powerful rein holding them in obedience and fear. It would give me the means of executing those royal orders it pleases you to send me and of checking the rebellions and seditions that are only too frequent in the city. (BN, MC, 112)

All the while, Colbert, his many kinsmen, and his other collaborators were relying on tax farmers who pocketed as much of the royal return as they could manage, on troops who received their orders and pay from contractors and semiautonomous regional officers rather than directly from the Crown, and on municipal or provincial officeholders who had much to lose by conforming to royal demands for money, credit, commodities, military support, or repression of their dissident citizens.

From day to day, furthermore, the Colbert team gave no sign of executing a master plan. They maneuvered frenetically to pay troops who would otherwise mutiny; to bargain or force enough tax payments for the monarchy's avoidance of bankruptcy; to keep smuggling, banditry, bribery, and plunder from getting completely out of hand; to contain the dangers of elite and popular rebellions; and to execute a few criminals and rebels in a sufficiently spectacular manner for deterrence of others. Only in distant retrospect could Louis XIV imagine the 1660s to be a time of well-planned reorganization in a disorderly country.

Yet a new order did emerge from the effort of that powerful duo, Colbert and Louis XIV (Dessert and Journet 1975; Dessert 1984). By 1714, Louis and his great administrative corps did in fact regularize taxation, circumscribe great financiers, subordinate most regional magnates to royal power, insert effective royally controlled intendants and other officers in their places, subdue noble-led private armies that had ravaged the seventeenth-century French countryside, reduce once-proud cities and provinces of Protestant hegemony to a few pockets of popular resistance, and enormously augment the power of king and ministers. They did so, to be sure, at the price of creating or confirming revenue-generating rights for nobles, officeholders, courts, parlements, clergy, municipalities, and guilds—rights that would eventually block further royal reorganization and contribute to the crisis opening the French Revolution of 1789. But Louis XIV, approaching death, could rightfully claim to have driven a momentous consolidation of royal power during his seven-decade reign. What he could *not* reasonably claim is to have anticipated the consequences of his agents' actions at each step along the rock-strewn road.

A seventeenth-century Robert Merton could have told him so. Merton's famous 1936 "Unanticipated Consequences of Purposive Social Action" initiated (no doubt in unanticipated fashion) a whole series of Mertonian ideas: on self-fulfilling prophecies, on social structure and anomie, on socially expected durations, on invisible colleges, on specified ignorance. Merton's article enumerates several reasons why purposive actions often fail to produce their expected outcomes: limits to existing causal knowledge, time and effort required to amass essential information, erroneous evaluation of the situation, blockage of analysis by interest, conformity of action to prescriptive values rather than means–end reasoning, influence of predictions on the actions of participants in outcomes. It then ends with a plea for systematic study of such obstacles to planning in the hope of specifying conditions in which wise planning remains possible. In the context of the New Deal that Franklin D. Roosevelt was then offering to Americans, we can read Merton's 1936 analysis either as a call for enlightened intervention or as a warning of disappointments to come.

Of course, with his unanticipated consequences—as the author of *On the Shoulders of Giants* was the first to declare—Merton picked up ideas that had been laid down by much earlier thinkers, including Adam Smith's conception of the "Invisible Hand" that fashions beneficent collective consequences from narrow self-interest, not to mention frequent conservative arguments concerning the generally perverse effect of deliberate social interventions (Hirschman 1977, 1991; Schneider 1975; Smith 1910; Wrigley 1987). Institutional and evolutionary economists who emphasize limits on optimization set by costs of acquiring information directly intersect one part of Merton's argument (Coase 1952, 1992; Nelson 1995; North 1991). With somewhat more indirectness, Merton also influenced such subsequent inquiries as Vilhelm Aubert's treatments of predictability and chance in social life (Aubert 1965). In 1936, Merton struck a resounding gong.

Nevertheless, Merton played only half the tune: he enumerated good reasons why purposive action so regularly produces unexpected outcomes, thus challenging all rational-action accounts of social behavior. But he left untouched the problem's other half: how purposive social action nonetheless produces systematic, durable social structure. The answer, it seems to me, lies first in substituting social *inter*action for individual action, then in applying four principles:

1. As gauged by intentions or by models available to the participants, all social interaction contains incessant errors, constantly corrected.
2. People draw their correction mechanisms from historically accumulated shared understandings, from culture.
3. Interaction occurs within constraining webs of previously established social relations, which it alters incrementally.
4. Both culture and social relations change systematically, interacting to lay down durable social structure.

System inheres not only in available alternatives and patterns of choice among them, but also in orderly constraints on error correction set by culture, social ties, their interaction, and their change.

Onetime Merton student Viviana Zelizer's superb analyses of life insurance, valuation of children, and monetary distinctions repeatedly demonstrate how ostensibly rationalizing institutions produce unexpected consequences through their intersection with shared understandings and established social ties. Where most students of monetization, for example, have supposed that it invariably depersonalizes the transactions involved, Zelizer shows us how people recast money itself to represent different varieties of social relations (Zelizer 1994). Instead of the conventional three-way distinction among rational action, chance, and irrationality, Zelizer insists on a fourth possibility: social involvements of actors that produce their own patterned consequences, thus baffling chance, irrationality, and stark rationalization alike. An effective Zelizerian sequel to Merton's article might bear the title "The Unanticipated—but Systematic—Consequences of Purposive Social Interaction."

For the Invisible Hand, let's substitute the Invisible Elbow. Coming home from the grocery store, arms overflowing with food-filled bags, you wedge yourself against the doorjamb, somehow free a hand to open the kitchen door, enter the house, then nudge the door closed with your elbow. Because elbows are not prehensile and, in this situation, not visible either, you sometimes slam the door smartly, sometimes swing the door halfway closed, sometimes miss completely on the first pass, sometimes bruise your arm on the wood, sometimes shatter the glass, and sometimes— responding to one of these earlier calamities—spill groceries all over the kitchen floor.

You, your elbow, the groceries, and the kitchen have systematic properties that strongly limit the likely consequences of your attempted nudge. Over many trips to the grocery store, which of these outcomes occurs forms a frequency distribution with stable probabilities modified by learning. With practice, you may get your door-closing average up to .900. After a calamitous elbow shot, however, you tell a story not of frequency distributions, but of good intentions frustrated by bad circumstances: the floor was wet, children left toys just inside the door, the grocery bagger put heavy items on top, or something of the sort. Thus we latter-day Louis XIVs save the belief in rational action, at least our own.

Don't hear my analysis as an irrationalist model of social life. Despite the fact that batters rationally aim to hit safely on almost every swing, over the long run, few major-league baseball players ever maintain batting averages even a third of the way to .900. As Herbert Simon has taught us to understand, instead of true maximizing, most of us mostly "satisfice" by settling for the first outcome of our efforts that falls within an acceptable zone (Simon 1976, 1991). Despite the appeal of solipsism to postmodernists and paranoids, faulty everyday talk contains enough redundancy and error correction to convey meanings from one person to another. Even great dancers make constant adjustments to their own and their partners' almost imperceptible deviations from choreographed movements. Life is like that. The big differences among persons and groups lie not in the frequency with which they make mistakes, but in the speed, frequency, and manner of their correction. Smart people correct their many errors fast and well.

All life, I am claiming, fills with erroneous interactions, therefore with unanticipated consequences. But life also teems with error correction and responses, sometimes almost instantaneous, to unexpected outcomes. In conversation, we incessantly utter mistakes, receive signals from ourselves or others that mark our errors, then repair them so quickly and well that no one notices unless a witness replays the tape. Erving Goffman delighted in collecting errors and repairs in radio announcing, for example:

> Disc Jockey: "And now a record by Little Willie John . . . here's 'Sleep-Sleep-Sleep' . . . By the way, did you get any last night? . . . (*pause*) . . . SLEEP, that is! (Goffman 1981: 217)

Or the more subtle:

> So all you do when you are on your way home is, stop by at Korvette's and leave your odor . . . ORDER!!! (Goffman 1981: 216)

Only transcription of the text, or replay of the tape, captures the odor of the disorder.

Mention of "the tape" recalls a Toronto experience. I came to Toronto in 1966 after teaching at Harvard, where I could hardly get through a sentence without a question or challenge from one of my students. What a shock to lecture Toronto students and find them dutifully and silently writing down whatever nonsense I spoke! Looking at the tops of Canadian heads bent over paper so unnerved me that a few lectures into my course on cities, I stopped my presentation to say, "Let's make a deal. If you'll agree not to take notes, I'll agree to tape my lectures and give you full transcripts." The students accepted my proposal. I did my part, they did theirs, and an unanticipated ordeal began.

Tapes and transcripts revealed something I should have known, but had never quite recognized: lecturing from notes, however orderly, I hardly ever uttered a complete sentence. Even intact sentences often mixed metaphors or switched grammatical direction. I interrupted myself, introduced new points that suddenly came to mind, modified or even contradicted arguments incessantly. When students intervened—as they now did more frequently—syntax fled in disarray. I had discovered the difference between writing and conversation. I could not bear to distribute accurate transcripts and found myself staying up very late, like Louis XIV, to rewrite the record of what had happened in my domain. I never taped another course.

Nevertheless, my recasting of those lectures had systematic properties resulting from interplay between conventions of English prose and messages I sought to impress, however erroneously, on my Toronto audience. Here, distinctions among conformity, error, and innovation began to blur. They operate under similar constraints from shared understandings and established social relations. Note African Americans' recent move toward innovative and African-sounding names for newborn children. Stanley Lieberson and Kelly Mikelson show that, on the average, such names incorporate sound patterns and gender markers that correspond closely not to African, but to American English, patterns (Lieberson and Mikelson 1995). Innovation gains its intelligibility from relations to previously established practices.

When working in Toronto, I asked my three eldest children to draw maps of the city from memory (Tilly 1967). Seven-year-old Laura drew an area bounded on the west (left) and the north (up) by the closest major thoroughfares to our house, placed the block containing our house prominently in the lower left (southwest) corner, displayed two more adjacent blocks (one with major areas marked "playground," "grass," and "working"), and sketched in a few other schematic streets, both vertical and horizontal. Nine-year-old Kit bounded her map vertically with the southward-flowing Humber and Don Rivers, placed the McDonald-Cartier Freeway at the northern limits, and limned in a gridwork of vertical and horizontal streets centering almost precisely on our home block. Chris, then eleven, produced a wondrously detailed map of the metropolis, complete with north, east, south, and west compass points. In Lake Ontario, he placed a presentable outline of Toronto Island, then next to it a blob labeled "this represents all other islands." All three children innovated delightfully. But all three also followed conventions of mapmaking they had somehow absorbed from schooling and everyday practice: north to the top, streets horizontal and vertical within that frame, major boundaries defined by waterways and big thoroughfares.

Of course, my children were responding not just to convention, but to verifiable features of the Toronto cityscape, all of which they had observed piecemeal even if they had never regarded all of them simultaneously. Indeed, their maps identified common features of Toronto, Cleveland, Chicago, Milwaukee, and other lakeside cities—features that themselves resulted from the interplay of topography, city-building conventions, and the incremental error-filled interactions of local residents. At all these levels, innovation, error, and conformity alike operate within constraints set by previous understandings and practices; they thereby produce intelligible structure.

Here, we encounter another paradox, for those very regularities define possibilities that could occur, but do not—at least not yet. Sound social science concerns counterfactuals: explaining what actually occurs, which ironically requires specifying what did *not* occur but could have occurred, then comparing factual with counterfactual. The central work of social science consists of specifying nonexistent social structures and processes that were possible, that are now possible, that under specifiable circumstances will be possible. Strong explanations do just that, comparing observed states with other possible states, using known cuases to account for the differences. Game theory and Markov processes gain some of their intuitive appeal as representations of social life because they explicitly represent choice points, hence counterfactuals.

Counterfactual explanation makes social science a powerful complement to ethics and politics. In his renowned lecture "Science as a Vocation," Max Weber touched on this realization, but reduced it to the observation that if you choose a certain end, scientific experience can teach "you have to use such and such a *means* in order to carry out your conviction practically" (Gerth and Mills 1946: 151). If actors could actually anticipate consequences of their chosen actions and then produce the actions without error, we would indeed only need to sort intentions and preferences.

Much more, however, lies beyond that point. Every ethical or political proposal imports, however covertly, a theory of the possible, a selection among alternative actions that theory names as possible, and causal arguments relating actions to outcomes. To advocate turning away aspiring immigrants in order to protect your country's existing workers against unfair competition invokes a theory of competition, an argument concerning the probable effects of immigration and suppositions about the efficacy of anti-migration controls.

Even short of adjudicating fairness, social scientists have much to say about ethically implicated theories of possibility, selections among possible actions, and causal arguments. However one comes down on the question, to the extent that it generates reliable knowledge of causes and possibilities, social science obviously bears on ethical and political choices. For that very reason, assertions of social science's explanatory power regularly stir passions rarely seen in discussions of astronomy and geology: they constitute claims to pronounce on the possibility assumptions of religious, moral, and political doctrines.

Incessant error intersects with counterfactual explanation at two different points. First, the order-producing imbrication of error-filled interaction in shared understandings and interpersonal networks constitutes a causal domain requiring explanation of what actually happens along with what else might have happened. Second, the implicit computation of possible interactions and their possible outcomes that inheres in every initiation of interaction, erroneous or otherwise, takes place within limits set by the actor's social location and the previous history of the interaction in question. That constraint on decision making itself requires counterfactual explanation. Any explanation of social processes worth its salt must account both for social interaction and for its consequences in the face of omnipresent constraint and error.

I certainly didn't discover these principles. Merton's analysis of unanticipated consequences more or less implies them. Camouflaged, they frequently enter literary territory as might-have-beens, as speculations on other available choices one could have made, other possible outcomes of choices actually made. In a self-congratulatory mode, Robert Frost told the story of having to decide between two roads that branched in the woods, never to know the other one's itinerary:

> I shall be telling this with a sigh,
> Somewhere ages and ages hence:
> Two roads diverged in a wood, and I—
> I took the one less traveled by,
> And that has made all the difference.
> ("The Road Not Taken," in Frost 1916: 9)

But grimmer variants also recur, reducing competing possibilities to chance or questioning whether one trajectory has any more meaning than another. Poet-novelist Paul Auster voices the despairing version powerfully:

> It comes down to this: that everything should count, that everything should be a part of it, even the things I do not or cannot understand. The desire, for example, to destroy everything I have written so far. Not from any revulsion at the inadequacy of these words (although that remains a distinct possibility), but rather from the need to remind myself, at each moment, that things do not have to happen this way, that there is always another way, neither better nor worse, in which things might take shape. I realize in the end that I am probably powerless to affect the outcome of even the least thing that happens, but nevertheless, and in spite of myself, as if in an act of blind faith, I want to assume full responsibility. (Auster 1988: 110)

Somewhere between boastful Frost and despairing Auster we hear the music of chance, the counterfactual canticle of modest successful persons, pleading for contradiction: "I've just been lucky; I was in the right place at the right time," which implies strongly that something else could just as easily have happened and that someone else in the same location would have done as well. Joseph Conrad put it well:

> I follow the instincts of vainglory and humility natural to all mankind.
> For it can hardly be denied that it is not their own deserts that men are
> most proud of, but rather of their prodigious luck, of their marvellous
> fortune, of that in their lives for which thanks and sacrifices must be
> offered on the altars of the inscrutable gods. (Conrad 1995: 4)

To challenge such self-deprecation does not necessarily deny the other possibilities; the heroine gains even more credit if her grit, wit, or resourceful-
ness explains why she did not fall into the counterfactuals. (Although fear
of having to explain what I do for a living and why has always kept me
away from school reunions, they fascinate me as occasions for observing
what other paths one might have followed from the same point of origin.)
In social science itself, the idea of alternative possibilities spreads far beyond
game theory and Markov chains. It appears in the recurrent impulse to
contrast meaningful but fallible human agency with both random behavior
and instrumental rationality.

Responses to error, in any case, are neither instinctual nor random;
they draw on historically accumulated shared understandings, on culture.
They also take place within constraining webs of previously established
social relations and, in the process, alter those webs incrementally. Culture
and social relations, however, do not alter unpredictably; they interact, and
they obey strong constraints as they interact.

Take the analogy with mechanical inventions (Petroski 1992; see also
Norman 1990): the vast majority of inventions emerge from criticism of
previous devices meant for similar purposes. Inventors design and justify
new can openers as superior versions of previous can openers, new engines
as superior versions of previous engines. As patent applications testify elo-
quently, inventions therefore incorporate many existing features of those
devices, not to mention accumulated understandings concerning how they
work and what uses they serve. Because their effectiveness depends on the
fit among elements, as well as on their articulation with the receiving social
environment, new devices often work less well than their predecessors, at
least initially. For that reason, even famous industrial designer Raymond
Loewy declared that he aimed not for the limit of what current technology
made possible, but for the "most advanced yet acceptable" design (Petroski
1992: 248). Such connections make invention a culturally conditioned,
intensely path-dependent process. They belie any distinction between
technology and culture.

Adoption of new inventions, accordingly, depends intimately on inventors' or, more often, entrepreneurs' access to existing networks connecting potential users. Invention and improvement of the sewing

machine's successive versions, for instance, depended heavily on interaction between such inventor-entrepreneurs as Isaac Singer and various possible customers for different variants of the machine. Others invented sewing machines well before Singer without being able to secure their widespread adoption. Singer was no technical genius, but he had a sharp eye for possible adaptations of his product to new uses; he spent much of his time seeking out potential users, creating appropriate variants of his machine, and selling their adoption. He facilitated the interplay between technology and market (Thomson 1984).

The combination of cultural path-dependency and network embeddedness, in short, means the consequences of all social interaction, erroneous from the actors' viewpoint or otherwise, pass through powerful, systematic constraints, modifying established patterns instead of striking out alone in an empty causal space. Even revolutions depend heavily for their form and content on the regimes they replace (Goodwin 1994a, 1994b). How much more so for everyday error-filled social interaction!

Similar ideas motivate my recent studies of contentious repertoires: arrays of means by which actors within a polity make collective claims on other actors—claims that, if realized, would affect their objects' interests. Careful catalogs of gatherings in which people made collective claims in Great Britain from the 1750s to the 1830s provide strong evidence of significant variation and change in contentious repertoires. But they also establish two points of greater importance for present purposes:

> *First,* for any given pair of political actors at a given time, the range of collective claim-making performances they could stage reduced to a tiny number compared with the interactions that in principle they could have produced.
>
> *Second,* changes in such repertoires of claim-making performances occurred in bursts, as products of intense strategic interaction, as innovations at the edge of established performances.

Over the long run of the eighteenth and nineteenth centuries, British contenders largely abandoned donkeying, seizures of grain, Rough Music, and related once-prevalent ways to make claims in favor of demonstrations, marches, public meetings, and the now-familiar apparatus of social movements. But in doing so, they moved incrementally, never disposing of more than a few claim-making routines at a time, and always innovating, like designers of mechanical devices, at edges of existing performances, most often in response to perceived inadequacies of performances, thereby reproducing most features of performances and their underlying social relations as they did so.

Need I add that British contenders' actions always brought unanticipated consequences, that they spent much of their energy in error correction, that because of their embeddedness in shared understanding and constraining social relations they nevertheless generated systematic social structure, that to explain changes in contentious repertoires entails close examination of counterfactuals, of paths not taken, of events that never happened?

Remember, however, that error-filled interaction produces orderly consequences. During the 1660s, members of Colbert's combine produced systematic change despite day-to-day desperation. They did so not because they acted efficiently in conventional means-end terms, but because shared understandings concerning power, prerogative, and possible forms of action, embedded in networks of kinship and patronage, enormously limited what they could do and what their doing would produce. Ruthlessly they used patronage and force—the king's—to combat other people's patronage and force, thus moving the entire polity toward patronage and force emphatically centered on the king. After the fact, Louis XIV could claim to have intended and foreseen the whole process.

As analysts of social processes, we must distinguish ex post facto rationalization (for all its great importance as social cement) from systematic explanation. Systematic explanation requires much greater attention to errors, their consequences, and their rectification than social scientists have given them so far. I should know: instead of invisible hands, invisible elbows are the story of my life.

NOTES

This chapter is a revised version of address to the TillyFest, University of Toronto, 6–8 October 1995. Thanks to Barry and Beverly Wellman for organizing that warm, lively affair. I am grateful to Robert K. Merton, Barry Wellman, and Viviana Zelizer for criticism of previous drafts.

REFERENCES

Aubert, Vilhelm. 1965. *The Hidden Society.* Totowa, NJ: Bedminster Press.

Auster, Paul. 1988. *Disappearances: Selected Poems.* Woodstock, NY: Overlook Press.

Coase, Ronald. 1952. "The Nature of the Firm." *Economica* 4: 386–405; reprinted in George Stigler and Kenneth Boulding, *Readings in Price Theory.* Chicago, IL: Irwin, 1937.

———. 1992. "The Institutional Structure of Production." *American Economic Review* 82: 713–719.

Conrad, Joseph. [1917] 1995. "Author's Note." In *Youth. Heart of Darkness. The End of the Tether.* London: Penguin.

Dessert, Daniel. 1984. *Argent, pouvoir et société au Grand Siècle.* Paris: Fayard.

Dessert, Daniel, and Jean-Louis Journet. 1975. "Le lobby Colbert: Un royaume ou une affaire de famille?" *Annales: Economies, Sociétés, Civilisations* 30: 1303–1336.

Frost, Robert. 1916. *Mountain Interval.* New York: Holt.

Gerth, H. H., and C. Wright Mills, eds. and trans. 1946. *From Max Weber: Essays in Sociology.* New York: Oxford University Press.

Goffman, Erving. 1981. *Forms of Talk.* Oxford: Blackwell.

Goodwin, Jeff. 1994a. "Old Regimes and Revolutions in the Second and Third Worlds: A Comparative Perspective." *Social Science History* 18: 575–604.

———. 1994b. "Toward a New Sociology of Revolutions." *Theory and Society* 23: 731–766.

Hirschman, Albert O. 1997. *The Passions and the Interests: Political Arguments for Capitalism before its Triumph.* Princeton, NJ: Princeton University Press.

———. 1991. *The Rhetoric of Reaction: Perversity, Futility, Jeopardy.* Cambridge, MA: Harvard University Press.

Lieberson, Stanley, and Kelly S. Mikelson. 1995. "Distinctive African American Names: An Experimental, Historical, and Linguistic Analysis of Innovation." *American Sociological Review* 60: 928–946.

Merton, Robert K. 1936. "The Unanticipated Consequences of Purposive Social Action." *American Sociological Review* 1: 894–904.

———. [1965] 1993. *On the Shoulders of Giants: A Shandean Postscript.* New York: Free Press.

———. 1977. "The Sociology of Science: An Episodic Memoir." In Robet K. Merton and Jerry Gaston, eds., *The Sociology of Science in Europe.* Carbondale and Edwardsville: Southern Illinois University Press.

———. 1984. "Socially Expected Durations: A Case Study of Concept Formation in Sociology." In W. W. Powell and Richard Robbins, eds., *Conflict & Consensus: A Festschrift for Lewis A. Coser.* New York: Free Press.

———. 1987. "Three Fragments from a Sociologist's Notebooks: Establishing the Phenomenon, Specified Ignorance, and Strategic Research Materials." *Annual Review of Sociology* 13: 1–28.

———. 1989. "Unanticipated Consequences and Kindred Sociological Ideas: A Personal Gloss." In Carlo Mongardini and Simonetta Tabboni, eds., *L'Opera di R. K. Merton e la Sociologia Contemporanea.* Genoa: Edizioni Culturali Internazionali.

———. 1994. "A Life of Learning." American Council of Learned Societies Occasional Paper 25.

Nelson, Richard R. 1995. "Recent Evolutionary Theorizing about Economic Change." *Journal of Economic Literature* 33: 48–90.

Norman, Donald A. 1990. *The Design of Everyday Things.* New York: Doubleday/Currency; first published as *The Psychology of Everyday Things* (New York: Basic Books, 1988).

North, Douglass C. 1991. "Institutions." *Journal of Economic Perspectives* 5: 97–112.

Petroski, Henry. 1992. *The Evolution of Useful Things.* New York: Knopf.

Prisching, Manfred. 1995. "The Limited Rationality of Democracy: Schumpeter as the Founder of Irrational Choice Theory." *Critical Review* 9: 301–324.

Resnick, Mitchel. 1996. "Beyond the Centralized Mindset." *Journal of the Learning Sciences* 5: 1–22.

Schneider, Louis. 1975. "Irony and Unintended Consequences." In *The Sociological Way of Looking at the World.* New York: McGraw-Hill.

Simon, Herbert. [1945] 1976. *Administrative Behavior: A Study of Decision-Making Processes in Administrative Organization.* New York: Free Press.

———. 1991. "Organizations and Markets." *Journal of Economic Perspectives* 5: 25–44.

Smith, Adam. [1776] 1910. *The Wealth of Nations.* 2 vols. London: J. M. Dent.

Thomson, Ross. 1984. "The Eco-Technic Process and the Development of the Sewing Machine." In Gary Saxonhouse and Gavin Wright, eds., *Technique, Spirit, and Form in the Making of the Modern Economies: Essays in Honor of William N. Parker.* Research in Economic History, Supplement 3. Greenwich, CT: JAI Press.

Tilly, Charles. 1967. "Anthropology on the Town." *Habitat* 10: 20–25.

Wrigley, E. A. 1987. *People, Cities, and Wealth.* Oxford: Blackwell.

Zelizer, Viviana A. 1979. *Morals and Markets: The Development of Life Insurance in the United States.* New York: Columbia University Press.

———. 1985. *Pricing the Priceless Child: The Changing Social Value of Children.* New York: Basic Books.

———. 1994. *The Social Meaning of Money.* New York: Basic Books.

· *Part Two* ·

Contention and Social Change

· 4 ·

THE MODERNIZATION OF POLITICAL
CONFLICT IN FRANCE

MODERNIZATION[1]

Modernization is like raising children; it takes longer, and costs more, than anyone imagines before he begins. The very emergence of the blurry word *modernization* in discussions of contemporary nations that used to employ sharper terms like *industrialization* and *urbanization* suggests as much.[2] Industrialization turns out to be much chancier, and urbanization much more complicated, than the hopeful commentators of the 1940s used to say. To speak of modernization is to point to a broader, longer, more complicated set of changes.

Not that as an analytical tool the concept of modernization serves more effectively than the concepts of industrialization and urbanization. The opposite is true. Modernization is too big and slippery for deft manipulation. Its virtue is as a warning: pay attention to *what else* happens before, and while, industrialization or urbanization occurs. Our adoption of the term *modernization* signals (1) that the development of an industrial labor force, an educated population, an urban way of life or widespread participation in national politics entails far wider changes than any of these terms suggests in itself, and (2) that these—and other—transformations depend on one another closely enough to justify imagining another grand process comprehending all of them. These signals (and thus the term *modernization*) became more important as students of contemporary nations began to realize that promoting economic growth was a risky and complicated business; that many other things might have to happen before stable and/or democratic government would even begin to emerge in new states; and that in the Western experience, the appropriate analogies to current changes in non-

This chapter was first published as "The Modernization of Political Conflict in France," in Edward B. Harvey, ed., *Perspectives on Modernization* (Toronto: University of Toronto Press, 1972), pp. 51–95. © 1972 by Charles Tilly. Reprinted with permission.

Western countries might be the emergence of governments, national markets, bureaucracies, and the like in the eighteenth century and earlier, rather than the swirling urban-industrial growth of the nineteenth and twentieth centuries. So the turn to the larger agenda signaled by the word *modernization* included a turn toward reconsideration of the Western experience over a long sweep of time.

One portion of this reconsideration that has not gone far enough is the study of political conflict. In the contemporary world, poor countries appear to be much more turbulent than rich ones, despite all the recent wrangling and protesting in the richest countries.[3] That could be because wealth (or industrialization, or urbanization, or something else that goes along with wealth) pacifies people. It could be that political conflict changes form—becomes more subtle, shifts away from physical force—with advancing wealth. Or it could be an illusion based on bad information or faulty definitions. Whichever applies, it raises the question whether the historical experience of Western countries points to the same conclusions. Did modernization reliably transform political conflict? If it did, we could reasonably compare the historical evidence with the implications of the contemporary comparisons.

In Western countries, modernization clearly did not *eliminate* political conflict, even in its more violent forms. Within the most modern nations, men are fighting and protesting still. Just as clearly, modernization in those countries did bring changes in the issues, the styles, the personnel of political conflict. No one could mistake the Peasants' War for the Nazi revolution, or the struggle of Tudor factions for the jockeying of twentieth-century Parliament members. The critical questions lie between those two extremes. Did political conflict in Western countries change in some regular way attributable to standard features of modernization? Did its intensity and disruptiveness diminish in consequence?

Let us take a serious look at those questions in a single country, France. We shall thereby run the risk of mistaking French idiosyncrasies for Western universals. In compensation, we get the opportunity to follow the well-documented actual experience of a turbulent country continuously over a considerable span of time. One might think that the seventeenth-century Frenchmen who blamed the bickering and bloodshed of their time on an enduring moral weakness of their people were not only correct but prescient. The eighteenth century, after all, brought a revolution more far-reaching than the seventeenth-century Fronde; the nineteenth century was full of protest; and the twentieth century—well, here we are, and France is still crackling with conflict.

Yet the character of political conflict has changed. The contenders, the issues, the occasions for conflict in contemporary France have little resemblance to those of the seventeenth and eighteenth centuries. France is no longer its old self; why should its conflicts remain the same? Some parts of the change are, nevertheless, hard to understand and worth trying to understand. The problem is to determine what essential features of conflict changed, how they changed, and what connection those changes had with the modernization of France, which was proceeding simultaneously and, presumably, interdependently.

This essay takes up only a portion of that problem. Despairing (at least for the moment) of any hope of treating *all* forms of conflict comprehensively, I shall sketch some of the major alterations in French society over the last few centuries, review some of the major shifts in the character of the more violent, public and political forms of conflict, and offer some ideas and evidence concerning the relationships between the two.

That means taking up themes that mattered a good deal to my late friend, colleague, and critic Ian Weinberg. I am taking up the themes in his memory, although not in perfect agreement with the conclusions he had reached. Ian Weinberg argued that over the long run, modernization had reduced (in Western countries) and would reduce (in others) the pervasiveness and violence of political conflict. As he put it:

> The impact of modernization was not simply to "break down" traditional authority systems as the literature so often puts it, because there was hardly any need to do this. What actually occurred in western political development was that the legitimacy of the political system itself was accepted as more of the population became participants. Institutional mechanisms were evolved which assured succession, opposition, and the greater effectiveness over time and in depth of governmental authority. The bureaucracy of government provided much of the stability because recruitment was more universalistic. France, for example was well-governed during the tempestuous Third Republic, even though the civil service was accused of harboring royalist elements. Intraelite aggression became oral and bureaucratized, or formalized into the duelling system. Elite schools began to emphasize seminars and tutorials, education to styles of verbal aggression, rather than the lecture system. The greater mobilization of the lower socioeconomic groups, with the expansion of the franchise meant that violence and riot as a political phenomenon began to decline. . . . The decline in violence intrinsic to the premodern political system is indicated by the romanticization of violence by intellectuals which begins in the nineteenth century. There were, and still are

breakdowns in the process of modernization, which produce internal
war and revolution. But persistent violence, as a common and pathologi-
cal problem at every level of society, has disappeared.[4]

Much of this argument is correct and valuable. The standard portrayal of
the emergence of modern politics as a "breakdown" of traditional systems
of authority does, indeed, obscure the way that emerging states accumulated authority where little had existed before. The bureaucratization of
government did promote a continuity and predictability of administration
that survived transfers of power. The style of elite conflict did become
more subtle, more verbal. Larger and larger segments of the population did
become directly involved in national politics.

There the difficulties begin. Two questions deserve scrutiny. First,
how smoothly did the participation of ordinary people in national systems
of power expand? I shall suggest that the whole process went on with
frequent fits, starts, and reversals, and that ordinary people often *resisted*
incorporation into national politics (which meant the subordination of
other political units to the national state) with rage and indignation.

Second, did the process of modernization somehow routinize and
mollify political conflict? I shall suggest that any particular form of conflict
did tend to routinize and become more predictable, if not more manage-
able, but that the structural processes we lump together under the name
modernization, in transforming the identities and interests of the principal
contenders for power, constantly threw up new forms of conflict to replace
the old.

Whether the overall amount of conflict declined in Western countries
over the long run of modernization is more doubtful. Final resolution of
that question will take far more agreement on the facts, the definitions, and
the measurements of conflict than is now in sight. I shall suggest that in
France, at least, violent conflict was just as prevalent in the twentieth century as in the nineteenth, although its form changed fundamentally from
one century to the next.

A QUICK VIEW OF THE HISTORY OF CONFLICT

In order to sense the magnitude and character of the change, let us go back
to a time before the urbanization and industrialization of the nineteenth
century. We stride through history in hundred-year boots. It is 1768, a year
of dearth in France. Louis XV, no longer excessively *bien-aimé,* still reigns.
When violence breaks out, it most often assumes the shape of a food riot.

In the food riot's most developed form, mixed crowds of ordinary people gather angrily before the shop of a miller, a merchant, or a baker; they complain about prices, seize the food on hand, cart it off to the market square, sell it to all comers (so long as they belong to the community) at a price they declare to be just, turn the cash over to the owner of the grain or bread, and go home saying they have done justice, as the authorities themselves should have done justice. That year, major disturbances following this pattern occur in Le Havre, Rouen, and Mantes; many more break out in the smaller market towns of Normandy.

A century earlier, the crowd would normally have smashed, manhandled, and looted. Sometimes they still do. But as merchants and royal ministers have painstakingly constructed a national market in grains (and thus assured the survival of monstrous Paris), ordinary people have shifted to more highly organized, more effective, and more nearly nonviolent ways of bargaining through the threat of force. Through a decree of 1763, the royal government has made its greatest effort so far to knock down barriers to the shipment of grain from town to town and province to province; "free trade" is the slogan, the prescription for France's economic ills.

Many provincial people see it differently. Confronted with a large and long-forecast food riot in April 1768, the Parlement of Rouen has reinstated many of the traditional controls—inventory of grains in private hands, requirement that all sales be made in the public market, strict control over the departure of grain from the community. It has declined to condemn the authorities of small Norman towns for actually setting the price of grain (no one questioned their setting the price of bread). And it has authorized the arrest of government commission agents sent out to buy wheat for Paris. The government's views of these "hindrances to trade" appear emphatically in a letter from the controller general of finances, l'Averdy, to the duc d'Harcourt:

> I see, Sir, by the report that M. Bertin made to the King a few days ago concerning the news he had from you on the present circumstances of the province of Normandy, that you were worried about the provisioning of the province and believe that it is completely stripped of grain. It gives me the greatest pain to see the state to which the province has been reduced by a very ill-considered decree of the Parlement of Rouen; for I cannot help thinking that it is the hindrance to the food trade brought about by that decree which produced the shortage about which people are complaining today. I do not know, Sir, if you have accurate information about the amount of grain which has arrived in Rouen since the tenth of this month and about the grain which is still expected. I am sure that when you have informed yourself on that score you will support the

measures taken by order of the King, which I made as prompt and effective as possible, and you will agree that it was impossible to do more than
was done in those unhappy circumstances. If the merchants had not been
discouraged and if they had thought it possible to take part in the free
competition guaranteed to them by government decree, they would
have made greater efforts and the rise in grain prices would have been
negligible in the province.[5]

But the provincials persist. In a letter of remonstrance of October 1768,
the Parlement goes so far as to intimate that the king is in cahoots with
hoarders and racketeers. The idea of a Pact of Famine is spreading.[6]

Behind this widespread belief in a conspiracy among merchants and
royal officials to profit from the starvation of the provinces exists the usual
refracted glimmer of truth. The king and his minions are bending every
effort to pry resources from the grip of provincial particularism, in order to
devote them to their own national ends: the feeding of Paris, the maintenance of the army, the payment of a growing bureaucracy, the creation
of a national market, the promotion of agriculture. The struggle pits the
centralizers not only against the holders of grain, but also against the hoarders of men, of land, of gold, and of loyalty.

The collective violence of the time expresses the titanic conflict. There
is still a substratum of very old-fashioned violence aligning members of one
more or less communal group against another: the brawl among rival
groups of artisans, the free-for-all setting two adjacent villages against each
other, and so on. In the mid-eighteenth century, however, the characteristic forms of collective violence involve angry resistance to demands from
the center. Food riots take first place, but revolts against conscription, tax
rebellions, and forcible invasions of lands closed off from communal use by
royal decree have essentially the same character. The century's largest series
of disturbances will be the garland of food riots draped around Paris in
1775, after Turgot's most vigorous efforts at freeing the grain trade. A very
large part of the collective action of the Revolution itself will take the
quintessential eighteenth-century forms.

We spring forward a century, to 1868, Napoleon III, no longer so
lustrous as when he seized power sixteen years ago, governs France. By
now, the French have virtually forgotten food riots and tax rebellions, although they were rife only twenty years ago. The gatherings that commonly turn violent nowadays are no longer casual congregations at markets
or fairs; they are deliberate assemblies of men belonging to special-purpose
associations. The International Workingmen's Association—later to be
called the First International—is four years old and actively organizing in

France. In June of this year, the empire finally legalizes public meetings, although it still requires prior authorization for them. As settings for collective violence, demonstrations and strikes now prevail.

Now is the time of massive strikes, the first important wave of the Second Empire, strikes of a scale and sophistication never before seen in France. The workers of Lille and its vicinity have been striking, on and off, for two years. This year's graffiti on the walls and urinals of Lille go:

Vive la République!

Des balles ou du pain

Aux armes, citoyen

Ci nous ne voulons pas nous laissés mourir ou mangé par les Anglais

Je suis républicain parce que le bonheur est dans la République[7]

All of which are, naturally, defined as "seditious slogans."

In this year of 1868, major strikes break out in the Nord, in Marseille, and through much of the industrial region of Lyon, Saint-Étienne, and Roanne. Many of them pass more or less peacefully, if not amicably. Some few produce violence—typically, strikers stoning the house of a mine's director, or scuffles between assembled strikers and the troops sent in to keep them in line. Although strikes have been more or less legal for four years, prefects are quick to aid the managers when workers show signs of turbulence and/or "socialism." However, the really bloody encounters of soldiers and workers—the so-called Massacres of la Ricamarie and Aubin in 1869, the struggles around the near-insurrectionary strikes of 1870, the Commune of 1871—have yet to come.

The deliberately organized demonstration is rapidly becoming the usual setting for collective violence. Toulouse, for example, has seen no disturbances of any note since its republicans' futile resistance to Louis Napoleon's 1851 coup d'état. But now the government is beginning to organize the militia (the *garde mobile*) in preparation for a possible war with Prussia. On 9 March, there is a minor demonstration at the prefecture: some singing, some stoning. On the following evening,

> a crowd of 1,500 to 2,000 persons sings the Marseillaise, and breaks the gas lamps. Then groups of young men go to the Prefecture, where the police station is broken into and sacked. They then run through the streets to shouts of Vive la République! Down with the Emperor!, break street lights and windows of public buildings, and besiege the mayor at his house, on which they fly a red flag. The next day . . . many workers stay away from the job, and new disturbances break out; many women

take part, thinking that the militia will be garrisoned far away . . . young-sters take to the streets with a red flag (a towel drenched in an ox's blood at the slaughterhouse) and try to build a barricade of wagons. Another gang breaks gaslights around the Place des Carmes. A third goes to the School of Law, breaks in and smashes a bust of the Emperor. The author-ities start preparing the military for action.[8]

Many of the disturbances of the time follow this script: a moderately disci-plined demonstration shatters into rioting and vandalism. As the reporter of the incident tells us, "It seems that the Republicans were behind the first demonstrations, but they were overwhelmed by the exuberance of the young people and the calculated intervention of a few troublemakers." The well-organized mass demonstration, in which the usual violence takes the form of struggles between the demonstrators and the police sent to disperse or contain them, has not yet come into its own.

One more hundred-year bound brings us to 1968. General de Gaulle has survived ten years as president, but his popularity seems frayed. Strikers still shake France's industrial life frequently. But this year, student rebellions steal the headlines. A series of student strikes blend agitation against the American war in Vietnam with demands for greater student participation in the running of universities. PROFESSEURS, VOUS ETES VIEUX, goes one of the slogans.

In May, the main action in Paris shifts from the new campus in the industrial suburb of Nanterre to the ancient one at the Sorbonne. After some vandalism and some threats of rough-and-tumble between militants of the far Left and the far Right, the rector asks police to surround, and then to disperse, a group of students meeting in the Sorbonne's courtyard to protest disciplinary action begun against some of the leaders at Nanterre. The clearing of the Sorbonne itself goes smoothly, but clashes between riot police and jeering students gathered just outside the old building began six extraordinary weeks of demonstrations, street fighting, strikes, sit-downs of a new style in schools and factories, speeches, elections, repression: the "Events of May." This year's graffiti have a more fantastic touch:

La culture est l'inversion de la vie

La lucidité est la blessure la plus proche du soleil

Haut-parleur = ambiance programme = répression

Quand le dernier des sociologues aura été pendu avec les tripes du
dernier bureaucrate, aurons-nous encore des problèmes?

L'anarchie, c'est je

And *l'anarchie* sometimes seems to be the point of it all. It turns out otherwise, at least in the short run. The elections at the end of June produce a Gaullist landslide. People are scared. Nevertheless, the Events involve far more than a handful of fanatics. In May and June, at least 20,000 Frenchmen take part in violent encounters with the police, perhaps 2,500 are wounded and 4,500 arrested during those encounters, and 5 men die as a more or less direct result of them. A far larger number of people join nonviolent strikes, sit-ins, and demonstrations.

The violence itself does not distinguish the Events of May from a number of other disturbances since World War II: the insurrectionary strikes of 1947, for example, or the riots at General Eisenhower's installation as SHAEF (Supreme Headquarters of the Allied Expeditionary Forces) commander in 1951, or the huge, bloody demonstrations during the Algerian war. For the great numbers involved, the destruction and casualties of May 1968 are slight. But the leadership of students, their reaching out to factory workers, the rejection of Communist patronage, the experiments with local control of schools and workplaces, the undercurrent of demands for communal autonomy within a complex society combine to give the Events a new and baffling character.

Veteran observer Raymond Aron finds the Events senseless and repellent, which is to say, baffling. Just after the fighting dies down, he rummages in his word bag for the right label and chooses *psychodrama*.

> The psychodrama brings into play the revolutionary propensity of the French people, the weakness of mediating institutions (accentuated by Gaulism, in which everything depends on General de Gaulle himself), the surge of irrational forces in a society which calls itself modern, probably the discontent of a number of Frenchmen in a phase of modernization lacking the morphine of inflation. There were enough frustrations, resentments and griefs among Frenchmen for a great outburst to occur, given the right circumstances. Is it the end of a civilization?[9]

No revolution, but mass hysteria, says Raymond Aron. No hysteria, but mass revolution, reply the students. Both agree that something deep in French society is coming to the surface. They disagree on whether it represents a change or a breakdown. A little later, Alain Touraine will tell us that it represents both, with the change in French society being the more fundamental:

> The movement of May is a new form of the class struggle. More than any other collective action of the last decades, this movement revealed and thus constituted the fundamental social conflict of our society. That

way of putting it is farther than it might seem from the proclamations of the participants themselves, for it means that we are dealing with a new social conflict, whose nature and participants are no longer the same as in the previous society, in truly capitalist society. . . . The French students, like those of Berlin and Berkeley, began a struggle against the apparatus of integration, manipulation and aggression. It is these words and not the word exploitation which best define the nature of the conflict.[10]

And so—as in 1768 and 1868–the analysis of the violent events quickly becomes an analysis of the society that produced them.

Our mythical journey is far from bootless. The two centuries we have paced off brought fundamental changes in the character of collective violence in France. That is the first and elementary lesson: collective violence has form—more than clumsy words like *riot* or *disturbance* convey. At any particular time and place, people have a limited and well-defined repertoire of violent forms. The repertoire changes systematically with time and place, as the basic forms of organization for *non*violent action vary. That is the second (and more contestable) lesson: the predominant forms of violence depend on the basic structure of collective action. No tragic chasm separates violence from nonviolence, in 1968 or 1768.

The third lesson follows directly from the first two, although it may be even harder to accept; it is that in the French experience, collective violence has been a cause, effect, and constituent element of the political process. If that is the case, it makes little sense to imagine violent protest as a geyser newly erupting through a weakened but level surface—as an expression of either "revolutionary propensities" or "accumulated tension." It then makes much sense, on the other hand, to suppose that if the nature of violent conflict changes significantly, other, much wider, changes in the political process must be going on. The rise of the food riot in the eighteenth century and the rise of the violent demonstration in the nineteenth signified far more general transformations of France's political structure. Perhaps the new features of the 1968 rebellion also signify more than an instant impulse.

Saying so, however, only poses the main questions more insistently. If there is some order to disorder, what is it? In the short run, how does the structure of nonviolent social relationships shape the structure of violence? In the long run, how do transformations of the social structure transform violent protest? And what, if anything, is peculiarly French about the French experience with these matters? These questions will guide the rest of our inquiry.

THE CENTRALIZATION OF POWER

Part of the answer lies in the broadest features of French political history. France has long stood out among nations for its centralizing verve. Although "Absolutism" went much farther in theory than in practice (and the theory itself was a weapon fashioned in the long battle of the Crown with provincial magnates), the center prevailed. Tocqueville saw in the royal centralization of power, wealth, and population in Paris the roots of the Revolution and the origins of the subsequent fragility of democratic institutions in France. Much more recently, Herbert Luethy has commented that nonparliamentary institutions of modern French government represent

> the state apparatus of the absolute monarchy perfected and brought to its logical conclusion under the First Empire. When the crowned heads fell, the real sovereignty was transferred to this apparatus. But it works in the background, unobtrusively, anonymously, remote from all publicity and almost in secret; a monarch, a monarch whose only surviving driving principle is routine. It is not so much a state within a state as the real state behind the facade of the democratic state.[11]

The French system has long subordinated local and regional authorities to direct national control. The departmental prefect is, of course, an agent of the central government. With the dissolution of the provincial National Guard units and the reduction of the Parisian Guard to ceremonial functions in 1852, the last legally armed forces not firmly under national control disappeared almost definitively—the deeply significant exception being 1870 and 1871. At about the same time as he tamed the National Guard, Louis Napoleon perfected an apparatus of spies, informers, and informants already assembled by earlier regimes. Later innovations in techniques of control—tanks, telephones, tear gas, automatic rifles—simply increased the technical advantages of the government over its challengers.

The administrative centralization promoted and fed on geographic centralization in Paris and its protuberance, Versailles. Paris has towered over all other French cities since there has been a France. The roads of France, and then the railroads of France, and then the airlines of France, grew up in the shape of a Parisocephalic octopus. Tocqueville entitled a pivotal chapter of *The Old Regime and the French Revolution* as follows: "How in France, more than in any other European country, the provinces had come under the thrall of the metropolis, which attracted to itself all that was most vital in the nation." (Indeed, a lexicon that permits *province* to mean every part of the country but a single city would be fantastic almost anywhere else.) Marx saw Parisian dominance as a major political fact: "If Paris, as a result of political centralization, rules France, the workers, in moments of revolutionary earthquake, rule Paris."[12] Blanqui, writing in the waning months of the Second Empire, elevated the political reality into a doctrine:

> A year of Parisian dictatorship in 1848 would have spared France and would have spared history the quarter of a century now drawing to a close. If it takes ten years of it this time, let us not hesitate. After all, the government of Paris is the government of the nation by the nation, and therefore the only legitimate one. Paris is not just a municipality entrenched in its own interests. It represents the nation.[13]

The sheer existence of such a doctrine illustrates the political centralization of France . . . and gives point to the old fear that monstrous Paris will devour all the nation.

The work of centralization went on for centuries. It did not stop with the Revolution and empire, but continued apace during the nineteenth century, as the state drew larger and larger parts of people's lives under its direct control through public education, universal military training, manhood suffrage, and programs of public welfare. Eventually the state seized control over substantial parts of the economy: railroads, airlines, radio, television, mines, utilities, important parts of banking, and automobile manufacturing. The great moment for that expansion came at the end of World War II. If Louis XIV declared, *L'Etat, c'est moi,* his successors announced, *L'Etat, c'est tout.* Today, much of the debate about governmental reform in France concerns ways of reversing, or at least arresting, a centuries-old process of centralization.

The Nationalization of Politics

In addition to a centralization of power, the France of the last two centuries has seen a nationalization of politics. The two processes have depended on each other. Ordinary Frenchmen led fairly active political lives within their own communities and provinces long before the Revolution; they elected local officials, apportioned the local tax burden, wrangled over the expenses of the religious establishment. But they had only intermittent contact with national politics through privileged intermediaries—and even then, more as subjects than as participants. The political reforms of 1787 and of the early Revolution actually restricted formal participation in community politics (by substituting an elected council for the assembly of all heads of households and imposing property qualifications for voting and office-holding). On the other hand, the Revolution enormously increased the opportunities and incentives for ordinary people to participate in national politics through voting, holding office, joining clubs, adopting revolutionary styles, demonstrating, reading, arguing, volunteering.

The fashionable word for this drawing of people into intensive communication on a national scale is *mobilization*.[14] After the early Revolution, the next great surge of political mobilization in France did not come until the Revolution of 1848. Then universal manhood suffrage, election campaigns, proliferating political associations, a relatively free national press, election campaigns, proliferating political associations, a relatively free national press, and a great acceleration of the movement of political information via telegraph and railroad drew men much further into national politics than they had ever gone before. Centralization itself promoted this process of nationalization by placing more and more of the resources and decisions that really mattered in the national capital or the national government.

THE INSTABILITY OF REGIMES

The centralization and nationalization of French politics did not, to be sure, proceed smoothly and without hesitation. The French moved from regime to regime through revolutions and coups; 1789, 1799, 1830, 1848, 1851, 1870, and 1958 are only the largest markers. Even today, French leaders and parties claim and contest the lines of descent from the eighteenth-century revolution with a passion resembling that of the Russians or the Chinese more than that of the Dutch or the English (to name four regimes of revolutionary genesis). Although the Radicals acquired a special position as protectors of secular republicanism under the Third Republic, no party has ever been able to establish a monopoly of revolutionary legitimacy, and few parties have avoided claiming one. As recently as 13 May 1958, the insurgents who seized power in Algiers, and ultimately brought down the Fourth Republic, sang the Marseillaise and formed a Committee of Public Safety.

Still, 1958 is an exception in one crucial regard. It is the only occasion since 1799 in which the professional French military have taken an autonomous and fundamental part in the overthrow of a regime. Men who acquired their renown as soldiers have periodically come to power in France and have periodically appeared as threats to democratic continuity: Boulanger, Petain, and de Gaulle are the celebrated examples; the two Napoleons are the Men on Horseback with whom they are most often compared. Louis Napoleon did use the army with grim effectiveness in his 1851 coup. The question of civilian control over the military did almost tear France apart during the Dreyfus affair. Yet the army as such has played only a small role in France's succession of revolutions and coups. In that respect, France's instability is unlike that of Spain or Brazil.

Under the Third and Fourth Republics, the quick turnover of cabinets combined with the memory of those coups and revolutions to give France a worldwide reputation for political instability. That French fickleness, as Raymond Aron points out, actually developed earlier than the Third Republic:

> Instability at the top is . . . less novel than the sociologists tend to think. In Tocqueville's time, during the July Monarchy, people joked about the same thing, and told the story of the ambassador who didn't know, when he left Paris, what ministry he would represent when he arrived at his post. The presence of a king, of an emperor or of a Charles de Gaulle temporarily removes the head of state from factional quarrels, but it does not do away with the quarrels. The head of state presides over our disputes more than he resolves them.[15]

Although by now a number of younger nations have thrown down serious challenges to France's supremacy in this line of endeavor, France's reputation for governmental discontinuity was well earned—with two important qualifications. The first is that the personnel of government, especially the state bureaucracy, persisted to a remarkable degree through changes of regime. Despite the sudden shift from heavy property qualifications for voting to manhood suffrage, a good half of the deputies elected in April 1848 had already served in prerevolutionary Chambers. At the level of departmental councils, the continuity was much greater. Administrative personnel at all levels survived the change of regime with very little perturbation.[16]

The second qualification is that *instability* does not equal *violence*. The French have had plenty of violent moments, but so have most other peoples, regardless of whether they live under "stable" or "unstable" governments. England, the United States, Canada, and Belgium have all, in their times, experienced collective violence of the same general varieties as France's; their daily lives, over the long run, may even have been more violent than France's. Certainly the sheer amount of bloodshed does not account for France's contentious reputation. Over the period from 1930 to 1960, for example, about 100 Frenchmen died in political disturbances, mostly at the hands of the police. During the same period, some 200,000 were killed in wars, and 600,000 died in accidents. Obviously, political disturbances create fear and trembling disproportionate to their toll in human life. France's distinction lies not in the amount of wounding and killing, but in the frequency with which violent protests have brought down governments and regimes.

That special political experience has produced a special set of political attitudes. As Philip Williams puts it:

> The Frenchman's approach to the problem of political authority is . . . shaped by three factors: a political struggle which has always been waged with sectarian bitterness and thoroughness, sparing no sector of the country's organized life; an experience of governments abusing their authority to maintain their position; and an immensely powerful administrative machine, which provides a standing temptation to such abuse. There is a latent totalitarianism in the French attitude to politics, which makes French democrats fear the power of government, and regard it as a source of potential dangers rather than of potential benefits.[17]

No doubt most people are ambivalent toward the state. French people, more than most.

France's political history is to some extent an explanation, and to some extent a result, of the changing character of its collective violence. The centralization of government, the nationalization of politics, the barriers to independent political action by the army, the revolutionary heritage, and the continuing vulnerability of regimes to challenge from the street give France a greater resemblance to, say, Italy than to England. A France with a more independent military might well resemble Spain or Argentina.

WEALTH

But only in some respects. The analogies of Italy, Spain, or Argentina lose some of their persuasiveness when it comes to matters of wealth, industrial structure, regional diversity, and urban population. The history of collective violence in France depends not only on the country's formal political structure, but also on the great transformation of other features of the social structure.

Before the Revolution, France was one of the world's most prosperous, industrial, urban nations. Since that time, a number of other countries have moved much faster than France along all of these dimensions. France still has a longer experience with comfortable levels of living than almost any other country in the world. With respect to income per capita, Holland and England no doubt pulled away from France as early as the seventeenth century. But the next-comers—Belgium, Germany, and the United States—did not pass it until fairly late in the nineteenth century.

All this is relative, of course. If we were to cast about the world of the mid-twentieth century for approximations of France's material condition at the beginning of the nineteenth century, we would have to seize on poor but civilized nations like Bulgaria, Yugoslavia, or Costa Rica. Even those analogies would touch on the grotesque; we would have to conjure up a Yugoslavia without railroads, without radios, without splashes of ultra-modern industry, with a class of titled landlords still wresting their incomes form tenant farmers, and another class of merchants, bankers, industrialists, and officials just coming into their own, with even fewer of its people in big cities than in contemporary Yugoslavia, yet prevailing in a world of nations poorer and less powerful than itself. The France of that era has no counterpart in the Western world today.

Over the long run since the Revolution, the wealth of France has accumulated slowly and surely. One informed guess at the long-run rate of growth of per capita income in France puts it at 1.25 percent per annum, about the same as England's.[18] Figure 4.1 presents three of the best-known national income series for France since 1810.[19] They display a relatively steady growth throughout the nineteenth century. The twentieth century brought greater swings in income. According to these estimates, the most notable periods of decline were the depression of the 1870s, the two world wars, and the depression of the 1930s. World War II shows up as an economic disaster, even compared to the depression it followed. The periods of most notable growth (discounting the curious implications of Colin Clark's estimates) run from around 1855 to 1869, 1922 to 1930, and, incomparably, 1946 to 1960 and beyond. These dates correspond satisfactorily to what we know otherwise about the timing of industrial expansion. The curves register the steady increase of the older industries up to 1850, the spurting growth (relying increasingly on steel, railroads, and other new industries) of the 1850s and 1860s, and the tremendous expansion both of modern industry and of services since that time.

The increase of national income that occurred meant more to the average French citizen than it would have to the average Briton or American because the population of France grew slowly. Fewer persons shared the spoils. (Of course, it may well be—and has often been argued—that a higher rate of population increase would have accelerated France's economic growth.) France did not draw anything like the hordes of immigrants who sailed to Canada or Argentina. Its birthrate dropped steadily

Figure 4.1. Estimates of Changes in French National Income, 1810–1950

from the Revolution to World War II, generally faster than the death rate. In whole regions of Burgundy, Normandy, and Languedoc, families began limiting births rather stringently well before the Revolution. As a result, France's natural increase was slow and uncertain. The birthrate did tend to recover somewhat in prosperous days: the 1860s, the 1920s, and, sensationally, the 1950s. But war and depression actually produced substantial natural *decreases* in 1870–1871, 1914–1919, and 1936–1955. Since World War II, on the other hand, with mortality still skidding down and fertility up to fin de siècle levels, the French have multiplied at rates unrivaled in at least two centuries. After a century of aging, this made the French population young again. Both demographically and industrially, the postwar change of pace far exceeded what happened earlier.

INDUSTRIALIZATION AND URBANIZATION

The same is true for the structure of employment. Figure 4.2 shows what a century and a half of industrialization did to the French labor force.[20] Some of the changes are factitious. The apparent decline of the total labor

Figure 4.2. The French Labor Force, 1825–1959

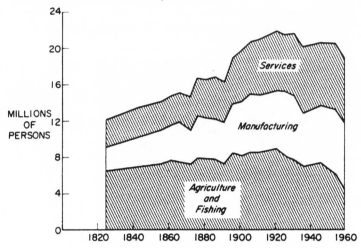

force after 1954, for example, resulted almost entirely from the application of stricter definitions to the agricultural population. Nevertheless, several facts come through:

1. Contrary to common notions of revolutionary and postrevolutionary France, close to half the labor force was already working outside of agriculture as early as 1825.
2. However, the absolute size of the agricultural population remained virtually constant for a century after 1825, began to slide after World War I, and has only fallen off rapidly since World War II.
3. As a consequence, France had an exceptionally high proportion of its labor force in agriculture, compared with other prosperous twentieth-century nations, right into the 1950s.
4. The shares of manufacturing and services grew constantly except around 1900 and during World War II. However, the pace of their growth depended on the general level of economic activity; the greater the prosperity, the faster the shift into manufacturing and services, and vice versa.
5. The shares of manufacturing and services have remained roughly equal over the entire period. France has not so far experienced the shift from secondary to tertiary industries supposed to characterize advanced industrial economies.

The period under examination, then, saw France transformed from a fairly poor, predominantly agrarian country to a prosperous industrial one, while a number of other countries traveled in the same general direction faster. Although in 1825, France already had long experience with traditional forms of manufacturing, the period since then is its essential time of industrialization.

France also urbanized. Revolutionary Paris, with its half million inhabitants, was one of the world's great cities. For centuries, Paris had been reaching out to control the men, mores, and markets of northeastern France; by the end of the eighteenth century, a vast area was pouring migrants and food into the city. Marseille, Lyon, Bordeaux, and Rouen, each with close to 100,000 people, dominated their own much smaller hinterlands. The great majority of the French, nonetheless, lived in villages.

For French statisticians, the word *urban* has traditionally singled out communes with at least 2,000 persons in the central settlement. By this criterion, about one-fifth of the French population lived in urban places in 1820, about three-fifths in 1960. As Figure 4.3 shows, the rural population has been declining both absolutely and relatively since around 1850.[21] Big-city France, the France of places with 50,000 or more persons, has fed on that decline: only 4 percent in 1821, 18 percent in 1901, 25 percent in 1962. The pace of urban growth was relatively even. Over the long run, it

Figure 4.3. Urban, Rural, and Total Population, 1821–1961

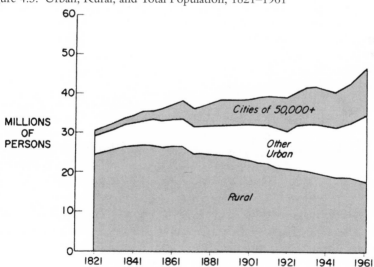

comes, like per capita income, to about 1.25 percent per year. The industrial expansion of the 1850s, the 1920s, and the 1950s and the slower industrialization from 1870 to World War I and during the depression braked it; the two wars and the loss of territory to Prussia in 1870 dented the curve, but not for long.

If the French population in agriculture reached its peak, as we have seen, around the time of World War I, while the rural population began a steady decline around 1850, the two cannot have been the same. In fact, a good proportion—perhaps a third—of the so-called rural population of postrevolutionary France was living from manufacturing, services, and other nonagricultural pursuits. The domestic textile industry (said in rural Meyenne, for example, to be the principal economic activity of the countryside before the Revolution) occupied far more people than its rivals, the wood-burning forges, woodworking, tanning, basketry, pottery. All these industries quickly moved to the city during the nineteenth century, leaving a once-humming countryside more bucolic than it had been for centuries. Rural areas deindustrialized.

It looks as though hundreds of thousands of rural artisans hung on in small towns through the first half of the nineteenth century, living on half wages, seasonal work in the fields, and dwindling hope for a return of the good old days. They and their descendants began to move off the land in growing numbers around 1850, as jobs in the new industrial centers became more plentiful, the railroads made travel to them easier, all rural industry expired, and traditional rights to glean, cut, and hunt in common fields or forests disappeared before the advance of calculating, capital-intensive agriculture. So the rural exodus so often deplored by French lovers of rustic virtue probably had three rather different, if overlapping, phases: (1) a draining of present and former workers in rural industry, peaking in the middle of the nineteenth century; (2) a tapping of "extra" children of farm families, especially during the period of relatively high natural increase up to 1890 or so; and (3) the movement of families displaced by the closing down and consolidation of farms since 1890, especially after 1930. The first movement had an air of desperation, the second offered a way out of poverty to several generations of young Frenchmen on the make, and the third went on rather smoothly except for the worst years of the 1930s. The three kinds of movement were bound to have very different impacts on agrarian protest.

The growth of cities and the draining of the rural population were no more evenly distributed across the map of France than was the development of industry on a large scale. Let us call "modern," for the sake of simplicity, those areas with high per capita incomes, productive agriculture, large manufacturing establishments, high literacy, extensive means of communication, and so on. In these terms, the geographical distribution of modernity in France has followed a curvilinear path since the Revolution. Modernity was then already somewhat concentrated in Paris and its hinterland, plus much smaller regions immediately around a handful of other big cities. It grew even more unequal during the nineteenth century as those regions (and more generally, the northeastern quadrant of the country) urbanized and industrialized. Slowly after World War I and rapidly after World War II, the fruits of modernity—bitter and sweet alike—spread outside those regions of initial importance, and a degree of equalization occurred.

One rather surprising feature of this process shows up in agricultural yields.[22] From the beginning, the hinterland of Paris has, under the stimulus of the metropolitan market, produced the highest yields per hectare. Regional disparities, especially the advantage of Paris, *increased* during the nineteenth century (despite the spread throughout France of new agricultural practices), only to give way to a much greater equalization during the twentieth.

Maps of road traffic in 1856–1857 and 1955 identify two points in a very similar progression: inequality at the beginning, growing inequality with the industrial urbanization of the north, eventual spread of traffic to larger and larger portions of the country.[23] The traffic maps suggest the extent to which this twentieth-century spread of modernity is occurring through the expansion and convergence of existing urban regions: Lyon and Marseille linking arms and reaching around to Nice; Toulouse and Bordeaux building their own metropolitan network; Paris extending its alliances in every direction.

The process touches everyday life. In an Angevin country town:

As the social networks in Chanzeaux have diminished in number, they have mostly because of the revolution in transportation, greatly increased their geographic spread. Whenever the people of Chanzeaux are not working, they are on the move, usually in order to visit friends, relatives, acquaintances of far-reaching networks. Eight years ago if we wanted to talk to a farmer, we would be sure to find him at home on Sunday afternoon, and our visit was welcome since he seemed to have nothing else to do. Now people are rarely at home when they have leisure time. If they stay at home, it is because they expect visitors. The traffic on all the roads of the Maine-et-Loire, especially the back roads leading to hamlets and farms, is surprisingly heavy on Sunday nowadays. Sometimes farmers—and townspeople—go even farther away for the weekend. Faligand visits his cousin in Paris. Bourdelle visits a friend with whom he has kept up since army days in Lille. The Massonneaus drive down from Paris to visit the Guitieres. Only the ill stay at home—and they have visitors. It used to be that on Sunday afternoon the Chanzeans who wanted to get away from home would walk along the Hyrome River to stop and drink with friends at the little wineshops along the way. Today one can walk the length of the path and see only an occasional fisherman. The people of Chanzeaux have broader contacts and interests.[24]

It is not so much that the French move *more* than they used to. Despite enduring myths to the contrary, rural communities in most sections of France have been experiencing rapid turnovers of population for at least a century. The big change is that the circles in which they travel, the networks they form, have spread and spread. This extension of social relations began with Paris and its hinterland, followed the growth of industrial metropolises in the nineteenth century, and has in recent decades been knitting all of France together.

I do not say the knit is smooth, regular, or harmonious. The French have shared a general experience of Western peoples: a shift of the crucial lines of division of wealth, prestige, power, social access, and solidarity from local to national. Division remains, the principles of division change. Particular attachments to this village or that, this family or that, even this faith or that have lost much of their importance as promoters or inhibitors of collective action, however much sentimental value they may have retained. Positions in national systems of occupation and wealth have come to matter a great deal more.

CLASS STRUCTURE

Though the long years we are considering here, the urbanization and industrialization of France have transformed its class structure in four interdependent ways:

1. Control over liquid wealth, complex organizations, and the industrial apparatus has largely supplanted control over land as the central criterion of class position.
2. The numbers of persons working in large organizations under bureaucratic control (whether, through style of work and style of life, we call them "working class" or "middle class") have enormously and steadily expanded.
3. As the French have moved cityward, position and acceptability within a particular community have lost much of their importance

as determinants of individual or group behavior: local notability, or notoriety, matters less and less as compared with position in the national occupational structure, membership in national associations, contacts and experiences outside the community.

4. Largely as a result of changing little while other things were changing much, positions as local representatives or interpreters of national structures—priest, notary, government functionary—have lost much of their prestige and power; by contrast, positions presuming technical expertise—scientist, engineer, doctor—have gained in luster.

Familiar trends, all.

The hand of history has erased a France of peasants and artisans, of landowning local notables linked (although not always happily) with urban officials and financiers. It has written in their place a France of farmers, bureaucrats, technicians, and industrial workers, dominated by professional organizers in a variety of specialties.

With some disgust, Balzac read the writing on the wall in the 1840s:

> The three orders have been replaced by what are nowadays called *classes*. We have lettered classes, industrial classes, upper classes, middle classes, etc. And these classes almost always have their own regents, as in the *college*. People have changed big tyrants into petty ones, that's all. Each industry has its bourgeois Richelieu named Laffitte or Casimir Perier.[25]

Just a few years later, Karl Marx wrote of the same transformations from a rather different perspective:

> French industry is more developed and the French bourgeoisie more revolutionary than that of the rest of the Continent. But was not the February Revolution levelled directly against the finance aristocracy? This fact proved that the industrial bourgeoisie did not rule France. The industrial bourgeoisie can rule only where modern industry shapes all property relations to suit itself, and industry can win this power only where it has conquered the world market, for national bounds are inadequate for its development. But French industry, to a great extent, maintains its command even of the national market only through a more or less modified system of prohibitive duties. While, therefore, the French proletariat, at the moment of a revolution, possesses in Paris actual power and influence which spur it on to a drive beyond its means, in the rest of France it is crowded into separate, scattered industrial centers, being almost lost in the superior numbers of peasants and petty bourgeois.[26]

The hand of history was, in short, busily producing a palimpsest.

Many traces of the Old Regime persisted into the twentieth century. That is what was special about France's version of a very general transformation of class structure in industrializing societies: in France, small-town life, marginal family farming, the family firm and the small shop all hung on tenaciously, only losing their grip under the battering of the depression and World War II. Politics grew to a national scale far faster, and far more decisively, than did routine social life. The result was the disparity between the nationalization of politics and the segmentation of solidarity, which Stanley Hoffmann considers the foundation of the "stalemate society" of France under the Third Republic.[27]

ORGANIZATION FOR COLLECTIVE ACTION

Hoffmann also argues that the poverty of French associational life contributed to the stalemate. On that score, I am not so sure. Throughout the interdependent transformations of demographic, economic, political, and class structures we have been reviewing, the French turned increasingly to complex organizations, including associations in the narrow sense of the word, as the means of getting their work done. The trend is obvious in the worlds of industry and government. The history of voluntary association for political and economic ends is more elusive, because successive governments from the Revolution to the beginning of the Third Republic set ponderous barriers in the way of private association. They did it selectively, so that employers long had the organizational advantage in dealing with their workers. Nevertheless, even under the forbidding eye of the minister of the interior, French workers, peasants, bourgeois, and political activists persisted in forming clubs, secret societies, *compagnonnages,* associations for mutual aid, rudimentary trade unions, and parties. As Henry Ehrmann says:

> the legal obstacles were frequently ignored; many categories did not wait for the change in legislation to form groups and to constitute in fact the "partial societies" condemned by Rousseau. But the necessity of achieving this by subterfuge was nevertheless bound to shape group practice and to spread doubts about the legitimacy of group activities.[28]

The proof that associational life was far from extinguished lies in the energy with which the spies of the Interior Ministry eavesdropped and infiltrated during regimes of relatively strict control, like the Restoration and the Second Empire, and in the startling speed with which such associations proliferated—or came out into the open—in times of relative freedom, like the spring of 1848.

Now, it appears that the pace, scale, and complexity of formal organization in France all increased rapidly as France urbanized and industrialized after 1840. The evidence is uncertain precisely because so much of the new organization took place in the shadows. Tocqueville did not detect it when writing *Democracy in America* in the 1830s; on the contrary, he considered the absence of associations a prime reason for the weakness of democratic institutions in France. Yet in his own time, the Saint-Simonians, Fourierists, Blanquists, and other sects teetering between reform and revolution had gone into frenzies of organization. As early as October 1831, a report of Paris's prefect of police, summarizing the reports of his spies, gives some of the flavor of organization in the capital:

> The society of *Amis du Peuple* is vigorously continuing its organization of *decuries*. They reproduce, under another name, the *ventes* of the Carbonari . . . [t]he *Société des Amis de l'Egalité* into the *Amis du Peuple*. Both of them are counting heavily for new recruits on the return of the students; but generally speaking the young people coming back from the provinces appear little inclined to rejoin the popular societies.[29]

At Lyon, mutual aid societies began to flourish in the late 1820s and came angrily to light in the insurrections of 1830 and 1834. In general, Paris preceded the other big cities in the nurturing of association, the big cities preceded the towns, and the towns preceded the countryside.

It was not, however, a simple function of industrialization, at least not in any narrow sense of the word. The workers in the new, expanding, factory-based nineteenth-century industries—steel, railroads, cotton textiles—organized slowly.[30] The industries breeding extensive organization were older, more artisanal, smaller in scale, with the egregious exception of mining. Four main conditions promoted organization, in industry and elsewhere: (1) the absence of hereditary memberships in community, family, and the like as bases for collective action; (2) a good-sized population in daily contact over a long period of time; (3) an accumulation of common lore, grievances, and political experience; (4) the visible presence of an antagonist. These conditions first obtained in traditional small-scale industries like typography and silk weaving. Eventually, they developed in factories and even among agricultural workers. Thus over the nineteenth century, the principal loci of working-class organization shifted from shops to factories, with a lag of several decades behind the shift of the labor force from one to the other.

Politics and industry set the standard for religion, sociability, and intellectual life; the Third Republic brought France into its golden age of association. Napoleon III had speeded the process, or at least conceded to it gracefully, by openly tolerating workers' associations throughout the 1860s, legalizing the strike in 1864, and considerably relaxing restrictions on public assembly in 1868. The real spate of organizing and joining came, however, after the French rid themselves of Napoleon III.

It is true that the French have perpetuated a myth to the contrary. Confronted with the evidence of ubiquitous semisecret lodges, sodalities, and religious associations in the south during the eighteenth and nineteenth centuries, Maurice Agulhon has postulated a *sociabilité méridionale* peculiar to that region.[31] In fact, we have no good reason to limit that "sociability" to the south. In our own time, French rural communities are reputed to resist voluntary association. But when calm observers look carefully, this turns out not to be the case. In the small, and ostensibly backward, French villages he studied, Laurence Wylie found fire companies, multiple church-based associations, political parties, *classes* of all young men eligible for conscription in a given year, and other special-purpose organizations to be active participants in community life. Robert T. Anderson and Barbara Gallatin Anderson, studying a village 16 kilometres from Paris, found voluntary associations proliferating from late in the nineteenth century:

> The decades on either side of the turn of the century saw four voluntary associations introduced and sustained: a hunting society, an unemployment-funeral insurance (mutuality) society, a musical society, and a voluntary fire-fighting society. We are more concerned here with the last four decades of abrupt changes when, under the impact of primary urban-industrial change, approximately forty associations were founded.[32]

The Andersons go on to note how regularly the formal associations parallel and grow from older, existing groups in the community: the shop, the farm, the family, the church, and the community as a whole. In a sense, the organization was already there; the association simply crystallized and formalized it.

In those times when the state blocked the formation of distinct special-interest associations (which means most of the time before 1901, plus most of that during World War II), the French tended to overload whatever existing, tolerated means of asssembly and collective action they had at hand. During the Revolution, church services were often the occasions for agitation, argument, and action. Under the Restoration and the July

Monarchy, not only church services, but funerals and theatrical performances, became important contexts for demonstrations of political sympathies. About a year after the July Revolution, for example, the Parisian public (including medal holders from the Revolution itself, who were deliberately seated together by the management) attending the provocatively titled *Voyage de la liberté* took the many veiled political allusions in the play as their opportunity to stomp, hoot, cheer, and otherwise display their opposition to the regime.[33] Often the crowd went further than that; the insurrection of 1832 began with the funeral of the popular General Lamarque. At the same time, Frenchmen were busily forming secret societies for mutual aid and political action. They seized whatever organizational means were at their disposal.

Two things are deceptive about French organizations: (1) they often form as offshoots of organizations already in existence—the Catholic Church, the Communist Party, and so on; (2) while coherent and active, many of them do not quite acquire formal, legal existence. Both conditions contribute to the illusion of underorganization in France. The state's long resistance to formally constituted voluntary associations of any kind, the consequent tendency to form such groups in the shadows, the consequent unwillingness of the state to collect and publish information on voluntary associations (even political parties) add to the illusion.

The long concentration of the French population in rural communities probably did slow the creation of autonomous voluntary associations. And the French probably are more loath to form communitywide associations, but more eager to form associations serving particular interests, than other people. Duncan MacRae points out that, while on the whole joining was less common in the France of the 1950s than in the United States, France differed little from Britain and Germany in that respect. Then he goes on to suggest that "organizations that reinforced existing social divisions were more typical in France, while those that cut across other divisions and made decisions at the community level were more characteristic of the United States."[34] So the history we are reviewing is peculiarly a history of special-interest associations. From the later nineteenth century forward, craftspeople, students, teachers, winegrowers, farmers, big businessmen, veterans, professional women, and innumerable others devised new formal organizations to pursue their interests on a national scale.

THE CHANGING STRUGGLE FOR POWER

This vast series of change in French social structure reshaped the struggle for political power in three fundamental ways. First, position in the national structure of power came to matter far more, for practically every purpose, than local position did. Second, the struggle increasingly took the form of contention or coalition among formal organizations specialized in the pursuit of particular interests; communal groups virtually disappeared from politics. Third, new contenders for power emerged as the class structure and the organizational structure of France evolved. The rise of organizations speaking for segments of the industrial working class was the most important single movement, but other bids for power came from representatives of assorted groups of peasants, of youths, of schoolteachers, of Catholic employers, of governmental employers, of shopkeepers. Even when old established wielders of power like landholders and churchmen contended for power, they adopted the new associational style.

As in other Western countries, the political parties that emerged to full activity in Third Republic France compounded diverse interests. The Radicals, the Socialists, and, for that matter, the Radical Socialists long represented curious mélanges of the French electorate. As compared with its neighbors, nevertheless, France always had a remarkable susceptibility to party fragmentation, an exceptional openness to new parties representing new or old but separate political interests, and a considerable tendency for parties to slim down to a single major interest. The Parti Ouvrier Français, the Parti Social Français, the Boulangists, the Christian Democrats, the Communists, the Poujadists represent different phases of this specialization of parties. Fragmentation was the normal condition of French parlements, alliance among fragments the parliamentary game. Genuine threats to the parliamentary system came less from this kind of splintering than from the occasional appearance of an important political force acting outside the parliamentary arena: the Ligue des Patriotes, the Croix de Feu, Algerian nationalists, sometimes the Gaullists or the Communists. Inside or outside Parlement, the twentieth-century political struggle pitted associations representing relatively narrow segments of the population against one another, and aligned them with or against the regime. Interest-group politics emerged in France.

Our France, the France of 1830 and after, never stopped transforming itself. Our review of social change in France has pointed out spurts of industrialization, urbanization, and demographic transformation after 1850, after 1920, and, preeminently, after 1945; they contrast with crises and reversals at the times of the Franco-Prussian War, the two world wars, and the depression of the 1930s. These are but ripples in a fast-flowing stream. An urban-industrial class structure built on liquid rather than landed wealth, separating owners and managers of large formal organizations (factories, governments, schools) from their employees, emphasizing position in the national labor market over local attachments, giving exceptional rewards to technical expertise, gradually emerged from a class structure based far more on land and locality; periods of urban-industrial growth accelerated this transformation of the class structure. The centralization of politics through the growth of a massive and powerful state apparatus continued trends already established centuries earlier, although the advent of Louis Napoleon after 1848 and the extension of controls over the economy in the 1940s speeded the process. The nationalization of politics through the shift of power and participation to an arena far larger than local went on more or less continuously, but the political mobilization of 1848, of the early Third Republic, of the Popular Front, and of the years just after World War II probably drew people into involvement in national politics faster than at other times. The shift of collective action—both political and nonpolitical—from communal to associational bases proceeded inexorably over the entire period, especially during those same periods of political mobilization. These changes transformed the struggle for power and thus transformed the character of collective violence.

BACK TO VIOLENCE

How? Most immediately, by changing the collective actions characteristically producing violence. Remember that group violence ordinarily grows out of collective actions that are not intrinsically violent—festivals, meetings, strikes, demonstrations, and so on. Without them, the collective violence could hardly occur. People who do not take part in them can hardly get involved in the violence. The groups engaging in collective action with any regularity usually consist of populations perceiving and pursuing a common set of interests. And collective action on any considerable scale requires coordination, communication, and solidarity extending beyond the moment of action itself. Now the urbanization and industrialization and political rearrangement of France from the Revolution onward utterly transformed the composition of the groups capable of collective action, their internal organization, their interests, their occasions for collective action, the nature of their opponents, and the quality of collective action itself. The transformation of collective action transformed violence.

Again, how? It is easy to illustrate and hard to analyze. The classic French tax rebellion, for example, took two forms, singly or in combination:

1. A group of taxpayers attacked the *matériel* of tax collection, typically by smashing tollgates and burning assessment records.

2. Many of the residents of a community greeted the tax collector by blocking his way, by beating him, or by running him out of town; if he brought an armed force, the villagers fought them.

A typical small version of the tax rebellion occurred at Saint-Germain (Haute-Vienne) in August 1830. The local tax collectors stopped a carter to check his load and collect their toll. A crowd of men, women, and children "armed with picks and with stones" surrounded them, shouted against the tax, and led away man and wagon from the helpless revenue men.[35] This elementary form of resistance sometimes expanded into widespread and grave rebellion, as in the years before the Fronde, during the early Revolution, and (for the last time) in 1849. Although the sheer difficulty of paying when times were hard certainly had something to do with this common form of resistance to the state, it is important to see how regularly and directly it centered on the very *legitimacy* of the tax. Not long before the Revolution of 1830, the procureur general of the judicial district of Poitiers reported that "seditious posters" had been appearing in the city of Fontenay (Vendée); "the content of the posters is always to forbid the payment of taxes before the ministers who voted the budget are brought to trial."[36] The same sort of campaign was gathering strength in other parts of France at the same time and continued through the Revolution, often operating secretly and without violence, but now and then showing up in a public confrontation. The tax rebellion rose in the sixteenth century, flourished in the seventeenth, continued through the eighteenth into the nineteenth, and recurred in 1789, 1830, or 1848 as new revolutionary officials sought to reimpose the state's authority; it vanished after 1849. Its history traced the government's long struggle to secure obedience and income.

Gabriel Ardant has identified the general conditions for waves of fiscal revolts in France: a sharp increase in the central government's demands for cash, a sharp decrease in the market for products of rural industry or agriculture (and hence in the ability of villagers to convert their surplus into cash), or, more serious still, both at once. He has also pointed to their clustering in areas of "closed economy"—not necessarily poor, but little involved in production for the market, typically composed of largely self-sufficient farms. As he sums it up for the Massif Central:

> The proportion of the population in agriculture remains relatively large. No doubt some industries have grown up in the Massif Central near the coalfields, but the coalfields themselves are less productive than those of the North and the East. Furthermore, the factories do not have the ad-

vantage of channels of communication comparable to the networks of rivers and canals in the North and the East. In any case, industries like agriculture are far from the important markets of the North, the East and the Parisian region. From all this comes a larger tendency than elsewhere to live in a closed economy. Thus we can explain that the regions of the Massif Central have been perpetual zones of fiscal rebellion, that movements like those of the Croquans have periodically reappeared in Limousin, Perigord and Quercy, that in 1848 and 1849 the resistance to taxation developed in these same provinces. In our own time the Poujadist movement started out from Haut-Quercy (now the department of Lot), and the first departments affected were the adjacent ones, the locales of fiscal sedition under the old regime.[37]

Tax revolts grouped together in time and space, largely because the changes in national policy that incited them affected many localities sharing common characteristics at more or less the same time. The largest nineteenth-century bursts of tax revolts came in 1830, when the officials of the new monarchy sought to reimpose taxes on the provinces; in 1841, when the new minister of finance tried a special census as a step toward reorganizing the whole inequitable tax system; and—last and most—in 1848 and 1849, when another revolutionary government tried to put its fiscal affairs in order.

The tax rebellion often succeeded in the short run. The taxman fled, the tollgates fell. Its success, its timing, its personnel, its very form, however, depended on the solidarity of small, local groups of taxpayers and on the vulnerability of a system of control that relied on agents dispatched from cities into treacherous hinterlands. While the French have shrewdly finagled and dissimulated to avoid taxes up to our own day, their capacity for *collective* resistance to the tax collector sank fast after the middle of the nineteenth century. When antitax movements did revive with winegrowers after 1900, small distillers in the 1930s, or shopkeepers in the 1950s, the groups that joined the combat were no longer the taxpayers of a single commune, then of the next, but specialized regional and national associations responding to centralized direction. Marcelin Albert's Comité de Defense Viticole (in the first period), Henri Dorgère's Comités de Défense Paysanne (in the second), and Pierre Poujade's Union de Défense des Commerçants et Artisans (in the third) all adopted the defensive stance of earlier tax rebels, right down to their titles; all left violence aplenty in their wakes; but in these cases, the defensive actions and the violence came after the deliberate, strenuous organization of protest groups through substantial sections of small-town France.

That comparison provides a necessary clue. Around the middle of the nineteenth century, the scale and organizational complexity of the collective actions normally producing violence—and hence of violent action itself—both increased rapidly and decisively. That happened for two related reasons: (1) the scale and organizational complexity of the groups already contending for power increased rapidly and decisively, the expanding organization of industrial workers in the most notable case; and (2) communal groups dropped out of the struggle as the new associations, and new groups organized associationally, joined it. The organizational revolution reorganized violence.

There is something more, something the tax rebellion alone cannot reveal. Take the point of view of the state for a moment. From that perspective, the predominant forms of collective violence in France during the first half of the nineteenth century were *defensive*: tax rebellions fending off state employees, food riots beating back outside merchants, attacks on machines repelling technical innovations. The demonstrations, strikes, and rebellions that grew in importance over the century had a much larger *offensive* component; their participants reached for recognition, for a larger share, for greater power.

The crux of the contrast is the relationship of the participants to organization at the national scale: the national market, the national culture, and, preeminently, the national state. In the earlier, defensive phase, most of the participants were *resisting* the claims of national structures, especially the state; in the later, offensive phase, most of the participants were bidding for power over the operation of those national structures. In between, the nation won out.

We can be more exact. The nationalization of politics and economic life in France actually divided the major forms of collective violence into three main categories, which waxed and waned successively. The first we may call *primitive* collective violence. Primitive conflicts include the feud, the violent rivalries of adjoining villages, the recurrent ritual brawls of competing groups of artisans. They are the most visible form of the constant contention among communal groups within small-scale, local political systems. They predominated—at least in the statistical sense—in France before state makers like Mazarin and Colbert began pressing the claims of the national state and the national economy over local commitments and resources.

That bitter struggle of the state makers for control promoted defensive, resistant, backward-looking conflicts between different groups of local people, on the one hand, and agents of the nation, on the other. The word *reactionary* sums them up. The tax rebellion, the food riot, violent resistance to conscription, machine breaking, and invasions of enclosed land rose and fell in their own rhythms. They often occurred in the course of transfers of power that our comfortable retrospect permits us to treat as progressive revolutions. Yet they had in common a tendency to involve communal groups jostled and outraged by the commotion of state making.

The French state triumphed eventually over the major varieties of resistance to its claims. From that point on, what we may call *modern* forms of collective violence predominated. The deliberate attempt to seize control of the state qualifies. So does the demonstration, or the strike, which leads to a violent encounter. They differ from the reactionary forms of collective violence in several important ways: in pivoting on attempts to control, rather than resist, different segments of the national structure; by normally involving relatively complex special-purpose associations rather than communal groups; through a greater articulation of objectives, programs, and demands. These characteristics imply further contrasts with reactionary conflicts. One is a lesser dependency on natural congregations like markets, church services, and festivals in favor of deliberate assemblies and shows of strength (since special-purpose associations rarely draw all their members from the same round of life, but are often effective at calling together a diverse membership at crucial moments). Another is a tendency of the disturbances to be large and short; communal groups, once committed to a conflict, rarely mobilize large numbers of men, rarely have leaders with the authority to negotiate quick compromise settlements, and rarely can call off the action rapidly and effectively; associational groups, on the other hand, tend to become involved in violence as an outgrowth of brief, coordinated mass actions that are not intrinsically violent. Still another is a prevalence of indignation about the loss of specific rights and privileges in reactionary disturbances, as compared with a greater emphasis, in modern disturbances, on rights due on general principles.[38]

Two features of the shift from primitive to reactionary to modern forms of collective violence stand out: the change in *organization* of the participants and the change in *locus* of conflict. First, the groups taking part in collective violence became bigger, more complicated, more bureaucratized, more specifically committed to some public program or ideology, more open to new members prepared to support the group's special goals; earlier, I called this a transfer from communal to associational bases for collective action. Second, the locus of the conflicts involved moved away from the purely local toward the national, and even the international, scale; although the French were already making national revolutions and demonstrating in support of Poland in 1830, the great bulk of the violent conflict of the time aligned essentially local issues; by the 1930s, national issues and national antagonists took precedence. From a national perspective, this change seemed to involve a politicization of conflict. The trouble with that way of putting it is the fact that the primitive and reactionary forms of collective violence also grew out of well-developed struggles for power, out of political conflicts, on a smaller scale. The tax rebellion, the food riot, the invasion of fields, and even the artisans' brawl pivoted on local questions of rights, duties, and power. For that reason, we would be better off speaking of a nationalization of conflict, integrally related to the nationalization of political life. In our own day, we may have to speak of a further stage of internationalization.

It will not quite do, however, to picture primitive, reactionary, and modern collective violence as three distinct, exclusive stages. That image has two defects. First, some communal groups gradually acquire associational characteristics and retain their capacity for collective action throughout the process; a city's traditional elite joins a national pressure group, a religious community becomes a corporation. During the transformation, their characteristic *forms* of collective action, and thus of collective violence, change as well. Second, the modern forms of collective violence emerged early in those sectors of French society in which the national structures also emerged early: major cities, areas of advanced industry, the hinterland of Paris, and so on. At the center of the centralized French system, men had already begun struggling for control of the state and the national market centuries before their brothers at the periphery stopped fighting the expansion of the state and the market.[39] The rapid nineteenth-century transition from predominantly reactionary to predominantly modern forms of collective violence resembled the movement from one terrain to another rather than the passage of a guarded frontier. We might imagine the statistical distribution shown in Figure 4.4.

In the absence of reasonable criteria for the amount of collective violence and of reasonable data for the period before the nineteenth century, the exact shapes of the curves represent nothing but informed speculation. The biggest speculation is that the volume of reactionary collective violence swelled rapidly during the heroic state making of Louis XIII and Louis XIV; we know that popular rebellions of a reactionary form abounded at that time, but too little work has been done on conflicts well before and well after the Fronde to make the general timing sure. Figure 4.4 tests on a much firmer factual footing in illustrating that reactionary disturbances grew up to a nineteenth-century peak, instead of gradually diminishing.[40] The real point of the diagram, however, is to portray the slow displacement of primitive by reactionary collective violence as the French state extended its claims and the rapid displacement of reactionary by modern collective violence during the nineteenth-century nationaliza-

Figure 4.4. Hypothetical Evolution of Collective Violence in France

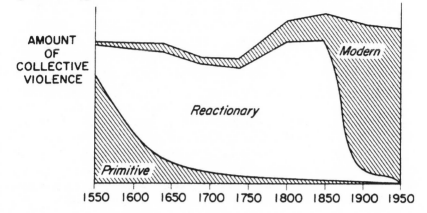

tion of the struggle for power. Only on the latter do we have much systematic information.

After the Revolution, the major periods of widespread collective violence in France were these: 1830–1882, beginning with the antecedents of the July Revolution and ending with a great miscellany of rebellions touching the whole range of French politics; 1846–1851, running from the last great round of food riots, through the February Revolution and the June Days of 1848, on past another mixture of tax rebellions, machine breaking, and other conflicts, all the way to the angry, unavailing response to Louis Napoleon's coup; 1869–1871, starting with massive, violent strikes and ending with the putting down of the Commune; 1934–1937, with its great, rowdy demonstrations and strikes of all varieties; 1947–1948, encompassing a wide range of postwar struggles for power; and, finally, the revolution (or coup, depending on your perspective) of 1958. The "Chronology" later in this chapter provides more details on the kinds of events making up each of these clusters of collective violence.

Several features of the calendar of violence deserve attention. First, the major bursts of violent conflict accompanied the largest realignment of the French political system, and vice versa; violence and political change depended on each other to an important extent. Second, the surprising durability of the superficially unstable Third Republic from 1870 to 1940 shows up again in its relative freedom from major crises of violence except at its birth and death; the 1890s and the early 1900s were turbulent years, but their incidents did not cumulate like those of the 1840s or the 1930s. Third, there was no particular tendency for violent protests to concentrate during or after the principal surges of urban expansion or industrial growth; the calendar offers no support for the idea that the pace of urbanization and industrialization itself determines the amount of protest. Fourth, the turbulence of 1846–1851 was the last in which reactionary collective violence played a large part; after that, the tax rebellion, food riot, machine breaking, and similar events virtually disappeared. Fifth, despite all the fluctuations, France remained violent in the twentieth century, as it had been in the nineteenth; advanced industrialism did not bring domestic peace. To be sure, the transformations wrought by industrialization changed the contenders, the style of conflict, and the prizes to be gained in French politics. But the rhythm of collective violence itself depended very little on the timing of population movements, changes in the organization of work, or the introduction of technological innovations; it depended very much on the shifts in the struggle for political power.

Figures 4.5 and 4.6 offer a closer look at the fluctuations in collective violence in France over two thirty-year segments, 1830–1860 and 1930–1960. In this case, a disturbance is any event in which at least one group of fifty persons or more took a direct part in an action in the course of which some persons or property were damaged or seized over resistance; the figures represent the numbers of such disturbances encountered in a day-by-day reading of two national newspapers over the entire period.[41] (The average size and duration of disturbances is sufficiently constant from one year to the next to permit the making of general inferences about the total

Figure 4.5. Number of Disturbances, 1830–1860

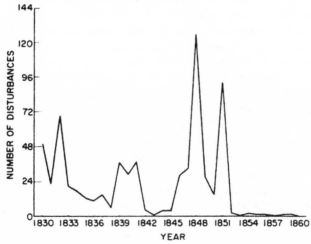

Figure 4.6. Number of Disturbances, 1930–1960

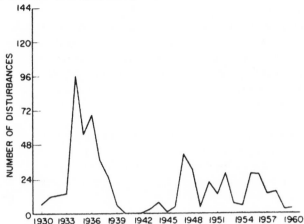

amount of time and numbers of persons involved from these curves.) More clearly than the simple chronology, the curves bring out the wide contrast among adjacent blocks of years, the presence of some periods (especially periods of extensive repression like the 1850s) with almost no collective violence at all, and the rough correspondence of major bursts of collective violence with major crises of the French political system. They also show that, although 1848 topped every other year in this series, the massive strikes and demonstrations of the 1930s produced as large a set of violent incidents as any comparable segment of the nineteenth century. The postwar was less turbulent in this respect than the 1930s, but far from calm. Collective violence did not trail away with modernization.

A ROUGH CHRONOLOGY OF
COLLECTIVE VIOLENCE IN FRANCE, 1830–1960*

1830 After few, small, and scattered disturbances during the first half of the year, the July Revolution in Paris, with immediate repercussions in Nantes, Bordeaux, Toulouse, Nîmes, and a few other places; later, tax re-

---

*This chronology is neither a complete nor a representative list of incidents. It characterizes the violence of the most turbulent years and mentions the largest *clusters* of disturbances. In fact, almost every single year produced at least a few violent incidents.

bellions, food riots, workers' protests, and violent demonstrations through many parts of France

1831 Continuation of smaller disturbances, many attacks on machines (e.g., Saint-Étienne, Bordeaux, Toulouse), multiple violent demonstrations in Paris and a few other big cities, silk workers' insurrection in Lyon

1832 Major rebellions in Paris, minor ones in a number of other cities, food riots in the east and southwest, large Legitimist protests at several points in the south, and an even larger Legitimist insurrection through important parts of the west

1834 Amid the usual small disorders here and there, another silk workers' rebellion in Lyon, with significant responses in Saint-Étienne and Paris

1839–1840 Frequent food riots, invasions of forests, several large conflicts in Paris, notably the abortive Insurrection of the Seasons (May 1839)

1841 Some tax rebellions and closely related resistance to the census, concentrated in the southwest

1846–1847 Exceptionally widespread food riots and similar conflicts, in a great semicircle around Paris

1848 February Revolution (especially Paris, but with a much wider response elsewhere than in 1830), continued rioting and agitation up to the June Days; attacks on machines and railroads, resistance to tax collectors, anti-Semitic violence, attacks on convents and châteaux through many parts of France

1849–1850 More tax rebellions (the Forty-Five Centime Revolt), forest disorders, and similar small-scale events, recurrent fighting between government forces and demonstrators, including one serious attempt at a coup, in Paris and a few other cities

1851 Armed resistance to Louis Napoleon's coup in almost a third of France's departments

1869–1870 Major strikes, leading to battles with police and troops, most bloodily at Saint-Étienne and Aubin

1870–1871 Insurrection in Alsace, revolution after the French defeat at Sedan beginning in Paris, with strong responses in Lyon and Marseille, further disturbances during and after the siege of Paris, followed by the Commune; similar but smaller rebellions in Marseille, Lyon, Toulouse, Limoges, Le Creusot, Saint-Étienne

1880 Numerous violent strikes

1891–1894 Many violent strikes and much terrorism attributed to anarchists, including the assassination of President Carnot in Lyon, 1894

1900–1901 Turbulent, insurrectionary strikes in Belfort, Monteau-les-Mines, Marseille, and elsewhere

1906–1907 Many violent strikes involving struggles with troops or retaliation against nonstrikers and bosses; winegrowers' protests in the south

1911   More violent confrontations of strikers, nonstrikers, owners, troops
1919–1920   Attempted general strikes and national workers' demonstrations leading to fights with troops, police, other workers
1934–1935   Large demonstrations of both Right and Left leading to frequent clashes among demonstrators, counterdemonstrators, and forces of order; attempted general strikes, violent meetings of peasant organizations
1936—1937   Great sit-down strikes, clashes between adherents of political extremes, particularly Communists and extreme right-wing organizations
1944   Extensive resistance activity, including a few large demonstrations and strikes
1947–1948   Violent resistance to fiscal controls; frequent rioting and conflicts with police based on protest demonstrations and on meetings of political extremes; insurrectionary strikes, including the occupation of railroad stations and public buildings, throughout France
1950–1952   Numerous clashes beginning with strikes, demonstrations, or political meetings, focusing on French and American foreign policies (e.g., violent demonstrations against Eisenhower in 1951), coupled with bombings and other terrorism directed mainly against Communists
1955–1956   Turbulent meetings, demonstrations, and street battles, featuring Poujadists and partisans of various policies in Algeria
1958   Coups in Algeria and Corsica, attempted coups elsewhere followed by street battles in Paris and other cities, eventuating in de Gaulle's coming to power

The curve of disturbances for the years from 1830 through 1860 has three high points: 1832, 1848, and 1851. Historians do not conventionally treat 1832 as a major crisis, yet it produced collective violence running from an unsuccessful insurrection in Paris to tax and food riots in many regions to widespread guerrilla action in the counterrevolutionary west. We already recognize 1848 as a revolutionary year. Yet many of the year's disturbances were food riots, tax revolts, and similar events coming well after the February Revolution and not belonging in any obvious way to the same action. The disturbances of 1851 occurred mainly in the course of the resistance to Louis Napoleon's coup d'état; seventy-six of the year's ninety-two disturbances came in December. After that, under the watchful eye and iron fist of the imperial police, collective violence on any scale virtually disappeared from France for over a decade.[42]

World War II breaks the second three-decade period in half. That violent interlude appears calm in the graph because I have excluded acts of international war, and because most of the terror and counterterror of

Occupation and Resistance involved very small, if deadly, groups of men. The great years for open, violent confrontation were 1934 (a year of constant demonstrations and of street fights growing out of them) and 1947 (a year of massive, often insurrectionary, strikes). The largest series of disturbances actually run from 1934 to 1937, and again from 1947 to 1952. In the first period, the French were battling over the place of labor and its representatives in the structure of power. In the second, an even more complex struggle over the form, strength, composition, and policy of French government was raging.

Summing up for each decade, I estimate the total number of persons taking part in these disturbances as:

1830–1839	300,000
1840–1849	500,000
1850–1860	100,000
1930–1939	750,000
1940–1949	250,000
1950–1960	750,000

If these numbers are approximately accurate, they mean that the number of people taking part in collective violence rose substantially over the century of modernization. A breakdown of these totals appears in Table 4.1. The table uses statistics similar to those commonly employed in the reporting of strikes. They show the disturbance rate in most decades to have run around seven or eight per million population (while strikes in contemporary countries like France, Britain, or Italy tend to be four or five times as frequent). They also show a considerable rise in the mean number of participants, a drop in the mean days the average participant spent in a

Table 4.1. Volume of Collective Violence in France, 1830–1860 and 1930–1960

Period	Number of Disturbances	Disturbances per Million Population	Mean Participants	Man-Days per Participant	Participants per Million Population	Man-Days per Million Population
1830–1839	259	7.7	1,150	1.6	8,700	13,900
1840–1849	202	8.2	1,750	1.9	14,300	27,300
1850–1860	114	3.2	950	1.6	3,000	4,700
1930–1939	333	7.9	2,200	1.0	17,500	17,500
1940–1949	93	2.3	2,400	1.0	5,500	5,500
1950–1960	302	7.1	2,200	1.0	15,600	15,600

disturbance, and, as a result, a fluctuation without trend in the total man-days spent in disturbances. With due allowance for the repeaters who returned for encounter after encounter, the figures make it appear possible that as many as one Frenchman out of a hundred took part in a collective action producing violence at some time during the average decade. If we took only adults, and only towns in which disturbances actually occurred, the figure would be more like one in twenty. In either case, a small minority, but not a negligible one.

The figures show that from the nineteenth to the twentieth century, the typical disturbance became shorter and bigger. As a consequence, the number of man-days absorbed by the average disturbance changed relatively little. To be sure, the decades varied considerably in the number of disturbances and, therefore, in the *total* man-days they brought into violent action. As a glance at the figures will show, the ten years from 1840 through 1849 produced the greatest volume of disturbances as measured by total man-days, but the 1930s produced a larger number of disturbances. The total energy flowing into collective violence and the kinds of particles in which the energy was emitted varied somewhat independently of each other.

We are actually dealing with two interlocking processes, one determining the shape of the typical disturbances, the other determining the frequency of disturbances. The long, slow process of association, the move from communal to associational bases for political action, lies behind the change in shape of the *typical* disturbance. In the 1830s, the typical disturbance (whether invasion of fields, tax rebellion, or food riot) would bring men, women, and children from the same small area out in anger for a day, and then another, and then perhaps still another. By the 1930s, the typical disturbance was the political party's one-day show of strength in a major city: a demonstration that often attracted determined counterdemonstrators and frequently led to scuffles, or pitched battles, with the police. Associations came to be the important mobilizers of collective action and thus the important participants in collective violence.

The other process affected the *number* of violent incidents at any particular time. It was (and is) a complex political process, governing, first, the occasions on which different contenders for power take collective action to assert their strength, defend their rights, or vent their anger and, second, the frequency with which such collective actions produce violence. The two questions are separate. A repressive government like that of Vichy holds down collective violence by making collective action of any sort difficult and costly. Whether repressive or not, a government faced with strikes, sit-ins, demonstrations, and other collective actions that, if illegal, are not intrinsically violent, has a considerable choice of tactics for dealing with them. Some tactics lead to frequent killing and wounding.

On the other side, when new contenders for power are appearing or old ones are losing their places, the frequency of collective action rises; the possibility of violence rises with it. And as associations become more prominent in the struggle for power, the people who lead them gain a certain ability both to move their followers around and to calculate the probability that one action or another will lead to violence. They therefore acquire some of the same control over the frequency of violence that the state ordinarily possesses. So the number of disturbances at a given point in time is a function of the intensity of the political struggle and the tactics of the contenders.

A similar pair of interlocking processes—one organizational, the other broadly political—seems to have determined the evolution of strike activity in France.[43] From the 1880s, when the first really comprehensive data on strikes became available, to World War II, the mean strikers per strike rose irregularly from 200 to around 700. After remaining around five or six days for decades, on the other hand, the median duration fell precipitously to a single day some time during or after the massive unionization of the Popular Front. Strikes also became big, but short. The timing is different from that of the transformations of collective violence, but the processes are surely related. In both cases, complex organizations not only capable of mobilizing men for protest, but also fairly effective in demobilizing them once the issue is decided, assumed a larger and larger role in the preparation of encounters between contenders and the authorities. The *number* of strikes at any given time and place, on the other hand, has fluctuated enormously in response to the intensity of grievances and the negotiating tactics of both labor and management. Over the very long run, aggregate strike activity has risen enormously in France as the labor force has industrialized, but within the industrial labor force itself, the rate has tended neither up nor down. Industrial conflict and collective violence have a lot in common. In both cases, the form of the individual conflict depends on the organization of the contenders and changes with that organization, while the frequency of conflicts depends more directly on the give-and-take of the struggle for power.

There is also a rough parallel in timing between strike activity and collective violence.[44] The evidence on strikes is mixed. Before 1855, we have fragmentary reports on strikes and fuller reports of persons criminally charged with striking; from 1885 on, we have relatively complete enumerations of strikes. From this evidence, the outstanding moments for strike activity were 1830–1834, 1847–1848, 1852–1856(?), 1890–1894, 1899–

1912, 1919–1920, 1936–1938, and 1947–1953, with the last period breaking all records for the sheer amount of time spent in strikes (see Figures 4.7
and 4.8). Those periods fit the calendar of disturbances to some extent.
The flurry of criminal charges in the 1850s may be due to Louis Napoleon's
clamping down at the beginning of his regime. The years before the Commune do not mark the statistics very heavily, but, in fact, there were great
strikes in 1869 and 1870, centering on Saint-Étienne, Mulhouse, and Le
Creusot, many of the authors of which escaped prosecution. Tentatively,
we may conclude that there has been some tendency for industrial conflict
and collective violence to occur together; indeed, at times, they have been
indistinguishable from each other.

However, it is *not* true that either strikes or collective violence ebbed

Figure 4.7. Number of Strikes and Number of Persons Charged for Strike Activity,
1825–1894

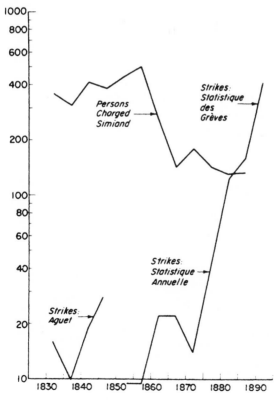

Figure 4.8. Number of Strikes, 1890–1960

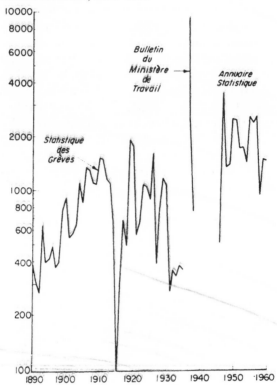

and flowed in response to the pace of structural change. We might look back to the signs we have already inspected. The great periods of economic expansion in France came between 1855 and 1870, 1920 and 1930, 1945 and 1960; the first period started quiet and ended raucous, the second produced little violent protest after a turbulent first year, the third an alternation of insurrectionary years with merely disorderly ones. The years of substantial downswing and depression were roughly 1870 to 1875, 1914 to 1920, 1931 to 1945 (with some small relief just before the war). The first period began, of course, with one of France's great revolutionary moments; the second, after the external disorder and internal order of World War I, ended with nationwide protests; and the third might have been continuously turbulent if a brutal war had not diverted French attention both inward and outward from the national political arena. One might possibly argue a complex connection between economic *contraction* and protest, with the immediate proviso that war counteracts even that connection. But the interdependence between collective violence and the timing of economic growth is clearly very weak, very complicated, or both.

During the period before 1860, there was some small correspondence between price swings and collective violence, mainly due to the rise of food riots in years of high prices. Figure 4.9 presents two composite price series for the years 1825–1860.[45] The score is about fifty-fifty: the high prices of 1838–1841 and 1846–1847 did correspond to the secondary bursts of protest in those years, and the lower prices of the mid-thirties and early forties did coincide with periods of relative peace; but neither 1830 nor 1848 was an especially high-priced year, and the great leap upward in prices of the 1850s may have distressed many people, but it did not lead

Figure 4.9. Wholesale Price Indexes, France, 1825–1860 (1914 = 100)

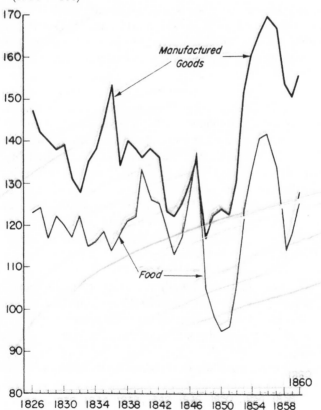

them into collective violence. (In fact, a last scattering of food riots occurred in 1853 and 1854, but they were small and few by comparison with 1847 or 1839.) In short, this comparison produces little more evidence of any straightforward determination of protest by economic fluctuation.

Since the timing of mechanization, of new industrial employment, of technical innovation, and even of urban growth followed approximately the same calendar as that of overall economic expansion, the conclusion is a more general one. If there is a connection between the pace of structural change and the frequency of violent conflict, it is not a direct, mechanical one. Fast social change does not, for all its bewilderments, incite disorder immediately or reliably. The relationship does not resemble that between the flushing of a toilet and the pulling of the handle. A better analogy might be the relationship between the performance of automobiles and the stamping of the dies used in making their parts: indelible but indirect.

Of course, it could still be true that collective violence, as one type of disorder, appears with other signs of social disintegration and thus reflects a general weakening of social cohesion and control. Do the variations of conventional indexes of social disorganization in France correspond to those of violent conflict? We can at least examine fluctuations in reported suicide and crime (Figure 4.10).

Since Emile Durkheim wrote his famous *Le Suicide,* sociologists have ordinarily been willing to accept the frequency of suicide as an indicator of the extent of social disintegration. France has long had an exceptionally high rate of suicide, a fact that seems to dovetail with its tendency to lapse into political chaos. But what of fluctuations in the reported rate?[46] During the nineteenth century, the rate of suicide marched inexorably upward, almost heedless of political transformations; during the twentieth, it has been relatively steady, except for the declines in suicide at the times of the two world wars. The all-time peak in the rate came near 1890, about the time Durkheim began his study of the phenomenon. Since then, the French have destroyed themselves (or, at least, have been reported as destroying themselves, the incompleteness of suicide reporting being considerable) less often. At this level, there is not detectable correspondence between suicide and collective violence. Does crime come closer?

Criminal statistics have some of the same weaknesses as suicide statistics. They ordinarily describe actions of the state—arrests, convictions, incarcerations, and so forth—rather than actions of its citizens. They therefore vary with the repressive powers and proclivities of the government. In the case at hand, the statistics include some of the direct responses of various French governments to political disturbances. In any case, the

Figure 4.10. Criminal Convictions, Vagrancy, and Suicide, 1826–1960

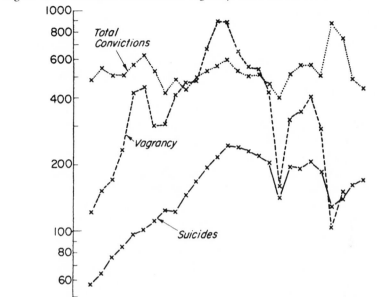

figures for total criminal convictions in France fit the temporal pattern of collective violence only a trifle better than the figures for suicide do. The maxima come around 1833, 1852, 1894, 1912, 1934, and 1942, which are at least in the vicinity of considerable clusters of violence. Their distribution might possibly justify the inference that repression tends to *follow* major upheaval, rather than that outbreaks of crime and political disturbances come together. However, the violent portions of the 1860s and 1870s were actually low points for criminal convictions, the turbulent period from 1944 to 1948 produced a significant decline in convictions, and the record crime levels of World War II surely had more to do with the repressive policies of Vichy and the Nazis than with any tendency for disorder to run rampant through France.

As for arrests for vagrancy, which one might expect to have some connection with the availability of insurrectionary masses, they did rise dramatically before 1848 and again before 1870, as well as less emphatically in the early 1930s. They reached their greatest height, on the other hand, around 1890, not the century's vintage year for violence. And they remained exceptionally low in the troubled years after World War II. So if there is a connection there, it is mediated and attenuated by other factors.

These negative conclusions clear the way for an assessment of the actual connections between modernization and changes in the character of conflict in France. The assessment must take the form of an argument—incompletely documented, but generally consistent with the evidence already reviewed. First, the conglomerate changes thrown together in the bin labeled "modernization" had no uniform effects whatsoever on the level, locus, form, or timing of political conflict in France, although some of the processes that observers ordinarily have in mind when using the sweeping term did have some well-defined effects. Second, rapid urbanization and industrialization alike generally depressed the level of conflict in the short run, because they destroyed various contenders' means and bases of collective action faster than they created new ones. Peasants who moved to cities, for example, ordinarily left settings in which they were sufficiently organized and aware of common interests to throw up repeated resistance to taxers, drafters, and grain buyers; in the industrial city, it commonly took them and their children a full generation to form the new organization and the new consciousness essential to renewed collective action. Third, urbanization and industrialization, nevertheless, directly stimulated political conflict when they diverted resources and control over resources from established groups that retained their internal organization; food rioters fighting the shipment of grain from their villages to cities and urban craftspeople fighting the threat of mechanization are two cases in point. When these changes proceeded faster than the dissolution of existing organization (which appears to have been the case in the 1840s, for example), the effect was actually to raise the level of group conflict. Fourth, the emergence of industrial capitalism, the development of a class structure organized around relations to a national market and the means of industrial production, the rise of bureaucracies and other formal organizations as the principal means of accomplishing collective ends combined to transform both the identities and the interests of the major contenders for power, and the form of their concerted action as well. Since conflict, including violent conflict, grows out of concerted action, the transformation of the contenders transformed the nature of contention in France. That series of transformations has occupied most of this essay's attention.

But what determined how *much* conflict there was? In those general terms, my inquiry into the French experience has produced no answer at all; without firmer establishing of types of conflict, and equivalencies among them, there is no way to rule out the possibility that conflict is constant in human life and that only its visage is variable. If we restrict our attention to the public, collective forms of conflict that commonly lead to violence, however, then we can see how much their frequency and outcome depends on the operation of the state.[47] The nineteenth-century centralization and nationalization of politics, as the state crushed its local rivals, incited widespread protest and durably shifted the focus of violent conflict. State repression of collective action by contenders for power diminished the frequency of violent conflicts during the 1850s and the two world wars, whereas the relaxation of that repression in the 1860s or the later 1940s permitted the contention to come back into the open. Throughout the two centuries, the state resisted the bids of new contenders for power in the name of those who already had established places in the structure of power; the tactics selected by the agents of the state (for example, in controlling hostile demonstrations) strongly determined the extent of violence. As a consequence, new contenders for power tended to pass through a cycle going from quiet organization to violent contention to conquest of a position within the structure of power to involvement in violence mainly through the proxies of police and soldiers. Enough new contenders came along, however, and enough of them were rebuffed to keep the level of violence high. Today, students, intellectuals, and technical workers seem to be hammering at the gates.

Samuel Huntington has interpreted part of this experience as a nineteenth-century peculiarity:

> In the nineteenth century in Europe and America industrial labor was radical and at times revolutionary because industrialization preceded unionization, the dominant groups in society often vigorously opposed unions, and employers and governments did what they could to resist the demands of labor for higher pay, shorter hours, better working conditions, unemployment insurance, pensions, and other social benefits. In these countries, the mobilization of labor easily outran the organization of labor, and consequently radical and extremist movements often gained support among the alienated working class before unions became strong. When unions were organized they were of this new class. Communist and other radical groups were strongest in labor movements which were

denied legitimacy and recognition by the political and economic elites.
. . . All these conditions are much less prevalent among countries industrializing later.[48]

The experience of France does not support the contention that "the mobilization of labor easily outran the organization of labor." Mobilization actually came as a consequence of organization. The French experience does,
on the other hand, fit Huntington's implicit argument that recognition and
legitimation diminish a contender's involvement in violent conflict. In his
argument, Huntington stresses the mollifying effect of (a) legitimate means
for the expression of demands and grievances, (b) the direct control that
"institutionalization" gives governments over contenders. There is more
to it than that. I would say it is also because recognition opens up new
means to the accomplishment of the contender's ends, because recognition
tends to commit the leaders to the maintenance of the structure they have
entered, because recognition was part of what they were seeking in the first
place, and because recognition restrains the state's repressive agents from
reacting violently to the new contender's displays of strength.

Question: is this a peculiarity of the nineteenth century, or of France
alone? The peculiarity, it seems to me, resides in the greater readiness of
the twentieth century's new states to preempt, coopt, and even stimulate
organization among emerging contenders for power as a means of keeping
them under control.[49] As it happens, the new states often fail, and violent
conflict is widespread among them. The underlying processes producing
collective violence in those countries have much in common with those at
work in nineteenth-century France.

In the twentieth century as well, France's collective violence shares a
number of traits with the collective violence of other industrial countries.
It probably shares causes as well. For example, the nearly simultaneous
swelling of separatist movements, student protests, and other strident demands for autonomy and release from state control in a wide variety of
Western countries, including France, probably tells us that both individu-
ally and collectively they are undergoing similar political transformations.
Marshall McLuhan, in an interview for a popular magazine, made an interesting stab at analysis:

PLAYBOY: On what do you base your prediction that the United States
will disintegrate?
MCLUHAN: Actually, in this case as in most of my work, I'm "predicting"
what has already happened and merely extrapolating a current process to
its logical conclusion. The Balkanization of the United States as a conti-

nental political structure has been going on for some years now, and racial chaos is merely one of several catalysts for change. This isn't a peculiarly American phenomenon; as I pointed out earlier, the electric media always produce psychically integrating and socially decentralizing effects, and this affects not only political institutions within the existing state but the national entities themselves.

All over the world, we can see how the electric media are stimulating the rise of ministates: in Great Britain, Welsh and Scottish nationalism are recrudescing powerfully; in Spain, the Basques are demanding autonomy; in Belgium, the Flemings insist on separation from the Walloons; in my own country, the *Québecois* are in the first stages of a war of independence; and in Africa, we've witnessed the germination of several ministates and the collapse of several ambitiously unrealistic schemes for regional confederation. These ministates are just the opposite of the traditional centralizing nationalisms of the past that forged within one national boundary. The new ministates are decentralized tribal agglomerates of those same ethnic and linguistic groups. Though their creation may be accompanied by violence, they will not remain hostile or competitive armed camps but will eventually discover that their tribal bonds transcend their differences and will thereafter live in harmony and cultural cross-fertilization with one another.[50]

I beg leave to doubt that "the electric media" lie behind the new minification. I lack McLuhan's confidence in a harmonious future. I miss, in this statement, some sense of the prevalence of communal, autonomist longings *outside* the traditional ethnic and linguistic groups. Yet the notion that the domestic troubles of our own time depend in an important way on a realignment of the international structure of politics—and, more exactly, on the national state's loss of power and autonomy—strikes me as worth serious consideration. Perhaps the emergence of huge blocs of states like those dominated by the United States or the Soviet Union, and those that show some signs of forming in Europe and around China, reduces the room for maneuver of the men who run any particular state, and thus simultaneously diminishes the value of membership in the national political system and encourages those who have their strongest investment in some smaller unit to throw off the weight of the state. If so, a new transformation in the character of political conflict is occurring. And, as before, the transformation nonetheless continues processes of change that began long before. That such a transformation should occur by no means follows ineluctably from the logic of this paper's argument. But it is the *kind* of transformation we have been discussing.

Ultimately, to be sure, much of the argument comes down to an awesome tautology. Political conflict changes as a consequence of changes in the political system. Since "the political system" is itself a name for the regularities in a series of conflicts and resolutions of conflict, the proposition comes close to reading: political conflict changes as a consequence of changes in political conflict. That apparently self-defeating result has more value than is evident. It calls attention to the intimate dependence on central political processes of protest, riots, and movements (like machine breaking and tax rebellions) that have frequently been considered nonpolitical and have commonly been portrayed as direct responses to the strains of economic change. It points up the continuity between the violent and nonviolent forms of political contention. It opens the way to the examination of the effects of different forms and degrees of state control of collective action on the character of political conflict, including the most violent forms of conflict. It finally leads to reconsideration of a crucial question barely raised in this paper: how does the nature of the conflict affect the distribution, or redistribution, of power?

For people articulate, advertise, and sometimes achieve their interests through conflict. That includes violent conflict. Ordinary French people, by rioting, force the authorities to hold down the price of bread. The great demonstrations and sit-down strikes of the 1930s did solidify the place of organized labor in the structure of power. Mass action did help produce significant transfers of power in 1789, 1830, 1848, 1870, and 1958. The use of the special word *revolution* for most of these dates should not obscure the fact that the collective action involved in the events shared the characteristics of the much larger number of collective actions of their own eras that did *not* produce transfers of power. The great bulk of the actions we now sum up as the Revolution of 1789 were, in fact, food riots, tax rebellions, and similar conflicts of exactly the same variety as prevailed in France for a century before 1789 and another half century after then. The continuities are so great as to indicate that those theorists of revolution who ask themselves how so rare a collective action as revolution could come about are chasing a will-o'-the-wisp. What we call revolutions in retrospect are whole chains of collective actions, many of them at cross-purposes. In the French experience, at least, they deeply resembled other collective actions far removed from revolution. The real question is why only a few of a large number of similar actions result in transfers of power.

Barrington Moore Jr. has theorized that the main conditions for revolution are:

1. the development of a widespread challenge to prevailing modes of thought and to the predominant explanations or justifications of human suffering;

2. the emergence of acute conflicts of interest within the dominant classes;
3. the elite's loss of unified control over army, police, and other instruments of violence;
4. the mobilization of a revolutionary mass either from the urban plebs or (more likely) the peasantry, which is most likely to occur with "a sudden increase in hardship coming on top of quite serious deprivations, together with the breakdown of the routines of daily life—getting food, going to work, etc.—that tie people to the prevailing order."[51]

The first three conditions have to do mainly with elite control over the political apparatus and its justifications; only the fourth refers directly to mass action. Moore distinguishes sharply (and, I believe, rightly) between the conditions under which regimes are vulnerable and the conditions under which ordinary people act against regimes. Only the convergence of the two makes revolution likely. Here, I have dealt almost entirely with the second sort of question: the conditions for mass action. At best, that amounts to only half the problem of accounting for 1789, 1848, or 1958.

If my analysis is correct, the immediate stresses and strains of technological changes, population movements, and other such components of "modernization" play a rather small part in the promotion of collective action. Nor does material hardship as such, or even the sudden increase of material hardship, seem to have had a primary role in France. The crucial exception is that when (as in the standard food riot) someone else appears to be creating or profiting by the new hardship and doing so through violations of his own duties and other people's rights, ordinary people often strike at the presumed profiteers in the name of justice. But it is justice—and conflicting conceptions of justice, at that—that is at the heart of violent conflict. That means violent conflict remains close to politics in origin as well as in impact. In that respect, France resembles other European nations.

Nonetheless, France has a particular history, and that history affects its political conflicts. The foundation of all its modern regimes on one version or another of a revolutionary tradition has, paradoxically, justified the government's taking on of exceptional powers when it could declare *la patrie en danger*. That has probably produced greater fluctuations in repression, and sharper distinctions between "ins" and "outs" in times of repression, in France than in most other Western countries. Likewise, the enormous centralization of power within the French system has probably defined more different kinds of struggles in France than elsewhere as confrontations between the state and its enemies—and as struggles the state could not afford to lose. Before broadcasting conclusions from French political history throughout the world, we must begin to treat these two features, the presence or absence of a revolutionary tradition and the degree of centralization of power, as major variables. That done, we have much to learn about modernization in general from the modernization of political conflict in France.

In the France of the last two centuries, political conflict did modernize, in the sense of shifting toward larger-scale, more highly organized forms of collective action. The changing relations of the French to a state that over at least half that period was increasing its hold over their everyday lives set one of the major rhythms: the change from primitive to reactionary to modern forms of collective violence. At the same time, men's everyday organization for collective action changed slowly as France urbanized and industrialized; the reorganization of everyday life transformed the character of collective conflict; that long-run reshaping of solidarities, rather than the immediate production of stress and strain, constituted the most important impact of structural change on political conflict. In the shorter run, the state's tactics of repression and accommodation strongly affected the intensity, form, locus, and outcome of conflict. Throughout the two centuries, the struggle to acquire or maintain established places in the structure of power, and thus to gain control over the conditions of their own existence, most regularly brought different groups of French people into violent conflict with one another. Even in modern France, the struggle continues.

NOTES

1. Substantial portions of this chapter came from early drafts of Charles Tilly, Louise Tilly, and Richard Tilly, *The Rebellious Century,* Cambridge: Harvard University Press, 1975.

2. See Ian Weinberg, "The Concept of Modernization: An Unfinished Chapter in Sociological Theory," unpublished paper presented to the annual meeting of the American Sociological Association, 1968; Reinhard Bendix, "Tradition and Modernity Considered," *Comparative Studies in Society and History* 9 (April 1967): 292–346.

3. For a review of the literature on this point, see Samuel P. Huntington, *Political Order in Changing Societies* (New Haven, CT: Yale University Press, 1968), pp. 39–59.

4. Ian Weinberg, "Social Problems Which Are No More," in Erwin O. Smigel, ed., *Handbook of Social Problems* (Chicago: Rand McNally, 1971), pp. 637–72.

5. Letter of 27 May 1768: C. Hippeau, *Le Gouvernement de Normandie au XVIIe et au XVIIIe siècle* (Caen: Goussiaume de Laporte, 1864), pt. 2, vol. 1, p. 478.

6. Georges Afanassiev, *Le commerce des céréales en France au dix-huitième siècle* (Paris: Picard, 1894), pp. 163–164.

7. Pierre Pierrard, *La Vie ouvrière à Lille sous le Second Empire* (Paris: Bloud & Gay, 1965), pp. 490–491.

8. Andrè Armengaud, *Les Populations de l'Est-Aquitaine au début de l'époque moderne* (Parish: Mouton, 1961), pp. 420–421.

9. Raymond Aron, *La Révolution introuvable* (Paris: Fayard, 1968), p. 44.

10. Alain Touraine, *Le Mouvement de mai ou le communisme utopique* (Paris: Le Seuil, 1968), p. 14.

11. Herbert Luethy, *France against Herself* (New York: Meridian, 1955), pp. 19–20. Consider, in the same connection, that Louis Napoleon had only to tighten well-established procedures to produce the repressive regime of the early Second Empire: Howard C. Payne, *The Police State of Louis Napoleon Bonaparte* (Seattle: University of Washington Press, 1966).

12. Karl Marx, *The Civil Wars in France* (New York: International Publishers, 1935), p. 39.

13. Auguste Blanqui, "La critique sociale," in *Textes choisis* (Paris: Editions Sociales, 1955), pp. 166–167.

14. See J. P. Nettl, *Political Mobilization* (London: Faber & Faber, 1967).

15. Raymond Aron, *Immuable et changeante, de la IVe à la Ve République* (Paris: Calmann-Levy, 1959), pp. 40–41.

16. André-Jean Tudesq, *Les Conseillers généraux en France au temps de Guizot* (Paris: Colin, 1967; Cahiers de la Fondation Nationale des Sciences Politiques, 157), pp. 85–102; ibid., *Les Grands notables en France* (Paris: Presses Universitaires de France, 1964; Publications de la Faculté des Lettres et Sciences Humaines de Paris, "Recherches," 21), II, 1065; George W. Fasel, "The French Election of April 23, 1948: Suggestions for a Revision," *French Historical Studies* 5 (Spring 1968): 285–298.

17. Philip Williams, *Politics in Post-War France,* 2nd ed. (London: Longmans, 1958), p. 2. Cf. Michel Crozier, *The Bureaucratic Phenomenon* (Chicago: University of Chicago Press, 1964), pp. 213–264.

18. W. A. Cole and Phyllis Deane, "The Growth of National Incomes," in *The Cambridge Economic History of Europe* (Cambridge, MA: Cambridge University Press, 1965), vol. 6, pt. 1, p. 12.

19. Sources for Figure 4.1: (1) Maurice Lévy-Leboyer, "La croissance économique en France au XIXe siècle, Résultats préliminaires," *Annales: Economies, Sociétés, Civilisations* 23 (July–August 1968): 788–807. The statistic is an index number (1890 + 100) for "global product" of agriculture, industry, and construction. It therefore excludes services, investment, government purchases, and net exports from among the items conventionally included in gross national product. (2) Colin Clark, *The Conditions of Economic Progress,* 3rd ed. (London: Macmillan, 1960), pp. 123–229. The figures represent real income (including the imputed value of agricultural products produced and consumed outside the market) in billions of International Units. Up to 1913, the figures are annual averages for decades centered on

the date shown. (3) Estimates of national income by Alfred Sauvy, 1901–1949 and, after 1949, extrapolation of Sauvy series at 1949, as reported in *Annuaire statistique de la France, résumé retrospectif,* 1966, table 14, p. 556. The units are billions of 1938 francs. The estimates of production made by the researchers of the Institut de Science Economique Appliquée (ISEA) yield a somewhat different timetable for expansion and contraction, most notably in attributing greater growth to the decade from 1835 to 1844 than to the decade after 1854. See Jean Marczewski, *Introduction à l'histoire quantitative française de 1789 à 1964—Conclusions générales* (Paris: ISEA, 1966; Cahiers de l'ISEA, AF, 7).

20. Source: J.-C. Toutain, *La population de la France de 1700 à 1959* (Paris: ISEA, 1963; Cahiers de l'ISEA, AF, 3), pp. 135, 161.

21. Sources: *Annuaire statistique de la France, résumé retrospectif,* 1966, table 3, p. 23; *Statistique de la France* (Paris: Imprimerie Royale, 1837), pp. 267–283. "Urban places" are communes with 2,000 or more persons in the central agglomeration. The figures for 1821 and 1836 are estimates from the ratio communes 2,000 + / communes 10,000 + for 1851, as applied to the actual total in communes of 10,000 or more in 1821 and 1836.

22. Paul-M. Bouju et al., *Atlas historique de la France contemporaine* (Paris: Colin, 1966), p. 56.

23. Ibid., pp. 72–73.

24. Laurence Wylie et al., *Chanzeaux* (Cambridge, MA: Harvard University Press, 1966), p. 341.

25. Honoré de Balzac, "Ce qui disparaît de Paris," in *Le Diable boiteux* (1845–1846); reprinted in *Les Parisiens comme ils sont* (Geneva: La Palatine, 1947), p. 158. Four or five decades later, Edward Goblot was to declare (prematurely, I believe) the end of the system Balzac had seen crystallizing: "So we see all artificial inequality, as well as false equality, disappearing little by little, giving way to natural inequalities: intelligence, knowledge, talent, taste, virtue and vice. In short, personal merit is overcoming class distinctions. For there could not be a *class* of bright men, or men of good will, or men of good taste. A class can only survive by making others believe it is an elite, and cannot become an elite by ceasing to be a class. Thus it is remarkable that this condition of unstable equilibrium has been able to maintain itself for nearly a century" (*La Barrière et le niveau* [Paris: Alcan, 1930], p. 160).

26. Karl Marx, "The Class Struggles in France, 1848–1850," in Karl Marx and Friedrich Engels, *Selected Works* (Moscow: Foreign Languages Publishing House, 1958), I, 148–149.

27. Stanley Hoffmann, "Paradoxes of the French Political Community," in Stanley Hoffmann et al., *In Search of France* (Cambridge, MA: Harvard University Press, 1963), pp. 1–117.

28. Henry W. Ehrmann, *Politics in France* (Boston: Little, Brown, 1968), p. 171.

29. Archives Nationales F^{1c}I 33, report of 14 October 1831.

30. Peter N. Stearns, "Patterns of Industrial Strike Activity in France during the July Monarchy," *American Historical Review* 70 (January 1965): 371–394.

31. Maurice Agulhon, *La Sociabilité méridionale*, 2 vols. (Aix-en-Provence: La Pensée Universitaire, 1966).

32. Robert T. Anderson and Barbara Gallatin Anderson, *Bus Stop for Paris* (Garden City, NY: Doubleday, 1965), pp. 224–225.

33. Archives Nationales F[lc]I 33, report of 20 July 1831.

34. Duncan MacRae Jr., *Parliament, Parties, and Society in France, 1946–1958* (New York: St. Martin's, 1967), pp. 29–30. See also Orvoell R. Gallagher, "Voluntary Associations in France," *Social Forces* 36 (December 1957): 153–160.

35. Archives Nationales BB[18]1186, 14 August 1830.

36. Archives Nationales BB[18]1181, report of 3 February 1830.

37. Gabriel Ardant, *Théorie sociologique de l'impôt* (Paris: SEVPEN, 1965), II, p. 784.

38. I have discussed and documented these contrasts at much greater length in "The Changing Place of Collective Violence," in Melvin Richter, ed., *Essays in Theory and History* (Cambridge, MA: Harvard University Press, 1970), and "Collective Violence in European Perspective," in Hugh Davis Graham and Ted Robert Gurr, eds., *Violence in America* (Washington, DC: Government Printing Office, 1969), pp. 5–34.

39. Sylvia Thrupp has pointed out to me that the typology also leaves no place for the extraordinary role that simultaneously communal and associational groups of the type of sworn brotherhoods played in the collective violence of the European Middle Ages.

40. I have put considerable evidence on this point into "How Protest Modernized in France, 1845–1855," in William O. Aydelotte, Allan Bogue, and Robert Fogel, eds., *The Dimensions of Quantitative Research in History* (Princeton: Princeton University Press, 1972).

41. Important qualification: the enumeration excludes acts of war with an external enemy and thus distorts the actual level of violence in the territory of France during 1870 and 1940–1944.

42. Comparisons of newspapers with major police series (notably BB[18] in the Archives Nationales) indicate that some of the apparent damping of violence in the 1850s was due to reduced reporting of conflict in the press. A number of brawls between Piedmontese and French railroad workers, for example, escaped notice in the national papers, as did a substantial peasant rising in the Beauce in December 1854 (BB[18]1537). Nevertheless, the archives also register a huge drop in the frequency of collective violence after 1851, lasting well into the 1860s.

43. These statements summarize some of the findings of an analysis of strike activity conducted by Edward Shorter and myself at the University of Toronto, the first report of which appears in a paper by Shorter and Tilly, "The Shape of Strikes in France, 1830–1968" (University of Toronto, 1969).

44. Sources: François Simiand, *Le Salaire, l'évolution sociale et la monnaie* (Paris: Alcan, 1932), III; Jean-Pierre Aguet, *Les Grèves sous la Monarchie de Juillet (1830–1847)* (Geneva: Droz, 1954); Direction du Travail, *Statistique des grèves et des recours à la conciliation*, 1893–1936; Direction du Travail, *Notices et comptes rendus*, nos. 3

and 7, 1890–1892; Ministère du Travail, *Bulletin,* 1937–1939; Institut National de la Statistique et des Etudes Economiques (INSEE), *Annuaire statistique de la France, résumé rétrospectif, 1966.*

45. Source: INSEE, *Annuaire statistique de la France, résumé rétrospectif, 1966.*

46. Sources: INSEE, *Annuaire statistique de la France, résumé rétrospectif, 1966,* tables 4 and 5, pp. 124–127, and tables 3–9, pp. 161–166. Emile Levasseur, *La Population française* (Paris: Rousseau, 1889–1893), II, p. 126. Maurice Halbwachs, *Les Causes du suicide* (Paris: Alcan, 1930), p. 92. "Total convictions" sums convictions in Cours d'assises, Tribunaux correctionnels and (after 1952), Cours d'appel; the figure is an annual average rate per 100,000 population over the five-year interval centering on the date shown. "Vagrancy" represents arrests for *mendicité* and *vagabondage;* it is also an annual average rate per 100,000 population over the same five-year intervals. "Suicide" is reported cause of death, calculated as an annual average rate per 10,000 population over the same five-year intervals.

47. The argument to follow resembles in many respects that laid out by William Gamson in "Stable Unrepresentation in American Society," *American Behavioral Scientist* 12 (November–December 1968): 15–21.

48. Huntington, *Political Order in Changing Societies,* p. 284.

49. In this connection, it is interesting to note that by far the most powerful factor in Ted Gurr's analysis of civil strife in 114 polities, 1961–1965, was "social and structural facilitation," which combines measures of internal geographic accessibility, legitimacy of the Communist Party, and the extent of external support for the initiators of strife (the first two being negatively related to the extent of strife, the third positively related to it), and most of the other significant variables have to do with the relations between the state and its citizenry, rather than, say, the extent of economic hardship or the prevalence of religious barriers within the population. As proportions of the total variance explained, the factors are: persisting deprivation, 24 percent; short-term deprivation, 12 percent; "institutionalization" (which really has to do with the representation of interests within the policy), 1 percent; legitimacy, 11 percent; coercive potential, 4 percent; social and structural facilitation, 48 percent. Ted Gurr, "A Causal Model of Civil Strife: A Comparative Analysis Using New Indices," *American Political Science Review* 62 (December 1968): 1104–1124. See also his "A Comparative Study of Civil Strife," in Graham and Gurr, eds., *Violence in America,* II, pp. 443–495.

50. "Playboy Interview: Marshall McLuhan," *Playboy* (March 1969): 68.

51. Barrington Moore Jr., "Revolution in America?" *New York Review,* 30 January 1969, pp. 6–12. Moore draws one conclusion that runs counter to the general argument of this paper: "Though the influence of prior forms of social organization, pre-existing habits, and general outlook is a topic that requires further investigation, I have come to suspect that it too plays a much less important role than immediate circumstances in creating a revolutionary mass" (p. 8).

· 5 ·

DOES MODERNIZATION BREED REVOLUTION?

A SICILIAN REVOLUTION

Eighteen forty-eight was one of Europe's vintage years for revolution. The first truly revolutionary situation of the year did not develop in the industrializing centers of France, Germany, or England. It formed in poor old Sicily. During the three decades since the settlement that had closed the Napoleonic Wars, Sicily had occupied a position subordinate to Naples in the newly created Kingdom of the Two Sicilies. Its bourgeoisie had long been pushing for Sicilian autonomy. Some of them, in tune (and, to some extent, in concert) with liberals elsewhere in Italy, had lately been entertaining ideas of political reform. And other groups of Sicilians opposed any strong government whatsoever.

Early in January 1848, the closing of the university, after student riots centering on calls for a new constitution, freed the young and educated for political action. The government decreed the arrest of some of the city's prominent liberals. Then the call for a revolt on the occasion of King Ferdinand's birthday celebration—January 12—began to spread through Palermo. A manifesto, passed from hand to hand on 9 January, read as follows:

> Sicilians! The time of useless supplications is past. Protests, requests, and peaceful demonstrations are useless. Ferdinand has scorned them all. Are we, a freeborn people reduced to shackles and misery, to delay any longer in reconquering our legitimate rights? To arms, sons of Sicily. The force of the people is omnipotent: the unity of the people will bring the fall of the king. The day of 12 January 1848, at dawn, will bring the glorious epoch of universal regeneration. Palermo will receive with delight those armed Sicilians who offer themselves in support of the common cause: to establish reforms and institutions proper to the progress of this century, reforms and institutions desired by Europe, by Italy, and by Pope Pius.

This chapter was first published as "Does Modernization Breed Revolution?" *Comparative Politics* 5 (1973): 425–447. Reprinted with permission.

Union, order, subordination to our leaders. Respect for property: theft is
a declaration of betrayal of the cause of the nation and will be punished
as such. He who lacks means will be given them. With these principles
Heaven will support the just cause. Sicilians, to arms![1]

The declaration was a little grander than the events that followed, but the
Palermitani did, indeed, begin a revolution on 12 January.

The people of Palermo had rebelled many times, and against a great
variety of governments, in the centuries before 1848. On this day, they
began with the formation of small crowds that listened to harangues,
sported the Italian tricolor, marched through the streets, and skirmished
with the troops and police. By the end of the day, a few demonstrators and
a few troops had died in combat, and barricades had put the rebels in
control of the Fieravecchia section of the city. The next day, the few hundreds of insurgents expanded their control over different points in the city
and found themselves reinforced by the arrival of *squadre* of agricultural
workers from the surrounding countryside. On 14 January, the establishment of four revolutionary committees created a kind of government for
Palermo and brought the liberal bourgeois and aristocrats directly into the
revolutionary movement. In the succeeding days, they held off the troops
and ships of the Bourbon monarchy and dislodged the old government
from its remaining toeholds within the city. As the Bourbon forces re-
treated from Palermo, insurrections sprang up all over Sicily. By the middle
of February, revolutionary committees had taken power almost everywhere. In the course of the following months, a revolutionary regime re-
suscitated the old Sicilian parliament, declared its attachment to the nascent
Italian federation, and established de facto autonomy for the island.

The revolutionary coalition, however, was disparate and uneasy. Many
of the early revolutionary actions consisted of seizures of agricultural land
by rural workers, acts of vengeance by them and others, and moves by
bosses of what would later be called Mafia, to secure their own positions
by diligent use of their strong-arm boys. The revolutionary committees
soon found themselves struggling to keep down some of their supposed
supporters and to hold the rest together. They organized a bourgeois National Guard to counter the irregulars who had assumed military duties
everywhere. They attempted to launch a program of modest liberal reforms
in the face of strenuous demands for land reform and other great transformations, and against equally strenuous resistance to any governmental intervention. Even the return of the Bourbon troops did not reunite the
revolutionaries. The National Guard dissolved as the Bourbons advanced.
By May 1849, those who had made the Sicilian revolution had fled, or

surrendered, or disguised their roles. Ferdinand II again ruled Sicily, at least in principle.

Put in the company of the English revolution of the seventeenth century, the Spanish of the nineteenth century, the Russian of the twentieth, or even of some of the other revolutions of 1848 itself, the Sicilian revolt was a petty affair. Yet its very incompleteness, ineffectuality, and reversal raise important questions about the nature of revolution that a concentration on the great standard examples ordinarily tempts us to answer in superficial, conventional ways. In what sense, if any, should we regard events such as those in Sicily as revolutionary? Do they constitute a number of separate revolutions, a single revolution, part of a larger revolution, or no revolution at all? What distinguishes them from the banditry, vendetta, rioting, warfare, and murder that have sometimes permeated Sicilian life? Do they have any connections? If the revolutions of 1848 were somehow promoted by the modernization of Europe, how does that generalization apply to cases like Sicily? Under what conditions might we reasonably have expected this revolution to succeed or to produce extensive structural change? How would we know which caused what?

The historical versions of these questions are challenging. The political history of Sicily always displays exotic complexities; it draws its practitioners into a sort of ethnography that rarely seems necessary on the more familiar terrain of Paris or Berlin. It also tests the limits of the standard general interpretations of 1848. Although disagreement on the character of the midcentury revolutions still thrives (within a range running from observations of the decay or incompetence of nineteenth-century political regimes to straightforward assertions of bourgeois revolution), almost everyone asserts the importance of: (a) some sort of bad fit between the political institutions shaped in the aftermath of the French Revolution and the aspirations and forms of life growing up within the urbanizing and industrializing European countries of the nineteenth century; (b) the short-run industrial and agricultural crisis of the later 1840s; and (c) the rise of new segments of the middle classes devoted to varying versions of liberalism, nationalism, and social reform. As Frederico Curato sums up for the Sicilian revolution:

> This insurrectional movement was based on economic causes not dissimilar to those prevailing elsewhere in Europe, but it had some special features which made it an unusual movement in the history of that year's insurrections. In fact it embodied not only a reaction against Naples . . . but also a reaction of the incipient Sicilian bourgeoisie to the introduction by the Neapolitan government of a unitary economic system for the

two parts of the Kingdom which, combined with the free coastal trade established in 1824, damaged the development of local industries which were incapable of meeting the competition of mainland industries. In Sicily, in the last analysis, the bourgeoisie sought power not because it had become the most important class and sought juridical and political recognition of its strength, but on the contrary in order simply to survive.[2]

The special features matter. Yet behind the particular interpretation of the Sicilian revolution we see a standard form of historical analysis that consists of identifying the principal actors, attributing to them appropriate incentives, outlooks, or calculations, and then settling them into motion. The conception is dramatic: the stage, the players, the impulses, the action. Revolution becomes a work of art.

Large structural transformations like the incipient industrialization of Europe figure only indirectly in this kind of analysis. They are neither actors nor actions. They simply condition the stage, the players, the impulses, the action. They may also result from the action, in the way that the installation of liberal regimes in 1848 facilitated the expansion of trade, the treatment of labor as a commodity, and so on. As a consequence, they tend to enter the account via theories (implicit or explicit) in which structural changes affect mentalities, mentalities guide actions, and actions produce further structural changes.

Those psychological theories are likely to fall into one of two classes. The first class of theory stresses the psychic impact of large-scale change: disorientation, rising expectations, relative deprivation, the diffusion of new ideologies. Thus, one standard interpretation of the revolutions of 1848 emphasizes the junction of two different responses to early industrialism: the bourgeois formation of a liberal-democratic-individualistic ideology and the working-class response of anger and fear. The second class of theory deals with the "fit" between political institutions and social situation, on the general grounds that where the fit is poor, people become dissatisfied, resentful, and rebellious. Another standard interpretation of the events of 1848 brings out the nineteenth-century inappropriateness or decay of political arrangements fashioned in the epic state-building of the preceding two or three centuries. Obviously, one can employ either or both of these lines of explanation in attempting to account for the Sicilian revolution of 1848: the small Sicilian bourgeoisie did share to some extent in the quasi-religious devotion of their mainland brothers to the market and to self-advancement (witness the acid portraits of these very traits of that period in Tomasi de Lampedusa's famous novel of Sicilian life *The*

Leopard), the agricultural workers of Sicily did find themselves being dispossessed (note the rapidity with which the day laborers of the island took advantage of each nineteenth-century hiatus in authority to repossess the lands that had been taken from them), and, for all its liberal facade, the Bourbon monarchy of the Two Sicilies was very much a dynastic state in the old style (witness the wry reports of British general William Bentinck, who had himself played an important part in the creation of the dual state).

Some Larger Questions

Despite the fascination of this sort of dramaturgic analysis of particular events, I want this essay to deal with the questions raised by the Sicilian case within a plane that is rather less historical, less colorful, more pretentious. With one eye fixed on the modern European experience, I want to ask myself whether modernization breeds revolution. (I should also like to ask, vice versa—does revolution breed modernization?—but within the compass of this chapter that is not possible.) That first formulation of the question is compact, but ambiguous. We shall, unfortunately, have to put a large part of our effort into the preliminary task of reducing the ambiguities. *Modernization* is a vague, tendentious concept. *Revolution* is a controversial one as well.

Instead of trying to pace off modernization precisely, I shall ordinarily substitute for it somewhat better-defined processes, such as industrialization or demographic expansion. Instead of trying to grasp the essential genius of revolution, I shall offer a rather arbitrary set of definitions that appears to me to have considerable theoretical utility. I shall compensate for my arbitrariness by discussing violence, instability, and political conflict more extensively than a strict concentration on revolution would justify.

There are, furthermore, quite a few different senses in which one can imagine large-scale structural change as breeding, shaping, causing, sparking, or resulting from major political conflicts. Instead of striving to catalog and assess them all, I shall take a critical look at one synthesis of the relationships that are most often proposed and try to communicate my reasons for thinking that (a) available theories that treat protest, conflict, violence, and revolution as direct responses to the stresses of structural change are wrong; (b) the strong effects of large-scale change on conflict run through the structure of power, especially by shaping the organizational means and resources available to different possible contenders for power; and (c) there are nevertheless certain kinds of short-run crises that tend to promote conflict, or even revolution, by affecting the likelihood that major participants in the political system will make or reject claims of great importance for the structure of power.

Pursuit of the first two problems (the conceptual difficulties and the direct relationships between structural change and revolution) will lead to a third set of questions: if the political process is so important after all, what *are* the political conditions for conflict, violence, and revolution? The discussion of that question will fall even shorter of a comprehensive reply than in the first two cases. But at least there will be some suggestions of relationships among war, domestic violence, revolution, and routine contention for power.

Huntington's Synthesis

One of the most sophisticated recent syntheses of the standard views concerning all these matters comes from Samuel Huntington. In his *Political Order in Changing Societies,* Huntington argues that the widespread domestic violence and instability of the 1950s and 1960s in many parts of the world "was in large part the product of rapid social change and the rapid mobilization of new groups into politics, coupled with the slow development of political institutions."[3] He goes on to portray an interaction among these elements:

> If a society is to maintain a high level of community, the expansion of political participation must be accompanied by the development of stronger, more complex, and more autonomous political institutions. The effect of the expansion of political participation, however, is usually to undermine the traditional political institutions and to obstruct the development of modern political ones. Modernization and social mobilization, in particular, thus tend to produce political decay unless steps are taken to moderate or to restrict its impact on political consciousness and political involvement. Most societies, even those with fairly complex and adaptable traditional political institutions, suffer a loss of political community and decay of political institutions during the most intense phases of modernization.[4]

Huntington deliberately applies this lead-lag model to Western revolutions, treating them as extreme cases of the conflicts that emerge when political institutionalization proceeds too slowly for the paces of large-scale social change (which Huntington treats as more or less identical with modernization) and of mobilization. Moreover, John Gillis has recently argued that the model applies specifically to the European modernizing revolutions of the eighteenth and nineteenth centuries.[5] It is therefore legitimate to ask how strong a grip on the Western experience with revolutions and violent conflict Huntington's analysis gives us. My answer is that the grip is needlessly weak: weak, because the scheme founders in tautologies, contradictions, omissions, and failures to examine the evidence seriously; needlessly, because several of the main arguments concerning mobilization, political participation, and conflict improve vastly on the usual socio-psychological tracing of "violence" or "protest" back to "strain" or "discontent."

Although it would be worth trying, this chapter will not attempt to wrench Huntington's theory into shape. I shall dwell on it in other ways, for other reasons, because in one manner or another it sums up most of the conventional wisdom connecting revolution to large-scale structural change; because Huntington places an exceptional range of contemporary and historical material within its framework; because the variables within it appear to be of the right kind; and because it is sturdy enough to exempt me from the accusation of having erected, and then burned, a straw man as I build up an alternative line of argument.

Huntington offers several criteria for the institutionalization of the existing political organization: adaptability, complexity, autonomy, coherence (with the latter essentially meaning consensus among the active participants in the political system). This sort of definition making increases the risk that Huntington's arguments will become tautological. To the extent that one judges adaptability, complexity, autonomy, and coherence on the basis of the absence or containment of domestic violence and instability, the circle of truth by definition will close.

Nevertheless, Huntington's balanced-development theory is appealing in its combination of three factors—rapid social change, mobilization, and political institutionalization—which other authors have employed separately in one-factor explanations of stability and instability. It does, furthermore, provide a plausible explanation of the twentieth-century concentration of revolution, governmental instability, and collective violence in the poorer (but not the poorest) countries of the world; the more plausible because it appears to dispose of the anomaly that, by many standards, the relatively peaceful richer countries are also the faster changing. Huntington's stress on the importance of group claims on the political system by mobilizing segments of the population is a distinct improvement over the more usual model of accumulating individual grievances. Indeed, the most attractive general feature of Huntington's scheme is its deliberate flight from psychologism, from the assumption that the central things to be explained by a theory of revolution are why, when, and how large numbers of individuals become discontented.

Not that I find the theory convincing, even where it escapes tautology. Its plausibility begins to wither as we examine the portion of the argument that deals directly with the political consequences of large-scale structural change: "Not only does social and economic modernization produce political instability, but the degree of instability is related to the rate of modernization. The historical evidence with respect to the West is overwhelming on this point."[6] I beg leave not to be overwhelmed by the available evidence. Almost all the sources habitually cited by Huntington and others in this regard refer to static cross-sectional comparisons of contemporary states during short spasms of recent years or the distribution of support for ostensibly radical political movements like Communists. In order to be even mildly persuaded, one would want to have reliable information on the effects of changes in the rate of "social and economic modernization" within the same countries.

Very few over-time studies of the problem have ever been done. The vast long-run analyses of Sorokin offer no particular support for the thesis that the pace of change governs the degree of instability.[7] Such longitudinal evidence as my collaborators and I have been able to assemble for European countries in the modern period displays plenty of violent conflict in the modern period. But it suggests either no direct relationship with the pace of structural change, or a negative one: rapid change, diminution of political conflict. In France since 1830, for example, we have discovered a broad tendency for times of rapid urbanization to produce *less* collective violence than the rest.

Among the big cross-sectional studies, Ted Gurr's analysis of 1,000-odd "strife events" occurring in 114 polities from 1961 through 1965—the most careful and comprehensive of its kind—offers little comfort to anyone who views the pace of change as a powerful determinant of the level of conflict.[8] Within his scheme, the variables that turn out to carry the explanatory weight have to do with the illegitimacy of the regime, the difficulty of communications within the country, the existence of foreign support for potential dissidents, the presence of an illegal but active Communist Party, economic discrimination, political discrimination, religious cleavage, dependence on private foreign capital, potential separatism, and so on. These detailed findings of Gurr's are doubly interesting. Like other investigators, in the preliminary stages of his analysis, Gurr found a considerable concentration of political conflict in the poorer countries, but not the poorest ones—the very "modernizing" countries whose high propensity to instability Huntington is seeking to account for. As the analysis of causal factors proceeded, Gurr generally ruled out the pace of industrialization, urbanization, and so on, in favor of a cluster of structural, organizational, and international relations characteristics that form the special burden of those poorer countries. Gurr's own interpretation of his findings runs in terms of relative deprivation, rising expectations, and the like. But it takes quite an inferential claim to go from the structural conditions he actually indexes to the psychic orientations with which his theory deals. Perhaps we can attach the greater importance to Gurr's findings because he eventually sharpened a rather different axe from the one he was grinding.

On a smaller scale, the exact connections that are usually alleged to tie instability to rapid structural change also turn out to be dubious. Rapid rural-to-urban migration has no particular tendency to excite protest; marginal urban populations are not the tinder of revolutions; the initial exposure of peasants to factories does not generate high levels of industrial conflict; and so on. Huntington himself happens onto some of the evidence with apparent surprise when he observes that the big-city lumpenproletariat in modernizing countries, contrary to theory, tends to be a passive, or even conservative, political force and when he goes on to speculate that urbanization may be negatively correlated with revolution.[9] Yet somehow this important qualification does not penetrate to the general statement of the theory.

To accept the Huntingtonian theory confidently, one would also want clear distinctions among radicalism, instability, violence, extent of protest, and propensity to revolution—not to mention a specification of their relationships to one another. That they are equivalent or closely related constitutes a theory to be tested, not a postulate from which theorizing may begin. As it happens, Huntington never quite clears away this difficulty. He succeeds in detaching revolution from the other phenomena by inflating it: "A revolution is a rapid, fundamental, and violent domestic change in the dominant values and myths of a society, in its political institutions, social structure, leadership, and government activity and policies."[10] By this standard, one might reasonably argue that no revolution has ever occurred, but one certainly would not confuse revolution with simple violence or protest. For the rest, however, Huntington willingly couples or confounds violence with "other forms of disorder."[11]

Oddly enough, all these failings eventually become irrelevant. As Huntington's arguments march on, the direct relationships between political conflict and structural change gradually drop out. At the end, the balanced-development theory is pitting rapid mobilization against institutionalization alone. Modernization now acts in a series of unspecified ways as a cause of mobilization. It does not directly produce conflict. The reformulation has the advantage of simplicity. In my view, it also has the advantage of greater proximity to the main conditions affecting the level of violent conflict: the interaction of the claims being made on the system by actual and aspiring participants, on the one hand, and the established arrangements for responding to such claims, on the other. The costs of Huntington's reformulation are twofold. First, we lose any strong sense of the political consequences of structural change because of the shapelessness of the theory linking mobilization to modernization; Marx, by contrast, told us exactly what kinds of groups we could expect to emerge as significant political actors out of the development of industrial capitalism. Second, the danger of truth by definition in such a two-factor theory is even greater than before. It becomes more crucial than ever to specify *mobilization* and *institutionalization* independently of each other.

Huntington on Revolution

Huntington restricts the term *revolution* to the deep and rapid transformations of whole societies, which others have called "Great Revolutions"; the French, Chinese, Mexican, Russian, and Cuban revolutions epitomize what he has in mind. Sicily's adventure of 1848 would not qualify. Nevertheless, Huntington's formulation asserts a fundamental continuity between revolution and lesser forms of conflict:

> Revolution is thus an aspect of modernization. It is not something which can occur in any type of society at any period in its history. It is not a universal category but rather an historically limited phenomenon. It will not occur in highly traditional societies with very low levels of social and economic complexity. Nor will it occur in highly modern societies. Like other forms of violence and instability, it is most likely to occur in societies which have experienced some social and economic development and where the processes of political modernization and political development have lagged behind the processes of social and economic change.[12]

Thus the imbalances that account for other forms of "disorder" also account for revolution: "The political essence of revolution is the rapid expansion of political consciousness and the rapid mobilization of new groups into politics at a speed which makes it impossible for existing political institutions to assimilate them. Revolution is the extreme case of the explosion of political participation."[13]

Huntington then distinguishes between an Eastern and a Western pattern of revolution. In the *Eastern,* new groups mobilize into politics, they fashion new political institutions, and they overthrow the old order; anticolonial revolutions are the type case. In the *Western,* the old political institutions disintegrate and only then new groups mobilize into politics, create new political institutions, and come to power. The Russian Revolution is typical. The "decay" of established institutions plays a large part in the Western pattern, according to Huntington, and a small part in the Eastern. As a result, the sequences are rather different. Nevertheless, in both cases, the immediate cause of revolution is supposed to be the discrepancy between the performance of the regime and the demands being made upon it. In both cases, that discrepancy is supposed to increase as a consequence of the mobilization of new groups into politics, which in turn occurs as a more or less direct effect of rapid social and economic change.

The danger of circular argument is just as apparent here as before. In his detailed argumentation, Huntington does not really escape the fateful circularity of judging the extent of the discrepancy from the character of the revolution that presumably resulted from the discrepancy. He tells us, for example, that:

> The great revolutions of history have taken place either in highly central-ized traditional monarchies (France, China, Russia), or in narrowly based military dictatorships (Mexico, Bolivia, Guatemala, Cuba), or in colonial regimes (Vietnam, Algeria). All these political systems demonstrated little if any capacity to expand their power and to provide channels for the participation of new groups in politics.[14]

Suppose we suppress the urge to blurt out questions about England in the 1640s or the United States in the 1860s and stifle suspicions that the implicit standard for great revolutions at work in this passage simply restricts them logically to centralized, authoritarian regimes. We still must wonder how we could have known before the fact of revolution that the expansive capacity of these governments was inferior to that of the many other monarchies, military dictatorships, and colonial regimes that did not experience revolutions.

Huntington does not answer. In its present form, his scheme does not, it appears, give us any social guidance in the anticipation or production of revolution—not even in the weak sense of projecting ourselves back into the France of 1788 or the Sicily of 1847, and saying how we would have gone about estimating the probabilities of revolution within the next few years. That is true of the whole argument, and not just of the treatment of revolution. Even in principle, the scheme is not really a predictive one. It is an orientation, a proposal to weigh several clusters of variables differently from the way they have been estimated in the past, and a presentation of an exceptionally wide range of observations in the light of the orientation and the weighing.

Alternatives

How else could we proceed? We should hold onto several of Huntington's perceptions: (a) that revolutions and collective violence tend to flow directly out of a population's central political processes, instead of expressing diffuse strains and discontents within the population; (b) that the specific claims and counterclaims being made on the existing government by various mobilized groups are more important than the general satisfaction or discontent of those groups and that claims for established places within the structure of power are crucial; (c) that large-scale structural change transforms the identities and structures of the potential aspirants for power within the population, affects their opportunities for mobilization, governs the resources available to the government, and through it to the principal holders of power. Accepting those insights would incline us to set our faces against such aggregate psychological hypotheses as those of James Davies[15] or Ted Gurr,[16] as well as against gross system-function hypotheses like those of Chalmers Johnson[17] or Neil Smelser.[18] It will encourage us to concentrate our analysis on processes of mobilization, on structures of power, and on the changing demands linking one to the other, in the manner of Barrington Moore,[19] Eric Wolf,[20] or William Gamson.[21]

We have to go further. By contrast with Huntington's global strategy, we must clearly distinguish among different forms of conflict before seeking to identify their connections; we must disaggregate revolution into its components instead of treating it as a unitary phenomenon; we must investigate the precise ways in which urbanization or political centralization affect the mobilization and demobilization of different segments of the population; and we must specify and trace the relations of each major segment to the changing structure of power.

Here, I simply want to sketch a line of argument embodying an attempt to move in the direction I call desirable. The argument grows from an effort to document and explain changes in the character of political conflict (especially in its violent forms) in European countries over recent centuries. On its home ground, the argument is ambiguous at some points and eminently debatable at others. Far too little systematic evidence is now available to put it to any comprehensive test. The formulations reflect modern European experience too directly to warrant any confidence that they apply to the rest of the world. I inflict them on my readers only because that European experience has, in fact, provided the bulk of the models for the analysis of revolution in the contemporary world, because the scheme does not help make sense of the European experience, because at some points the line of argument yields testable inferences, and because such small evidence as I have been able to accumulate from a few countries over a few centuries appears to support those inferences.

A MODEL OF POLITICAL CONFLICT

First, a simple model of political action. Let us distinguish three kinds of social unit within any specified population. A *government* is an organization that controls the principal concentrated means of coercion within the population; a *contender for power* is a group within the population that at least once during some standard period applies resources to influence that government; and a *polity* is the set of contenders that routinely and successfully lays claims on that government. (We may call these individual contenders *members* of the polity, while *challenger* is a good name for a contender laying claims in an irregular or unsuccessful fashion.) Almost any population beyond a very small scale will include more than one contender. Almost any large population will include more than one government, hence more than one polity. But many theoretically possible contenders will not contend during any particular period; some will never contend. A group gains the capacity to contend by mobilizing: by acquiring collective control over resources—land, labor, information, arms, money, and so on—that can be applied to influence the government; it loses that capacity by demobilizing, losing collective control over resources.

Every polity, then, collectively develops tests of membership. The tests always include the capacity to bring considerable numbers of people into action; they may also include the possession of wealth, certified birth, religious stigmata, and many other characteristics. Challengers acquire membership in the polity by meeting the tests, despite the fact that existing members characteristically resist new admissions and employ the government's resources to make admissions more difficult. The members also test one another more or less continuously; a member failing the tests tends to lose membership in the polity. Each change in membership moves the tests in a direction harmonious with the characteristics and capacities of the set of members emerging from the change. The members of the polity come to treat the prevailing criteria of membership as having a special moral virtue. Challengers denied admission tend to define themselves as being deprived of rights due them on general grounds. Members losing position tend, in contrast, to accent tradition, usage, and particular agreements in support of their claims to threatened privileges and resources. Thus contenders both entering and leaving the polity have a special propensity to articulate strongly moral definitions of their situations.

The model is simple and broad. I have compressed its presentation unmercifully, because its only function here is as a vehicle for the analysis of large-scale political conflicts. Even in précis, however, a large practical disadvantage becomes clear: the model's requirement for data concerning the mobilization, contention, and testing of a considerable number of different groups within a population of any size—not the sort of data drawn readily from a *World Handbook*. There are compensating advantages: the avoidance of that ill-defined entity called a "society" as the basic analytic unit; the well-defined connections among mobilization, contention, and conflict; the easy accommodation to the existence of multiple governments within the same population.

The scheme also permits us to specify the close relationship between collective violence and the central political process: (a) political life consists largely of making collective claims for resources and privileges controlled by governments; (b) collective violence is largely a by-product of situations in which one contender openly lays such claims and other contenders (or, especially, the government) resist these claims; (c) such situations occur with particular frequency when groups are acquiring or losing membership—that is, partly because testing tends to take that form, partly because the moral orientations of the groups whose memberships are disputed encourage the individuals within them to take exceptional risks of damage or injury, partly because the activation of the coercive forces of the government increases the likelihood of damage or injury to other participants; (d) hence collective violence tends to cluster around major or multiple entries and exits; (e) governments themselves act to maintain priority over substantial concentrations of coercive resources, so that a contender accumulating such resources outside the control of the government is quite likely to find itself in acute conflict with the agents of the government.

As a consequence, the common theories of violence that treat it as a product of the willingness of certain kinds of individuals or groups to "resort to violence" to express themselves or accomplish their ends fall wide of the mark. Those equally common theories that distinguish sharply between violent and orderly political actions fail just as badly. The one misses the extent to which collective violence is a contingent outcome of interactions among contenders and governments, in which the agents of government commonly have the greater discretion and do most of the injury and damage. The other misses the great continuity between nonviolent and violent political actions. In Europe of the last few hundred years, at least, the great bulk of collective violence has (a) involved agents of the government, (b) grown from collective actions (such as assemblies, demonstrations, or strikes) that were not intrinsically violent, indeed that usually went on without violence. Lovers of order and defenders of the state have obscured these facts by expanding the word *violence* to include not only physical damage, but also a wide range of illegal, unseemly, and symbolically repugnant behavior. In our own day as well, it is customary to puff up the idea of violence until it has little value as an analytic tool but carries great moral weight; thus, Jacques Ellul's provocative essay (called, simply, *Violence*) treats without distinction almost every form of coercion men employ.[22]

REVOLUTIONS

We now have the means of moving on to television. The multiplication of polities is the key. A revolution begins when a government previously under the control of a single, sovereign polity becomes the object of effective, competing, mutually exclusive claims from two or more separate polities. A revolution ends when a single polity—by no means necessarily the same one—regains control over the government. This multiple sovereignty can result from the attempt of one polity to subordinate another heretofore independent polity; from the assertion of sovereignty by a previously subordinate polity; from the formation of a bloc of challengers that seizes control of some portion of the government apparatus; from the fragmentation of an existing polity into blocs, each of which controls some part of the government. Many observers would prefer to restrict the label "revolution" to the action by challengers; many others would prefer to call each of these a different major type of revolution: civil war, national revolution, and so on. I begin with an exceptionally broad definition to call attention to the common properties of the various paths through multiple sovereignty.

This labeling is a delicate matter. As with violence, many groups want to define their own political objectives by reference to *revolution,* whether they fear or welcome an overturn of things as they are. Most debates over the scope of the term contain the germ of a debate over goals. Some readers will surely conclude that by calling any development of multiple sovereignty revolutionary, I cheapen a valuable word and erase crucial distinctions between true revolutions and mere coups, bootless rebellions, and simple brigandage. If there were, in fact, wide agreement in the scholarly and hortatory literature on the criteria for revolution, I would not hesitate to accept a narrower definition. But there is precious little agreement. The varieties of political discontinuity have a disconcerting tendency to overlap and run into one another, as illustrated by the far-reaching effects of the "mere coups" involved in the Meiji Restoration and the accession of Mustafa Kemal to power. As a consequence, there are strong advantages to beginning with the common denominator of a wide variety of phenomena—multiple sovereignty—and then creating types of revolution by subdivision. It is not hard to recreate all the major customary types by introducing the following variables: (1) extent of change in the structure of the polity; (2) composition of the rival polities in the period of multiple sovereignty; and (3) extent of structural change resulting from the revolution. These three variables fairly well exhaust the further distinctions that are most commonly made: success versus failure, proletarian versus bourgeois, colonial versus noncolonial, center-to-periphery versus periphery-to-center, and so on.

Conditions for Revolution

At one time or another, the building of European states led down all four paths to multiple sovereignty: (1) attempts of one polity to subordinate another independent polity—a standard situation in the dynastic and colonial war making of the sixteenth century and later; (2) the assertion of sovereignty by a previously subordinate polity—the diverse Habsburg Empire was peculiarly subject to this outcome, and the revolutions of the Netherlands and Catalonia are prime examples; (3) the formation of a bloc of challengers that seizes control of some portion of the government apparatus—the purest cases are peasant revolts, but every major revolution included some such action; (4) the fragmentation of an existing polity into blocs, each controlling some part of the government—with the important qualification that coalitions between members and challengers (in this case, especially working-class groups) were frequent and influential. This was the pattern in the Sicilian revolution with which we began, the standard pattern in 1848 as a whole, and, no doubt, the most common pattern among all modern Western revolutions.

What observable political conditions, then, ought to prevail before a revolution begins? Three conditions appear to be necessary, and a fourth strongly facilitating. The three apparently necessary conditions are:

1. The appearance of contenders or coalitions of contenders, advancing exclusively alternative claims to the control over the government currently exerted by the members of the polity;
2. commitment to those claims by a significant segment of the subject population;
3. unwillingness or incapacity of the agents of the government to suppress the alternative coalition or the commitment to its claims.

The strongly facilitating condition:

> 4. formation of coalitions between members of the polity and the contenders making the alternative claims.

Let me confess at once that the list contains little news not already borne by the definition of revolution as a state of multiple sovereignty. The purpose of the list is simply to focus the explanation of revolution on the structure of power and away from the general level of strain, discontent, disequilibrium, or mobilization. At first approach, the argument therefore resembles Huntington's; both of them attach great importance to encounters between existing political arrangements and specific mobilized groups making new and powerful demands on the government. This analysis veers away from Huntington's, especially in denying the significance of a discrepancy between the overall rates of mobilization and institutionalization; in attaching great importance to conflicts over claims, duties, privileges, and conceptions of justice embedded in particular contenders for power; and in drawing attention to the important possibility that the crucial contenders will be disaffected members of a polity rather than newcomers to power.

The explanation of revolution, within this formulation, becomes the identification of the probable causes for the three necessary conditions and the fourth facilitating condition: the appearance of a bloc advancing exclusive alternative claims, commitment to those claims, failure of repression, and formation of coalitions between the alternative bloc and members of the polity. An alternative bloc can come into being via three different routes: (a) the mobilization of a new contender outside the polity; (b) the turning away of an existing challenger from acceptance of the polity's current operating rules; (c) the turning away of an existing member from its established place in the polity. In order to gauge the probabilities of employment of any of the routes, we would have to know a good deal about the operating rules of the polities involved. But several general conditions very likely increase those probabilities: contraction of the resources available to the government for the meeting of its commitments, a shift in the direction of structural change within the base population such that not just new groups but new *kinds* of groups are coming into being, disappearance of the resources that make possible the membership in the polity, and the continuing collective life of some contender.

The expansion of commitment to the claims of the alternative bloc occurs both through their acceptance by groups and individuals not belonging to the bloc and through the further mobilization of the bloc itself.

The two undoubtedly reinforce each other. Acceptance of the alternative claims is likely to generalize when: the government fails to meet its established obligations; it greatly increases its demands on the subject population; the alternative claims are cast within the moral framework already employed by many members of the population; there is a strong alliance between the existing government and a well-defined enemy of an important segment of the population; and the coercive resources of the alternative bloc increase.

The literature of "counterinsurgency" (perhaps most notably, the work of Nathan Leites and Charles Wolf)[23] is full of attempts to analyze the tactics for producing or checking these outcomes. The Marxist account of the conditions for radicalization of the proletariat and the peasantry remains the most powerful general analysis of the process, expanding commitment to a revolutionary bloc.[24] Where it falls down is in not providing for contenders (communities, ethnic minorities, religious groups, and so on) that are not class-based and in obscuring the revolutionary importance of defensive reactions by segments of the population whose established positions are threatened. (Eric Wolf's superb study of twentieth-century peasant wars makes apparent the revolutionary potential of such defensive responses to land enclosure, expansion of the market, and the encroachment of capitalism; John Womack's biography of Zapata provides a heroic portrayal of one important leader of that reaction.)[25]

The agents of the government are likely to become unwilling or unable to suppress the alternative bloc and the commitment to its claims when their coercive resources contract, their inefficiency increases, and inhibitions to their use arise. Defeat in a war is a quintessential case, for casualties, defections, and military demobilization all tend to decrease the government's coercive capacity; the destruction of property, disruption of routines, and displacement of population in defeat are likely to decrease the efficiency of the established coercive means; and the presence of a conqueror places constraints on the government's use of coercion. (The routine of modern military occupation, however, tends to substitute the coercive capacity of the victors for that of the vanquished.) The end of any war, won or lost, tends to restore men with newly acquired military skill to most of the contenders in the political system. Where military demobilization proceeds rapidly, it is likely to shift the balance of coercive resources away from the government, and may shift it toward an alternative bloc. Even without war, the increase in the coercive resources of the alternative bloc (which can occur through theft, purchase, training, the imposition of military discipline, and the lending of support by outsiders) is equivalent to the contraction of the government's own coercive resources. The efficiency of governmental coercion is likely to decline, at least in the short run, when the character, organization, and daily routines of the population to be controlled change rapidly; this appears to be one of the most direct effects of large-scale structural change on the likelihood of revolution. Inhibitions to the use of coercion are likely to increase when the coercive forces themselves are drawn from (or otherwise attached to) the populations to be controlled, when new members of the polity act against the coercive means that were employed to block their acquisition of membership, and when effective coalitions between members of the polity and revolutionary challengers exist.

The final condition for revolution—this one strongly facilitating rather than necessary—is the formation of just such coalitions between polity members and revolutionary challengers. Modern European history, for example, provides many examples of temporary coalitions between professionals, intellectuals, or other fragments of the bourgeoisie well established within the polity and segments of the working class excluded from power. The revolutions of 1830 and 1848 display this pattern with particular clarity. The payoff to the challengers consists of a hedge against repression, some protection against the devaluation of their resources, and perhaps the transfer of information and expertise from the member. The payoff to the member consists of an expansion of the resources available for application to the government and to other members of the polity—not least, the ability to mount a credible threat of mass action. This sort of coalition formation is likely to occur, on the one hand, when a challenger rapidly increases the store of resources under its control and, on the other, when a member loses its coalition partners within the polity, or the polity is more or less evenly divided among two or more coalitions, or an established member is risking loss of membership in the polity through failure to meet the tests of other members.

REVOLUTION AND SOME OTHER FORMS OF CONFLICT

The conceptualization of revolution as the appearance of multiple sovereignty leaves some interesting cases at the margin: banditry, durable separatism, foreign intervention in domestic conflict, some varieties of war. At least those cases *belong* at the margin; they share some, but not all, features of revolutionary situations. They are nevertheless important, because they display the similarities and connections among superficially separate organized uses of force.

The similarities are easier to grasp. Eric Hobsbawm, in his beautifully executed brace of books, *Bandits* and *Primitive Rebels*,[26] has called attention to the common properties of social banditry and popular rebellion; each tends to involve a turning of the back to the state, a wide, tacit conspiracy among members of the population who are not directly engaged in the action, a theme of redressing wrongs committed by the powerful, a romantic ideology framed in terms of traditional obligations and customs, an acting out of "natural justice." Even the less romantic forms of piracy and banditry that flourished around the Mediterranean for centuries bore some striking resemblances to civil war, for they frequently amounted to de facto claims to sovereignty within particular geographic areas. In regions like southern Italy, the bandits sometimes exercised their claims in collusion with the duly constituted authorities of adjacent territories.

In the case of Italy, it also becomes clear that war and revolution have a good deal in common. We conventionally distinguish the two on the basis of (a) the status of each participant at the beginning and the end of the conflict, and (b) the means employed. But in nineteenth-century Italy, the "national revolution" that brought about unification consisted mainly of military conquests by Piedmont, coupled with risings led by such heroic invaders as Mazzini and Garibaldi, insurrections subsidized or even engineered by Piedmont, and further popular rebellions that broke out very widely after invasion had weakened the grips of the old state and the old elite. War or revolution? Both. The same conjunction appears in the multiple rebellions of conquered territories against Napoleon, the movements of resistance against the Nazis, the anti-Japanese phase of the Chinese Revolution, and a great many other important conflicts.

Not only similarities, but interconnections. I have already pointed out that the extent of damage and injury that results from collective violence depends largely on the organization and tactics of the government's own coercive forces. Within strong states, that relationship goes further. Repression often works. In the European experience of the last two centuries, the substantial periods of respite from collective violence within any particular country have generally been in the tenures of repressive regimes: the Spanish dictatorships of Primo de Rivera and Franco, the Bolsheviks in power, the heyday of Nazism, Italian fascism after 1925, France under Louis Napoleon and—the Resistance notwithstanding—under German occupation. Obviously, I am speaking strictly of collective violence that pits groups of individuals against one another, and not of terror, torture, individual repression, psychic punishment, or external war. The Nazis (among others) engaged in all of these terrible acts while internal collective violence was at its low point. Just as obviously, all these regimes began with widespread collective violence, and most of them ended with it. So the point is not that repressive regimes are kinder to life. It is, rather, that by deliberately demobilizing their most likely opponents and closely controlling the opportunities for collective action by any other contender, repressive regimes greatly reduce the chances that collective violence will grow out of contention for power.

Another connection comes to mind. In the West of the past five centuries, perhaps the largest single factor in the promotion of revolutions and collective violence has been the great concentration of power in national states. (I concede that the rise of the national state depended to such a large degree on the growth of production, the expansion of large-scale marketing, the strengthening of the bourgeoisie, and the proliferation of bureaucracy that such a statement commits a dramatic oversimplification.) This factor shows up most clearly in frequency of tax rebellions in Western countries over those centuries and in the prominence of grievances concerning taxation in revolutions, such as those of the 1640s or the 1840s. The frequency of violent resistance to military conscription points in the same direction. Violent resistance by separatist movements has commonly begun with attempts of national governments to increase their control over the periphery.

The connections are subtler and more debatable when it comes to food riots, land seizures, machine breaking, violent strikes, or religious conflicts, but in those cases as well, I think the influence of the concentration of power in national states is far from negligible. In any case, over that span of European history, one can see a long slope of resistance to central control followed by a fairly rapid transition (mainly in the nineteenth century) to struggles for control *over* the central state. In the records of collective violence, this shows up as a decisive shift away from localized tax rebellions and the like to conflicts involving contenders articulating national objectives, organized on a national scale, and confronting representatives of the national state.

But I have neglected one major connection. States are war makers, and wars are state makers. At least in modern Europe, the major increases in the scope and strength of national states (as indicated by national budgets, national debts, powers of intervention, and sizes of staffs) have, on the whole, occurred as a direct result of war making or preparation for war. What is more, the armed forces have historically played a large part in subordinating other authorities and the general population to the national state. They backed up the collection of taxes, put down tax rebellions, seized and disposed of the enemies of the crown, literally enforced national policy. The relationship was neatly reciprocal: war provided the incentive, the occasion, and the rationalization for strengthening the state, while war makers assured the docility of the general population and the yielding of the resources necessary to carry out the task. The fairly recent division of labor between specialized police forces for domestic control and military forces for the remaining tasks has not fundamentally changed the relationship.

The connection matters here because a series of important relationships between war and revolution also exists. It is not just that they overlap to some extent. In some circumstances, war promotes revolution. That assertion is true in several different ways: the extraction of resources for the prosecution of a war has repeatedly aroused revolutionary resistance; the defeat of states in war has often made them vulnerable to attacks from their domestic enemies; the complicity of some portion of the armed forces with the revolutionary bloc has been absolutely essential to the success of the modern revolution, and the most frequent variety of revolution—the coup—has depended mainly on the alignments of armed forces; the waning phases of major movements of conquest (the weakening of the Napoleonic regimes outside of France, the Nazi regimes outside of Germany, and the Japanese regimes outside of Japan being prime examples) are strikingly propitious for revolution; and the periods of readjustment immediately following large international conflicts also seem favorable to revolution, often with the collusion of major parties to the conflict. All of this suggests a strong connection between realignments in the international system and conflicts within individual countries, a connection mediated by the repressive policies and capacities of the governments involved.

Those who find at least some of the preceding analysis useful and plausible will do well to reflect on the sorts of variables that have been in play. Despite the many recent attempts to psychologize the study of revolution by introducing ideas of anxiety, alienation, rising expectations, and the like, and to sociologize it by employing notions of disequilibrium, role conflict, structural strain, and so on, the factors that hold up under close scrutiny are, on the whole, political ones. The structure of power, alternative conceptions of justice, the organization of coercion, the conduct of war, the formation of coalitions, the legitimacy of the state—these traditional concerns of political thought provide the main guides to the explanation of revolution. Population growth, industrialization, urbanization, and other large-scale structural changes do, to be sure, affect the probabilities of revolution. But they do so indirectly, by shaping the potential contenders for power, transforming the techniques of governmental control, and shifting the resources available to contenders and governments. There is no reliable and regular sense in which modernization breeds revolution.

NOTES

1. Giorgio Candeloro, *Storia dell' Italia moderna,* 2nd ed. (Milan: Teltrinelli, 1966), III, p. 122.

2. Federico Curato, "Il 1848 italiano ed europeo," in *Nuove questione di storia del Risorgimento e dell' Unità* (Milan, 1969), I, p. 682.

3. Samuel P. Huntington, *Political Order in Changing Societies* (New Haven, CT: Yale University Press, 1968), p. 4.

4. Ibid., pp. 85–86.

5. John R. Gillis, "Political Decay and the European Revolutions, 1789–1848," *World Politics* 22 (April 1970): 344–370.

6. Huntington, *Political Order,* p. 45.

7. Pitirim A. Sorokin, *Social and Cultural Dynamics III: Fluctuation of Social Relationships, War, and Revolution* (New York: Bedminster, 1962).

8. Ted Robert Gurr, *Why Men Rebel* (Princeton, NJ: Princeton University Press, 1970).

9. Huntington, *Political Order,* pp. 278–283, 299.

10. Ibid., p. 264.

11. Ibid., p. 358.

12. Ibid., p. 265.

13. Ibid., p. 266.

14. Ibid., p. 275.

15. James C. Davies, "Toward a Theory of Revolution," *American Sociological Review* 27 (1962): 5–19.

16. Gurr, *Why Men Rebel.*

17. Chalmers Johnson, *Revolutionary Change* (Boston: Little, Brown, 1966).

18. Neil J. Smelser, *Theory of Collective Behavior* (New York: Free Press, 1963).

19. Barrington Moore Jr., *Social Origins of Dictatorship and Democracy* (Boston: Beacon Press, 1966).

20. Eric Wolf, *Peasant Wars of the Twentieth Century* (New York: Harper & Row, 1969).

21. William A. Gamson, *Power and Discontent* (Homewood, IL: Dorsay, 1968).

22. Jacques Ellul, *Violence* (London: SCM Press, 1970).

23. Nathan Leites and Charles Wolf Jr., *Rebellion and Authority: An Analytic Essay on Insurgent Conflicts* (Chicago: Markham, 1970).

24. Karl Marx, "The Eighteenth Brumaire of Louis Bonaparte," in Karl Marx and Frederick Engels, *Selected Works* (Moscow, 1958), I, pp. 243–344.

25. John Womack Jr., *Zapata and the Mexican Revolution* (Cambridge, MA: Harvard University Press, 1969).

26. E. J. Hobsbawm, *Primitive Rebels* (Manchester: Manchester University Press, 1959) and *Bandits* (New York: Delacorte, 1969).

· 6 ·

CITIES, BOURGEOIS, AND REVOLUTION IN FRANCE

REVIVING ANATHEMIZED THEORIES

In a delightful dialectic, the decay of one social interpretation is giving rise to another. The pamphleteering Marxist account of the French Revolution, with its transfer of power grounded in a straightforward succession of ruling classes and modes of production, lies in tatters after a generation of critical flailing. The critique of that interpretation has often led away from any serious consideration of the actual processes by which France changed in the critical years after 1787. In its better moments, however, the critique has called attention to the importance of changes in state power Marxist historians long neglected, which in turn has made it possible to see that a "social interpretation" actually has a good deal of explanatory power. Although recent rhetoric has gone in quite a different direction, historians are on the way to rediscovering the bourgeois revolution in a more precise and sophisticated form. We find ourselves accepting Perry Anderson's great challenge:

> Today, when "history from below" has become a watch word in both Marxist and non-Marxist circles, and has produced major gains in our understanding of the past, it is nevertheless necessary to recall one of the basic axioms of historical materialism: that secular struggle between classes is ultimately resolved at the *political*—not at the economic or cultural—level of society. In other words, it is the construction and destruction of States which seal the basic shifts in the relations of production, so long as classes subsist. (Anderson 1974: 11)

This chapter was first published as "Cities, Bourgeois, and Revolution in France," in M'hammed Sabour, ed., *Liberté, Egalité, Fraternité: Bicentenaire de la Grande Révolution Française* (Joensuu, Finland: University of Joensuu, 1992), pp. 28–63. Reprinted with permission.

If we insert the French state's history in the general transformations of European states as we have long inserted the transformation of France's social classes in the general history of European capitalism, we will understand both better. Let me sketch a line of explanation that stresses the interaction of city-systems and state-systems, the shift from indirect to direct rule, and the place of capitalists in both momentous processes. It will give some reasons for thinking of revolution and counterrevolution as complementary elements of the same processes of state formation and for considering the French Revolution to have been a bourgeois revolution after all.

In its simplest form, my argument runs as follows. In France, as elsewhere in Europe, towns and cities formed two analytically distinct hierarchies: an imposed top-down hierarchy defined by coercion, conquest, and state power; a bottom-up hierarchy defined by capital, trade, and manufacturing. The two hierarchies linked the same places in different ways, with some centers such as Versailles occupying very high positions in the coercive hierarchy and relatively low positions in the top-down hierarchy, and crystallized it into a connected administrative structure. Soldiers and state administrators held power in the top-down hierarchy. Trade and manufacturing created the bottom-up hierarchy. Capitalists—those who made their living from the deployment of capital—held power. Transformations of the state inevitably affected the coercive hierarchy directly, but had lesser and more indirect effects on the hierarchy of capital.

Like other European states, the French state of the eighteenth century only extended its direct top-down rule to the level of the region, the level of the *subdélégation,* the *élection,* the *sénéchaussée,* the *grenier à sel,* and similar administrative units; at and below that level, the Old Regime state ruled indirectly, especially through the mediation of priests, nobles, and urban oligarchies. During the eighteenth century, in search of funds for past, present, and future military activity, state agents began pressing for various forms of direct rule that would bypass the privileges and resistance of the entrenched intermediaries. In the Revolution, the state's new managers, battling the old intermediaries for control of revenues, loyalty, and military power at the local and regional levels, improvised successive systems of direct rule in which capitalists broadly defined played a critical part. The creation of the new top-down administrative hierarchy drastically altered the relations between coercion and capital and incited a new series of struggle for power within regions. Revolutionary attempts to institute direct rule and to displace old intermediaries incited widespread resistance, which took the form of open counterrevolution where the intermediaries had large followings and the national network of capitalists had only thin support. The argument requires many explications, qualifications, and nuances. Yet it captures many implications of recent work on urban hierarchies, political processes, and struggle in France.

A Conceptual Interlude

Let us begin the explications with a distinction between *coercion* and *capital* as bases of social relations. Let us think of *capital* generously, including any tangible mobile resources, and enforceable claims on such resources. Capitalists, then, are people who specialize in the accumulation, purchase, and sale of capital. In eighteenth-century France, the word *bourgeois* applied fairly well to the capitalist class; even where they were landlords or lawyers, they stood out from other people especially by means of their use of capital. The main exception is that many eighteenth-century nobles were, by this criterion, capitalists even thought no one called them bourgeois.

Capitalists and bourgeois occupy the realm of *exploitation,* where the relations of production and exchange themselves yield surpluses, and capitalists capture them. Capitalists have often existed in the absence of capitalism, the system in which wageworkers produce goods by means of materials owned by capitalists. Through most of history, indeed, capitalists have worked chiefly as merchants, entrepreneurs, and financiers, rather than as the direct organizers of production. The system of capitalism itself arrived late in the history of capital. It grew up in Europe after 1500, as capitalists seized control of production. It reached its apex—or, depending on our perspective, its nadir—after 1750, when capital-concentrated manufacturing became the basis of prosperity in many countries. For millennia before then, capitalists had flourished without much intervening in production.

The processes that accumulate and concentrate capital also produce cities. Cities figure prominently in my analysis, both as favored sites of capitalists and as organizational forces in their own right. To the extent that the survival of households depends on the presence of capital through employment, investment, redistribution, or any other strong link, the distribution of population follows that of capital. (Capital, however, sometimes follows cheap labor; the relationship is reciprocal.) Trade, warehousing, banking, and production that depends closely on any of them all benefit from proximity to one another. Within limits set by the productivity of agriculture, that proximity promotes the formation of dense, differentiated populations having extensive outside connections—cities. When capital both accumulates and concentrates within a territory, urban growth tends to occur throughout the same territory—more intensely at the greatest points of concentration, and secondarily elsewhere.

What of coercion? Coercion includes all concerted application, threatened or actual, of action that commonly causes loss or damage. (The cumbersome definition excludes inadverted, indirect, and secret damage.) Where capital defines a realm of exploitation, coercion defines a realm of *domination*. The means of coercion center on armed force, but extend to facilities for incarceration, expropriation, humiliation, and publication of threats. Europe created two major overlapping groups of specialists in coercion: soldiers and great landlords; when they merged and received ratification from states in the form of titles and privileges they crystallized into nobilities, who in turn supplied the principal European rulers for many centuries. Coercive means, like capital, can both accumulate and concentrate: some groups (such as monastic orders) have few coercive means, but those few are concentrated in a small number of hands; others (such as armed frontiersmen) have many coercive means that are widely dispersed. Coercive means and capital merge where the same objects (e.g., workhouses) serve exploitation and domination. For the most part, however, they remain sufficiently distinct to allow us to analyze them separately.

When the accumulation and concentration of coercive means grow together, they produce states; they produce distinct organizations that control the chief concentrated means of coercion within well-defined territories and exercise priority in some respects over all other organizations operating within those territories:

CONCENTRATION OF COERCIVE MEANS

▲

▲
GROWTH OF STATES
▼

ACCUMULATION OF COERCIVE MEANS

Efforts to subordinate neighbors and fight off more distant rivals create state structure in the form not only of armies, but also of civilian staffs that gather the means to sustain armies and that organize the ruler's day-to-day control over the rest of the civilian population.

CHINA, EUROPE, AND FRANCE

Unexpectedly, a comparison of Europe with China helps clarify what is at issue. G. William Skinner portrays the social geography of imperial China as the intersection of two sets of central-place hierarchies (Skinner 1977: 275–352; see also Schram 1985, 1987; Whitney 1970). The first, constructed largely from the bottom up, emerged from exchange; its overlapping units consisted of larger and larger market areas centered on towns and cities of increasing size. The second, imposed mainly from the top down, resulted from imperial control; its nested units comprised a hierarchy of administrative jurisdictions. Down to the level of the *hsien,* or county, every city had a place in both the commercial and the administrative hierarchy. Below that level, even the mighty Chinese Empire ruled indirectly via its gentry. In the top-down system, we find the spatial logic of coercion; in the bottom-up system, the spatial logic of capital.

In some Chinese regions, imperial control was relatively weak and commercial activity relatively strong; there, cities generally occupied higher ranks in the order of markets than in the imperial order. Elsewhere (especially at the empire's periphery, where regions were typically more valuable to the center for security than for revenue), imperial control placed a city higher than did commercial activity. Skinner sketches some critical correlates of a city's relative position in the two hierarchies; for example, imperial administrators assigned to cities occupying relatively high positions in the market hierarchy accomplished more of their work by dealing with "parapolitical" networks of merchants and other prospering notables than did their colleagues in less well-favored areas, while the regions including those major market cities financed more than their share of candidates for the imperial examinations that led to careers in the bureaucracy. Many other consequences flowed from that interplay of the top-down and bottom-up systems.

How did China differ from Europe? In a pamphlet published in 1637, Jesuit Giuldo Aldeni reported that his Chinese friends often asked of Europe, "If there are so many kings, how can you avoid wars?" He reported answering, naively or disingenuously, "The kings of Europe are all connected by marriage, and therefore live on good terms with one another. If there is a war, the Pope intervenes; he sends out envoys to warn the belligerents to stop fighting" (Bunger 1987: 320). This in the middle of the frightful Thirty Years' War, which eventually drew the vast majority of European states into the bloodletting. The difference is critical: China had once lived through an era of warring states that had much in common with the international anarchy of Europe; most of the time, a single center dominated much of Chinese space, a zone that was unimaginably large by European standards. Empire was for long China's normal condition. In Europe, fragmentation into multiple competing states has prevailed over all of the last millennium.

Although Russian czars eventually commanded a huge expanse of Asia, Europe itself never hosted an empire on the scale of China's at its prime. After the fragmentation of Rome's domains, nonetheless, many rulers attempted to build empires in Europe, or to extend them into Europe. A succession of Muslim empires reached into Spain and the Balkans, but got no farther. Byzantine, Bulgarian, Serbian, and Ottoman Empires sometimes straddled the Balkans and the Middle East, while Mongols and other Asian invaders left an imperial heritage in Russia. In Europe's heartlands, Charlemagne pieced together a fissiparous empire, Normans made several attempts at empire building, and both a Holy Roman Empire (de jure) and a Hapsburg Empire (de facto) made their presences felt. Yet these imperial efforts all fell far short of grasping the entire continent. After Rome, no large section of Europe felt the rule of another empire on a Roman, much less a Chinese, scale.

Nevertheless, Europe experienced in its own more segmented way the interplay of the two processes Skinner detects in China: the bottom-up building of regional hierarchies based on trade and manufacturing, the top-down imposition of political control. What Bernard Lapetit calls two "models" of urban systems actually constitute two different sets of relations among cities. Europe's urban networks represented the hierarchy of capital; they comprised the higher levels of commercial connections that reached into towns and villages, linked by *colporteurs* (etymologically, those who carried goods on their shoulders), peddlers (etymologically, those who walked their goods from place to place), and other more substantial merchants who made their business capital accumulation through local and regional trade. As an English king or a Burgundian duke reached into the countryside for taxes and soldiers, he found well-established commercial connections he had played little part in creating and could not completely control. Indeed, Europe's bottom-up hierarchies long remained more complete, connected, and extensive than its top-down structures of political control. That was a major reason for the failure of the many post-Roman attempts to build empires spanning the continent.

R. Bin Wong's comparison of struggles over food in Europe and China suggest some important Skinnerian parallels between the experiences of the two continents (Wong 1983; Wong and Perdue 1983). Despite significant differences in structure, people in both regions seem to have been especially likely to seize food forcefully in times of shortage and/or high prices where and when the gap was widening between the extent of food marketing and the degree of governmental control over food supply. Poor people who depended on local markets for their food substituted themselves for authorities who could or would no longer enforce the locality's claims to food stored, marketed, or shipped within its perimeter. Eighteenth- and nineteenth-century China experienced a decline in imperial control as markets held their own or even expanded, and local people blocked shipments, bullied merchants, or seized stored grain to enforce their claims to the supply.

Eighteenth- and nineteenth-century Europe, for its part, saw the marketing of food expand even faster than the local strength of governments: its local people seized grain to enforce claims that *their* officials would no longer respect (Bohstedt 1983; Charlesworth 1983; L. Tilly 1971). No one has done a sufficiently broad geography of grain seizures in Europe to determine whether they followed an appropriately Skinnerian pattern. Given the marked tendency of grain seizures to ring major cities and ports, however, such a pattern is quite plausible. China's banditry, rebellion, and other forms of collective conflict also showed marked regional differences that bear at least a rough correspondence to the joint distribution of imperial and mercantile activity. From that fact, we might reasonably search for similar geographic inequalities within Europe. Popular collective action might well display a Skinnerian logic.

The patterns of political covariation Skinner describes have European counterparts: the administrative capitals in the regions of scanty commerce in which a viceroy held power through direct military control but could produce little revenue for the king, the lower-ranking royal officials surrounded by prosperous landlords and merchants with whom they had no choice but to negotiate. Consider the contrast between eastern Prussia, where the state's administrative apparatus overwhelmed merchants in favor of great landlords, and western Prussia, where a similar apparatus almost dissolved in the region's commercial activity. Gabriel Ardant pointed out many years ago that the "fit" between fiscal system and regional economy determines the cost and effectiveness of attempts to tax. In an area with little market activity, a land tax based on estimated value and levied in cash is likely to cost a great deal to collect, strike the population very inequitably, miss a good deal of potential revenue, and incite widespread resistance. In a highly commercialized area, in contrast, a flat head tax generates less revenue at higher cost than a comparable tax designed to fit the loci of capital and paths of commerce.

On the other hand (as Ardant did not observe), with a high level of commercial activity, merchants often hold considerable political power, and they are therefore in a position to prevent the creation of a state that will seize their assets and cramp their transactions. In Europe, as we have seen, the extent of commercial activity strongly affected the viability of the various tactics used to build state strength. Outside of Gdansk, which prospered with the quickening of Baltic trade, Polish merchants were unable to break the grip of the great landlords. (Ironically, the power of Polish landlords also cramped Poland's elected king, and thereby made him an attractive suzerain for Prussian cities that were trying to escape the more demanding tutelage of the Teutonic Knights.) But the merchants of Amsterdam, Dubrovnik, Venice, and Genoa, high points in the commercial hierarchy, could dictate the terms on which any state would operate in their territories. Thus Skinner's model of China sheds light on the geography of state formation in Europe.

What drives the geography of top-down hierarchy? Under most circumstances, the spatial distribution of state activity that serves military purposes well differs sharply from the spatial distribution that serves the production of revenues. So long as a state is operating through conquest and tribute in a contiguous territory, the discrepancy need not be large; occupying soldiers can then serve as monitors, administrators, and tax collectors. Beyond that point, however, four interests pull in different directions: (1) the placement of military forces between their likely sites of activity and their major sources of supplies; (2) the distribution of state officials who specialize in surveillance and control of the civilian population in a pattern that compromises between spatial completeness and correspondence to the population distribution; (3) the proportioning of state revenue-collecting activities to the geography of trade, wealth, and income, and (4) the distribution of state activities resulting from bargaining over revenues according to the spatial structures of the parties to the bargains.

Obviously, the resulting geography of state activity varies with its relation to all four of these forces; navies concentrate in deepwater locations along a state's periphery, while post offices cling to one another. The bigger the military establishment, the greater its orientation to war outside the state's own territory; and the more extensive the apparatus of extraction and control that grows up to support it, the greater the discrepancy between their geographies and the more distant the ideal military geography from one that gives the armed forces substantial day-to-day control over the civilian population.

Both geographies alter as a result of conquest. When states conquer regional rulers—both inside and outside their own nominal territories—they rarely displace those rulers entirely, at least in the short run, and they often make compacts with regional power holders that confirm their positions, maintain existing boundaries, and incorporate them wholesale into the conquering state. As a result, important deviations from the spatial logics of efficient military activity and policing appear within state administrative structures. Given regional power holders, the geographic distribution of policing is likely to change more slowly than that of military organization, with the probable consequence of greater discrepancies between the two.

The geographic discrepancy encourages the creation of separate organizations for each activity, including the division of armed forces into armies and police forces. The distribution of police forces comes to approximate the geography of the civilian population, while the distribution of troops isolates them from civilians and places them where international strategy dictates. Indeed, the French model divides land forces into three parts: soldiers grouped into garrisons located for administrative and tactical convenience; gendarmes (remaining under military control and mobilizable into the military in wartime) spread across the communications lines and thinly settled segments of the territory; and police stationed in the country's larger agglomerations. Soldiers then patrol the frontiers, protect the sites of national power, intervene overseas, but rarely take part in control of crime or civilian conflicts.

Except for highways, gendarmes deal chiefly with those portions of the territory in which private property occupies most of the space, and they therefore spend most of their time patrolling communication lines and responding to calls from civilians. Urban police, in contrast, crisscross territories dominated by public space and those having valuable property within reach of that public space; they correspondingly spend more of their effort reaching out to control and apprehend without calls from civilians. Ultimately, any such geographic division separates the military from political power and makes it dependent for survival on civilians whose preoccupations include fiscal soundness, administrative efficiency, public order, and the keeping of political bargains as well as (perhaps even instead of) military efficacy. This complex logic strongly affected the spatial differentiation of European states.

INDIRECT AND DIRECT RULE

A widespread movement from indirect to direct rule occurred with the nationalization of military power. It offered a seductive but costly opportunity to ordinary people. After 1750, states began moving aggressively from a nearly universal system of indirect rule to a new system of direct rule: unmediated intervention in the lives of local communities, households, and productive enterprises. As rulers shifted from the hiring of mercenaries to the recruitment of warriors from their own national populations, and as they increased taxation to support the great military forces of eighteenth-century warfare, they bargained out access to communities, households, and enterprises, sweeping away autonomous intermediaries in the process.

Through much of European history, city-states, autonomous bishoprics, petty principalities, and other microstates ruled in a relatively direct way: agents who were immediately responsible to the Crown and served at the monarch's pleasure collected taxes, administered courts, tended Crown property, and maintained day-to-day contact with local communities falling under the Crown's jurisdiction. Larger states, however, invariably opted for some form of indirect rule, coopting local power holders and confirming their privileges without incorporating them directly into the state apparatus.

Before the seventeenth century, every large European state ruled its subjects through powerful intermediaries who enjoyed significant autonomy, hindered state demands that were not to their own interest, and profited on their own accounts from the delegated exercise of state power. The intermediaries were often privileged members of subordinate populations and made their way by assuring rulers of tribute acquiescence from those populations. In southeastern Europe especially, the presence of multiple populations mixed by centuries of conquest and Mediterranean trade combined with the characteristic forms of Muslim rule through semiautonomous subordinates to produce a vast zone of indirect rule, the traces of which remain today in the region's cultural heterogeneity and its continuing struggles over the rights of minorities. Crucial intermediaries included clergy, landlords, urban oligarchies, and independent professional warriors, in proportions that varied along the continuum from capital-intensive to coercion-intensive regions. The centrality of these various intermediaries identified alternative systems to indirect rule.

Any system of indirect rule set serious limits on the quantity of resources rulers could extract from the ambient economy. Beyond that limit, intermediaries acquired an interest in impeding extraction, even in allying themselves with ordinary people's resistance to the state's demands. In the same circumstances, however, rulers developed an interest both in undermining the autonomous powers of intermediaries and in making coalitions with major segments of the subject population. As war demanded greater resources, emphatically including manpower, and as the threat of conquest by the largest states grew more serious, ever more rulers bypassed, suppressed, or coopted old intermediaries and reached directly into communities and households to seize the wherewithal of war. Thus national standing armies, national states, and direct rule caused one another.

Before then, how much autonomy power holders enjoyed varied significantly from state to state; after its early phase of conquest and military administration, the Ottoman Empire installed two successive forms of rule in the Balkans, the second even more indirect than the first. Into the seventeenth century, sultans drew tribute from their vassal states, but within their own domains divided substantial parts of their lands into *timars,* grants held by warriors so long as they continued to serve in the armed forces. The *timarlis* (grant holders) drew their own revenues from the land, collected taxes for the sultan, ran the civil administration, and controlled the Christian serfs, but gained no right to alienate the land or pass it on to their children. Sixteenth- and seventeenth-century wars, however, killed off many *timarlis,* and the demand to collect more and more taxes for increasingly expensive war making made the grants less attractive to warriors. Sultans turned increasingly to tax farmers, who used their leverage to convert the lands they taxed into their own property. As that happened, other groups demanded and received the right to buy and own lands that paid taxes; *chiftliks,* private lands, displaced *timars* (Roider 1987: 133–134).

Thus the Ottomans inadvertently installed a classic system of indirect rule. That system later turned against both subjects and rulers by virtue of the power it put into the hands of semi-independent warriors. At the peace of Sistova between the Ottoman and Austrian Empires (1791), for example:

> the janissaries and the irregular military units (in Serbia) found themselves unemployed. They thus turned and preyed on the population. Bands of these men seized villages and their lands and converted the property into their own estates. Others joined rebel *avans* or bandit organizations and plundered peaceful Muslims and Christians alike. (Jelavich and Jelavich 1977: 27)

The autonomy and predation of the Janissaries eventually hindered Ottoman rule so seriously that in 1826, the sultan's troops, at his behest, joined with the crowds of Constantinople in slaughtering the remainder of their corps. The great risks of indirect rule were predation by intermediaries, which incited resistance to the intermediaries by the general population, and resistance by the intermediaries, which incited resistance of whole regions to national rule.

Most of the time, however, local rulers governed in a relatively stable fashion and bought insulation for the local population through the timely payment of tribute to the Ottoman state. Meanwhile, Prussian junkers served simultaneously as masters of their own great estates, judges, military commanders, and spokesmen of the Crown, as the English gentry, nobility, and clergy divided the work of civil administration outside of the capital.

Under favorable circumstances, the middlemen thus empowered mitigated the effects of state expansion on the social organization and wealth of their subjects. The nature of their mediation differed significantly between two types of regions: those having an indigenous nobility and those dominated by aliens. Where the nobility shared religion, tongue, and tradition with the peasantry (as in Austria and Bohemia), some possibility of regional solidarity against the Crown's demands existed. Where nobles were foreigners (as in the European portion of the Ottoman Empire through much of its history), village headmen and tribal elders frequently linked local people to national authorities. In such regions, the empire's collapse left peasants, merchants, and professionals in direct contact with the state (Berend and Ránki 1977: 29–36).

Whether indigenous or alien, middlemen were usually tyrants within their own zones of control. As the *chiftlik* system displaced the *timars* in Ottoman territory, even the appeal to Moslem courts officials disappeared as a resource, and absentee landlords frequently pressed their peasants harder their their military predecessors (Roider 1987: 134). When the center's power declined—as it did generally during the nineteenth century—landlords acquired increasing control of local affairs. In nineteenth-century Bosnia and Serbia, Muslim landlords drove their Christian tenants into serfdom (Donia 1981: 4–5). In those circumstances, banditry became rampant in the Balkans. As a result of exploitation by middlemen, an alliance with the distant king or his agents often seemed an attractive alternative to exploitation close at hand; villagers then appealed to royal agents, took their cases against landlords to royal courts, and cheered the curtailment of urban privileges. In the short run, they sometimes gained by these choices. But in the long run, the destruction of intermediate barriers made them more vulnerable to the state's next round of war-generated demands.

The growth of domestically recruited standing armies offered a strong stimulus to direct rule. Although rented troops persisted in some armies through the eighteenth century, rulers in regions of capitalized coercion—especially in France, Prussia, and England—began to move away from wholesale engagement of mercenary armies during the seventeenth. Mercenaries had the severe drawbacks of being unreliable when poorly paid, seeking booty and rapine when not closely supervised, causing widespread trouble when demobilized, and costing a great deal of cash. The effort to maintain substantial armies in peacetime, pioneered by such rulers as Prussia's Frederick William in the seventeenth century, exceeded most states' ability to tax the essential revenues, especially in the face of competition from regional power holders. These circumstances encouraged rulers to establish durable domestic military administrations, and then to conscript, coopt, and penetrate. These steps bypassed intermediaries and led the way from indirect to direct rule.

The domestic recruitment of large standing armies entailed serious costs. While discharged mercenaries had few enforceable claims on any states, veterans of a national force did, especially if they had incurred disabilities in the nation's service. Families of dead or wounded warriors likewise acquired benefits such as preference in the state-run sale of tobacco and matches. The garrisoning of troops within the country involved military officials and their civilian counterparts in food supply, housing, and public order. Eventually, the health and education of all young males, which affected their military effectiveness, became governmental concerns. Thus military reorganization entered a wedge for expansion of activity into what had previously been local and private spheres.

In one of their more self-conscious attempts to engineer state power, rulers frequently sought to homogenize their populations in the course of installing direct rule. From a ruler's point of view, a linguistically, religiously, and ideologically homogenous population presented the risk of a common front against royal demands; homogenization made a policy of divide and rule more costly. But homogeneity had many compensating advantages: within a homogenous population, ordinary people were more likely to identify with their rulers, communication ran more efficiently, and an administrative innovation that worked in one segment was likely to work elsewhere as well. People who sensed a common origin, furthermore, were more likely to unite against external threats. Spain, France, and other large states recurrently homogenized by giving religious minorities—especially Muslims and Jews—the choice between conversion and emigration; in 1492, shortly after the completed conquest of Granada, for example, Ferdinand and Isabella gave Spanish Jews just that choice; Portugal followed suit in 1497. As it happened, Jewish exiles from Iberia, the Sephardim, constituted a trade diaspora elsewhere in Europe, using their existing connections to set up a powerful system of long-distance credit and communication that allowed them to establish near-monopolies in precious stones, sugar, spice, and tobacco at various times in the succeeding centuries (von Greyerz 1989).

The Protestant Reformation gave rulers of smaller states a splendid opportunity to define their nation's distinctness and homogeneity vis-à-vis the great empires, not to mention a chance to coopt the clergy and their administrative apparatus in the service of royal ends. Sweden set an early example, with large chunks of public administration placed in the hands of Lutheran pastors. (Today's Swedish historians still benefit from the long series of parish registers, complete with information about literacy and changes of residence, that those pastors prepared faithfully from the seventeenth century onward.) Over and above any possible influence on beliefs about the state's legitimacy, a shared clergy and a common faith linked to the sovereign provided a powerful instrument of rule.

THE FRENCH REVOLUTION: FROM INDIRECT TO DIRECT RULE

European states began forcing the choice between local and national loyalties during the eighteenth century. Although Enlightenment "reforms" often had the effect of reinforcing direct rule, the most sensational move in direction was no doubt the work of the French Revolution and Empire. French actions from 1789 to 1815 forwarded the general European transition from indirect to direct rule in two ways: by providing the model of centralized government that other states emulated, and by imposing variants of that model wherever France conquered. Even though many of the period's innovations in French government emerged from desperate improvisations in response to threats of rebellion and bankruptcy, their battle-tested forms endured beyond the Revolution and empire.

What happened to France's system of rule during the revolutionary years? Before 1789, the French state, like almost all other states, ruled indirectly at the local level, relying especially on priests and nobles for mediation. From the end of the American war, the government's efforts to collect money to cover its war debts crystallized an antigovernmental coalition that initially included the parlements and other power holders, but changed toward a more popular composition as the confrontation between the regime and its opponents sharpened (Comninel 1987; Doyle 1986; Egret 1962; Frêche 1974; Stone 1981). The state's visible vulnerability in 1788–1789 encouraged any group that had a stifled claim or grievance against the state, its agents, or its allies to articulate its demands and join others in calling for change. The rural revolts—the Great Fear, grain seizures, tax rebellions, attacks on landlords, and so on—of the spring and summer of 1789 occurred disproportionately in regions with large towns, commercialized agriculture, navigable waterways, and many roads (Markoff 1985). Their geography reflected a composite but largely bourgeois-led settling of scores.

At the same time, those whose social survival depended most directly on the Old Regime state—nobles, officeholders, and higher clergy are the obvious examples—generally aligned themselves with the king (Dawson 1972: chap. 8). Thus a revolutionary situation began to form: two distinct blocs both claimed power and both received support from some significant part of the population. With significant defections of military men from the Crown and the formation of militias devoted to the popular cause, the opposition acquired a force of its own. The popular bloc, connected and often led by members of the bourgeoisie, started to gain control over parts of the state apparatus.

The lawyers, officials, and other bourgeois who seized the state apparatus in 1789–1790 rapidly displaced the old intermediaries: landlords, seigneurial officials, venal officeholders, clergy, and sometimes municipal oligarchies as well. "[I]t was not a rural class of English-style gentlemen," declares Lynn Hunt, "who gained political prominence on either the national or the regional level, but rather thousands of city professionals who seized the opportunity to develop political careers" (Hunt 1984: 155; see also Hunt 1978; Vovelle 1987). At the local level, the so-called Municipal Revolution widely transferred power to enemies of the old rulers; patriot coalitions based in militias, clubs, and revolutionary committees and linked to Parisian activists ousted the old municipalities. Even where the old power holders managed to survive the Revolution's early turmoil, relations between each locality and the national capital altered abruptly. Village "republics" of the Alps, for example, found their ancient liberties—including ostensibly free consent to taxes—crumbling as outsiders clamped them into the new administrative machine (Rosenberg 1988: 72–89). Then Parisian revolutionaries faced the problem of governing without intermediaries; they experimented with the committees and militias that had appeared in the mobilization of 1789, but found them hard to control from the center. More or less simultaneously, they recast the French map into a nested system of departments, districts, cantons, and communes, while sending out *représentants en mission* to forward revolutionary reorganization. They installed direct rule.

Given the unequal spatial distribution of cities, merchants, and capital, furthermore, the imposition of a uniform geographic grid altered the relations between cities' economic and political power, placing insignificant Mende and Niort at the same administrative level as mighty Lyon and Bordeaux (Lepetit 1988: chap. 6; Margadant 1988a, 1988b; Ozouf-Marignier 1986; Schultz 1982). Bernard Lepetit has established a "functional" hierarchy for the prerevolutionary period that unfortunately compounds commercial importance with administrative position, but gives pride of place to administration; we can therefore take the discrepancy between a city's size and its position on Lepetit's scale as a rough indication of its relative emphasis on trade. Within Old Regime France, cities whose commercial rank exceeded their administrative stature included, for example, Nîmes, Saint-Étienne, Roubaix, and Castres, and those occupying higher administrative than commercial rank included, for example, Tulle, Saint-Amand-en-Berry, Saint-Flour, and Soissons (Lepetit 1988: 167–168).

The Revolution reordered that relationship. For that period, Lepetit considers "functional" rank, size, and wealth as measured by municipal revenues. Among capitals of the eighty-six original *départements,* Lepetit inexplicably provides information for only eighty-five. Of these, fifty-four were indisputably the dominant cities within the new jurisdictions, three won out through size over others that had higher administrative and fiscal ranks under the Old Regime, six maintained their administrative priority despite smaller size, twelve became capitals despite being neither the largest nor the highest ranking of their regions, and ten were too close to call (Lepetit 1988: 203–204). Larger cities that failed to win departmental capitals clustered disproportionately in northern France, with Atlantic and Mediterranean ports likewise having more than their share (Lepetit 1988: 208). The great discrepancies, however, did not appear on the local level, but as inequalities among the eighty-six capitals, now all nominally occupying identical administrative relations to the national capital.

As a result, the balance of forces in regional capitals shifted significantly: in the great commercial centers, where merchants, lawyers, and professionals already clustered, departmental officials (who frequently came, in any case, from the same milieux) had no choice but to bargain with the locals. Where the National Assembly carved departments out of relatively uncommercialized rural regions, the Revolution's administrators overshadowed other residents of the new capitals and could plausibly threaten to use force if they were recalcitrant. But those regions lacked the bourgeois allies who helped their confrères do the Revolution's work elsewhere and confronted old intermediaries who still commanded significant followings.

In great mercantile centers such as Marseille and Lyon, the political situation was very different. By and large, the federalist movement, with its protests against Jacobin centralism and its demands for regional autonomy, took root in departmental capitals whose commercial positions greatly outraced their administrative rank. In dealing with these alternative obstacles to direct rule, Parisian revolutionaries improvised three parallel, and sometimes conflicting, systems of rule: (1) the committees and militias; (2) a geographically defined hierarchy of elected officials and representatives; and (3) roving commissioners from the central government. To collect information and gain support, all three relied extensively on the existing personal networks of lawyers, professionals, and merchants.

As the system began to work, revolutionary leaders strove to routinize their control and contain independent action by local enthusiasts, who often resisted. Using both cooptation and repression, they gradually squeezed out the committees and militias. Mobilization for war put great pressure on the system, incited new resistance, and increased the national leaders' incentives for a tight system of control. Starting in 1792, the central administration (which until then had continued in a form greatly resembling that of the Old Regime) underwent its own revolution: the staff expanded enormously, and a genuine hierarchical bureaucracy took shape. In the process, revolutionaries installed one of the first systems of direct rule ever to take shape in a large state.

That shift entailed changes in system of taxation, justice, public works, and much more. Consider policing. Outside of the Paris region, France's Old Regime state had almost no specialized police of its own; it dispatched the Maréchaussée to pursue tax evaders, vagabonds, and other violators of royal will and occasionally authorized the army to quell rebellious subjects, but otherwise relied on local and regional authorities to deploy armed force against civilians. The revolutionaries changed things. With respect to ordinary people, they moved from reactive to proactive policing and information gathering: instead of simply waiting until a rebellion or collective violation of the law occurred, and then retaliating ferociously but selectively, they began to station agents whose job was to anticipate and prevent threatening popular collective action. During the Revolution's early years, Old Regime police forces generally dissolved as popular committees, National Guards, and revolutionary tribunals took over their day-to-day activities. But with the Directory, the state concentrated surveillance and apprehension in a single centralized organization. Fouché of Nantes became minister of police in the year 1799 and thenceforth ran a ministry the powers of which extended throughout France and its conquered territories. By the time of Fouché, France had become one of the world's most closely policed countries.

Going to war accelerated the move from indirect to direct rule. Almost any state that makes war finds that it cannot pay for the effort from its accumulated reserves and current revenues. Almost all war-making states borrow extensively, raise taxes, and seize the means of combat—including men—from reluctant citizens who have other uses for their resources. Prerevolutionary France followed these rules faithfully, to the point of accumulating debts that eventually forced the calling of the Estates General. Nor did the Revolution repeal the rules: once France declared war on Austria in 1792, the state's demands for revenues and manpower excited resistance just as fierce as that which had broken out under the Old Regime. In overcoming that resistance, revolutionaries built yet another set of centralized controls.

The French used their own new system as a template for the reconstruction of other states. As revolutionary and imperial armies conquered, they attempted to build replicas of that system of direct rule elsewhere in Europe. Napoleon's government consolidated the system and turned it into a reliable instrument of rule. The system survived the Revolution and empire in France and, to some degree, elsewhere; Europe as a whole shifted massively toward centralized direct rule with at least a modicum of representation for the ruled.

Resistance and counterrevolutionary action followed directly from the process by which the new state established direct rule. Remember how much change revolutionaries introduced in a very short time. They eliminated all previous territorial jurisdictions, consolidated many old parishes into larger communes, abolished the tithe and fuedal dues, dissolved corporations and their privileges, constructed a top-bottom administrative and electoral system, imposed expanded and standardized taxes through that system, seized the properties of emigrant nobles and of the Church, disbanded monastic orders, subjected clergy to the state and imposed upon them an oath to defend the new state church, conscripted young men at an unprecedented rate, and displaced both nobles and priests from the automatic exercise of local leadership. All this occurred between 1789 and 1793.

Subsequent regimes added more ephemeral changes such as the revolutionary calendar and the cult of the Supreme Being, but the early Revolution's overhaul of the state endured into the nineteenth century and set the pattern for many other European states. The greatest reversals concerned the throttling of local militias and revolutionary committees, the restoration or compensation of some confiscated properties, and Napoleon's concordat with the Catholic Church. All in all, these changes constituted a dramatic, rapid substitution of uniform, centralized direct rule for a system of government mediated by local and regional notables. What is more, the new state hierarchy consisted largely of lawyers, physicians, notaries, merchants, and other bourgeois.

Like their prerevolutionary counterparts, these fundamental changes attacked many existing interests and opened opportunities to groups that had previously had little access to state-sanctioned power—especially the village and small-town bourgeoisie. As a result, they precipitated both resistance and struggles for power. Artois (the department of Pas-de-Calais) underwent a moderate version of the transition (Jessenne 1987). Before the Revolution, Artesian nobles and churchmen held a little over half of all land as against a third for peasants. Up to 60–80 percent of all farms had fewer than 5 hectares (which implies that a similar large majority of farm operators worked part-time for others), and a quarter of household heads worked primarily as agricultural wage laborers. Taxes, tithes, rents, and feudal dues took a relatively low 30 percent of the income from leased land in Artois, with a fifth of rural land on sale with the revolutionary seizure of church and noble properties. Agricultural capitalism, in short, was well advanced by 1770.

In such a region, large leaseholders dominated local politics, but only within limits set by their noble and ecclesiastical landlords. The Revolution, by sweeping away the privileges of those patrons, threatened the leaseholders' power. They survived the challenge, however, as a class, if not as a particular set of individuals: many officeholders lost their posts during the struggles of the early Revolution, especially when the community was already at odds with its lord. Yet their replacements came disproportionately from the same class of comfortable leaseholders. The struggle of wage laborers and smallholders against the *coqs de village* that Georges Lefebvre discovered in the adjacent Nord was less intense, or less effective, in the Pas-de-Calais. Although the larger farmers, viewed with suspicion by national authorities, lost some of their grip on public office during the Terror and again under the Directory, they regained it later and continued to rule their roosts through the middle of the nineteenth century. By that time, nobles and ecclesiastics had lost much of their capacity to contain local power holders, but manufacturers, merchants, and other capitalists had taken their places. The displacement of the old intermediaries opened the way to a new alliance between large farmers and bourgeoisie.

Under the lead of Paris, the transition to direct rule went relatively smoothly in Artois. Elsewhere, intense struggle accompanied the change. The career of Claude Javogues, agent of the Revolution in his native department of the Loire, reveals that struggle and the political process that incited it (Lucas 1973). Javogues was a huge, violent, hard-drinking roustabout whose close kin were lawyers, notaries, and merchants in Forez, a region not far to the west of Lyon. The family was on the ascendant in the eighteenth century, and in 1789, Claude himself was a well-connected thirty-year-old *avocat* at Montbrison. The Convention dispatched this bourgeois bull to the Loire in July 1793 and recalled him in February 1794. During those six months, Javogues relied heavily upon his existing connections, concentrated on repression of the Revolution's enemies, acted to a large degree on the theory that priests, nobles, and rich landlords were enemies, neglected and bungled administrative matters such as the organization of food supply, and left behind him a reputation for arbitrariness and cruelty.

Yet Javogues and his coworkers did, in fact, reorganize local life. In following his action in the Loire, we encounter clubs, surveillance committees, revolutionary armed forces, commissars, courts, and *représentants en mission*. We see almost unbelievable attempts to extend the direct administrative purview of the central government to everyday individual life. We recognize the importance of popular mobilization against the Revolution's enemies—real or imagined—as a force that displaced the old intermediaries. We therefore gain insight into the conflict between two objectives of the Terror: extirpation of the Revolution's opponents and forging of instruments to do the work of the Revolution. We discover again the great importance of control over food as an administrative challenge, as a point of political contention, and as an incentive to popular action.

Direct Rule and Counterrevolution

Contrary to the old image of a unitary people welcoming the arrival of long-awaited reform, local histories of the Revolution make clear that France's revolutionaries established their power through struggle, and frequently over stubborn popular resistance. Most of the resistance, it is true, took the form of evasion, cheating, and sabotage rather than outright rebellion. But people through most of France resisted one feature or another of revolutionary direct rule. In the bustling port of Collioure, on the Mediterranean close to the Spanish border, popular collective action during the Revolution "consciously or not, pursued the goal of preserving a certain cultural, economic, and institutional independence. In other words, popular action sought to challenge the French state's claims to intervene in local life in order to raise troops for international wars, to change religious organization, or to control trade across the Pyrenees" (McPhee 1988: 247). The issues differed from region to region as a function of previous history, including the previous relations of capital and coercion. Where the fault lines ran deep, resistance consolidated into counterrevolution: the formation of effective alternative authorities to those put in place by the Revolution. Counterrevolution occurred not where everyone opposed the Revolution, but where irreconcilable differences divided well-defined blocks of supporters and opponents on a large geographic scale.

France's south and west, through similar processes, produced the largest zones of sustained counterrevolution (Lebrun and Dupuy 1985; Nicolas 1985; Lewis and Lucas 1983). The geography of executions under the Terror provides a reasonable picture of counterrevolutionary activity. The departments having more than 200 executions included: Loire Inférieure (3,548), Seine (2,639), Maine-et-Loire (1,886), Rhône (1,880), Vendée (1,616), Ille-et-Vilaine (509), Mayenne (495), Vaucluse (442), Bouches-du-Rhône (409), Pas-de-Calais (392), Var (309), Gironde (299), and Sarthe (225). These departments accounted for 89 percent of all executions under the Terror (Greer 1935: 147). Except for the Seine and the Pas-de-Calais, they concentrated in the south, the southwest and, especially, the west. In the south and southwest, Languedoc, Provence, Gascony, and the Lyonnais hosted military insurrections against the Revolution, insurrections the geography of which corresponded closely to support for federalism (Forest 1975; Hood 1971, 1979; Lewis 1978; Lyons 1980; Scott 1973). Federalist movements began in the spring of 1793, when the Jacobin expansion of the foreign war—including the declaration of war on Spain—incited resistance to taxation and conscription, which in turn led to a tightening of revolutionary surveillance and discipline. The autonomist movement peaked in commercial cities that had enjoyed extensive liberties under the Old Regime, notably Marseille, Bordeaux, Lyon, and Caen. Sustained rural counterrevolution, on the other hand, broke out chiefly in regions the revolutionary capitals of which had occupied relatively low ranks in the Old Regime's administrative, fiscal, and demographic hierarchies and the bourgeois of which therefore had relatively weak influence in the surrounding regions (Lepetit 1988: 222). In those two kinds of cities and their hinterlands, France fell into bloody civil war.

In the west, guerilla raids against republican strongholds and personnel unsettled Brittany, Maine, and Normandy from 1792 to 1799, while open armed rebellion flared south of the Loire in parts of Brittany, Anjou, and Poitou beginning in the fall of 1792 and likewise continuing intermittently until Napoleon pacified the region in 1799 (Bois 1981; Le Goff and Sutherland 1984; Martin 1987). The western counterrevolution reached its high point in the spring of 1793, when the Republic's call for troops precipitated armed resistance through much of the west. That phase saw massacres of "patriots" and "aristocrats" (as the proponents and opponents of the Revolution came to be called), invasion and temporary occupation of such major cities as Angers, and pitched battles between armies of Blues and Whites (as the armed elements of the two parties were known).

The west's counterrevolution grew directly from the efforts of revolutionary officials to install a particular kind of direct rule in the region: a rule that practically eliminated nobles and priests from their positions as partly autonomous intermediaries; that brought the state's demands for taxes, manpower, and deference to the level of individual communities, neighborhoods, and households; that gave the region's bourgeois political power they had never before wielded. They consolidated their power through struggle. On 12 October 1790, at la Chapelle de Belle-Croix, Vendée, a number of people from neighboring parishes arrived for Mass and vespers armed with clubs. "Seeing the local National Guard with their regular uniforms and arms, the strangers came up to them and said they had no right to wear the national uniform, that they were going to strip it from them, that they supported the cause of clergy and nobility and wanted to crush the bourgeois who, they said, were taking bread from priests and nobles." They then attacked the guards and the Maréchaussée of Palluau, who only fought them off with difficulty (Chassin 1892: II, 220). In the mouths of Vendeans, to be sure, the word *bourgeois* conflated class and urban residence; nevertheless, the people of that counterrevolutionary region saw clearly enough that the two connected intimately. In seeking to extend the state's rule to every locality, and to dislodge all enemies of that rule, French revolutionaries started a process that did not cease for twenty-five years. In some ways, it has not yet ceased today.

In these regards, for all its counterrevolutionary ferocity, the west conformed to France's general experience. Everywhere in France, bourgeois—not owners of large industrial establishments, for the most part, but merchants, lawyers, notaries, and others who made their livings from the possession and manipulation of capital—were gaining strength during the eighteenth century. Throughout France, the mobilization of 1789 brought disproportionate numbers of bourgeois into political action. As the revolutionaries of Paris and their provincial allies displaced nobles and priests from their critical positions as agents of indirect rule, the existing networks of bourgeois served as alternate connections between the state and thousands of communities across the land. For a while, those connections rested on a vast popular mobilization through clubs, militias, and committees. Gradually, however, revolutionary leaders contained or even suppressed their turbulent partners. With trial, error, and struggle, the ruling bourgeoisie worked out the system of rule that reached directly into local communities and passed chiefly through administrators who served under the scrutiny and budgetary control of their superiors.

This process of state expansion encountered three huge obstacles. First, many people saw opportunities to forward their own interests and settle old scores opened up in the crisis of 1789. They either managed to capitalize on the opportunity or found their hopes blocked by competition from other actors; both categories lacked incentives to support further revolutionary changes. Second, the immense effort of warring with most other European powers strained the state's capacity at least as gravely as had the wars of the Old Regime kings. Third, in some regions the political bases of the newly empowered bourgeois were too fragile to support the work of cajoling, containing, inspiring, threatening, extracting, and mobilizing that revolutionary agents carried on everywhere; resistance to demands for taxes, conscripts, and compliance with moralizing legislation occurred widely in

France, but where preexisting rivalries placed a well-connected bloc in opposition to the revolutionary bourgeoisie, civil war frequently developed. In these senses, the revolutionary transition from indirect to direct rule embodied a bourgeois revolution and engendered a series of antibourgeois counterrevolutions.

NOTES

I have pillaged large sections of this paper from "The Geography of European Statemaking and Capitalism since 1500," in Eugene Genovese and Leonard Hochberg, eds., *Geographic Perspectives in History* (Oxford: Blackwell, 1989); "State and Counter-Revolution in France," *Social Research* 56 (1989): 71–98; and *Coercion, Capital, and European States, A.D. 990–1990* (New York: Blackwell, 1990). In addition to the items cited in the paper, the following bibliography includes an overview of the relevant literature.

BIBLIOGRAPHY

Anderson, Perry. 1974. *Lineages of the Absolutist State*. London: NLB.

Ardant, Gabriel. 1965. *Théorie sociologique de l'impôt*. 2 vols. Paris, SEVPEN.

———. 1975. "Financial Policy and Economic Infrastructure of Modern States and Nations." In Charles Tilly, ed., *The Formation of National States in Western Europe*. Princeton, NJ: Princeton University Press.

Aubert, Jacques, and Raphaël Petit. 1979. *La Police en France. Service public*. Paris: Berger-Levrault.

Aubert, Jacques, et al. 1979. *L'Etat et la police en France (1789–1914)*. Geneva: Drotz.

Aydelot, Philippe, Louis Bergeron, and Marcel Roncayolo. 1979. *Industrialisation et croissance urbaine dans la France du XIXe siècle*. Paris: Centre de Recherches Historiques, Ecole des Hautes Etudes en Sciences Sociales.

Bairoch, Paul. 1977. *Taille des villes, conditions de vie et développement économique*. Paris: Editions de l'Ecole des Hautes Etudes en Sciences Sociales.

Batchelder, Ronald W., and Herman Freudenberger. 1983. "On the Rational Origins of the Modern Centralized State." *Explorations in Economic History* 20: 1–13.

Beik, William H. 1985. *Absolutism and Society in Seventeenth-Century France*. Cambridge: Cambridge University Press.

Berend, Iván, and György Ránki. 1977. *East Central Europe in the 19th and 20th Centuries*. Budapest: Akademiai Kiado.

————. 1982. *The European Periphery and Industrialization, 1780–1914.* Budapest: Akademiai Kiado.

Best, Geoffrey. 1982. *War and Society in Revolutionary Eruope, 1770–1870.* London: Fontana.

Bohstedt, John. 1983. *Riots and Community Politics in England and Wales, 1790–1810.* Cambridge, MA: Harvard University Press.

Bois, Paul. 1981. "Apercu sur les causes des insurrections de l'Ouest à l'époque révolutionnaire." In J.-C. Martin, ed., *Vendée-Chouannerie.* Nantes: Reflets du Passé.

Bosher, J. F. 1970. *French Finances, 1770–1795: From Business to Bureaucracy.* Cambridge: Cambridge University Press.

Bossenga, Gail. 1988. "City and State: An Urban Perspective on the Origins of the French Revolution." In Keith Michael Baker, ed., *The French Revolution and the Creation of Modern Political Culture.* Vol. 1: *The Political Culture of the Old Regime.* Oxford: Pergamon.

Bulst, Neithard, and Jean-Philippe Genet, eds. 1988. *La Ville, la bourgeoisie, et la genèse de l'Etat moderne (XIIe–XVIIIe siècles).* Paris: Editions du Centre National de la Recherche Scientifique.

Bunger, Karl. 1987. "Concluding Remarks on Two Aspects of the Chinese Unitary State as Compared with the European State System." In Stuart Schram, ed., *Foundations and Limits of State Power in China.* London: School of Oriental and African Studies, University of London, and Hong Kong: Chinese University Press, Chinese University of Hong Kong.

Cameron, Iain A. 1977. "The Police of Eighteenth-Century France." *European Studies Review* 7: 47–75.

Centre de la Méditerranée Moderne et Contemporaine. "Villes de l'Europe méditerranée et de l'Europe occidentale du Moyen Age au XIXe siècle." *Annales de la Faculté des Lettres et Sciences Humaines de Nice,* nos. 9–10. Saint-Brieuc: Les Belles Lettres.

Charlesworth, Andrew, ed. 1983. *An Atlas of Rural Protest in Britain, 1548–1900.* London: Croom Helm.

Chassin, Charles-Louis. 1892. *La Préparation de la guerre de Vendée.* 3 vols. Paris: Dupont.

Church, Clive H. 1981. *Revolution and Red Tape: The French Ministerial Bureaucracy, 1770–1850.* Oxford: Clarendon Press.

Cobb, Richard. 1970. *The Police and the People*. Oxford: Oxford University Press.

Comninel, George C. 1987. *Rethinking the French Revolution: Marxism and the Revisionist Challenge*. London: Verso.

Connelly, Owen. 1965. *Napoleon's Satellite Kingdoms*. New York: Free Press.

Dann, Otto, and John Dinwiddy, eds. 1988. *Nationalism in the Age of the French Revolution*. London: Hambledon.

Dawson, Philip. 1972. *Provincial Magistrates and Revolutionary Politics in France, 1789–1795*. Cambridge, MA: Harvard University Press.

Donia, Robert J. 1981. *Islam under the Double Eagle: The Muslims of Bosnia and Hercegovina, 1878–1914*. New York: Columbia University Press for Eastern European Monographs.

Doyle, William. 1986. *The Ancien Régime*. Atlantic Highlands, NJ: Humanities Press.

Duchacvo D. 1986. *The Territorial Dimension of Politics: Within, among, and across Nations*. Boulder, CO: Westview.

Duffy, Michael, ed. 1980. *The Military Revolution and the State, 1500–1800*. Exeter Studies in History, vol. 1. Exeter: University of Exeter.

Dupuy, Roger. 1988. *De la Révolution à la Chouannerie: Paysans en Bretagne, 1788–1794*. Paris: Flammarion.

Egret, Jean. 1962. *La pré-Révolution française*. Paris: Presses Universitaires de France.

Eisenstadt, S. N. 1963. *The Political Systems of Empires: The Rise and Fall of the Historical Bureaucratic Societies*. Glencoe: Free Fress.

Forest, Alan. 1975. *Society and Politics in Revolutionary Bordeaux*. Oxford: Oxford University Press.

Frêche, Georges. 1974. *Toulouse et la région Midi-Pyrénées au siècle des Lumières* (vers 1670–1789). Paris: Cujas.

Genet, Jean-Philippe, and Michel Le Mené, eds. 1987. *Genèse de l'état moderne: Prélèvement et Redistribution*. Paris: Editions du Centre National Recherche Scientifique.

Genovese, Eugene, and Leonard Hochberg. 1989. *Geographic Perspectives in History*. Oxford: Blackwell.

Greer, Donald. 1935. *The Incidence of the Terror during the French Revolution*. Cambridge, MA: Harvard University Press.

Heper, Metin. 1985. "The State and Public Bureaucracy: A Comparative and Historical Perspective." *Comparative Studies in Society and History* 27: 86–110.

Hinrichs, Ernst, Eberhard Schmitt, and Rudolf Vierhaus, eds. 1978. *Vom Ancien Régime zur französischen Revolution: Forschungen und Perspektiven.* Göttingen: Vandenhoeck & Ruprecht.

Hohenberg, Paul, and Lynn Hollen Lees. 1985. *The Making of Urban Europe. 1000–1850.* Cambridge, MA: Harvard University Press.

Hood, James N. 1971. "Protestant-Catholic Relations and the Roots of the First Popular Counter-Revolutionary Movement in France." *Journal of Modern History* 43: 245–275.

———. 1979. "Revival and Mutation of Old Rivalries in Revolutionary France." *Past and Present* 82: 82–115.

Hunt, Lynn. 1978. *Revolution and Urban Politics in Provincial France: Troyes and Reims, 1786–1790.* Stanford, CA: Stanford University Press.

———. 1984. *Politics, Culture and Class in the French Revolution.* Berkeley: University of California Press.

Jelavich, Charles, and Barbara Jelavich. 1977. *The Establishment of the Balkan National States, 1804–1920.* Seattle: University of Washington Press.

Jessenne, Jean-Pierre. 1987. *Pouvoir au village et Révolution: Artois, 1760–1848.* Lille: Universitaires de Lille.

Johnston, R. J. 1982. *Geography and the State.* New York: St. Martin's Press.

Juillard, Etienne, and Henri Nonn. 1976. *Espaces et régions en Europe Occidentale.* Paris: Editions du Centre National de la Recherche Scientifique.

Kettering, Sharon. 1986. *Patrons, Brokers, and Clients in Seventeenth-Century France.* New York: Oxford University Press.

Kim, Kyong-Won. 1987. *Revolution and International System.* New York: New York University Press.

Ladurie, Emmanuel Le Roy. 1981. *La Ville Classique de la Renaissance aux Révolutions.* Vol. 3 of Georges Duby, *Histoire de la France Urbaine.* Paris: Le Seuil.

Langlois, Claude. 1987. "La Révolution malade de la Vendée." *Vingtième Siècle* 14: 63–78.

Lebrun, François, and Roger Dupuy, eds. 1985. *Les résistances à la Révolution.* Paris: Imago.

Le Goff, T. J. A., and D. M. G. Sutherland. 1974. "The Revolution and the Rural Community in Eighteenth-Century Brittany." *Past and Present* 62: 96–119.

————. 1983. "The Social Origins of Counter-Revolution in Western France." *Past and Present* 99: 65–87.

————. 1984. "Religion and Rural Revolt in the French Revolution: An Overview." In János M. Bak and Gerhard Benecke, eds., *Religion and Rural Revolt*. Manchester: Manchester University Press.

Lepetit, Bernard. 1982. "Function administrative et armature urbaine: Remarques sur la distribution des chef-lieux de subdélégation en France à l'Ancien Régime." Institut d'Histoire Economique et Sociale de l'Université de Paris I. *Recherches et Travaux* 2: 19–34.

————. 1988. *Les villes dans la France moderne (1740–1840)*. Paris: Albin Michel.

Lewis, Gwynne. 1978. *The Second Vendée: The Continuity of Counter-Revolution in the Department of the Gard, 1789–1815*. Oxford: Clarendon Press.

Lewis, Gwynne, and Colin Lucas, eds. 1983. *Beyond the Terror: Essays in French Regional and Social History, 1794–1811*. Cambridge: Cambridge University Press.

Livet, Georges, and Bernard Vogler, eds. 1983. *Pouvoir, ville, et société en Europe, 1650–1750*. Paris: Ophrys.

Lucas, Colin. 1973. *The Structure of the Terror: The Example of Claude Javogues and the Loire*. Oxford: Oxford University Press.

————. 1988. "The Crowd and Politics between *Ancient Regime* and Revolution in France." *Journal of Modern History* 60: 421–457.

Lyons, Martyn. 1980. *Révolution et Terreur à Toulouse*. Toulouse: Privat.

Margadant, Ted. 1988a. "Politics, Class, and Community in the French Revolution: An Urban Perspective." Paper presented to conference on Revolutions in Comparison, University of California, Los Angeles.

————. 1988b. "Towns, Taxes, and State-Formation in the French Revolution." Paper presented to the Irvine Seminar on Social History and Theory, April.

Markoff, John. 1985. "The Social Geography of Rural Revolt at the Beginning of the French Revolution." *American Sociological Review* 50: 761–781.

————. 1986. "Contexts and Forms of Rural Revolt. France in 1789." *Journal of Conflict Resolution* 30: 253–289.

Martin, Jean-Clément. 1987. *La Vendée et la France*. Paris: Le Seuil.

McPhee, Peter. 1988. "Les formes d'intervention populaire en Roussillon: L'exemple de Collioure, 1789–1815." In *Centre d'Histoire Contempora-*

ine du Languedoc Méditerranéen et du Roussillon, Les pratiques politiques en province à l'époque de la Révolution francaise. Montpellier: Publications de la Recherche, Université de Montpellier.

Meyer, David R. 1986. "System of Cities, Dynamics in Newly Industrializing Nations." *Studies in Comparative International Development* 21: 3–22.

Meyer, Jean. 1983. *Le poids de l'Etat.* Paris: Presses Universitaires de France.

Meyer, Jean, et al. 1983. *Etudes sur les villes en Europe Occidentale.* 2 vols. Paris: Société d'Edition d'Enseignement Supérieur.

Nicolas, Jean, ed. 1985. *Mouvements populaires et conscience sociale, XVIe–XIXe siècles.* Paris: Maloine.

Ozouf-Marignier, Marie-Vic. 1986. "De l'universalisme constituant aux intérêts locaux: Le débat sur la formation des départements en France (1789–1790)." *Annales: Economies, Sociétés, Civilisations* 41: 1193–1214.

Petitfrére, Claude. 1979. *Blancs et bleus d'Anjou (1789–1793).* Paris: Maloine.

———. 1988. "The Origins of the Civil War in the Vendée." *French History* 2:187–207.

Robinson, E. A. G., ed. 1969. *Backward Areas in Advanced Countries.* London: Macmillan.

Roider, Karl. 1987. "Origins of Wars in the Balkans, 1660–1792." In Jeremy Black, ed., *The Origins of War in Early Modern Europe.* Edinburgh: John Donald.

Rosenberg, Harriet G. 1988. *A Negotiated World: Three Centuries of Change in a French Alpine Community.* Toronto: University of Toronto Press.

Roubaud, Francois. 1983. "Partition économique de la France dans la première moitié du XIXe siècle (1830–1840)." Institut d'Histoire Economique et Sociale de l'Université de Paris I Panthéon-Sorbonne. *Recherches et Travaux* 12: 33–58.

Rowe, William. 1985. "Approaches to Modern Chinese Social History." In Oliver Zunz, ed., *Reliving the Past.* Chapel Hill: University of North Carolina Press.

Schmal, H., ed. 1981. *Patterns of European Urbanization since 1500.* London: Croom Helm.

Schram, Stuart R., ed. 1985. *The Scope of State Power in China.* Published for European Science Foundation by School of Oriental and African Studies. London: University of London and Hong Kong: Chinese University Press of Hong Kong.

———. 1987. *Foundations and Limits of State Power in China*. Published for European Science Foundation by School of Oriental and African Studies. London: University of London, and Hong Kong: Chinese University Press of Hong Kong.

Schultz, Patrick. 1982. *La décentralisation administrative dans le département du Nord (1790–1793)*. Lille: Presses Universitaires de Lille.

Schwartz, Robert M. 1988. *Policing the Poor in Eighteenth-Century France*. Chapel Hill: University of North Carolina Press.

Scott, William. 1973. *Terror and Repression in Revolutionary Marseilles*. New York: Barnes & Noble.

Shue, Vivienne. 1988. *The Reach of the State: Sketches of the Chinese Body Politic*. Stanford, CA: Stanford University Press.

Skinner, G. W. 1964. "Marketing and Social Structure in Rural China." *Journal of Asian Studies* 24: 3–43.

———. 1985. "The Structure of Chinese History." *Journal of Asian Studies* 44: 271–292.

———, ed. 1977. *The City in Late Imperial China*. Stanford, CA: Stanford University Press.

Skocpol, Theda. 1979. *States and Social Revolutions: A Comparative Analysis of France, Russia, and China*. Cambridge: Cambridge University Press.

Smith, Carol A. 1976. "Analyzing Regional Systems." In Carol A. Smith, ed., *Regional Analysis*. Vol. 2: *Social Systems*. New York: Academic Press.

Stone, Bailey. 1981. *The Parlement of Paris, 1774–1789*. Chapel Hill: University of North Carolina Press.

Sutherland, Donald. 1982. *The Chouans: The Social Origins of Popular Counter-Revolution in Upper Brittany, 1770–1769*. Oxford: Clarendon Press.

Thbaut, Louis. 1971. "Les Voies navigables et l'industrialisation du Nord de la France." *Journal of Interdisciplinary History* 2: 23–57.

Tilly, Louise A. 1971. "The Food Riot as a Form of Political Conflict in France." *Journal of Interdisciplinary History* 2: 23–57.

von Greyerz, Kaspar. 1984. "Portuguese *Conversos* on the Upper Rhine and the *Converso* Community of Sixteenth-Century Europe." *Social History* 14: 59–82.

Vovelle, Michel. 1988. "L'Historiographie de la Révolution française à la veille du Bicentenaire." *Annales Historiques de la Révolution française* 272: 119.

————, ed. 1987. *Bourgeoisies de province et Révolution*. Grenoble: Presses Universitaires de Grenoble.

Vries, Jan de. 1984. *European Urbanization, 1500–1800*. Cambridge, MA: Harvard University Press.

————. 1985. *The Great Enterprise: The Manchu Reconstruction of Imperial Order in Seventeenth-Century China*. 2 vols. Berkeley: University of California Press.

————. 1988. "Barges and Capitalism: Passenger Transportation in the Dutch Economy, 1632–1839." *A.A.G. Bijdragen* 21: 33–398.

Wakeman Jr., Frederic. 1985. *The Manchu Reconstruction of Imperial Order in Seventeenth-Century China*. 2 vols. Berkeley: University of California Press.

Whitney, Joseph B. R. 1970. *China: Area, Administration, and Nation Building*. Research Paper 123. Chicago: Department of Geography, University of Chicago.

Wong, R. Bin. 1983. "Les émeutes de subsistances en Chine et en Europe Occidentale." *Annales: Economies, Sociétés, Civilisations* 38: 234–258.

Wong, R. Bin, and Peter C. Perdue. 1983. "Famine's Foes in Ch'ing China." *Harvard Journal of Asiatic Studies* 43: 291–332.

· Part Three ·

POWER AND INEQUALITY

WAR MAKING AND STATE MAKING
AS ORGANIZED CRIME

WARNING

If protection rackets represent organized crime at its smoothest, then war making and state making—quintessential protection rackets with the advantage of legitimacy—qualify as our largest examples of organized crime. Without branding all generals and statespeople as murderers or thieves, I want to urge the value of that analogy. At least for the European experience of the past few centuries, a portrait of war makers and state makers as coercive and self-seeking entrepreneurs bears a far greater resemblance to the facts than do its chief alternatives: the idea of a social contract, the idea of an open market in which operators of armies and states offer services to willing consumers, the idea of a society the shared norms and expectations of which call forth a certain kind of government.

The reflections that follow merely illustrate the analogy of war making and state making with organized crime from a few hundred years of European experience and offer tentative arguments concerning principles of change and variation underlying the experience. My reflections grow from contemporary concerns: worries about the increasing destructiveness of war, the expanding role of great powers as suppliers of arms and military organization to poor countries, and the growing importance of military rule in those same countries. They spring from the hope that the European experience, properly understood, will help us to grasp what is happening today, perhaps even to do something about it.

The Third World of the twentieth century does not greatly resemble Europe of the sixteenth or the seventeenth century. In no simple sense can

---

This chapter was first published as "War Making and State Making as Organized Crime," in Peter Evans, Dietrich Rueschemeyer, and Theda Skocpol, eds., *Bringing the State Back In* (Cambridge: Cambridge University Press, 1985), pp. 169–191. Reprinted with permission.

we read the future of Third World countries from the pasts of European countries. Yet a thoughtful exploration of European experience will serve us well. It will show us that coercive exploitation played a large part in the creation of the European states. It will show us that popular resistance to coercive exploitation forced would-be power holders to concede protection and constraints on their own action. It will therefore help us to eliminate faulty implicit comparisons between today's Third World and yesterday's Europe. That clarification will make it easier to understand exactly how today's world is different and what we therefore have to explain. It may even help us to explain the current looming presence of military organization and action throughout the world. Although that result would delight me, I do not promise anything so grand.

This essay, then, concerns the place of organized means of violence in the growth and change of those peculiar forms of government we call national states: relatively centralized, differentiated organizations the officials of which more or less successfully claim control over the chief concentrated means of violence within a population inhabiting a large, contiguous territory. The argument grows from historical work on the formation of national states in Western Europe, especially on the growth of the French state from 1600 onward. But it takes several deliberate steps away from that work, wheels, and stares hard at it from theoretical ground. The argument brings with it few illustrations and no evidence worthy of the name.

Just as one repacks a hastily filled rucksack after a few days on the trail—throwing out the waste, putting things in order of importance, and balancing the load—I have repacked my theoretical baggage for the climb to come; the real test of the new packing arrives only with the next stretch of the trail. The trimmed-down argument stresses the interdependence of war making and state making and the analogy between both of those processes and what, when less successful and smaller in scale, we call organized crime. War makes states, I shall claim. Banditry, piracy, gangland rivalry, policing, and war making all belong on the same continuum—that I shall claim as well. For the historically limited period in which national states were becoming the dominant organizations in Western countries, I shall also claim that mercantile capitalism and state making reinforced each other.

DOUBLE-EDGED PROTECTION

In contemporary American parlance, the word *protection* surrounds two contrasting tones. One is comforting, the other ominous. With one tone, protection calls up images of the shelter against danger provided by a powerful friend, a large insurance policy, or a sturdy roof. With the other, it evokes the racket in which a local strongman forces merchants to pay tribute in order to avoid damage—damage the strongman himself threatens to deliver. The difference, to be sure, is a matter of degree: A hell-and-damnation priest is likely to collect contributions from his parishioners only to the extent that they believe his predictions of brimstone for infidels; our neighborhood mobster may actually be, as he claims to be, a brothel's best guarantee of operation free of police interference.

Which image the word *protection* brings to mind depends mainly on our assessment of the reality and externality of the threat. Someone who produces both the danger and, at a price, the shield against it is a racketeer. Someone who provides a needed shield but has little control over the danger's appearance qualifies as a legitimate protector, especially if his price is no higher than his competitors'. Someone who supplies reliable, low-priced shielding both from local racketeers and from outside marauders makes the best offer of all.

Apologists for particular governments and for government in general commonly argue, precisely, that they offer protection from local and external violence. They claim that the prices they charge barely cover the costs of protection. They call people who complain about the price of protection "anarchists," "subversives," or both at once. But consider the definition of a racketeer as someone who creates a threat and then charges for its reduction. Governments' provision of protection, by this standard, often qualifies as racketeering. To the extent that the threats against which a given government protects its citizens are imaginary or are consequences of its own activities, the government has organized a protection racket. Since governments themselves commonly simulate, stimulate, or even fabricate threats of external war, and since the repressive and extractive activities of governments often constitute the largest current threats to the livelihoods of their own citizens, many governments operate in essentially the same way as racketeers. There is, of course, a difference: racketeers, by the conventional definition, operate without the sanctity of governments.

How do racketeer governments themselves acquire authority? As a question of fact and of ethics, that is one of the oldest conundrums of political analysis. Back to Machiavelli and Hobbes, nevertheless, political observers have recognized that, whatever else they do, governments organize and, wherever possible, monopolize violence. It matters little whether we take violence in a narrow sense, such as damage to persons and objects, or in a broad sense, such as violation of people's desires and interests; by either criterion, governments stand out from other organizations by their tendency to monopolize the concentrated means of violence. The distinction between "legitimate" and "illegitimate" force, furthermore, makes no difference to the fact. If we take legitimacy to depend on conformity to an abstract principle or on the assent of the governed (or both at once), these conditions may serve to justify, perhaps even to explain, the tendency to monopolize force, they do not contradict the fact.

In any case, Arthur Stinchcombe's agreeably cynical treatment of legitimacy serves the purposes of political analysis much more efficiently. Legitimacy, according to Stinchcombe, depends rather little on abstract principle or assent of the governed: "The person *over whom power is exercised* is not usually as important as *other power-holders.*"[1] Legitimacy is the probability that other authorities will act to confirm the decisions of a given authority. Other authorities, I would add, are much more likely to confirm the decisions of a challenged authority that controls substantial force; not only fear of retaliation, but also desire to maintain a stable environment recommend that general rule. The rule underscores the importance of the authority's monopoly of force. A tendency to monopolize the means of violence makes a government's claim to provide protection, in either the comforting or the ominous sense of the word, more credible and more difficult to resist.

Frank recognition of the central place of force in governmental activity does not require us to believe that governmental authority rests "only" or "ultimately" on the threat of violence. Nor does it entail the assumption that a government's only service is protection. Even when a government's use of force imposes a large cost, some people may well decide that the government's other services outbalance the costs of acceding to its monopoly of violence. Recognition of the centrality of force opens the way to an understanding of the growth and change of governmental forms.

Here is a preview of the most general argument: power holders' pursuit of war involved them willy-nilly in the extraction of resources for war making from the populations over which they had control and in the promotion of capital accumulation by those who could help them borrow and buy. War making, extraction, and capital accumulation interacted to shape European state making. Power holders did not undertake those three momentous activities with the intention of creating national states—centralized, differentiated, autonomous, extensive political organizations. Nor did they ordinarily foresee that national states would emerge from war making, extraction, and capital accumulation.

Instead, the people who controlled European states and states in the making warred in order to check or overcome their competitors and thus to enjoy the advantages of power within a secure or expanding territory.

To make more effective war, they attempted to locate more capital. In the short run, they might acquire that capital by conquest, by selling off their assets, or by coercing or dispossessing accumulators of capital. In the long run, the quest inevitably involved them in establishing regular access to capitalists who could supply and arrange credit and in imposing one form of regular taxation or another on the people and activities within their spheres of control.

As the process continued, state makers developed a durable interest in promoting the accumulation of capital, sometimes in the guise of direct return to their own enterprises. Variations in the difficulty of collecting taxes, in the expense of the particular kind of armed force adopted, in the amount of war making required to hold off competitors, and so on, resulted in the principal variations in the forms of European states. It all began with the effort to monopolize the means of violence within a delimited territory adjacent to a power holder's base.

VIOLENCE AND GOVERNMENT

What distinguished the violence produced by states from the violence delivered by anyone else? In the long run, enough distinguished them to make the division between "legitimate" and "illegitimate" force credible. Eventually, the personnel of states purveyed violence on a larger scale, more effectively, more efficiently, with wider assent from their subject populations, and with readier collaboration from neighboring authorities than did the personnel of other organizations. But it took a long time for that series of distinctions to become established. Early in the state-making process, many parties shared the right to use violence, the practice of using it routinely to accomplish their ends, or both at once. The continuum ran from bandits and pirates to kings via tax collectors, regional power holders, and professional soldiers.

The uncertain, elastic line between "legitimate" and "illegitimate" violence appeared in the upper reaches of power. Early in the state-making process, many parties shared the right to use violence, its actual employment, or both at once. The long love/hate affair between aspiring state makers and pirates or bandits illustrates the division. "Behind piracy on the seas acted cities and city-states," writes Fernand Braudel of the sixteenth century. "Behind banditry, that terrestrial piracy, appeared the continual aid of lords."[2] In times of war, indeed, the managers of full-fledged states often commissioned privateers, hired sometime bandits to raid their enemies, and encouraged their regular troops to take booty. In royal service,

soldiers and sailors were often expected to provide for themselves by prey-
ing on the civilian population: commandeering, raping, looting, taking
prizes. When demobilized, they commonly continued the same practices,
but without the same royal protection; demobilized ships became pirate
vessels, demobilized troops, bandits.

It also worked the other way: a king's best source of armed supporters
was sometimes the world of outlaws. Robin Hood's conversion to royal
archer may be a myth, but the myth records a practice. The distinctions
between "legitimate" and "illegitimate" users of violence came clear only
very slowly, in the process during which the state's armed forces became
relatively unified and permanent.

Up to that point, as Braudel says, maritime cities and terrestrial lords
commonly offered protection, or even sponsorship, to freebooters. Many
lords who did not pretend to be kings, furthermore, successfully claimed
the right to levy troops and maintain their own armed retainers. Without
calling on some of those lords to bring their armies with them, no king
could fight a war; yet the same armed lords constituted the king's rivals
and opponents, his enemies' potential allies. For that reason, before the
seventeenth century, regencies for child sovereigns reliably produced civil
wars. For the same reason, disarming the great stood high on the agenda of
every would-be state maker.

The Tudors, for example, accomplished that agenda through most of
England. "The greatest triumph of the Tudors," writes Lawrence Stone,

> was the ultimately successful assertion of a royal monopoly of violence
> both public and private, an achievement which profoundly altered not
> only the nature of politics but also the quality of daily life. There oc-
> curred a change in English habits that can only be compared with the
> further step taken in the nineteenth century, when the growth of a police
> force finally consolidated the monopoly and made it effective in the
> greatest cities and the smallest villages.[3]

Tudor demilitarization of the great lords entailed four complementary campaigns: eliminating their great personal bands of armed retainers, razing
their fortresses, taming their habitual resort to violence for the settlement
of disputes, and discouraging the cooperation of their dependents and tenants. In the Marches of England and Scotland, the task was more delicate,
for the Percys and Dacres, who kept armies and castles along the border,
threatened the Crown but also provided a buffer against Scottish invaders.
Yet they, too, eventually fell into line.

In France, Richelieu began the great disarmament in the 1620s. With

Richelieu's advice, Louis XIII systematically destroyed the castles of the great rebel lords, Protestant and Catholic, against whom his forces battled incessantly. He began to condemn dueling, the carrying of lethal weapons, and the maintenance of private armies. By the later 1620s, Richelieu was declaring the royal monopoly of force as doctrine. The doctrine took another half century to become effective.

> Once more the conflicts of the Fronde had witnessed armies assembled by the "grands." Only the last of the regencies, the one after the death of Louis XIV, did not lead to armed uprisings. By that time Richelieu's principle had become a reality. Likewise in the Empire after the Thirty Years' War only the territorial princes had the right of levying troops and of maintaining fortresses. . . . Everywhere the razing of castles, the high cost of artillery, the attraction of court life, and the ensuing domestication of the nobility had its share in this development.[4]

By the later eighteenth century, through most of Europe, monarchs controlled permanent, professional military forces that rivaled those of their neighbors and far exceeded any other organized armed force within their own territories. The state's monopoly of large-scale violence was turning from theory to reality.

The elimination of local rivals, however, posed a serious problem. Beyond the scale of a small city-state, no monarch could govern a population with his armed force alone, nor could any monarch afford to create a professional staff large and strong enough to reach from him to the ordinary citizen. Before quite recently, no European government approached the completeness of articulation from top to bottom achieved by imperial China. Even the Roman Empire did not come close. In one way or another, every European government before the French Revolution relied on indirect rule via local magnates. The magnates collaborated with the government without becoming officials in any strong sense of the term, had some access to government-backed force, and exercised wide discretion within their own territories: junkers, justices of the peace, lords. Yet the same magnates were potential rivals, possible allies of a rebellious people.

Eventually, European governments reduced their reliance on indirect rule by means of two expensive but effective strategies: (a) extending their officialdom to the local community and (b) encouraging the creation of police forces that were subordinate to the government rather than to individual patrons, distinct from war-making forces, and therefore less useful as the tools of dissident magnates. In between, however, the builders of national power all played a mixed strategy: eliminating, subjugating, dividing, conquering, cajoling, buying as the occasions presented themselves. The buying manifested itself in exemptions from taxation, creations of honorific offices, the establishment of claims on the national treasury, and a variety of other devices that made a magnate's welfare dependent on the maintenance of the existing structure of power. In the long run, it all came down to massive pacification and monopolization of the means of coercion.

PROTECTION AS BUSINESS

In retrospect, the pacification, cooptation, or elimination of fractious rivals to the sovereign seems an awesome, noble, prescient enterprise, destined to bring peace to a people; yet it followed almost ineluctably from the logic of expanding power. If a power holder was to gain from the provision of protection, his competitors had to yield. As economic historian Frederic Lane put it decades ago, governments are in the business of selling protection . . . whether people want it or not. Lane argued that the very activity of producing and controlling violence favored monopoly, because competition within that realm generally raises costs, instead of lowering them. The production of violence, he suggested, enjoyed large economies of scale.

Working from there, Lane distinguished between (a) the monopoly profit, or *tribute,* coming to owners of the means of producing violence as a result of the difference between production costs and the price exacted from "customers," and (b) the *protection rent* accruing to those customers— for example, merchants—who drew effective protection against outside competitors. Lane, a superbly attentive historian of Venice, allowed specifically for the case of a government that generates protection rents for its merchants by deliberately attacking their competitors. In their adaptation of Lane's scheme, furthermore, Edward Ames and Richard Rapp substitute the apt word *extortion* for Lane's *tribute.* In this model, predation, coercion, piracy, banditry, and racketeering share a home with their upright cousins in responsible government.

This is how Lane's model worked: if a prince could create a sufficient armed force to hold off his and his subjects' external enemies and to keep the subjects in line for 50 megapounds but was able to extract 75 megapounds in taxes from those subjects for that purpose, he gained a tribute of $(75 - 50 =) 25$ megapounds. If the 10-pound share of those taxes paid by one of the prince's merchant-subjects gave him assured access to world markets at less than the 15-pound shares paid by the merchant's foreign competitors to *their* princes, the merchant also gained a protection rent of (15 − 10 =) 5 pounds by virtue of his prince's greater efficiency. That reasoning differs only in degree and in scale from the reasoning of violence-wielding criminals and their clients. Labor racketeering (in which, for example, a shipowner holds off trouble from longshoremen by means of a timely payment to the local union boss) works on exactly the same principle: the union boss receives tribute for his no-strike pressure on the longshoremen, while the shipowner avoids the strikes and showdowns longshoremen impose on his competitors.

Lane pointed out the different behavior we might expect of the managers of a protection-providing government owned by

1. citizens in general
2. a single self-interested monarch
3. the managers themselves

If citizens in general exercised effective ownership of the government—O distant ideal!—we might expect the managers to minimize protection costs and tribute, thus maximizing protection rent. A single self-interested monarch, in contrast, would maximize tribute, set costs so as to accomplish that maximization of tribute, and be indifferent to the level of protection rent. If the managers owned the government, they would tend to keep costs high by maximizing their own wages, to maximize tribute over and above those costs by exacting a high price from their subjects, and likewise to be indifferent to the level of protection rent. The first model approximates a Jeffersonian democracy, the second a petty despotism, and the third a military junta.

Lane did not discuss the obvious fourth category of owner: a dominant class. If he had, his scheme would have yielded interesting empirical criteria for evaluating claims that a given government was "relatively autonomous" or strictly subordinate to the interests of a dominant class. Presumably, a subordinate government would tend to maximize monopoly profits—returns to the dominant class resulting from the difference between the costs of protection and the price received for it—as well as tuning protection rents nicely to the economic interests of the dominant class. An autonomous government, in contrast, would tend to maximize managers' wages and its own size as well and would be indifferent to protection rents. Lane's analysis immediately suggests fresh propositions and ways of testing them.

Lane also speculated that the logic of the situation produced four successive stages in the general history of capitalism:

1. a period of anarchy and plunder;
2. a stage in which tribute takers attracted customers and established their monopolies by struggling to create exclusive, substantial states;
3. a stage in which merchants and landlords began to gain more from protection rents than governors did from tribute; and
4. a period (fairly recent) in which technological changes surpassed protection rents as sources of profit for entrepreneurs.

In their new economic history of the Western world, Douglass North and Robert Paul Thomas make the second and third stages—those in which state makers created their monopolies of force and established property rights that permitted individuals to capture much of the return from their own growth-generating innovations—the pivotal moment for sustained economic growth. Protection, at this point, overwhelms tribute. If we recognize that the protected property rights were mainly those of capital and that the development of capitalism also facilitated the accumulation of the wherewithal to operate massive states, that extension of Lane's analysis provides a good deal of insight into the coincidence of war making, state making, and capital accumulation.

Unfortunely, Lane did not take full advantage of his own insight. Wanting to contain his analysis neatly within the neoclassical theory of industrial organization, Lane cramped his treatment of protection: treating all taxpayers as "customers" for the "service" provided by protection-manufacturing governments, brushing aside the objections to the idea of a forced sale by insisting that the "customer" always had the choice of not paying and taking the consequences of nonpayment, minimizing the problems of divisibility created by the public-goods character of protection, and deliberately neglecting the distinction between the costs of producing the means of violence in general and the costs of giving "customers" protection by means of that violence. Lane's ideas suffocate inside the neoclassical box and breathe easily outside it. Nevertheless, inside or outside, they properly draw the economic analysis of government back to the chief activities that real governments have carried on historically: war, repression, protection, adjudication.

More recently, Richard Bean has applied a similar logic to the rise of European national states between 1400 and 1600. He appeals to economies of scale in the production of effective force, counteracted by diseconomies of scale in command and control. He then claims that the improvement of artillery in the fifteenth century (the cannon made small medieval forts much more vulnerable to an organized force) shifted the curve of economies and diseconomies to make larger armies, standing armies, and centralized governments advantageous to their masters. Hence, according to Bean, military innovation promoted the creation of large, expensive, well-armed national states.

HISTORY TALKS

Bean's summary does not stand up to historical scrutiny. As a matter of practice, the shift to infantry-backed artillery sieges of fortified cities oc-curred only during the sixteenth and seventeenth centuries. Artillery did improve during the fifteenth century, but the invention of new fortifica-tions, especially the *trace italienne,* rapidly countered the advantage of artil-lery. The arrival of effective artillery came too late to have *caused* the increase in the viable size of states. (However, the increased cost of fortifi-cations to defend against artillery did give an advantage to states enjoying larger fiscal bases.)

Nor is it obvious that changes in land war had the sweeping influence Bean attributes to them. The increasing decisiveness of naval warfare, which occurred simultaneously, could well have shifted the military advan-tage to small maritime powers such as the Dutch Republic. Furthermore, although many city-states and other microscopic entities disappeared into larger political units before 1600, such events as the fractionation of the Habsburg Empire and such facts as the persistence of large but loosely knit Poland and Russia render ambiguous the claim of a significant increase in geographic scale. In short, both Bean's proposed explanation and his state-ment of what must be explained raise historical doubts.

Stripped of its technological determination, nevertheless, Bean's logic provides a useful complement to Lane's, for different military formats do cost substantially different amounts to produce and do provide substantially different ranges of control over opponents, domestic and foreign. After 1400, the European pursuit of larger, more permanent, and more costly varieties of military organization did, in fact, drive spectacular increases in princely budgets, taxes, and staffs. After 1500 or so, princes who managed to create the costly varieties of military organizations were, indeed, able to conquer new chunks of territory.

The word *territory* should not mislead us. Until the eighteenth century, the greatest powers were maritime states, and naval warfare remained cru-cial to international position. Consider Fernand Braudel's roll call of succes-sive hegemonic powers within the capitalist world: Venice and its empire; Genoa and its empire; Antwerp, Spain; Amsterdam, Holland; London, En-gland; New York, the United States. Although Brandenburg, Prussia, offers a partial exception, only in our own time have such essentially land-bound states as Russia and China achieved preponderant positions in the world's system of states. Naval warfare was by no means the only reason for that bias toward the sea. Before the later nineteenth century, land transportation was so expensive everywhere in Europe that no country could afford to supply a large army or a big city with grain and other heavy goods without having efficient water transport. Rulers fed major inland centers such as Berlin and Madrid only at great effort and at considerable cost to their hinterlands. The exceptional efficiency of waterways in the Netherlands undoubtedly gave the Dutch great advantages at peace and at war.

Access to water mattered in another important way. Those metropolises on Braudel's list were all major ports, great centers of commerce, and outstanding mobilizers of capital. Both the trade and the capital served the purposes of ambitious rulers. By a circuitous route, that observation brings us back to the arguments of Lane and Bean. Considering that both of them wrote as economic historians, the greatest weakness in their analyses comes as a surprise: both of them understate the importance of capital accumulation to military expansion. As Jan de Vries says of the period after 1600:

> Looking back, one cannot help but be struck by the seemingly symbiotic relationship existing between the state, military power, and the private economy's efficiency in the age of absolutism. Behind every successful dynasty stood an array of opulent banking families. Access to such bourgeois resources proved crucial to the princes' state-building and centralizing policies. Princes also needed direct access to agricultural resources, which could be mobilized only when agricultural productivity grew *and* an effective administrative and military power existed to enforce the princes' claims. But the lines of causation also ran in the opposite direction. Successful state-building and empire-building activities, plus the associated tendency toward concentration of urban population and government expenditure, offered the private economy unique and invaluable opportunities to capture economies of scale. These economies of scale occasionally affected industrial production but were most significant in the development of trade and finance. In addition, the sheer pressure of central government taxation did as much as any other economic force to channel peasant production into the market and thereby augment the opportunities for trade creation and economic specialization.[5]

Nor does the "symbiotic relationship" hold only for the period after 1600. For the precocious case of France, we need only consider the increase in royal expenditures and revenues from 1515 to 1785. Although the rates of growth in both regards accelerated appropriately after 1600, they also rose substantially during the sixteenth century. After 1550, the internal Wars of Religion checked the work of international expansion that Francis I had begun earlier in the century, but from the 1620s onward, Louis XIII and Louis XIV (aided and abetted, to be sure, by Richelieu, Mazarin, Colbert, and other state-making wizards) resumed the task with a vengeance. "As always," comments V. G. Kiernan, "war had every political recommendation and every financial drawback."[6]

Borrowing and then paying interest on the debt accounts for much of the discrepancy between the two curves. Great capitalists played crucial parts on both sides of the transaction: as the principal sources of royal credit, especially in the short term, and as the most important contractors in the risky but lucrative business of collecting royal taxes. For this reason, it is worth noticing that

> for practical purposes the national debt began in the reign of Francis I. Following the loss of Milan, the key to northern Italy, on September 15, 1522, Francis I borrowed 200,000 francs . . . at 12.5 percent from the merchants of Paris, to intensify the war against Charles V. Administered by the city government, this loan inaugurated the famous series of bonds based on revenues from the capital and known as *rentes sur l'Hôtel de Ville*.[7]

(The government's failure to pay those *rentes*, incidentally, helped align the Parisian bourgeoisie against the Crown during the Fronde, some twelve decades later.) By 1595, the national debt had risen to 300 million francs; despite governmental bankruptcies, currency manipulations, and the monumental rise in taxes, by Louis XIV's death in 1715, war-induced borrowing had inflated the total to about 3 billion francs, the equivalent of about eighteen years in royal revenues.[8] War, state apparatus, taxation, and borrowing advanced in tight cadence.

Although France was precocious, it was by no means alone. "Even more than in the case of France," reports the ever-useful Earl J. Hamilton,

> the national debt of England originated and has grown during major wars. Except for an insignificant carry-over from the Stuarts, the debt began in 1689 with the reign of William and Mary. In the words of Adam Smith, "it was in the war which began in 1688, and was concluded by the treaty of Ryswick in 1697, that the foundation of the present enormous debt of Great Britain was first laid."[9]

Hamilton, it is true, goes on to quote the mercantilist Charles Davenant, who complained in 1698 that the high interst rates promoted by government borrowing were cramping English trade. Davenant's complaint suggests, however, that England was already entering Frederic Lane's third stage of state-capital relations, when merchants and landowners receive more of the surplus than do the suppliers of protection.

Until the sixteenth century, the English expected their kings to live on revenues from their own property and to levy taxes only for war. G. R. Elton marks the great innovation at Thomas Cromwell's drafting of Henry VIII's subsidy bills for 1534 and 1540: "1540 was very careful to continue the real innovation of 1534, namely that extraordinary contributions could be levied for reasons other than war."[10] After that point as before, however, war making provided the main stimulus to increases in the level of taxation as well as of debt. Rarely did debt and taxes recede. What A. T. Peacock and J. Wiseman call a "displacement effect" (and others sometimes call a "ratchet effect") occurred: when public revenues and expenditures rose abruptly during war, they set a new, higher floor beneath which peacetime revenues and expenditures did not sink. During the Napoleonic Wars, British taxes rose from 15 to 24 percent of national income and to almost three times the French level of taxation.[11]

True, Britain had the double advantage of relying less on expensive land forces than its continental rivals and of drawing more of its tax revenues from customs and excise—taxes that were, despite evasion, significantly cheaper to collect than land taxes, property taxes, and poll taxes. Nevertheless, in England as well as elsewhere, both debt and taxes rose enormously from the seventeenth century onward. They rose mainly as a function of the increasing cost of war making.

What Do States Do?

As should now be clear, Lane's analysis of protection fails to distinguish among several different uses of state-controlled violence. Under the general heading of organized violence, the agents of states characteristically carry on four different activities:

1. War making: eliminating or neutralizing their own rivals outside the territories in which they have clear and continuous priority as wielders of force.
2. State making: eliminating or neutralizing their rivals inside those territories.
3. Protection: eliminating or neutralizing the enemies of their clients.

4. Extraction: acquiring the means of carrying out the first three activities—war making, state making, and protection.

The third item corresponds to protection as analyzed by Lane, but the other three also involve the application of force. They overlap incompletely and to various degrees; for example, war making against the commercial rivals of the local bourgeoisie delivers protection to that bourgeoisie. To the extent that a population is divided into enemy classes and the state extends its favors partially to one class or another, state making actually reduces the protection given some classes.

War making, state making, protection, and extraction each take a number of forms. Extraction, for instance, ranges from outright plunder to regular tribute to bureaucratized taxation. Yet all four depend on the state's tendency to monopolize the concentrated means of coercion. From the perspectives of those who dominate the state, each of them—if carried on effectively—generally reinforces the others. Thus, a state that successfully eradicates its internal rivals strengthens its ability to extract resources, to wage war, and to protect its chief supporters. In the earlier European experience, broadly speaking, those supporters were typically landlords, armed retainers of the monarch, and churchmen.

Each of the major uses of violence produced characteristic forms of organization. War making yielded armies, navies, and supporting services. State making produced durable instruments of surveillance and control within the territory. Protection relied on the organization of war making and state making but added to it an apparatus by which the protected called forth the protection that was their due, notably through courts and representative assemblies. Extraction brought fiscal and accounting structures into being. The organization and deployment of violence themselves account for much of the characteristic structure of European states.

The general rule seems to have operated like this: the more costly the activity, all other things being equal, the greater was the organizational residue. To the extent, for example, that a given government invested in large standing armies—a very costly, if effective, means of war making—the bureaucracy created to service the army was likely to become bulky. Furthermore, a government building a standing army while controlling a small population was likely to incur greater costs, and therefore to build a bulkier structure, than a government within a populous country. Brandenburg-Prussia was the classic case of high cost for available resources. The Prussian effort to build an army matching those of its larger continental neighbors created an immense structure; it militarized and bureaucratized much of German social life.

In the case of extraction, the smaller the pool of resources and the less commercialized the economy, other things being equal, the more difficult was the work of extracting resources to sustain war and other governmental activities; hence, the more extensive was the fiscal apparatus. England illustrated the corollary of that proposition, with a relatively large and commercialized pool of resources drawn on by a relatively small fiscal apparatus. As Gabriel Ardant has argued, the choice of fiscal strategy probably made an additional difference. On the whole, taxes on land were expensive to collect as compared with taxes on trade, especially large flows of trade past easily controlled checkpoints. Its position astride the entrance to the Baltic gave Denmark an extraordinary opportunity to profit from customs revenues.

With respect to state making (in the narrow sense of eliminating or neutralizing the local rivals of the people who controlled the state), a territory populated by great landlords or by distinct religious groups generally imposed larger costs on a conqueror than one of fragmented power or homogeneous culture. This time, fragmented and homogeneous Sweden, with its relatively small but effective apparatus of control, illustrates the corollary.

Finally, the cost of protection (in the sense of eliminating or neutralizing the enemies of the state makers' clients) mounted with the range over which that protection extended. Portugal's effort to bar the Mediterranean to its merchants' competitors in the spice trade provides a textbook case of an unsuccessful protection effort that nonetheless built up a massive structure.

Thus, the sheer size of the government varied directly with the effort devoted to extraction, state making, protection, and, especially, war making, but inversely with the commercialization of the economy and the extent of the resource base. What is more, the relative bulk of different features of the government varied with the cost/resource ratios of extraction, state making, protection, and war making. In Spain, we see hypertrophy of Court and courts as the outcome of centuries of effort at subduing internal enemies, whereas in Holland, we are amazed to see how small a fiscal apparatus grows up with high taxes within a rich, commercialized economy.

Clearly, war making, extraction, state making, and protection were interdependent. Speaking very, very generally, the classic European state-making experience followed this causal pattern:

In an idealized sequence, a great lord made war so effectively as to become dominant in a substantial territory, but that war making led to increased extraction of the means of war—men, arms, food, lodging, trans-

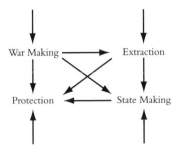

portation, supplies, and/or the money to buy them—from the population within that territory. The building up of war-making capacity likewise increased the capacity to extract. The very activity of extraction, if successful, entailed the elimination, neutralization, or cooptation of the great lord's local rivals; thus, it led to state making. As a by-product, it created organization in the form of tax-collection agencies, police forces, courts, exchequers, account keepers; thus it again led to state making. To a lesser extent, war making likewise led to state making through the expansion of military organization itself, as a standing army, war industries, supporting bureaucracies, and (rather later) schools grew up within the state apparatus. All of these structures checked potential rivals and opponents. In the course of making war, extracting resources, and building up the state apparatus, the managers of states formed alliances with specific social classes. The members of those classes loaned resources, provided technical services, or helped ensure the compliance of the rest of the population, all in return for a measure of protection against their own rivals and enemies. As a result of these multiple strategic choices, a distinctive state apparatus grew up within each major section of Europe.

How States Formed

This analysis, if correct, has two strong implications for the development of national states. First, popular resistance to war making and state making made a difference. When ordinary people resisted vigorously, authorities made concessions: guarantees of rights, representative institutions, courts of appeal. Those concessions, in their turn, constrained the later paths of war making and state making. To be sure, alliances with fragments of the ruling class greatly increased the effect of popular action; the broad mobilization of gentry against Charles I helped give the English Revolution of 1640 a far greater impact on political institutions than did any of the multiple rebellions during the Tudor era.

Second, the relative balance among war making, protection, extraction, and state making significantly affected the organization of the states that emerged from the four activities. To the extent that war making went on with relatively little extraction, protection, and state making, for example, military forces ended up playing a larger and more autonomous part in national politics. Spain is perhaps the best European example. To the extent that protection, as in Venice or Holland, prevailed over war making, extraction, and state making, oligarchies of the protected classes tended to dominate subsequent national politics. From the relative redominance of state making sprang the disproportionate elaboration of policing and surveillance; the Papal States illustrate that extreme. Before the twentieth century, the range of viable imbalances was fairly small. Any state that failed to put considerable effort into war making was likely to disappear. As the twentieth century wore on, however, it became increasingly common for one state to lend, give, or sell war-making means to another; in those cases, the recipient state could put a disproportionate effort into extraction, protection, and/or state making and yet survive. In our own time, clients of the United States and the Soviet Union provide numerous examples.

This simplified model, however, neglects the external relations that shaped every national state. Early in the process, the distinction between "internal" and "external" remained as unclear as the distinction between state power and the power accruing to lords allied with the state. Later, three interlocking influences connected any given national state to the European network of states. First, there were the flows of resources in the form of loans and supplies, especially loans and supplies devoted to war making. Second, there was the competition among states of hegemony in disputed territories, which stimulated war making and temporarily erased the distinctions among war making, state making, and extraction. Third, there was the intermittent creation of coalitions of states that temporarily combined their efforts to force a given state into a certain form and position within the international network. The war-making coalition is one example, but the peacemaking coalition played an even more crucial part: from 1648, if not before, at the ends of wars all effective European states coalesced temporarily to bargain over the boundaries and rulers of the recent belligerents. From that point on, periods of major reorganization of the European state system came in spurts, at the settlement of widespread wars. From each large war, in general, emerged fewer national states than had entered it.

WAR AS INTERNATIONAL RELATIONS

In these circumstances, war became the normal condition of the international system of states and the normal means of defending or enhancing a position within the system. Why war? No simple answer will do; war as a potent means served more than one end. But surely part of the answer goes back to the central mechanisms of state making: the very logic by which a local lord extended or defended the perimeter within which he monopolized the means of violence, and thereby increased his return from tribute, continued on a larger scale into the logic of war. Early in the process, external and internal rivals overlapped to a large degree. Only the establishment of large perimeters of control within which great lords had checked their rivals sharpened the line between internal and external. George Modelski sums up the competitive logic cogently:

> Global power . . . strengthened those states that attained it relatively to all other political and other organizations. What is more, other states competing in the global power game developed similar organizational forms and similar hardiness: they too became nation-states—in a defensive reaction, because forced to take issue with or to confront a global power, as France confronted Spain and later Britain, or in imitation of its obvious success and effectiveness, as Germany followed the example of Britain in Weltmacht, or as earlier Peter the Great had rebuilt Russia on Dutch precepts and examples. Thus not only Portugal, the Netherlands, Britain and the United States became nation-states, but also Spain, France, Germany, Russia and Japan. The short, and the most parsimonious, answer to the question of why these succeeded where "most of the European efforts to build states failed" is that they were either global powers or successfully fought with or against them.[12]

This logic of international state making acts out on a large scale the logic of local aggrandizement. The external complements the internal.

If we allow that fragile distinction between "internal" and "external" state-making processes, then we might schematize the history of European state making as three stages: (a) the differential success of some power holders in "external" struggles establishes the difference between an "internal" and an "external" arena for the deployment of force; (b) "external" competition generates "internal" state making; (c) "external" compacts among states influence the form and locus of particular states ever more powerfully. In this perspective, state-certifying organizations such as the League of Nations and the United Nations simply extended the European-based process to the world as a whole. Whether forced or voluntary, bloody or peaceful, decolonization simply completed that process by which existing states leagued to create new ones.

The extension of the Europe-based state-making process to the rest of the world, however, did not result in the creation of states in the strict European image. Broadly speaking, internal struggles such as the checking of great regional lords and the imposition of taxation on peasant villages produced important organizational features of European states: the relative subordination of military power to civilian control, the extensive bureaucracy of fiscal surveillance, the representation of wronged interests via petition and parliaments. On the whole, states elsewhere developed differently. The most telling feature of that difference appears in military organization. European states built up their military apparatus through sustained struggles with their subject populations and by means of selective extension of protection to different classes within those populations. The agreements on protection constrained the rulers themselves, making them vulnerable to courts, to assemblies, to withdrawals of credit, services, and expertise.

To a larger degree, states that have come into being recently through decolonization or through reallocations of territory by dominant states have acquired their military organization from outside, without the same internal forging of mutual constraints between rulers and ruled. To the extent that outside states continue to supply military goods and expertise in return for commodities, military alliance, or both, the new states harbor powerful, unconstrained organizations that easily overshadow all other organizations within their territories. To the extent that outside states guarantee their boundaries, the managers of those military organizations exercise extraordinary power within them. The advantages of military power become enormous, the incentives to seize power over the state as a whole by means of that advantage very strong. Despite the great place that war making occupied in the making of European states, the old national states of Europe almost never experienced the great disproportion between military organization and all other forms of organization that seems the fate of client states throughout the contemporary world. A century ago, Europeans might have congratulated themselves on the spread of civil government throughout the world. In our own time, the analogy between war making and state making, on the one hand, and organized crime, on the other, is becoming tragically apt.

NOTES

1. Arthur L. Stinchcombe, *Constructing Social Theories* (New York: Harcourt, Brace & World, 1968), p. 150; italics in the original.

2. Fernand Braudel, *La Méditerranée et le monde méditerranéen à l'époque de Philippe II* (Paris: Armand Colin, 1966), vol. 2, pp. 88–89.

3. Lawrence Stone, *The Crisis of the Aristocracy* (Oxford: Clarendon Press, 1965), p. 200.

4. Dietrich Gerhard, *Old Europe: A Study of Continuity, 1000–1800* (New York: Academic Press, 1981), pp. 124–125.

5. Jan de Vries, *The Economy of Europe in an Age of Crisis, 1600–1750* (Cambridge: Cambridge University Press, 1976).

6. V. G. Kiernan, *State and Society in Europe, 1550–1650* (Oxford: Blackwell, 1980), p. 104. For French finances, see Alain Guery, "Les Finances de la Monarchie Française sous l'Ancien Régime," *Annales: Economies, Sociétés, Civilisations* 33 (1978): 227.

7. Earl J. Hamilton, "Origin and Growth of the National Debt in France and England," in *Studi in onore de Gino Luzzato* (Milan: Giuffre, 1950), vol. 2, p. 254.

8. Ibid., pp. 247, 249.

9. Ibid., p. 254.

10. G. R. Elton, "Taxation for War and Peace in Early-Tudor England," in *War and Economic Development: Essays in Memory of David Joslin*, ed. J. M. Winter (Cambridge: Cambridge University Press, 1975), p. 42.

11. Peter Mathias, *The Transformation of England: Essays in the Economic and Social History of England in the Eighteenth Century* (New York: Oxford University Press, 1979), p. 122.

12. George Modelski, "The Long Cycle of Global Politics and the Nation State," *Comparative Studies in Society and History* 20 (1978): 231.

BIBLIOGRAPHY

Ames, Edward, and Richard T. Rapp. "The Birth and Death of Taxes: A Hypothesis." *Journal of Economic History* 37 (1977): 161–178.

Ardent, Gabriel. "Financial Policy and Economic Infrastructure of Modern States and Nations." In *The Formation of National States in Western Europe*, ed. Charles Tilly. Princeton, NJ: Princeton University Press, 1975.

Badie, Bertrand. *Le développement politique*. 2nd ed. Paris: Economica, 1980.

Badie, Bertrand, and Pierre Birnbaum. *Sociologie de l'Etat*. Paris: Bernard Grasset, 1979.

Bayard, Francoise. "Fermes et traités en France dans la première moitié du XVIIe siècle (première esquisse 1631–1653)." *Bulletin du Centre d'Histoire, Economique, et Sociale de la Region Lyonnaise*, no. 1 (1976): 45–80.

Bean, Richard. "War and the Birth of the Nation State." *Journal of Economic History* 33 (1973): 203–221.

Blockmans, W. P. "A Typology of Representative Institutions in Late Medieval Europe." *Journal of Medieval History* 4 (1978): 189–215.

Blok, Anton. *The Mafia of a Sicilian Village, 1860–1960: A Study of Violent Peasant Entrepreneurs.* Oxford: Blackwell, 1974.

Booney, Richard. *Political Change under Richelieu and Mazarin, 1624–1661.* Oxford: Oxford University Press, 1978.

Braudel, Fernand. *La Méditerranée et le monde méditerranéen à l'époque de Philippe II.* 2nd ed. 2 vols. Paris: Armand Colin, 1966.

———. *Civilisation matérielle, économie, et capitalisme, XVe–XVIIIe siècle.* 3 vols. Paris: Armand Colin, 1979.

Braun, Rudolf. "Taxation, Sociopolitical Structure, and State-Building: Great Britain and Brandenburg-Prussia." In *The Formation of National States in Western Europe,* ed. Charles Tilly. Princeton, NJ: Princeton University Press, 1975.

———. "Steuern und Staatsfinanzierung als Modernisierungsfaktoren: Ein deutsch-englischer Vergleich." In *Studien zum Beginn der modernen Welt,* ed. Reinhard Koselleck. Stuttgart: Keltt-Cotta, 1977.

Carneiro, Robert. "Political Expansion as an Expression of the Principle of Competitive Exclusion." In *Origins of the State,* ed. Ronald Cohen and Elman R. Service. Philadelphia: Institute for the Study of Human Issues, 1978.

Carsten, F. L. *The Origins of Prussia.* Oxford: Clarendon Press, 1954.

Chapman, Brian. *Police State.* London: Pall Mall, 1970.

Cipolla, Carlo M. *Guns, Sails, and Empires: Technological Innovation and the Early Phases of European Expansion, 1400–1700.* New York: Pantheon Press, 1965.

Clark, Sir George. "The Social Foundations of States." In *The New Cambridge Modern History,* vol. 5, *The Ascendancy of France, 1648–88,* ed. F. L. Carsten. Cambridge: Cambridge University Press, 1969.

Cooper, J. P. "Differences between English and Continental Governments in the Early Seventeenth Century." In *Britain and the Netherlands,* ed. J. S. Bromley and E. H. Kossmann. London: Chatto & Windus, 1960.

———. "General Introduction." In *The New Cambridge Modern History,* vol. 4, *The Decline of Spain and Thirty Years War, 1609–58/59,* ed. J. P. Cooper. Cambridge: Cambridge University Press, 1970.

Davis, Lance E. "It's a Long, Long Road to Tipperary, or Reflections on

Organized Violence, Protection Rates, and Related Topics: The New Political History." *Journal of Economic History* 40 (1980): 1–16.

Dent, Julian. *Crisis in Finance: Crown, Financiers, and Society in Seventeenth-Century France.* Newton Abbot, United Kingdom: David & Charles, 1973.

Dickson, P. G. M. *The Financial Revolution in England: A Study in the Development of Public Credit, 1688–1756.* London: St. Martin's Press, 1967.

Elton, G. R. "Taxation for War and Peace in Early-Tudor England." In *War and Economic Development: Essays in Memory of David Joslin,* ed. J. M. Winter. Cambridge: Cambridge University Press, 1975.

Finer, Samuel E. "State-Building, State Boundaries, and Border Control." *Social Science Information* 13 (1974): 79–126.

———. "State- and Nation-Building in Europe: The Role of the Military." In *The Formation of National States in Western Europe,* ed. Charles Tilly. Princeton, NJ: Princeton University Press, 1975.

Fueter, Edward. *Geschichte des europäischen Staatensystems von 1492–1559.* Munich: Oldenbourg, 1919.

Gerhard, Dietrich. *Old Europe: A Study of Continuity, 1000–1800.* New York: Academic Press, 1981.

Gooch, John, *Armies in Europe.* London: Routledge & Kegan Paul, 1980.

Guénée, Bernard. "Y a-t-il un Etat des XIVe et XVe siècles?" *Annales: Economies, Sociétés, Civilisations* 36 (1981): 399–406.

Guery, Alain. "Les finances de la monarchie française sous l'Ancien Régime." *Annales: Economies, Sociétés, Civilisations* 33 (1978), 216–239.

Hale, J. R. "Armies, Navies, and the Art of War." In *The New Cambridge Modern History,* vol. 2, *The Reformation, 1520–1559,* ed. G. R. Elton. Cambridge: Cambridge University Press, 1968.

———. "Armies, Navies, and the Art of War." In *The New Cambridge Modern History,* vol. 3, *The Counter-Reformation and Price Revolution, 1559–1610,* ed. R. B. Wernham. Cambridge: Cambridge University Press, 1968.

Hamilton, Earl J. "Origin and Growth of the National Debt in France and England." In *Studi in onore di Gino Luzzato,* vol. 2. Milan: Giuffre, 1950.

Harding, Robert R. *Anatomy of a Power Elite: The Provincial Governors of Early Modern France.* New Haven, CT: Yale University Press, 1978.

Hechter, Michael, and William Brustein. "Regional Modes of Production and Patterns of State Formation in Western Europe." *American Journal of Sociology* 85 (1980): 1061–1094.

Hintze, Otto. *Staat und Verfassung: Gesammelte Abhandlungen zur allgemeinen Verfassungsgeschichte.* Ed. Gerhard Oestreich. Göttingen: Vandenhoeck & Ruprecht, 1962; originally 1910.

Howard, Michael. *War in European History.* Oxford: Oxford University Press, 1976.

James, M. E. *Change and Continuity in the Tudor North: The Rise of Thomas First Lord Wharton.* Borthwick Papers no. 27. York: St. Anthony's Press, 1965.

———. "The First Earl of Cumberland (1493–1542) and the Decline of Northern Feudalism." *Northern History* 1 (1966): 43–69.

———. "The Concept of Order and the Northern Rising, 1569." *Past and Present* 60 (1973): 49–83.

John, A. H. "Wars and the British Economy, 1700–1763." *Economic History Review,* 2nd ser., 7 (1955): 329–344.

Kiernan, V. G. "Conscription and Society in Europe before the War of 1914–18." In *War and Society: Historical Essays in Honour and Memory of J. R. Western, 1928–1971,* ed. M. R. D. Foot. London: Elek Books, 1973.

———. *State and Society in Europe, 1550–1650.* Oxford: Blackwell, 1980.

Klaveren, Jacob von. "Die historische Erscheinung der Korruption." *Vierteljahrschrift für Sozial- und Wirtschaftsgeschichte* 44 (1957): 289–324.

———. "Fiskalismus—Merkantilismus—Korruption: Drei Aspekte der Finanz- und Wirtschaftspolitik während des Ancien Regime." *Vierteljahrschrift für Sozial- und Wirtschaftsgeschichte* 47 (1960): 333–353.

Landero Quesado, Miguel Angel. "Les finances royales de Castille à la veille des temps modernes." *Annales: Economies, Sociétés, Civilisations* 25 (1970): 775–788.

Lane, Frederic C. "Force and Enterprise in the Creation of Oceanic Commerce." In *The Tasks of Economic History* (Supplemental issue of the *Journal of Economic History* 10 [1950]), pp. 19–31.

———. "Economic Consequences of Organized Violence." *Journal of Economic History* 18 (1958): 401–417.

———. "The Economic Meaning of War and Protection." In *Venice and History: The Collected Papers of Frederic C. Lane.* Baltimore, MD: Johns Hopkins University Press, 1966; originally 1942.

———. "The Role of Government in Economic Growth in Early Modern Times." *Journal of Economic History* 35 (1975): 8–17; with comment by Douglass C. North and Robert Paul Thomas, pp. 18–19.

Levi, Margaret. "The Predatory Theory of Rule." In *The Microfoundations of Macrosociology,* ed. Michael Hechter. Philadelphia: Temple University Press, 1983.

Lüdtke, Alf. "Genesis und Durchsetzung des modernen Staates: Zur Analyse von Herrschaft und Verwaltung." *Archiv für Sozialgeschichte* 20 (1980): 470–491.

Lyons, G. M. "Exigences militaires et budgets militaires aux U.S.A." *Revue Française de Sociologie* 2 (1961): 66–74.

Mathias, Peter. "Taxation and Industrialization in Britain, 1700–1870." In *The Transformation of England: Essays in the Economic and Social History of England in the Eighteenth Century,* ed. Peter Matthias. New York: Oxford University Press, 1979.

Michaud, Claude. "Finances et guerres de religion en France." *Revue d'Histoire Moderne et Contemporaine* 28 (1981): 572–596.

Modelski, George. "The Long Cycle of Global Politics and the Nation-State." *Comparative Studies in Society and History* 20 (1978): 214–235.

Nef, John U. *War and Human Progress: An Essay on the Rise of Industrial Civilization.* Cambridge, MA: Harvard University Press, 1952.

———. *Industry and Government in France and England, 1540–1640.* Ithaca, NY: Cornell University Press, 1965; originally 1940.

North, Douglass C., and Robert Paul Thomas. *The Rise of the Western World: A New Economic History.* Cambridge: Cambridge University Press, 1973.

O'Donnell, Guillermo. "Comparative Historical Formations of the State Apparatus and Socio-economic Change in the Third World." *International Social Science Journal* 32 (1980): 717–729.

Parker, Geoffrey. *The Army of Flanders and the Spanish Road, 1567–1659.* Cambridge: Cambridge University Press, 1972.

Peacock, Alan T., and Jack Wiseman. *The Growth of Public Expenditure in the United Kingdom.* Princeton, NJ: Princeton University Press, 1961.

Poggi, Gianfranco. *The Development of the Modern State: A Sociological Introduction.* Stanford, CA: Stanford University Press, 1978.

Polisensky, Josef V. *War and Society in Europe, 1618–1648.* Cambridge: Cambridge University Press, 1978.

Pounds, Norman J. G., and Sue Simons Ball. "Core-Areas and the Development of the European States System." *Annals of the Association of American Geographers* 54 (1964): 24–40.

Ramsey, G. D. *The City of London in International Politics at the Accession of Elizabeth Tudor.* Manchester: Manchester University Press, 1975.

Redlich, Fritz. *The German Military Enterpriser and His Work Force.* 2 vols. Wiesbaden: Steiner, 1964–1965. *Vierteljahrschrift für Sozial- und Wirtschaftsgeschichte,* Beiheften 47, 48.

Riemersma, Jelle C. "Government Influence on Company Organization in Holland and England (1550–1650)." *The Tasks of Economic History* (Supplemental issue of the *Journal of Economic History* 10 [1950]), pp. 31–39.

Romano, Salvatore Francesco. *Storia della mafia.* Milan: Sugar, 1963.

Rosenberg, Hans. *Bureaucracy, Aristocracy, and Autocracy: The Prussian Experience, 1660–1815.* Cambridge, MA: Harvard University Press, 1958.

Russett, Bruce M. *What Price Vigilance? The Burdens of National Defense.* New Haven, CT: Yale University Press, 1970.

Schelling, Thomas C. "Economics and Criminal Enterprise." *The Public Interest* 7 (1967): 61–78.

Steensgaard, Niels. *The Asian Trade Revolution of the Seventeenth Century: The East India Companies and the Decline of the Caravan Trades.* Chicago: University of Chicago Press, 1974.

Stein, Arthur A., and Bruce M. Russett. "Evaluating War: Outcomes and Consequences." In *Handbook of Political Conflict: Theory and Research,* ed. Ted Robert Gurr. New York: Free Press, 1980.

Stinchcombe, Arthur L. *Constructing Social Theories.* New York: Harcourt, Brace & World, 1968.

Stone, Lawrence. "State Control in Sixteenth-Century England." *Economic History Review* 17 (1947): 103–120.

———. *The Crisis of the Aristocracy, 1558–1641.* Oxford: Clarendon Press, 1965.

Tenenti, Alberto. *Piracy and the Decline of Venice, 1580–1615.* Berkeley: University of California Press, 1967.

Torsvik, Per, ed. *Mobilization, Center-Periphery Structures, and Nation-Building: A Volume in Commemoration of Stein Rokkan.* Bergen: Universitetsforlaget, 1981.

Vries, Jan de. "On the Modernity of the Dutch Republic." *Journal of Economic History* 33 (1973): 191–202.

———. *The Economy of Europe in an Age of Crisis, 1600–1750.* Cambridge: Cambridge University Press, 1976.

———. "Barges and Capitalism: Passenger Transportation in the Dutch Economy, 1632–1839," *A.A.G. Bijdragen* 21 (1978): 33–398.

Wijn, J. W. "Military Forces and Warfare, 1610–48." In *The New Cam-*

bridge Modern History, vol. 4, *The Decline of Spain and the Thirty Years War, 1609–58/59,* ed. J. P. Cooper. Cambridge: Cambridge University Press, 1970.

Williams, Penry. "Rebellion and Revolution in Early Modern England." In *War and Society: Historical Essays in Honour and Memory of J. R. Western, 1928–1971,* ed. M. R. D. Foot. London: Elek Books, 1973.

Wolfe, Martin. *The Fiscal System of Renaissance France.* New Haven, CT: Yale University Press, 1972.

Zolberg, Aristide R. "Strategic Interactions and the Formation of Modern States: France and England." *International Social Science Journal* 32 (1980): 687–716.

· 8 ·

DEMOCRACY IS A LAKE[1]

TIME FOR DEMOCRACY

Once theorists thought vibrant, viable democracy emerged from centuries of struggle or maturation. In such formulations as Barrington Moore's, class and politics interacted over hundreds of years to create democracy or its alternatives.[2] Disillusioned by the failure of various revolutionary programs during the previous two decades, bemused by the cold war's ending, and enticed by the opportunity to prescribe programs of political change for Eastern Europe, Latin America, or Africa, recent theorists of democracy have moved away from the populism and revolutionism of the 1960s toward a remarkable elitism: suppositions that the masses have little to do with the making of democracy, that (however regrettably) presidents, priests, political patrons, planters, police chiefs, paratroop commanders, and plutocrats perform the essential operations producing durable democratic institutions.

Not all the change resulted from disillusion. Impressed by the rapid displacement of authoritarian regimes set in place by Franco, Salazar, or Brazilian generals, and pressed to formulate futures for Eastern Europe, Latin America, and Africa, recent theorists have accelerated the tempo so that at times the transition to democracy looks almost instantaneous: put the pact in gear and go. After decades of bottom-up, deterministic, long-term theories, we now see top-down models, instrumental and constructivist approaches to democratization, and short-run analyses beginning to prevail. Top-down models specify what rulers and leaders must do to promote democracy, instrumental ideas make democratization seem a matter of social engineering (whoever serves as engineer), constructivist ap-

This chapter was first published as "Democracy is a Lake," in George Reid Andrews and Herrick Chapman, eds., *The Social Construction of Democracy* (New York: New York University Press, and London: Macmillan, 1995), pp. 365–387. Reprinted with permission.

proaches assert that democracy depends on certain kinds of social beliefs, and short-run analyses say how politics move toward democracy today, this month, or this year rather than at a scale of centuries.

Timescale matters both theoretically and practically. Theoretically, democracy's time could resemble that of an oil field, a cultivated garden, or something in between. An oil field, the specific product of millennial history, conforms to regularities strong enough that petrogeologists can spot likely untapped deposits or explain how an oil well works. Yet experts cannot produce a new oil field at will wherever they want. The presence of oil fields depends on long, long conjunctions of circumstances that appear rarely in history and are little amenable to human manipulation.

Gardens are different. They will not flourish everywhere, but given adequate soil, sun, and precipitation, many different sorts of gardens grow in a variety of environments. As in the cases of oil fields, specialists in gardens are perfectly capable of explaining how they work, indeed of making contingent predictions about what will happen if X or Y happens first.

In both cases, experts know enough to intervene, within clear limits, to produce desired results with considerable probability. They know what aspects they cannot influence. They even know enough to identify a wide range of interventions that, however well meaning, are likely to fail. Differences between the cases do not concern the phenomenon's regularity or intelligibility, but the nature and timescale of the regularities involved, which in turn determine the phenomenon's susceptibility to deliberate promotion. We have no a priori warrant to think of democracy as resembling gardens more than oil fields. If oil fields offer the proper analogy, valid explanations of the presence or absence, waxing and waning, of democracy will combine very long histories with dense accounts of short-term dynamics. In that case, we might well conclude that Barrington Moore tells us how to analyze the foundations of democratization better than recent short-term planners.

Practically, the promotion of oil field democracy will require the transformation of environments, indeed the creation of whole histories, over centuries or even millennia. Both planned ruling-class intervention and popular collective action will be irrelevant to the success or failure of democratic projects. The cultivation of garden-style democracy, on the other hand, can occur in a wide variety of environments with relative rapidity through many combinations of elite and popular action. If the garden analogy holds, the secret will be to find or create those environments that can support some sort of democracy, then adapt the design and cultivation to the capacities of each environment. Two essential points follow: (1) the validity of various theories and metatheories of democracy depends on the general character and timescale of the phenomenon, which remain highly contested; (2) the validity of theories and metatheories of democracy has profound practical implications. Both points are at issue in the effort to create a sound social history of democracy, constructed or otherwise.

A short timescale typically couples with an instrumental, top-down view of democratization. Distinguishing between "elite ascendant" and "mass ascendant" paths to democracy in Latin America, for example, Terry Karl declares that

> To date, however, *no* stable political democracy has resulted from regime transitions in which mass actors have gained control, even momentarily, over traditional ruling classes. . . . Thus far, the most frequently encountered types of transition, and the ones which have most often resulted in the implantation of a political democracy, are "transitions from above."[3]

In a similar vein, Eva Etzioni-Halevy argues that

> A central historical condition for the emergence of stable Western democracy was the development of the relative autonomy of elites from and within the state. Without it the chances for the stabilization of such democracy—whatever its achievements and drawbacks—would have been greatly diminished, and the chances for democratic breakdown would have been much increased.[4]

From Adam Przeworski we hear that "It seems as if an almost complete docility and patience on the part of organized workers are needed for a democratic transformation to succeed."[5] In place of yesterday's bottom-up histories of democratization, today only top-down views vie for acceptance. In today's context, the massive historical-comparative analysis of Dietrich Rueschemeyer, Evelyne Huber Stephens, and John D. Stephens, with its long timescale and its strong emphasis on working-class contributions to democracy, reads as a startling exception, an obvious holdover from the era of Barrington Moore.[6]

Recent views have an instrumentalist edge, assuming that leaders can engineer democracy, or at least foster conditions for its appearance. Giuseppe Di Palma's characteristically titled *To Craft Democracies,* for a case in point, sometimes refers to "the popular sector" as a party to democratization, but in general presents the crafty creators of democracy as "actors" or "players" in a game more closely resembling chess than rugby. Although it often fails, the creation of democracy becomes work for self-conscious fashioners of collective bargains, not for social classes or armies engaged in battles to the death.[7]

Instrumentalism couples oddly but firmly to the increasingly popular argument that democracy is, or results from, a social construction. The argument has many variants, but in essence claims that the basic operations constituting or creating democracy consist of changes in shared beliefs; from shared beliefs follow the necessary institutions and constitutions. The shift toward social construction then encourages a comforting conclusion: the way to build democracy is to change people's minds about what is politically proper and possible. Everything depends, of course, on how plastic and subject to deliberate alteration such ideas turn out to be. At the extreme, all hope of concerted action disappears in the grip of overpowering, autonomous, slow-moving ideas. Nevertheless, in principle, the emphasis on social construction complements the top-down, instrumental view of democratization.

People actually *construct* democracy, however, in two different senses of the word. First, they create a set of political arrangements the effects of which are democratic, however we define democracy. This sense of *construct* has the misleading connotation of blueprints and carpenters, when over the last few hundred years, the actual formation and deformation of democratic regimes has more often resembled the erratic evolution of a whole city than the purposeful building of a single mansion. Still, the first sense draws our attention to the ways that human agency, however consciously, produces and destroys the objective conditions for democracy.

The second sense of *construction* refers to the shared understandings, the culture, that people create for themselves. Extreme versions of linguistic skepticism reduce all social reality to construction in this sense, on an argument that conflates epistemology and ontology: if social existence can only be known through language, it does not exist independently of language. Short of that extreme, however, even hard-nosed realists recognize that people do construct shared understandings concerning their political arrangements. Indeed, shared understandings affect how those arrangements work. In the case of democracy, as Robert Dahl points out repeatedly, much depends on the readiness of political actors who lose in the current round of struggle to believe that they will get another reasonably fair chance to win later on. Adam Przeworski makes just such an institutionalization of uncertainty the hallmark of democracy.[8] That shared belief is a social product.

More generally, ideas of justice, of due process, of official propriety, of efficiency, of collective interest, of property, of rights, and of history pervade every set of political arrangements, including those of democracy. No system of parliamentary democracy, for example, can survive the generalization of a belief (however false) that its elections are fraudulent and its officials powerless. The real questions are: (1) how such beliefs and their democracy-sustaining antitheses form, wax, or wane; (2) exactly what relation they bear to the political system's operation, routine or otherwise.

In principle, either form of construction—the deliberate creation or the imaginative formulation—could proceed at the timescale of an oil field, of a garden, or in between. One can imagine with Max Weber that age-old and slowly changing beliefs shape political institutions as they channel economic enterprise, with the consequence that only some select metaphysical traditions offer—and will ever offer—hospitable ground for democratic institutions. Thus some advocates argue that Islam has a unique affinity for democracy, while others consider Islam to be inherently authoritarian. Either view rests on oil field reasoning. But garden-variety construction also offers a plausible model, as sweeping changes rush across the world transforming beliefs and social relations simultaneously. In short, an emphasis on the social construction of democracy does not resolve, theoretically or empirically, the choice among timescales for its analysis.

Meanwhile, a historical puzzle arises. Broad-based democracy on a large scale first took shape in Western Europe. In the past, durable democratic institutions emerged out of repeated, long-term struggles in which workers, peasants, and other ordinary people were much involved, even where the crucial maneuvers involved an elite's conspiring in small concessions to avoid large ones. Revolutions, rebellions, and mass mobilizations made a significant difference to the extent of democracy in one country or another. Yet current theories of democratization give little place to popular collective action, emphasize instrumental maneuvers and bargains among elites, stress promulgated beliefs, and stage the critical political changes in the short run. Is the history revealed to us by Barrington Moore, Reinhard Bendix, or Stein Rokkan an illusion? Or have the conditions promoting democracy changed fundamentally?

To Conceptualize Democracies

Before examining that question, let us do some conceptual construction. In order to get to democracy, we must work our way down a chain including state, polity, rights, and citizenship. Here is the chain:

> *State:* an organization controlling the principal concentrated means of coercion within a delimited territory and exercising priority in some respects over all other organizations within the same territory.

> *Polity:* the set of relations among agents of the state and all major political actors within the delimited territory.
>
> *Rights:* enforceable claims, the reciprocal of *obligations.*
>
> *Citizenship:* rights and mutual obligations binding state agents and a category of persons defined exclusively by their legal attachment to the same state.

With that conceptual chain in place, we can begin hauling up an idea of democracy as a particular form of citizenship. Democracy combines *broad and relatively equal citizenship with (a) binding consultation of citizens in regard to state personnel and policies as well as (b) protection of citizens from arbitrary state action.*

This definition stands between those emphasizing ideal outcomes and those stipulating institutional arrangements. Robert Dahl speaks of "a political system in which the members regard one another as political equals, are collectively sovereign, and possess all the capacities, resources, and institutions they need in order to govern themselves."[9] As Dahl himself stresses, such a definition is not only problematic in detail (do children, convicts, and students from other countries, for instance, all qualify as "members"?), but also empirically empty (no large state has ever met its requirements). Yet it states a standard against which we can array real political arrangements.

Rueschemeyer, Stephens, and Stephens, on the other hand, offer an eminently institutional definition of democracy:

> It entails, first, regular, free and fair elections of representatives with universal and equal suffrage, second, responsibility of the state apparatus to the elected parliament (possibly complemented by direct election of the head of the executive), and third, the freedoms of expression and association as well as the protection of individual rights against arbitrary state action.[10]

For some questions (for example, what political arrangements are worth sacrificing for?), the ideal definition serves best, while for others (for example, what sort of government should we now organize in our new country?), the institutional definition makes much more sense. My definition lies between the two.

An intermediate definition, on the one hand, makes problematic the relationship between institutions and their consequences or correlates, whereas it facilitates, on the other hand, the linking of theories of democratization with theories of nationalism, citizenship, revolution, political conflict, and change in state structure. I claim that different institutional arrangements—town meetings in some settings, secret ballots for party-nominated candidates in others, and so on—promote democracy within different sorts of social structure, hence that strictly institutional criteria of democracy yield misleading conclusions on a large scale. To repeat, democracy consists of *broad and relatively equal citizenship with (a) binding consultation of citizens in regard to state personnel and policies as well as (b) protection of citizens from arbitrary state action.*

Notice what this conception does *not* do. It does not make general equality of means or opportunity a criterion of democracy; equality only refers to claims on and from the state in a person's capacity as citizen. As much as it invites a search for institutions guaranteeing democratic outcomes, it does not stipulate any particular political institutions as defining features of democracy. It ignores the unequal treatment of noncitizens, disregarding any disabilities they suffer with respect to binding consultation and protection from arbitrary state action. It certainly does not require intelligent communication, patriotism, legitimacy, happiness, or prosperity. It leaves theoretically and empirically open the relationship of democracy to general economic equality, care for noncitizens, social justice, communication, and innumerable other features that people sometimes consider inseparable from democracy. It excludes many connotations of the word *democracy* on the ground that including them all would bar any effective theoretical or empirical investigation of the subject.

The proposed conception of democracy *does,* on the other hand, declare that a polity is undemocratic to the degree that citizens' political rights and obligations vary by gender, race, religion, national origin, wealth, or any other general set of categories, that it is likewise undemocratic to the extent that large numbers of people subject to the state's jurisdiction lack access to citizenship. It makes binding consultation and protection from arbitrary state action, furthermore, matters of degree—recognizing, for example,that in large democratic states, the sheer existence of parliaments limits consultation and state agents sometimes commit injustices. Even breadth and equality, after all, have their limits; when Paul Peterson proposes "that all citizens, even our youngest, should cast votes or have their votes cast for them by their parents or guardians," even he must concede that the infants his proposal would enfranchise generally lack the reasoned political self-interest his argument requires; hence the extra votes his scheme entrusts to parents and guardians.[11] The definition, in short, simply allows us to designate polities as democratic *insofar* as they embody broad, equal citizenship that gives its beneficiaries binding consultation and protection from arbitrary state action.

Figure 8.1 represents the basic idea. The four criteria—equality,

Figure 8.1. Components of Democracy

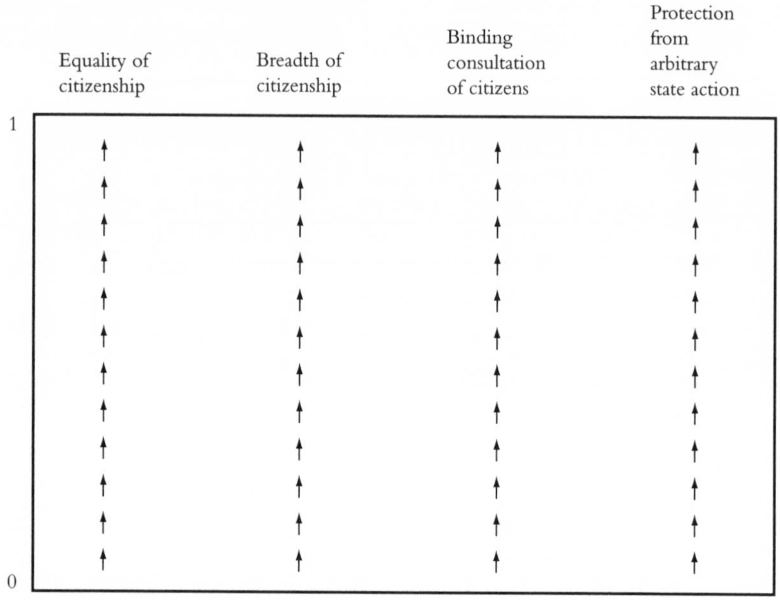

	Equality of citizenship	Breadth of citizenship	Binding consultation of citizens	Protection from arbitrary state action

breadth, consultation, and protection—form continua from none (0) to complete (1). All real polities lie somewhere between. For conceptual clarification, nevertheless, we can conveniently split each of the four dimensions into Yes (1) and No (0). That step allows us to diagram competing forms of political organization in the same terms, as in Figure 8.2. There, patrimonialism appears as 0000: narrow, unequal citizenship with little or no consultation and protection. Oligarchy (0010) likewise entails narrow, unequal citizenship and little protection of citizens from arbitrary state action, but involves binding consultation of the small number who possess citizenship.

Dictatorship (1100) looks much different: equal, broad citizenship but little or no consultation and protection. Democracy comes out, then, as 1111, high on all four criteria. Aristotle's idea concerning the devolution of genuine political forms into perverted forms reads, in his terms, as:

Kingship → Tyranny:	0001 → 0000
Aristocracy → Oligarchy:	0011 → 0010
Polity → Democracy:	1111 → 1110

Figure 8.2. Contrasting Political Arrangements

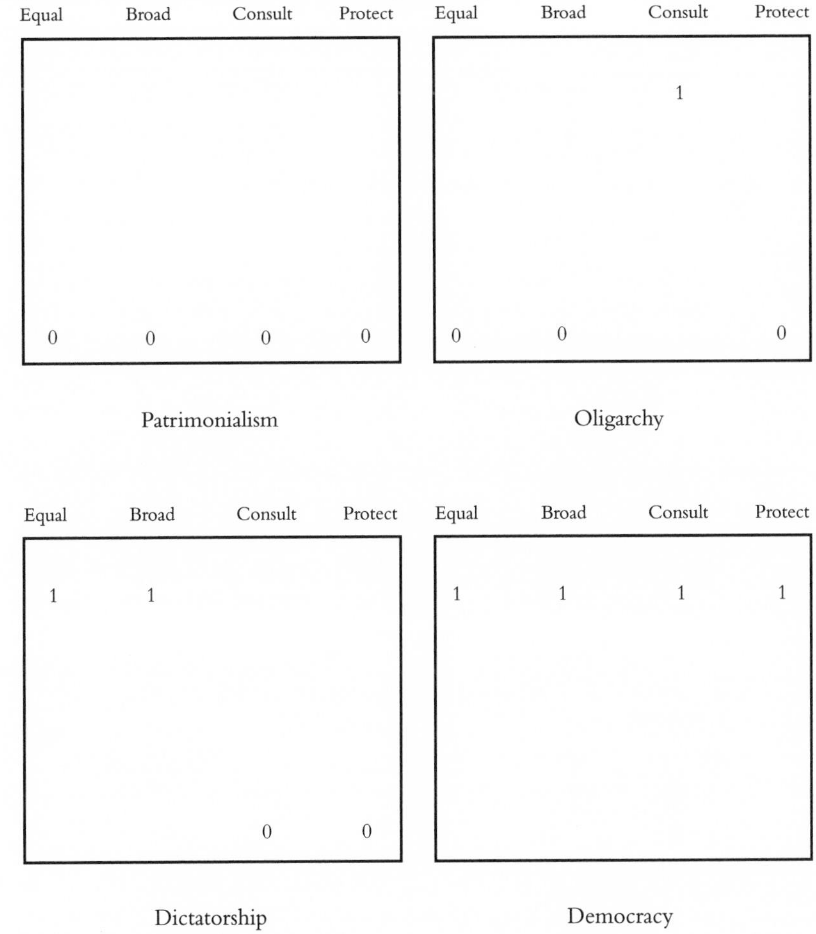

Equal	Broad	Consult	Protect
0	0	0	0

Patrimonialism

Equal	Broad	Consult	Protect
		1	
0	0		0

Oligarchy

Equal	Broad	Consult	Protect
1	1		
		0	0

Dictatorship

Equal	Broad	Consult	Protect
1	1	1	1

Democracy

My representation of the transition polity → democracy displays the limits of a dichotomous formulation, since Aristotle actually argued that something like 0.25, 0.25, 1, 1 (many substantial citizens ruling collectively in rough equality on behalf of the entire population—i.e., polity) ran the risk of degenerating into rule by the poor in their own interest (Aristotle's conception of democracy), which might then read 0.75, 1.0, 1.0, 0. In each case, nevertheless, Aristotle sees a danger in any faction's, including a faction of the poor, mistaking its own interest for the population's general interest. Mass society theorists have gone a step beyond Aristotle in fearing that:

$$1111 \rightarrow 1110 \rightarrow 1100 \rightarrow 0000$$

Here, extensive democracy degenerates into a corrupt form without protections, which devolves into a dictatorship over equally powerless citizens, a move that eventually eradicates citizenship itself in favor of subjection to a tyrant.

Table 8.1 generalizes the conceptualization by identifying a number of other types among the sixteen possible permutations of the four elements. (With values intermediate between 0 and 1 or with fluctuation in values between 0 and 1, we could produce still more types to our hearts' content.) A *patriciate* (1011), for example, looks a lot like a democracy, except that it adopts a narrow definition of citizenship. A *tutelary democracy* (1101) combines broad, relatively equal citizenship with substantial protections but has little binding consultation of citizens; state agents proceed quite autonomously. One might dispute my labels, but the main point remains: even in a simple dichotomous form, the four variables do a fairly effective job of distinguishing major types of polities and of placing democracy among them.

Missing patterns also deserve notice. So far as I can tell, combinations 1001, 1010, 1000, 0110, 0101, 0100, and 0011 are either evanescent or nonexistent. Contrary to mass society theorists and many conservatives, the pattern suggests that 10XX (narrow but equal) and 01XX (broad but unequal) have inherent instabilities. If so, the explanation is probably simple:

Table 8.1. Pure Types of Polity

Configuration	Equality	Breadth	Consult	Protect
Democracy	1	1	1	1
Corrupt democracy	1	1	1	0
Tutelary democracy	1	1	0	1
Dictatorship	1	1	0	0
Patriciate	1	0	1	1
Corporatism	0	1	1	1
Oligarchy	0	0	1	0
Paternalism	0	0	0	1
Patrimonialism	0	0	0	0

inequality and narrow citizenship reinforce each other through a process of coalition and exclusion. The movement of the Venetian Republic from a partial democracy of merchants to an oligarchy (1011 → 0010) through the narrowing of its already unequal citizenship and the reduction of protections for lesser citizens against arbitrary state action illustrates the transformation.

Despite the apparent existence of unstable types and empty cells, the wide variety of types that *have* existed raises doubts about any proposition that democracy appears and disappears as an interdependent package. Protection for citizens from arbitrary state action, for example, is compatible with broad and narrow definitions of citizenship, just as binding consultation of citizens combines with both equal and unequal definitions. Although it is conceivable that transitions among types follow some regular sequence (for example, that patriciates commonly precede full democracies, with the broadening of citizenship the last feature of democracy to arrive), each of the four elements very likely has a partly separate set of causes, sustaining conditions, and political consequences.

Let us distinguish tautologically necessary conditions for democracy from contingent conditions that may produce or sustain it. My proposed definition requires two interlocked conditions: a substantial state and citizenship relating people to that state. Citizenship has no substantial meaning in the absence of a relatively powerful and centralized state. It follows—likewise tautologically, but still usefully—that the forms of the state and of citizenship that have grown up in a given region or era prior to the formation of democratic institutions strongly affect the day-to-day operation of democracy. We can expect democratization and democracy to proceed differently as a function of variation in the prior trajectories of states and citizenship.

In European experience, at least, citizenship in the sense of rights and mutual obligations binding state agents and a category of persons defined by their legal attachment to the same state only became a widespread phenomenon during the nineteenth century. Before then, small units such as the city-states of the Low Countries, the Rhineland, and Italy had sometimes sustained patriciates of the rich and powerful; with respect to the state, these narrow segments of the total population had enjoyed relative equality, binding consultation, and protection from arbitrary action. But large states all ruled indirectly until the eighteenth or nineteenth century; they relied for troops, revenues, and compliance with state directives chiefly on regional power holders who maintained substantial autonomy and dealt with populations having distinctive traditions, cultures, and rights.

In these circumstances, neither citizenship nor democracy existed at a national scale in any strong sense of the words. At most, nobles and priests constituted a semicitizenry in countries such as England (but not Great Britain or, even less, the British Isles) where a skeletal administrative structure and a unitary state church intertwined. The greatest exception appeared in Sweden, where the articulation of a domestically recruited army, a state church, and direct peasant representation vis-à-vis the Crown produced quasi citizenship as early as the seventeenth century.[12] Given its great inequality and its limits to binding consultation, however, Sweden's polity remained far from democracy until the twentieth century. Extensive democracy awaited strong pressure from organized workers allied with fragments of the bourgeoisie and the popular movements that proliferated during the nineteenth century.[13]

For centuries, to be sure, many Europeans had exercised something like citizenship and even democracy in smaller units such as villages and municipalities. There, heads of propertied households commonly governed collectively or at least shared power with priests and nobles; they frequently led burgher militias as well. In very small states, the government of the capital city thereby established a narrow quasi citizenship at a national scale. With its cantonal structure, Switzerland federated a set of partial democracies in this style beginning with the sixteenth century.[14] In such countries as the Dutch Republic, eighteenth-century revolutionary movements commonly took that municipal experience as a model for political transformation.[15]

After the middle of the eighteenth century, and especially during the nineteenth, the abandonment of intermittent mercenary armies in favor of large standing armies drawn from, and supported by, national populations engaged rulers in vast struggles with their reluctant subjects. The settlements of those struggles, in their turn, created the rudiments of citizenship. In large states, the French Revolution and the wars of 1792–1815 marked the crucial break. The revolutionary and conquering French provided a model of citizenship, a stimulus to military mobilization, and—in their areas of conquest—a compulsion to reorganize on the French model. Thus citizenship went from being rare and chiefly local in Europe to being a predominant model of political organization.

With citizenship, limited democracy did not by any means become a necessity; plenty of European states developed political arrangements more closely approximating oligarchy or paternalism with some trappings of representation. Democracy did, however, become an option and a persistent program for reformers and revolutionaries. All over Europe, they began to demand equal, broad citizenship with binding consultation and protection for citizens from arbitrary state action. They began to demand democracy. Some even had their way.

European experience suggests strong hypotheses concerning the social bases of democracy's components:

1. *Protection from arbitrary state action* depends on (a) subordination of the military to civilian control, (b) class coalitions in which old power holders ally with relatively powerless but large segments of the population (for example, bourgeois and workers), thus extending old privileges and protections.
2. *Binding consultation* depends on (a) subordination of the military to civilian control, (b) extensive domestic taxation (as opposed, for example, to state revenues drawn directly from exports), (c) representation with respect to the assessment and collection of taxes.
3. *Equal citizenship* depends on (a) broad class coalitions including power holders, (b) creation and expansion of electoral systems.
4. *Broad citizenship* depends on (a) extensive domestic taxation, (b) broad class coalitions, (c) direct recruitment of large military services from the domestic population.

We might reasonably hypothesize that the relative strength of these factors prior to democratization also affects the kind of democracy that emerges, for example, that systems growing up chiefly through subordination of the military via defeat in war, military occupation, or some other cause will emphasize protection and breadth more than equality or binding consultation, while domestic taxation alone will promote binding consultation and breadth of citizenship while leaving equality and protection more uncertain. As Hanspeter Kriesi has pointed out, democracy operates quite differently in Switzerland and the Netherlands as a result of the contrast between Switzerland's federal coalescence and the transformation of the Dutch state under French conquest in the 1790s. The Dutch creation of a centralized bureaucracy and a subordinated military promoted a greater emphasis on breadth and equality of citizenship, which in turn led to the incorporation of the population's competing segments by means of "pillarization" in parallel organizations rather than the creation of multiple local niches for different kinds of politics. The Swiss system operates quite differently, tolerating considerable inequality among geographically segregated niches.[16]

DEMOCRACY AND CITIZENSHIP IN GREAT BRITAIN

The unlikely case of Great Britain illustrates the ties among democratization, citizenship, and changes in the state. The British case seems unlikely because analysts have so regularly pigeonholed Britain as an example of political transformation in the absence of a strong state. John Brewer has demolished that conception of British political history during the eighteenth century, but his stopping around 1780 has left unclear how much the war-led growth he describes accelerated during the great wars with France after 1792.[17] In fact, the creation of large military forces, their supply with men, goods, and services, the repression of domestic dissidence, and expansion of the fiscal system wrought great changes in British government between 1790 and 1815: not only a large net increase in military forces and government expenditures despite the demobilization of 1815–1816 and a remarkable tightening of the central bureaucracy, but also a dramatic shift of political power from the king, his clients, and other great patrons toward Parliament.[18] Under Pitt the Younger, Grenville, Portland, Perceval, and Liverpool, the state swelled in importance, and Parliament grew within it like a goiter.

This process of expansion had enormous importance for citizenship. Remember that by *citizenship* we still mean rights and mutual obligations binding state agents and a category of persons defined exclusively by their legal attachment to the same state. Between 1750 and 1815, such rights and obligations multiplied as a result of the state's pursuit of war. War had its most visible effects in the realms of taxation and military service. Total taxes collected rose from about £17 million in 1790 to almost £80 million in 1815, a 371 percent increase during a period when the cost of living was rising by about 45 percent; war-driven taxes reached an extraordinary height: about 35 percent of Britain's total commodity output.[19]

Military service, including civil defense, likewise expanded enormously in scope. As Linda Colley sums up:

> In Great Britain, as in other major European powers, it was training in arms under the auspices of the state that was the most common collective working-class experience in the late eighteenth and nineteenth centuries, not labour in a factory, or membership of a radical political organization or an illegal trade union.[20]

Through the increasingly visible presence of the tax collector, the recruiting sergeant, the militia commander, and the member of Parliament, ordinary British people acquired much more extensive direct contact with the state than they had experienced since the revolutionary period of 1640–1660. This time it lasted.

From multiplied encounters with agents of the state, Britons acquired a growing sense of Britishness, which did not keep many of them from attacking press gangs, evading tax collectors, or joining radical movements; on the contrary, the nationalization of daily life and consciousness nationalized British struggles and resistance to authorities as well. In the process, direct obligations between subjects and state gained enough scope and intensity to merit the name citizenship. As a revolution and a vast military mobilization were creating French citizens across the Channel, reaction to them were creating British citizens in England, Scotland, and Wales.

What of democracy? As of 1750, we can plausibly describe Great Britain as a 0001, a paternalistic polity involving narrow, unequal citizenship and only partial binding consultation of those aristocrats and gentry who enjoyed something like citizens' privileges, but substantial protections from arbitrary state action for them. The narrowness of citizenship did not reside so much in the small parliamentary electorate as in the mediation of most Britons' relations with the state through local and regional notables such as the justices of the peace, who enjoyed great autonomy in their exercise of state-authorized positions.

By 1835, Great Britain had moved closer to 1001 or even 1011, as a broader, but arguably more unequal, citizenry enjoyed extensive rights to assemble, associate, and communicate their grievances directly to the state, although the exclusion of the population's vast majority from the suffrage made binding consultation questionable. The Reform Act of 1832 had not greatly expanded the electorate, despite shifting the basis of representation from chartered privilege to population and wealth. But contention of the previous seventy-five years had significantly enlarged citizenship by establishing numerous channels, including mass associations, election campaigns, and public assemblies, through which even nonvoters exercised strong collective claims to be heard directly by agents of the state. The working-class Chartist program of 1838–1848 demanded an extension of democracy by means of equalization: universal suffrage, secret ballots, annual elections, salaried members of Parliament, no property qualification for members, and equal electoral districts—a call for 1111 (with the unstated presumption that British subjects already enjoyed a measure of protection from arbitrary state action). The movement collapsed in 1848, but its program gradually passed into law through the acts of 1867–1868, 1885, 1918, and auxiliary legislation. Through struggle from inside and outside the polity, the breadth and equality of citizenship increased as popular consultation—chiefly in the form of periodic elections—became more binding and protections extended as well.

Military mobilizations continued to inflate the state and expand the range of citizenship during the twentieth century.[21] By the enactment of female suffrage in 1918, Great Britain edged into the category of 1111 (in a more differentiated scale, perhaps 0.75, 0.80, 0.60, 0.75), by no means a "full" democracy, but nonetheless unusually democratic among the states of its time.[22] Thereafter, the chief alterations in citizenship consisted of openings to residents of former colonies and extensions of the state services or payments to which citizens had a right. If we included Ireland or British overseas colonies in the evaluation of democracy, to be sure, Britain's democracy scores would all plummet. Still, that makes the point: even in the days of the British Empire and the United Kingdom of Great Britain and Ireland (roughly 1800–1945), the polity commanding Wales, Scotland, and England remained somewhat distinct from the rest, and within its own confines significantly more democratic than them.

In a telling simplification, T. H. Marshall described the whole process of democratization as a movement from civic to political to social rights.[23] Marshall's formulation misleads us in two important ways: by substituting a neat succession for a tangled intertwining of civic, political, and social rights, and by erasing many curtailments of rights, for example, the massive repression of 1795–1799 and the defeat of Chartism in the 1840s. Nevertheless, Marshall's scheme rightly calls attention to the alternation among relative emphases on the breadth of citizenship, its equality, its protections against arbitrary state action, and control of citizens over state personnel and policy. British history of the last two centuries illustrates the truism that changes in the character of the state and of citizenship entail alterations in the extent and character of democracy.

Once we recognize the importance of military activity to the British state's transformation, British history takes on a delightful irony. In the world as a whole, autonomous militaries generally inhibit democracy, even when they seize power in the name of democratic programs. They regularly inhibit democracy by diminishing the protections of citizens against arbitrary state action and often by blocking the definitiveness of popular consultation—annulling or falsifying elections, bypassing or intimidating parliaments, evading public surveillance of their activities. Yet in Britain, militarization of the state indirectly fostered democratization. It did so through the struggle and bargaining it generated, which fortified citizenship and subordinated military activity to parliamentary control.

The process began in the sixteenth century with Tudor checking of great lords' private armies and fortified castles. It ended, for practical purposes, in the nineteenth century with the elimination of press gangs. An aristocratically led military continued to draw a major share of the state budget, retained great freedom of action in Ireland and the colonies, and enjoyed great prestige at home, yet as such, never wielded autonomous power in domestic politics after 1660. The reliance of the British military on Parliament for finance and supply—still an acute issue in the struggles that led up to the revolution of 1640—eventually subordinated the army and navy to civilian, parliamentary control. In retrospect, we can see the crucial importance of that subordination to the later creation of British democracy.

Parallel processes produced military subordination, and thereby promoted democracy, elsewhere in Europe. Where they had less force, as in Iberia and the Balkans, autonomous militaries posed barriers against democracy into the twentieth century. In Iberia, the weakening of the monarchy through Napoleon's conquest and the subsequent resurgence of military leaders in the peninsula's reconquest facilitated military intervention throughout the nineteenth century, while in the Balkans, both the casting off of Ottoman control and the promotion of local military resistance to the Ottomans by neighboring powers such as the Russian Empire similarly fortified the long-term involvement of militaries in politics. *Per contra,* Iberian and Balkan experiences underline the crucial importance of military subordination to democracy.

Democracy Resembles a Lake

The exploration of tautologically necessary conditions for democracy—states and citizens—clears the way for thinking about contingent causes and concomitants of democracy. No one has so far succeeded in separating common correlates of democratic arrangements from nontautologically necessary, sufficient, or contingently causal conditions. The task is difficult for three main reasons: *first,* because the crucial relationships are almost certainly multiple and complex; *second,* because democracy-promoting and democracy-sustaining conditions have most likely varied and changed from one historical setting to another; *third,* because the presence of compelling historical models such as Great Britain or Switzerland makes it so tempting to pack the whole of British or Swiss history, culture, and social organization into our theories of democracy, on the true but misleading ground that history, culture, and social organization all mark the ways those democratic systems work.

The problem resists solution because democracy does not resemble an oil field or a garden, but a lake. A lake—a large inland body of water—can come into being because a mountain stream feeds into a naturally existing basin, because someone or something dams up the outlet of a large river, because a glacier melts, because an earthquake isolates a segment of the ocean from the main body of water, because people deliberately dig an enormous hole and channel nearby watersheds into it, or for a number of other reasons. Once it exists, nevertheless, a lake nurtures characteristic ecosystems and maintains characteristic relations with its surroundings, so much so that limnologists have built a scientific specialty around the study of those regularities. Democracy behaves like a lake: although it has distinguishing properties and a logic of its own, it forms in a variety of ways, each of which retains traces of its singular history in the details of its current operation.

Quick! Let's abandon the simile before it drowns us! Here is the point: we have absolutely no a priori reason to believe that only one set of circumstances produces and sustains democracy, even if during the last few hundred years' experience, particular circumstances have often nurtured democracy. The most we can reasonably hope to get from scrutinizing historical cases of democratization is a map of alternative paths by which the process has occurred, an indication of sufficient—not necessary—conditions for that transformation, and a specification of general mechanisms that play a part in producing or sustaining democratic institutions when they form.

From their outstanding comparative study of democratization within four sets of states (Western and Central Europe, British settler states, mainland Latin America, and Central America/Caribbean), Rueschemeyer, Stephens, and Stephens draw important conclusions. They confirm Barrington Moore's assertion that the political power of labor-controlling landlords inhibited democratization while denying Moore's association of democratization with a politically strong bourgeoisie. Instead, they show, workers allied with others (who were often bourgeois) and pushed much more reliably for democracy, sometimes over the resistance of bourgeois who preferred more limited forms of political participation.

Rueschemeyer et al. conclude that in general capitalism does, as often alleged, promote democracy, but not because capitalists prefer democratic government; all other things equal and enemies such as landlords absent, capitalists prefer something like oligarchies of wealth: 0010, not 1111. Such oligarchies allow them to use state power to control workers. But capitalism generates both working classes and the conditions under which they are likely to mobilize; working classes then press for enlargements of citizens' rights and full inclusion of workers among citizens. Given powerful allies, they often succeed. Rueschemeyer and colleagues do not quite recognize their argument's implication: not capitalism itself, but proletarianization constitutes the crucial conditions for democratization. To the extent that proletarianization occurs by noncapitalist means, all other things equal, it still promotes democratization. The relatively noncapitalist proletarianization that occurred in Russia with and after the abolition of serfdom (1861), for example, created strong pressures toward democratic enlargements of rights between then and 1917.[24]

Rueschemeyer et al. also understate the importance of their most powerful finding: armed men who exercise autonomous state power inhibit democracy. The finding connects closely with the inhibitory power of landed classes. For so long as great landlords command large numbers of peasants and serfs, they provide an alternative source of military manpower. Where landlords supply and command military units directly, they retain great political power. As my précis of British history suggests, one of the more surprising and crucial effects of expanding capitalism was that it allowed prosperous states to buy off their militaries, supplying and paying them well but subordinating them to tax-authorizing parliaments and civilian bureaucracies. Stirred by fears of armed workers, those states also disarmed the civilian population and created demilitarized police forces specializing in control of civilians. The result was to reduce the chances for any armed group to wrest power, locally or nationally, from civilian hands. Even in poor agrarian states such as Costa Rica, reduction of the autonomous power of military men has facilitated democratization.

More so than the other factors to which they draw attention, military power and autonomy depend on the polity's transnational connections: whether it includes powerful agrarian actors depending on labor-repressive export agriculture, whether foreign powers arm the state, whether foreign capital forwards the repression of workers. (This set of observations links to the contemporary propensity for militarization of states receiving protection from great powers and/or exporting valuable commodities, notably oil, the revenues of which state agents control.)[25] Yet the domestic history of military activity likewise matters; in the age of mass military service, victorious wars strengthened ruling coalitions, while lost wars shook the grip of rulers. Lost wars therefore created openings to democracy in authoritarian systems, openings to authoritarianism in democratic systems.

As my tale of Great Britain suggests, Rueschemeyer et al. find that mass military mobilization empowers the classes supplying the bulk of military manpower, both in Europe and elsewhere:

> In the United States, soldiers' demands for suffrage rights at the time of the wars against Britain accelerated the broadening of suffrage. Over one hundred years later, the presence of black soldiers in the armed forces during World War II and afterward contributed to the movement which eventually resulted in the extension of suffrage to southern blacks. In Canada, the mass mobilization for World War I was critically implicated

in the institution of universal suffrage there. In nineteenth century Latin America, on the other hand, repeated involvement in wars led to a build-up of the military and increased the political weight of the military.[26]

The formula does not run, then: war, hence democracy. If it did, every state in bellicose Europe would have democratized by the sixteenth or seventeenth century. Instead, the path runs something like this:

mass mobilization under the state's direct auspices

↓   ↓

civilian bureaucracy   bargaining with supplying populations

↓   ↓

containment of military   concession of rights and citizenship

↓   ↓

openings for democracy

The existence of openings does not guarantee passage through them. As Rueschemeyer, Stephens, and Stephens argue, in the absence of favorable class configurations such as an effective worker-bourgeois coalition, the path of mass militarization easily leads to authoritarian repression of the populace.

In any case, the militaristic itinerary constitutes only one road to democracy. Others pass through the federation of small-scale democracies, the defeat or self-destruction of authoritarian regimes, and the imposition of constitutions by outside powers. These alternatives define distinct processes that have, in their times and places, encouraged the formation of polities that afforded binding consultation and protection from arbitrary state action to relatively broad and equal citizenries. Each historic journey left its mark on the travelers: Swiss, Canadian, and Japanese democracies operate in quite different ways. In most of them, contrary to recent theorizing, bottom-up action, unintended consequences, and long-term transformations play a fundamental part. But in all of them, social construction matters greatly.

How, then, does social construction matter? It matters through its impact on shared understandings, as often tacit as publicly acknowledged. It matters because all four components of democracy—equality, breadth, consultation, and protection—concern the past and present less than the future. They concern expectations: that agents of the state will in the future honor the relatively equal rights of a broad citizenry, that they will yield to citizens' collective decisions, that they will protect citizens from arbitrary state action. Of course, past and present performance in these regards provides much of the evidence from which citizens project these futures. But the secret of democracy lies in the expectation that one's day will come, that today's loss is only a temporary setback, that everyone eventually gets a chance.

Even in a smoothly operating democracy, a lost war, or a deep depression, the formation of an authoritarian mass movement, economic dependency on an outside power, or the acquisition of autonomy by military forces sometimes undermines that expectation rapidly, as the experiences of Italy and Germany after World War I illustrate vividly. Expectations, however much based on realistic observation, depend heavily on social construction and remain subject to social deconstruction. That is why democracy, once formed, does not stay in place forever. That is why sites of democracy always display the sign Under Construction.

Notes

1. An earlier version of this chapter circulated as "Of Oilfields, Lakes, and Democracy," Working Paper 152, Center for Studies of Social Change, New School for Social Research, November 1992. I am grateful to Viviane Brachet, Marshall Johnson, Ariel Salzmann, Kumru Toktamis, Pavel Tychtl, and Viviana Zelizer for criticism and encouragement, and to the National Science Foundation for support of the research concerning Great Britain on which the chapter draws.

2. Barrington Moore Jr., *Social Origins of Dictatorship and Democracy* (Boston: Beacon Press, 1966).

3. Terry Lynn Karl, "Dilemmas of Democratization in Latin America," *Comparative Politics* 23 (1990): 1–21.

4. Eva Etzioni-Halevy, "Democratic-Elite Theory: Stabilization versus Breakdown of Democracy," *Archives européennes de sociologie* 31 (1990): 317–350.

5. Adam Przeworski, "Some Problems in the Study of the Transition to Democracy," in Guillermo O'Donnell, Philippe C. Schmitter, and Laurence Whitehead, eds., *Transitions from Authoritarian Rule: Comparative Perspectives* (Baltimore: Johns Hopkins University Press, 1986). p. 63.

6. Dietrich Rueschemeyer, Evelyne Huber Stephens, and John D. Stephens, *Capitalist Development and Democracy* (Chicago: University of Chicago Press, 1992).

7. Giuseppe Di Palma, *To Craft Democracies: An Essay on Democratic Transitions* (Berkeley: University of California Press, 1990).

8. Przeworski, "Some Problems"; Robert A. Dahl, *Polyarchy: Participation and Opposition* (New Haven, CT: Yale University Press, 1971), and *Democracy and Its Critics* (New Haven, CT: Yale University Press, 1989).

9. Dahl, *Democracy and Its Critics,* p. 1.

10. Rueschemeyer, Stephens, and Stephens, *Capitalist Development and Democracy*, p. 43.

11. Paul E. Peterson, "An Immodest Proposal," *Daedalus*, 121, no. 4 (1992): 151–174.

12. See Gunnar Artéus, Ulf Olsson, and Kerstin Stromberg-Back, "The Influence of the Armed Forces on the Transformation of Society in Sweden, 1600–1945," *Kungl. Krigsvetenskaps akademius Bihafte—Militarhistorisk Tidskrift* (1981): 133–144; Klaus-Richard Böhme, "Schwedische Finanzbürokratie und Kriegsführung 1611 bis 1721," in Goran Rystad, ed., *Europe and Scandinavia: Aspects of the Process of Integration in the 17th Century* (Lund: Esselte Studium, 1983); Jan Lindegren, "The Swedish 'Military State,' 1560–1720," *Scandinavian Journal of History* 10 (1985): 305–336; Sven A. Nilsson, "Imperial Sweden: Nation-Building, War, and Social Change," in Sven A. Nilsson et al., *The Age of New Sweden* (Stockholm: Livrustkammaren, 1988).

13. Matti Alestalo and Stein Kuhnle, "The Scandinavian Route: Economic, Social, and Political Developments in Denmark, Finland, Norway, and Sweden," Research Report no. 31, Research Group for Comparative Sociology, University of Helsinki, 1984; Helga Hernes, "Scandinavian Citizenship," *Acta Sociologica* 31 (1988): 199–215; Sven Lundqvist, *Folkrörelserna i det svenska samhället, 1850–1920* (Stockholm: Almqvist & Wiksell, 1977); Bo Öhngren, *Folk i rörelse: Samhällsutveckling, flyttningsmonster och folkrörelser i Eskilstuna, 1870–1900* (Uppsala, 1974. Studia Historica Upsaliensia, 55).

14. Thomas A. Brady, *Turning Swiss: Cities and Empire, 1450–1550* (Cambridge: Cambridge University Press, 1985).

15. Maarten Prak, "Citizen Radicalism and Democracy in the Dutch Republic: The Patriot Movement of the 1780s," *Theory and Society* 20 (1991): 73–102; Wayne Te Brake, *Regents and Rebels: The Revolutionary World of the 18th Century Dutch City* (Oxford: Blackwell, 1989), and "How Much in How Little? Dutch Revolution in Comparative Perspective," *Tijdschrift voor Sociale Geschiedenis* 16 (1990): 349–363.

16. Hanspeter Kriesi, "Federalism and Pillarization: The Netherlands and Switzerland Compared," *Acta Politica* 25 (1990): 433–450.

17. John Brewer, *The Sinews of Power: War, Money, and the English State, 1688–1783* (New York: Knopf, 1989).

18. Norman Chester, *The English Administrative System, 1780–1870* (Oxford: Clarendon, 1981); Eric J. Evans, *The Forging of the Modern State: Early Industrial Britain, 1783–1879* (London, 1983); Michael Mann, *States, War, and Capitalism* (Oxford: Blackwell, 1988); Peter Mathias and Patrick O'Brien, "Taxation in Britain and France, 1715–1810: A Comparison of the Social and Economic Incidence of Taxes Collected for the Central Governments," *Journal of European Economic History* 5 (1976): 601–650; Patrick K. O'Brien, "Power with Profit: The State and the Economy, 1688–1815," inaugural lecture, University of London, 1991.

19. Mathias and O'Brien, "Taxation in Britain and France"; Patrick K. O'Brien, "The Political Economy of British Taxation, 1660–1815," *Economic History Review* 41 (1988): 1–32, and "The Impact of the Revolutionary and Napoleonic Wars,

1793–1815, on the Long-Run Growth of the British Economy," *Economic History Review* 12 (1989): 335–395; Peter H. Lindert and Jeffrey G. Williamson, "English Workers' Living Standards during the Industrial Revolutions: A New Look," *Economic History Review*, 2nd ser., 36 (1983): 1–25.

20. Linda Colley, *Britons: Forging the Nation, 1707–1837* (New Haven, CT: Yale University Press, 1992).

21. James E. Cronin, *The Politics of State Expansion: War, State, and Society in Twentieth-Century Britain* (London: Routledge, 1991).

22. James E. Cronin, "Politics, Class Structure, and the Enduring Weakness of British Social Democracy," *Journal of Social History* 16 (1983): 123–142.

23. T. H. Marshall, *Citizenship and Social Class* (Cambridge: Cambridge University Press, 1950).

24. Theodor Shanin, *The Roots of Otherness: Russia's Turn of Century*, 2 vols. (New Haven, CT: Yale University Press, 1986).

25. Charles Tilly, "War and the Power of Warmakers in Western Europe and Elsewhere," in Peter Wallensteen, Johan Galtung, and Carlos Portales, eds., *Global Militarization* (Boulder, CO.: Westview, 1985); "War and State Power," *Middle East Report* 21, no. 171 (July–August 1991): 38–40.

26. Rueschemeyer, Stephens, and Stephens, *Capitalist Development and Democracy*, p. 279.

· 9 ·

PARLIAMENTARIZATION OF POPULAR CONTENTION
IN GREAT BRITAIN, 1758–1834

During his trip to Manchester in July 1835, Alexis de Tocqueville jotted in his *carnet de route* a note on political centralization:

> There is a great deal of centralisation in England; but of what sort? Legislative and not administrative; governmental rather than administrative; but as with us it sometimes extends down to very small, puerile details. The mania for *regimentation,* which is not a French mania, but one of *men* and of *power,* is found here as elsewhere. But it can only have a single, passing effect, and can only very imperfectly achieve its object. That is because the *centralising* power is in the hands of the legislature, not of the *executive.*[1]

Three years past the Reform Act of 1832, Tocqueville saw clearly how much the United Kingdom's political life swirled not around the government's administrative offices, but around Parliament and, increasingly, around the House of Commons. He remarked that great magnates and the Crown vied vigorously for power, but ultimately conceded authority to the nationally elected assembly. He did not recognize, however, how much more central to British public life Parliament had become during the previous half century.

From the time of the Magna Carta and even before, regularly constituted assemblies of notables had played significant parts in English politics at local, regional, and national scales. As English influence extended over Wales, Scotland, and Ireland, the English Parliament and parallel bodies assumed prominence in those regions' political lives as well. By comparison with France or Russia, the British Isles had accumulated long, broad experience with deliberative bodies representing local and regional power holders, if not the general population.

Nevertheless, Great Britain (England, Wales, and Scotland) had also gone through extended periods of executive centralization. Britain's seventeenth-century civil wars and revolutions pivoted on relations between a power-seeking Crown and a resistant Parliament, but ended with plenty of executive power in royal hands. During the eighteenth century, moreover, Hanoverian kings used their patronage effectively in limiting Parliament's autonomy. The aristocratic politics that consolidated during the eighteenth century left little room for popular intervention at a national scale. Indeed, as Edmund Burke argued strenuously, the eighteenth-century Parliament operated as an agent of virtual, not direct, representation; authorities strongly resisted any suggestion that members of Parliament spoke for their constituencies, much less that constituencies could instruct their votes.[2] They prosecuted, moreover, efforts to organize assemblies, associations, or campaigns they deemed to usurp Parliament's exclusive right to speak for the nation. A hypothetical predecessor of Tocqueville who journeyed through England fifty years earlier would have noticed many more political resemblances to Old Regime France than Tocqueville saw.

Between the 1780s and the 1830s, British politics parliamentarized dramatically. Parliamentarization had three major components: (1) within Great Britain as a whole, increase in the central government's influence over decisions and resources; (2) within central government, relative and absolute increase of Parliament's command over decisions and resources; and (3) in political life outside the central government, increasing centrality of Parliament and its members to struggles for power. British parliamentarization matters both for itself and for its effects. For itself, British experience of parliamentarization constitutes an early, visible, and very influential model of a process that eventually shaped governments throughout the Western world and in Western colonies as well. In its effects, it defined an important possible path to democratic government—to broad, relatively equal citizenship affording citizens considerable protection from arbitrary state action, as well as significant collective control over the personnel and decisions of government.[3] Possible, not even probable: many oligarchies and tyrannies have coexisted with supine or venal parliaments; but as compared with their absence, the presence of powerful representative institutions facilitates popular struggle for direct voice at a national scale.

Far from seeking to document or explain British parliamentarization in general, this chapter takes up only one portion of the massive process. It shows how the increasing centrality of Parliament in national affairs affected popular politics, especially its discontinuous forms: not so much the day-to-day play of favors, preferment, discussion, and cultural expression as the more intermittent, public, collective voicing of demands, complaints, enmities, solidarities, and humble petitions. Parliament's great expansion of powers during the French wars of 1792 to 1815 durably shaped the forms and objects of popular contention.

Figure 9.1 suggests what a long-term observer of British politics could have seen happening between 1758 and 1834, the year before Tocqueville's own observation. The graph comes from an inventory of occasions on which people outside the government made collective claims on other people, including agents or segments of the government, during scattered years from 1758 through 1820 in southeastern England plus all years from 1828 through 1834 in Great Britain as a whole; separate results for southeastern England from 1828 to 1834 show essentially the same trend. It displays a massive, if irregular, increase in the proportion of all such claims taking as their objects either Parliament as a whole or individual members of Parliament (MPs). The share of the two combined rose from a typical 5 or 10 percent before the 1790s to over 40 percent in the 1830s. Britain experienced a massive parliamentarization of popular politics—a great increase in the centrality of Parliament, especially the elected House of Commons, over a wide range of issues and actors.

By collective claim making (synonym: contention) I mean the public, joint expression by word and deed of desires that concrete other parties act in certain ways, ways that would affect their interests. In eighteenth- and nineteenth-century Great Britain, the relevant "desires" ranged in heat from humble petitions or pledges of allegiance to boisterous demands or complaints backed by violent attacks. Participants, observers, and critics

Figure 9.1. Objects of Claims: Contentious Gatherings, 1758–1834

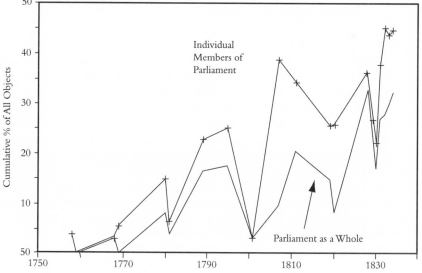

gave the various interactions in question such names as Rough Music, turn-out, strike, riot, disturbance, demonstration, meeting, procession, deputation, and march. Popular contention is deeply cultural, in the sense that it relies on and transforms shared understandings concerning what forms and ends of action are desirable, feasible, and efficacious; collective learning and memory strongly limit the claims that people make and how they make them.

Whatever its labels and forms, contention pivoted (as it still pivots) on rights and justice, often on conflicting definitions of rights and justice. Contention links doubly with rights; first, because rights consist of claims the enforcement of which third parties regularly support; and second, because collective claim making commonly asserts or defends rights against challenges to them. Although at a given moment we may only notice one actor making claims, over the longer run, contention always involves rights-tinged relations among political actors.

British parliamentarization of contention had four overlapping elements, increases in the frequency with which:

1. Parliament became the object of ordinary people's contention;
2. parliamentary action incited ordinary people's claim making, whether directed to Parliament or elsewhere;
3. issues currently being considered by Parliament became more central to popular contention;
4. connections with Parliament became more central in a wide range of claim making.

This chapter documents the parliamentarization of British popular contention between the 1750s and 1830s, offers tentative explanations for the momentous bundle of changes, then goes on to sketch the significance of parliamentarization for political life as a whole.

Figure 9.2 summarizes what happens during an idealized course of parliamentarization: popular politics undergoes a net shift from a local toward a national scale, while representation of ordinary people becomes more direct. Instead of orienting their claims chiefly to fellow members of local communities or to local power holders (and, through local power holders, to great patrons including the nobility and the Crown), ordinary people increasingly band together for claims on Parliament. Meanwhile, Parliament acts increasingly in response to mobilized segments of the general population. In the process, landlords, priests, and other local power holders lose some of their influence as brokers and mediators, while established national patron-client chains become less effective. Political entrepreneurs

Figure 9.2. Parliamentarization: As Changing Objects of Claims

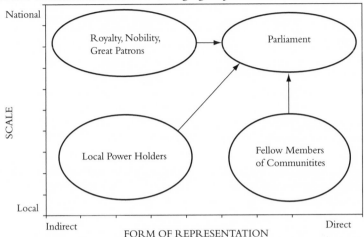

who can organize constituencies—party leaders, social-movement activists, reform journalists, and others—gain significant advantages for their causes.

Such a scheme describes major political trends not just in England, Great Britain, or the United Kingdom, but over a wide range of Western states from the eighteenth to twentieth centuries.[4] National representative institutions generally became more prominent as political actors and, therefore, as objects of popular claims. Direct rule by agents of the central state displaced indirect rule through relatively autonomous regional and local power holders. Meaningful citizenship developed: enforceable rights and obligations between state agents and whole categories of people defined chiefly by their relationship to the state. Broadening of citizenship included extensions to (some) ordinary people of claims on parliamentary institutions—for example, rights to vote and to run for election—ruling classes had previously enjoyed alone.

As a result of these changes, democracy—relatively broad and equal citizenship coupled with binding consultation of citizens in regard to state personnel and policy as well as with protection of citizens from arbitrary state action—likewise became possible at a national scale. (Possible, not necessary: the installation of direct rule and citizenship also made new varieties of tyranny possible.) These changes, in turn, promoted the expansion of paraparliamentary politics: political parties, citizens' association, pressure groups, and social movements. Visibly, parliamentarization played a crucial part in the creation of mass national politics such as many twentieth-century states have known, such as no large states knew before the nineteenth century. Although the path, context, and consequences of parliamentarization differed substantially from one country to another, popular contention and legislative activity acquired closer bonds through most of Europe and areas of European settlement.

In Great Britain, parliamentarization altered relations among a number of nonparliamentary actors. It weakened the autonomy and power of the Crown and of great lords, reduced direct involvement of troops and other repressive forces in claim making, and diminished the importance of local dignitaries both as objects of contention and as vehicles for the relaying of claims to higher authorities. Surprisingly, however, it also fortified the positions of local assemblies such as wardmotes (i.e., ward assemblies) and vestries, which became major bases for the mobilization and expression of shared claims on Parliament. Increasingly, contention centered on the deliberate organization of meetings, demonstrations, and other public manifestations of political preferences; more and more, those gatherings transmitted collective complaints, demands, proposals, and expressions of support or disapproval to Parliament by means of petitions, resolutions, and publicity. All this activity, in its turn, augmented the involvement and influence of political entrepreneurs at the national, regional, and local levels in the coordination of claim making.

Why did it happen? So far as I can tell, three major causal strands intertwined to produce British parliamentarization. First, the rising scale and cost of war—with other European powers in the Seven Years' War, with the Americans, and then, far weightier, with France of the Revolution and Napoleon—expanded the power of Parliament, which then intervened in a greatly increased range of economic and political activity. Second, increased capitalization of industry and agriculture (the latter accelerated by wartime labor and import shortages) augmented the demand of both capitalists and proletarianizing workers for political representation by other means than established webs of patronage. Third, in the presence of a system that already made Parliament the central locus of political decision making and that protected several forms of speech, association, and public deliberation, innovations within the forms of contention driven by collective learning and political entrepreneurship themselves tightened the connections between parliamentary action and popular claim making by means of local assemblies. The evidence for these causal influences remains more elusive than the documentation of changes in the forms and relations of claim making, but it indicates that all three chains contributed to parliamentarization.

WHAT HAPPENED?

My central body of evidence comes from a catalog of 8,088 "contentious gatherings" (CGs) that occurred in southeastern England (Kent, Middlesex, Surrey, or Sussex) during thirteen-year spreads from 1758 through 1820 and in Great Britain as a whole during the seven years from 1828 through 1834.[5] A CG is an occasion on which a number of people (in the instance, ten or more) outside the government gathered in a publicly accessible place and made visible collective claims bearing on the interests of at least one person outside their own number. The machine-readable catalog contains truncated, edited textual transcriptions of such events reported in *Gentleman's Magazine,* the *Annual Register,* and/or the *London Chronicle* for 1758, 1759, 1768, 1769, 1780, and 1781; in those publications plus the *Times* of London for 1789, 1795, 1801, 1807, 1811, 1819, and 1820; and in *Gentleman's Magazine,* the *Annual Register, Morning Chronicle, Times, Mirror of Parliament, Hansard's Parliamentary Debates,* and/or *Votes and Proceedings of Parliament* for 1828–1834. My group and I also scanned these sources over the first six months of 1835 for retrospective reports on 1834 and earlier years. Although for purposes of comparison we prepared a separate chronology of CGs for Great Britain as a whole over the entire period 1758–1834 from a wide variety of historical works, and although I have frequently consulted archival material and historical works for further detail and context, the enumeration analyzed here consists exclusively of qualifying events reported in the periodicals.

Each time a bundle of reports drawn from our basic periodicals qualified an event as a CG, my collaborators and I prepared a machine-readable record containing these parts:

1. a general description of the *event,* one per CG, for a total of 8,088 records;
2. a description of each *formation*—each person or set of persons acting in a distinguishable manner—within each CG (27,184 records);
3. a description of each *action*—any participating formation's movement or change with respect to the claims being made, including new utterances, cheers, or displays of sentiments—within each CG (50,875 records); when two or more formations changed action simultaneously, as in the outbreak of a fight, we transcribed their doings as separate actions within the same action phase;
4. an identification of each *source* (including sources supplementary

to our standard periodicals) we consulted in preparing the event for coding (21,030 records);

5. an identification of each *location* in which any part of the CG took place (11,054 records);
6. an enumeration of additional *names* the sources gave any formation (28,995 records);
7. an enumeration of *individuals* mentioned as members of any formation (26,318 records);
8. supplementary information on the geographical or numerical *size* of any formation (18,413 records);
9. the detailed *texts* from which we drew summary descriptions of actions (76,189 records); and
10. *comments* on any aspect of the CG or its description (5,450 records).

Except for straightforward items such as day of the week or county name, these records do not contain codes in the usual sense of the term; on the whole, we transcribed words from the texts or (when that was not feasible) paraphrases of those words, tagging those paraphrases so they would always stand out from direct quotations. Instead of coding names given to formations into broad categories, for example, we transcribed the actual terms used in our sources. Thus the transcription of each action includes the actor's name as reported in the source, a verb characterizing the action, and (where an object appeared) the name given for the action's object. For purposes of analysis, however, I generally regroup some of these elements into categories. This paper employs highly aggregated categories for actions, formations, and types of event.

My research group minimized inferences and syntheses concerning events and their contexts, with the idea that it was better to leave the machine-readable record as a reduced, but relatively faithful, transcription of the texts and to encourage users of the records to make their inferences or syntheses systematic and self-conscious. We divided the record into reported actions before, during, and after the CG itself—that is, before any two participating formations began interacting on that occasion, and after the last two stopped interacting. ("Before" actions included announcements of meetings, advance planning, precipitating events, and the like, while "after" actions sometimes extend to arrests, retaliation, and prosecution long after the central action.) This report treats "during" actions only.

Splicing together evidence from scattered years from 1758 to 1820 for southeast England alone with a continuous series for Great Britain as a whole from 1828 to 1834 might seem a perilous enterprise risking spurious indications of change. On average, events in the rest of Great Britain did differ in distribution from those in London and its hinterland, notably, in the larger part played by workers' struggles in Britain's industrial regions. But trends inside and outside the southeast ran quite parallel to each other, as we can establish directly for 1828–1834 and by comparison with other sources for earlier years.[6] In the analyses that follow, I often lump together evidence from Great Britain as a whole with that from the southeast alone, but treat the southeast separately where the risk of confusion appears significant.

Elsewhere, much of my inquiry concerns how and why the array of means for claim making—the available *repertoires* of contention—altered so greatly between the 1750s and the 1830s.[7] Table 9.1 gives some indication of the alteration's magnitude. It presents a rough classification of the occasions on which CGs occurred, consolidating observations for southeast England (1758–1820) and all of Great Britain (1828–1834). The categories run as follows:

> *Violent gathering:* attacks on poorhouses, affrays of hunters with game wardens, public shaming of renegade workers, pulling down of dishonored or dangerous houses, beatings of informers, and other direct applications of force.

Table 9.1. Occasions of Contentious Gatherings, 1758–1834

Year	Violent Gathering	Other Unplanned Gathering	Election Meeting	Authorized Assembly	Association Meeting	Other Public Meeting	Other*	Total	Number
1758	85.7	0.0	0.0	14.3	0.0	0.0	0.0	100.0	14
1759	75.0	0.0	0.0	8.3	8.3	0.0	8.3	99.9	12
1768	69.4	21.6	0.9	1.8	0.9	1.8	3.6	100.0	111
1769	28.4	19.4	11.9	32.8	3.0	1.5	3.0	100.0	67
1780	74.3	2.9	0.0	20.0	0.0	1.4	1.4	100.0	70
1781	48.3	6.9	3.4	37.9	3.4	0.0	0.0	99.9	29
1789	15.4	19.2	3.8	51.9	5.8	1.9	1.9	99.9	52
1795	15.7	13.9	0.9	55.6	6.5	4.6	2.8	100.0	108
1801	25.5	36.4	0.0	16.4	10.9	9.1	1.8	100.1	55
1807	13.0	8.3	30.6	22.2	9.3	12.0	4.6	100.0	108
1811	16.7	10.4	2.1	31.3	18.8	18.8	2.1	100.2	48
1819	8.2	6.3	3.9	66.4	6.6	8.2	0.4	100.0	256
1820	8.0	15.3	4.4	40.1	8.8	13.9	9.5	100.0	274
1828	12.6	1.2	2.2	7.6	48.2	19.8	8.4	100.0	595
1829	19.8	6.4	0.8	20.1	22.9	24.6	5.3	99.9	641
1830	30.0	8.2	5.3	18.2	12.1	21.6	4.6	100.0	1164
1831	11.0	4.7	9.9	36.9	6.4	17.3	3.8	100.0	1645
1832	13.2	5.3	22.6	39.4	7.0	9.0	3.4	99.9	1111
1833	11.0	7.7	5.7	47.6	8.8	16.0	3.3	100.1	674
1834	8.3	4.0	5.9	42.0	6.4	26.9	6.5	100.0	1054
Total	16.4	6.6	8.2	34.9	11.9	17.3	4.6	99.9	8088
N	1327	532	663	2826	966	1399	375	8088	

*"Other" = celebration, delegation, parade, demonstration, strike, or turnout.

Other unplanned gathering: nonviolent market conflicts; responses to the arrivals of dignitaries, heroes, or blackguards; popularly initiated public celebrations of major events; and other instances of assembly and claim making without substantial prior planning.

Election meeting: gatherings to endorse candidates, hear campaign speeches, or attend elections themselves.

Authorized assembly: offering demands, complaints, or expressions of support with respect to others in regularly constituted bodies such as vestry meetings, wardmotes, and city councils.

Association meeting: similar claim making in official sessions of explicitly named associations, including religious, economic, and political organizations.

Other public meeting: previously announced discussions of public issues open to the general citizenry (or sometimes the "respectable inhabitants") of a locality.

Other: organized celebration, delegation, parade, demonstration, strike, or turnout.

The rubrics cover the main occasions on which ordinary Britons made collective claims during the eighteenth and nineteenth centuries.

This way of presenting the evidence has significant limits: the categories overlap, as in the small number of routine meetings forcibly broken up by opponents, which appear here not as meetings, but as violent gatherings. The absence of breakdowns by location, group, and issue hides the uneven selectivity by which changes occurred in different niches of the British polity. The forms themselves were evolving, so that elements of what would become the demonstration—a performance absent as such in the 1760s but fairly well delineated by the 1830s—actually show up in elections, holiday celebrations, and turnouts of the 1760s. The catalog itself greatly underestimates the frequency of turnouts and strikes, thereby understating workers' overall involvement in claim making. All these features make the summary quite schematic.

Despite its limitations, the statistical evidence establishes a substantial decline in the proportion of violent gatherings from roughly 1789 onward—from 75 percent or so of all events in the early years to an order of 15 percent during the 1830s. Other unplanned gatherings fluctuated more than violent incidents, with a weak, irregular diminution after 1801. Collective acts of retaliation, resistance, and direct physical control lost much of the prominence they had assumed in the 1750s and 1760s. Except for a resurgence of agrarian and industrial conflict in 1829–1830 (especially the Swing rebellion of 1830), by the end of the Napoleonic Wars in 1815, aggressive direct action had receded to a minor share of all CGs.

Nonviolent, indirect, annunciatory, and preplanned actions waxed much more than violent events waned. Authorized assemblies such as wardmotes, elections, religious ceremonies, vestry meetings, and scheduled gatherings of ratepayers became mainstays of claim making by 1769 and occupied even larger shares of all events from 1789 onward; they reached a maximum two-thirds of all CGs in 1819. Meetings of named associations (e.g., Society of Supporters of the Bill of Rights, Hampden Clubs, Catholic Association) grew more important over time, although they never surpassed the proportions of local assemblies, except for the Catholic emancipation campaign of 1828–1829. Other public meetings (often organized by associations, but open to the general public) grew much more prominent after 1800, and by the 1830s, they played a large part in claim making. Meanwhile, elections fluctuated trendlessly as a function of parliamentary history and royal successions. The crude figures indicate a decisive shift from spur-of-the-moment provocation and violent retribution toward planned gatherings aimed at declaring collective positions with regard to the public issues.

Table 9.2 amplifies the picture. Using very broad categories and grouping the year span into four periods, it presents the central verbs in all 25,239 actions having identifiable objects—a little over half of all actions in the catalog. As Figure 9.1 indicates, the period 1758–1801 features slow, irregular parliamentarization, 1807–1820 marks a great acceleration of the trend, while the split between 1828–1831 and 1832–1834 roughly repre-

Table 9.2. Frequencies of Major Verb Categories, 1758–1834
(Verbs with objects only)

	% of All Verbs in Period				
Category	1758–1801	1807–1820	1828–1831	1832–1834	Total
Claim	8.8	7.6	21.9	14.1	17.2
Attack	26.0	9.1	15.3	14.9	15.5
Control	24.9	9.0	17.1	10.3	14.9
Cheer	7.0	16.5	14.6	16.4	14.7
Communicate	6.7	5.2	5.8	6.9	6.1
Deliberate	15.2	47.2	16.2	29.9	23.1
Enter	6.7	2.1	4.8	4.0	4.4
Other	4.8	3.4	4.3	3.5	4.0
Total	100.0	100.0	100.0	100.0	100.0
Number of Verbs	2021	2365	13333	7520	25239

sents "before" and "after" for passage of the great Reform Bill in June 1832.

The data in Table 9.2 show a marked decline in actions of attack and control, including both physical and verbal forms of abuse. Attack and control declined in favor of pacific claim making, deliberation, and expressions of support. As the tabulation of occasions for CGs has already forecast, the major shift from attack and control occurred between 1801 and 1820—more precisely, during the later, more intense years of the Napoleonic Wars. The minor resurgence of attack and control in 1828–1831 resulted chiefly from the Swing rebellion of 1830, during which landless laborers marched, burned, smashed agricultural machinery, and demanded wage rises through much of southeastern England.

Networks of Contention

Rather than tracing fluctuations in the forms of contentious action, however, this report focuses on changing relations among actors. Each claim, indeed each transitive action, constituted a transaction that we can conveniently think of as cumulating into ties defining social networks among claimants and objects of claims. In this sort of network, relations to "self" have meaning, since workers often made claims on other workers, local officials on other local officials, and so on. What is more, relations often ran in both directions: assembled citizens made claims on local authorities, but local authorities responded with claims of their own. Our evidence about claim-making networks is of course truncated, both (a) because claim making occurred outside of CGs and (b) because we excluded not only legislative assemblies as such, but also the few gatherings we encountered in which agents of government acting in their governmental capacity made the only reported claims. Yet the catalog provides rich information about the claim-making networks connecting ordinary people to one another and to various centers of power.

More precisely, we can conceive of each verb category as defining a separate matrix, a somewhat different set of relations among categories of actors. To make such an analysis practical, I aggregated the catalog's roughly 12,000 different formation names into sixty-four categories according to my judgment of formations' similarity in political position as of the early nineteenth century. I then grouped the sixty-four categories into larger blocks according to the same sorts of judgment, tested those judgments by means of block modeling with Ronald Burt's structure program, revised the blocks in accordance with block-modeling results, and on a third round, arrived at the fifteen blocks listed in Table 9.4: church, constables, crowd, electors, government, inhabitants, interest, locals, officials, pariahs, Parliament, repressive, royalty, trade, and workers. Block modeling tests the hypothesis that a given partition of all actors divides them into structurally equivalent sets: variously named actors maintaining essentially similar relations to all other actors.[8] After two rounds of minor adjustments to category boundaries, that hypothesis fits the data extremely well.

In the course of block modeling, for example, within repressive forces, I discovered an unexpected split between the gamekeepers, militia, New Police, sheriffs, and constables I have labeled "Constables" and the troops and older police forces I have dubbed "Repressive." I likewise responded to discrepancies in the first models by realigning the boundaries among inhabitants (e.g., residents of _____), locals (e.g., churchwardens, clergy, beadles, mayors, parishioners, vestries), and officials (essentially, London's deliberative bodies, plus high-ranking royal officers outside the ministry). The analyses reported here, then, concern 64-by-64 matrices over four distinct periods and 1758–1834 as a whole. Earlier matrices distinguish among major verb categories and the sixty-four classes of formations, while later ones sum over all verbs and aggregate into fifteen blocks of structurally equivalent actors.

Figures 9.3 and 9.4 illustrate what the matrices show. For major verb categories, they display the more frequent relations—those constituting at least 0.5 percent of relations defined by all verbs—during our first (1758–1801) and last (1832–1834) periods. As Table 9.2 indicates, verb categories "Claim," "Attack," "Control," "Cheer," and "Deliberate" account for about 85 percent of all actions over the entire period under study, although their proportions shift markedly. The network diagrams document large alterations in the social relations of claim making.

In the case of "Claim" (depute, petition, appeal, address, and so on), only the demands of crowds (assemblage, crowd, mob, gang, multitude, boys, someone, etc.) on other formations (notably, single persons identified by name) reached the threshold of 0.5 percent in 1758–1801. By 1832 to 1834, on the other hand, similar verbs connected churches, interests, electors, and assemblies of inhabitants to royalty and, especially, to Parliament, while assemblies of inhabitants also made demands of local officials and other nearby constituted bodies. Within the zone of "Claim," parliamentarization clearly occurred.

"Attack" behaved differently. As we might now expect, many more relatively frequent relations appeared in this zone during the period 1758–1801, but in both periods, crowds stood at the center of action. In the earlier period, relations of crowds with repressive forces, on the one hand,

Figure 9.3. Relations Defined by "Claim," "Attack," and "Control," 1758–1801 and 1832–1834 (Relations including 0.5% or more of all claims in period)

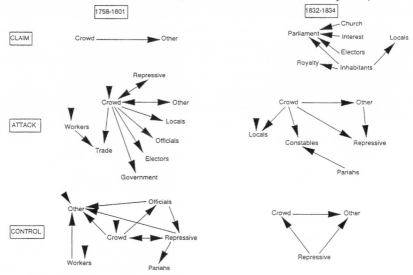

Note: ▼ = within same category.

and of crowds with "Other" formations ran strongly in both directions. Crowds also attacked other crowds, and workers other workers, with considerable frequency. The diagram for 1832–1834 shows a thinned set of relations, changed most notably in the addition of attacks by pariahs (poachers, smugglers, Irish, prisoners, vagrants, and so on) on constables, gamekeepers, militia, and similar agents of law enforcement.

A parallel thinning occurred with respect to "Control": apprehend, arrest, donkey, oppose, defy, and so forth. Although the mutual tie between repressive and crowd formations that characterized attacks likewise appeared in actions of control for 1758–1801, "Other" formations—again, especially named individuals—figured centrally. Officials and repressive forces, furthermore, initiated many more controlling actions than they did attacks. By 1832–1834, only the triangle repressive-crowd-other survived among the more frequent relations, and none of those relations was reciprocal. By that time, a sort of political symbiosis had emerged: crowds and others attacked repressive forces, who acted to control crowds and others.

"Cheer" (applaud, approve, thank, and so on) moved from lesser to greater complexity. In 1758–1801, Figure 9.4 shows us two small, separate relations: locals cheer officials, crowds cheer royalty. In 1832–1834, Parlia-

Figure 9.4. Relations Defined by "Cheer" and "Deliberate," 1758–1801 and 1832–1834 (Relations including 0.5% or more of all claims in period)

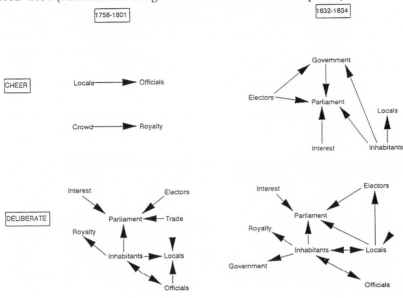

ment (not only the body as a whole or one of its chambers, but also individual MPs) stood at the system's center, receiving expressions of support from electors, members of defined interests, assemblies of inhabitants, and government dignitaries—nobles, gentry, ministers, and so on—acting outside their governmental roles. In the later period, we also see government dignitaries and local bodies, but not royalty, receiving frequent expressions of support from assemblies of inhabitants. Broadly speaking, the evolutions of "Claim" and "Cheer" paralleled each other, moving from relatively local and isolated relations to recurrent situations in which an interested group of citizens (notably, an assembly of inhabitants) gathered to send a message to Parliament.

Relations defined by "Deliberate" (chair, address, meet, resolve, and so on) changed less. Between 1758 and 1801, general meetings of inhabitants frequently formed and addressed claims to the Crown, high officials, local bodies, or Parliament. Local officers and bodies such as vestries, wardmotes, mayors, and churchwardens likewise assembled to address one another; by 1832–1834, their claims on Parliament had become frequent as well. Two things happened to deliberative actions: (1) they popularized, drawing in a much wider range of citizens; and (2) they came to center even more definitively on single-topic meetings organized to convey a collective desire to some branch of government, especially to Parliament.

Summing over all verbs, Table 9.3 shows the effect of these changes on connections defined by claim making. "Three-step relation strength" refers to the ratio of all a given formation's existing connections with other formations via one, two, or three steps, weighted for proximity, to all such

Table 9.3. Proportionate Relation Strengths[a] for Selected Actors,[b] 1758–1834

Actor	1758–1801	1807–1820	1828–1831	1832–1834	Total
Aldermen	.041	.068	.031	.054	.025
Crowd	.027	.116	.049	.039	.049
Electors	.010	.025	.038	.124	.057
Freeholders	.065	.015	.061	.026	.047
House of Commons	.039	.031	.008	.074	.031
Individual name	.145	.038	.116	.062	.124
Inhabitants	.151	.449	.271	.317	.296
Local officials	.039	.107	.066	.079	.051
MPs	.008	.105	.055	.135	.093
Ministers	.023	.025	.027	.059	.035
Mob	.378	.080	.140	.114	.176
Other	.033	.033	.026	.037	.029
Parliament	.067	.112	.212	.200	.193
Persons	.094	.033	.062	.026	.045
Police	.031	.022	.039	.066	.031
Protestants	.002	.004	.025	.014	.027
Royalty	.107	.261	.117	.090	.110
Society	.010	.031	.031	.057	.029
Supporters	.032	.058	.019	.022	.028
Trade	.146	.038	.048	.045	.060
Troops	.074	.005	.012	.021	.026
Workers	.098	.005	.012	.040	.033

[a]Proportionate relation strength: ratio of existing three-step connections, weighted for proximity, to all possible three-step connections with specified action, range 0–1.
[b]All categories of actors having relation strengths of .025 + for the period as a whole.

connections that could, in theory, exist. Thus in 1758–1801, the formation "Mob," which forms part of the larger block "Crowd," shows a high relation strength of .378—more than a third of its theoretically possible one-, two-, and three-step relations. (Reminder: "Mob" is not my term, but the label my group found in our sources.) Over the same period, the House of Commons shows a relation strength of .039, roughly a tenth of the mob's reading. Between 1758 and 1801, claim-making crowds connected much more closely with other participants in popular contention than did the House of Commons.

As the diagrams of claims, attacks, control, cheers, and deliberations might lead us to expect, the formations that lost significant relation strength over time include "Mob," "Trade," and "Troops." Large gainers include "Inhabitants," "MPs," and "Parliament." During the eighteenth-century years, the claim-making system clustered around freeholders, inhabitants, mobs, persons, trades, troops, workers, Parliament, royalty, and named individuals. In the 1830s, the system centered on electors, inhabitants, local officials, police, MPs, and Parliament itself, although named individuals, mobs, and royalty had not disappeared from the scene.

Table 9.4 indicates that formations fell into larger structurally equivalent blocks, with one significant change. "Structural equivalence" means similarity of a given actor's external relations to those of other actors; whether directly connected or not, strictly equivalent actors have identical relations with others. Reliabilities in the table (correlations among the outside relations of individual block members expressed as percentages of the maximum correlations possible) show impressively high and stable values. From period to period, members of the fifteen designated blocks occupied nearly identical positions in the overall network of claim making. The major exception is the block called "Parliament," composed of MP, Parliament, House of Commons, and House of Lords. Unlike any other block, that block's reliability declined from 93.9 to 89.5 to 73.4 to 51.6.

What happened? As Table 9.5 records, the relatively homogeneous position of Parliament's elements fell apart during the vast mobilization for parliamentary reform in 1830 and 1831, when concerted pressure on the resistant House of Lords became reformers' central strategy. The Lords managed to prevent passage of the Reform Bill until June 1832, when they finally buckled under the popularly inspired ministerial and royal threat to pack the House with new peers. The Lords' resistance then isolated them from the country's claim-making business as never before. Parliamentarization, as it developed in Great Britain, included a major shift of power and centrality within Parliament itself.

Table 9.4. Reliabilities of Three-Step Block Models for Subject-Object Relations, 1758–1834

Block	1758–1801	1807–1820	1828–1831	1832–1834	Total
Interest	98.9	99.6	98.2	98.5	99.3
Church	99.6	100.0	97.6	99.1	97.4
Workers	95.4	100.0	98.7	99.0	99.6
Trade	75.6	99.6	98.8	99.0	98.8
Crowd	85.2	96.3	92.7	95.9	91.9
Constables	99.3	100.0	97.8	99.1	99.4
Repressive	92.6	99.4	96.0	94.4	99.6
Locals	98.5	96.1	98.3	98.2	99.3
Officials	92.2	92.9	99.1	88.7	98.4
Electors	96.5	99.5	97.4	86.6	95.9
Government	97.6	98.6	99.2	97.8	98.6
Parliament	93.9	89.5	73.4	51.6	73.2
Pariahs	99.2	99.8	99.9	99.4	99.8
Inhabitants★	100.0	100.0	100.0	100.0	100.0
Royalty★	100.0	100.0	100.0	100.0	100.0

★Single category, therefore 100 percent reliable by definition. "Other" excluded from block models.

Members of Blocks:
Interest: farmers, firm, friendly society, interest, procession, society
Church: Catholics, church, Protestants
Workers: blacklegs, laborers, weavers, workers
Trade: masters, trade
Crowd: crowd, mob, numbers, persons, someone
Constables: constables, gamekeepers, militia, New Police, sheriff
Repressive: police, troops
Locals: churchwardens, clergy, committee, local officials, mayor, opponents, parishioners, party, select vestry, supporters, wardmote
Officials: aldermen, common council, judge, official
Electors: deputation, electors, freeholders
Government: gentlemen, government, ministers, nobles
Parliament: House of Commons, House of Lords, MP, Parliament
Pariahs: hunters, Irish, poor, prisoners, wrongdoers
Inhabitants: inhabitants
Royalty: royalty
Other: individual name, other

Table 9.5. Reliabilities of Actor Positions within "Parliament" Block, 1758–1834
(Based on three-step relations)

| Actor | Southeast England | | | | Other Britain | | Total |
	1758–1801	1807–1820	1828–1831	1832–1834	1828–1831	1832–1834	1758–1834
House of Lords	.954	.884	.977	.138	.960	.282	.823
MP	.972	.993	.845	.971	.923	.947	.917
Parliament	.974	.828	.400	.764	.814	.834	.606
House of Commons	.922	.977	.725	.830	.825	.866	.896
Total	93.94	89.48	73.37	51.56	79.67	56.04	73.20

TIMING

In two distinct senses of the word, parliamentarization entailed a profound alteration in contention's timing. First, ordinary people moved away from forms of action that often accomplished their objectives in the very course of claim making toward other forms of action having peculiar properties:

1. they could almost never, even in principle, accomplish their proclaimed objectives in the short run;
2. they depended for effectiveness on extensive anticipation, cumulation, and coordination of efforts by multiple actors, often substantially removed from one another in time and space.

Eighteenth-century shaming performances such as donkeying and Rough Music, for example, often drove a nonconforming worker out of his trade or broke up a disapproved sexual liaison almost immediately. Although they usually sprang from informal consultation, rumor, and strategic planning by local organizers, furthermore, they drew heavily on established local routines of assembly and circulation.

Public meetings, authorized assemblies, associational marches, demonstrations, and similar actions, in contrast, displayed shared support for demands, complaints, programs, and persons, but required intensive prior organizing, involved skilled political entrepreneurs, frequently depended on clandestine negotiation with police or other power holders, and rarely had any hope of achieving their aims in a single action. As paraparliamentary actions, indeed, they conveyed news not so much about what people were doing now as about what they might do if Parliament did not behave properly—how the electors among them might vote, how they might block governmental action, how they might support the government's enemies' action, and, at the extreme, how they might even rise in rebellion. All this meant an enormous expansion and forward movement of contenders' time horizons.

Timing's second alteration concerned relationships between claim making and parliamentary activity. During the nineteenth century, both contentious issues and the actual periodicity of collective claim making came to depend much more closely on rhythms of parliamentary elections and decision making. Political entrepreneurs became adept at coordinating public campaigns of support or disapproval with parliamentary consideration of bills concerning such matters as the slave trade, rights of religious minorities, workers' associations, and parliamentary reform. By the 1830s, these campaigns had crystallized into social movements, with their meetings, marches, demonstrations, slogans, banners, colors, pamphlets, and special-interest associations orbiting around one major issue at a time. Parliamentary elections, furthermore, increasingly attracted active expressions of support and opposition from broad segments of the nonvoting public— support and opposition often linked to social-movement issues such as workers' rights and parliamentary reform.

We can see a blurred reflection of this increasing temporal coordination in Table 9.6, which relates the timing of different sorts of CGs to presence/absence of elections and parliamentary sessions in a given month. It presents mean monthly frequencies of events by broad category according to whether in a given month (a) Parliament sat for at least one day and (b) an election campaign was under way, as indicated by the presence of at least one CG the major issue of which concerned an election. (In general, election campaigns took place when Parliament was not in session, but Parliament could recess and a campaign could begin in the same month.) Using eta squared as a test of mean differences, the table shows that on the whole differences between months of parliamentary sessions or electoral campaigns and other months increased substantially after 1800, more substantially for various sorts of public meeting. Before 1832, even violent CGs occurred more frequently in months of parliamentary activity; that relationship reversed in 1832–1834. The connection between parliamentary activity and associational meetings intensified in 1828–1831, when the issues of Catholic emancipation and parliamentary reform brought out such organizational behemoths as the Catholic Association, the Anti-Catholic Brunswick Clubs, and the Metropolitan Political Union.

Throughout our period, authorized assemblies such as vestry meetings and wardmotes played important parts in claim making. Yet they became much more frequent: from two or so per month in southeast England during 1758–1801 to twenty or so per month in 1832–1834. After 1800,

Table 9.6. Monthly Mean Frequencies of Selected Types of Event by Presence or Absence of Elections and Parliamentary Sessions, 1758–1801

Type of Event	Period	No Election or Parliament	No Parliament but Election	No Election but Parliament	Both Election and Parliament	Eta Squared
Violent	1758–1801	2.30	1.94	0.60	3.83	.01
	1807–1820	0.78	1.48	1.33	1.75	.03
	1828–1831	2.67	4.59	4.67	10.00	.07
	1832–1834	5.63	4.15	3.20	2.30	.25★
	Total	2.59	2.42	2.50	5.55	.03
Association meeting	1758–1801	0.03	0.25	0.00	0.50	.07
	1807–1820	0.78	1.28	1.17	2.50	.09
	1828–1831	1.58	6.35	2.67	11.85	.22★★
	1832–1834	4.00	4.62	3.40	4.70	.03
	Total	1.00	1.76	1.82	6.48	.14★★
Authorized assembly	1758–1801	0.87	1.53	2.60	3.00	.03
	1807–1820	7.00	5.38	8.83	23.75	.20★
	1828–1831	4.25	11.47	10.83	17.46	.07
	1832–1834	15.88	17.69	37.00	20.20	.16
	Total	4.53	5.43	14.36	16.42	.11★★
Other meeting	1758–1801	0.07	0.19	0.00	0.17	.03
	1807–1820	0.67	1.83	1.79	4.75	.23★★
	1828–1831	4.17	8.65	8.50	10.62	.11
	1832–1834	2.50	4.31	16.60	5.80	.41★★
	Total	1.32	2.13	6.59	6.55	.14★★

★$p < .05.$ ★★$p < .01.$

Note: Table data reflect answers to questions: (1) Did at least one CG this month involve an electoral campaign? (2) Did Parliament sit at least one day this month?

they also concentrated increasingly in periods of parliamentary activity. Similarly, the deliberately called single-issue public meeting culminating in some form of message to Parliament, government, or king not only multiplied after 1800, but also adhered much more closely to parliamentary activity. We see taking shape the dialogue between linked, planned local gatherings publicizing positions on public issues and the decision making of Parliament itself.

RAMIFICATIONS AND IMPLICATIONS

Two analytically separable but empirically interdependent streams of causes promoted parliamentarization. One consisted of transformations in the British state and economy, the other of mutations within the organization of claim making. On the side of state and economy, increases in the agrarian power of landlords, rapid capitalization of manufacturing, and intensification of large-scale commerce nationalized economic interests, while within the state an enormous expansion of military activity—especially from the 1790s through 1815—increased the political salience of parliament's tax-authorizing powers, hence the relative weight of parliament as compared with king, ministers, and their clients. (That parliament continued disproportionately to represent the landed interest does not gainsay the organizational shift in political decision making forwarded by the state's fiscal expansion.) Figure 5 summarizes one feature of those large changes: dramatic increases in governmental expenditure on military activity with the Seven Years' War, the American Wars, wars of the French Revolution, and especially the Napoleonic Wars, accompanied by a long-term rise in debt and expenditure on civil government, followed in peacetime not by a major contraction but by a much higher level of total governmental expenditure; a much larger central government, increasingly dominated by Parliament, emerged during those years of war. The correspondence between Figure 5 (governmental expenditure) and Figure 1 (claims on parliament) is striking.

In a context of capitalization and state expansion, however, the cumu-

Figure 9.5.   Government Budgets, 1750–1840
           (Deflated values)

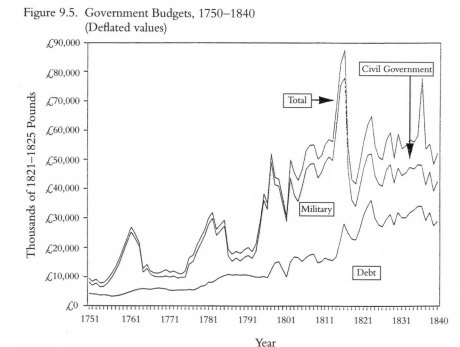

Year

lative history of contention itself promoted parliamentarization.[9] From much earlier than 1750, ordinary people's rights, opportunities, and incentives for contention depended on parliamentary writ in the form of guarantees for assembly, association, and petition within limits set by such legislation as the Riot Act and Vagrancy Act. Protected legal institutions such as parish governments, religious congregations, and ratepaying bodies likewise contained, but also authorized, public claim making. Elections— likewise protected occasions for public assembly—increasingly gave even nonvoters opportunities to voice support or opposition for governmental actions and personnel.

As of the 1750s, wealthy and powerful citizens enjoyed the privilege of forming nonreligious special-interest associations, a privilege generally denied to workers and other ordinary people. But between the 1750s and the 1830s, a double movement occurred: (1) privileged opponents of the government such as John Wilkes and Lord George Gordon sought allies and supporters among the less privileged and promoted associational life among them, then governmental defenders (e.g., antirevolutionaries of the 1790s) took up similar strategies to counter the dissidents; and (2) in the course of struggles with authorities and power holders, ordinary people and reformist-to-radical political entrepreneurs made a series of innovations in claim making that eventually cumulated into creation of the mass meeting, the popular political association, the petition march, the demonstration, and a series of related forms that had not existed in the 1750s—at least not in anything like their nineteenth-century versions. These forms of action connected ordinary people much more directly to the national government and to Parliament.

Parliamentarization describes a net movement, not an irreversible unilinear trend. The Swing Rebellion of 1830, for example, temporarily moved claim making away from Parliament and the national government as southeastern England's landless laborers attacked large farmers and local power holders in an attempt to defend themselves against declining job security and income. The rebellion only ended, nevertheless, when the government sent troops to quell rural workers. In 1831 and 1832, furthermore, Parliament acted to illegalize the sequestering of farmers that had occurred during Swing and to make the general populations of local areas collectively responsible for damages due to machine breaking. Thus even a nonparliamentary campaign of claim making eventually involved Parliament.

Parliamentarization of contention involved little legislation and even less constitutional change. It chiefly entailed judicial and practical accommodations on the side of authorities, organizational and tactical innovations on the part of popular claim makers. Yet it did lead past some legislative landmarks: abolition of the Combination Acts (1824 and 1825), repeal of the Test and Corporation Acts (1828), passage of Catholic emancipation (1829) and, incomparably, the Reform Act of 1832. These parliamentary actions served as both causes and effects: facilitating new relations between segments of the general population and Parliament, but also responding in part to augmented popular pressure on Parliament and the government.

British contention's parliamentarization joined with and facilitated a number of other changes in popular politics: generalization of mass associations as the basis of claim making; parallel establishment of national trade unions coordinating both local contention and demands on the government; formation of durable, election-mongering political parties; routinization of electoral campaigning on the issues rather than simply in terms of candidates' personal qualities; expansion of political reporting in the national press; creation of social movements as ways of organizing pressure on the government; and demands for popular sovereignty, instead of indirect or virtual representation.

These conjoined changes help explain one of the great ironies of British history between the 1750s and the 1830s: that the government's very effort to block infringement of Parliament's privilege as sole voice of national will generated antiparliamentary and paraparliamentary action in the form of popular attempts to establish a Mass Platform, a National Convention, nationwide associations, and simultaneous meetings throughout the land. They also help explain the anomaly of Chartism, a mass workers' movement, the demands of which consisted not of directly economic changes but entirely of further parliamentary reform: manhood suffrage, salaries and no property qualifications for MPs, annual elections, secret ballots, equal electoral districts. In short, parliamentarization constituted one element of expanded demands for democratic rule and actually forwarded democratic rule in some respects.

Parliamentarization did not spell unmitigated gain for all popular interests. In moving toward claims on Parliament, ordinary people abandoned a whole array of claim-making means that had produced substantial results in the short run and on the local scale; price-fixing seizures of grain, public shaming of workers who accepted less than the going wage, direct attacks on poorhouses, and similar enforcing actions accomplished their objectives in many cases. Social-movement tactics, in contrast, always depended on cumulation from action to action and place to place; required difficult planning, coordination, entrepreneurship, and anticipatory negotiation with authorities; frequently failed; and, even when successful, often demanded years of sustained effort.

Parliamentary contention, furthermore, disadvantaged clients in patronage chains, workers in localized crafts, and people whose welfare depended on community moral pressure. Landless laborers, for example, lost out badly until their numbers started dwindling and their successors began forming national unions during the later nineteenth century. The Poor Law of 1834—direct fruit of parliamentarization and parliamentary reform—greatly curtailed the claims of village paupers, including the seasonally unemployed. No one should confuse parliamentarization with the advent of justice and democracy.

In Great Britain, nevertheless, parliamentarization greatly increased the involvement of ordinary people in national politics. It augmented their collective influence over the national government as well. Remember the elements of parliamentarization: increases in the frequency with which

1. Parliament became the object of ordinary people's contention;
2. parliamentary action incited ordinary people's claim making, whether directed to Parliament or elsewhere;
3. issues currently being considered by Parliament became more central to popular contention;
4. connections with Parliament became more central in a wide range of claim making.

As we have seen, all of these changes occurred in Great Britain between the 1750s and the 1830s, accelerating dramatically during the years of intense war with France. Together, they accomplished a significant transformation of popular politics.

Can we generalize British experience in these regards? No and yes. Only to the extent that initial conditions and environing histories resemble those prevailing in eighteenth- and nineteenth-century Great Britain can we reasonably expect parliamentarization elsewhere to parallel the British path. But the causal processes at work in Great Britain operate very generally. Everywhere changes in the character and extent of state power, alterations of economic organization, and the cumulative history of claim making itself interact to produce shifts in relations between citizens and states.

Consider again the implications of parliamentarization for democracy, conceived of as (1) broad citizenship, (2) relatively equal citizenship, (3) binding consultation of citizens with respect to state policies and personnel, and (4) protection of citizens, especially members of minorities, from arbitrary state action. Speaking only of the national scale, parliamentarization promoted each of the four democratic elements. It broadened the category of people who had publicly recognized rights and obligations vis-à-vis agents of the state—that is, who exercised citizenship. It effected a mild equalization of those rights, although the Reform Bill's exclusion of most workers and all women from the vote certainly limited equality. It increased the extent and influence of popular consultation on Parliament and the national executive not only through elections and contact with MPs, but also through social movements and the routine operation of special-interest associations. With regard to assembly and association, at least, it increased the protection of citizens, including religious minorities, against arbitrary deprivation of their rights. Parliamentarization did important democratic work in Great Britain.

Still, in the world at large, democracy rests on other conditions—for example, subordination of armed forces to civilian rule—that by no means result reliably from the establishment of parliamentary institutions or the involvement of ordinary people in them. Many an election-holding military regime has proved otherwise. Parliamentarization, furthermore, has occurred in many other ways than the intersection of state expansion, capitalization, and popular struggle that characterized eighteenth- and nineteenth-century Great Britain. During the same period, Americans created parliamentary institutions and popular involvement in them through revolutionary seizure or circumvention of consultative councils designed for colonial rule, while French revolutionaries wrought the very different Estates General into something like a parliament and used a vast web of committees and clubs to connect ordinary people with it. In multiple regions of Western and Central Europe, varying coalitions of insurrectionary bourgeois and workers seized power from existing rulers in 1848, then installed sudden, if generally temporary, parliamentary representation and popular participation. After the Ottoman Empire's disintegration in World War I, Kemal Ataturk and his party installed Western-style institutions and enforced popular involvement in them from the top down. Following World War II, as European colonies became independent, they generally created the forms of democratic participation, including parliaments and widespread suffrage, only to see them give way to military and/or one-party regimes. These diverse experiences gainsay any idea of a single path to parliamentarization, or of a necessary connection with democracy.

Yet diversity makes its point. For in all these cases and more, the *relation* between parliamentary institutions and the expansion of popular participation in national politics defines the possibilities for democracy. Where popular struggle and hard bargaining loomed larger, it seems, democracy had a greater chance. In any case, the diverse experiences of parliamentarization open the way to a promising comparative inquiry. To ask how and why parliamentarization occurred in a particular national setting takes us to the heart of democratic possibilities.

NOTES

Both the Workshop on Language, Culture, and Social Structure (Columbia University) and the Proseminar on Political Mobilization and Conflict (New School for Social Research) provided searching critiques of earlier drafts. I am especially grateful for criticism and editorial advice to Robert Franzosi, Dan Friel, Jeff Goodwin, Perry Grossman, Jason Kaufman, John Mohr, Tony Pereira, Harrison White, and Viviana Zelizer.

   1. Alexis de Tocqueville *Journeys to England and Ireland,* J. P. Mayer, ed. (London: Faber & Faber, 1958), p. 109; italics in original.

   2. Peter J. Stanlis, ed., *Edmund Burke: Selected Writings and Speeches* (Garden City, NY: Doubleday Anchor, 1963); see also Conor Cruise O'Brien, *The Great Melody: A Thematic Biography and Commented Anthology of Edmund Burke* (Chicago: University of Chicago Press, 1992).

   3. Charles Tilly, "Democracy Is a Lake," in George Reid Andrews and Herrick Chapman, eds., *The Social Construction of Democracy* (New York: New York University Press, and London: Macmillan, 1995), pp. 365–387.

   4. See, for example, Matti Alestalo and Stein Kuhnle, "The Scandinavian Route: Economic, Social, and Political Developments in Denmark, Finland, Norway, and Sweden," Research Report no. 31, Research Group for Comparative Sociology, University of Helsinki, 1984; Gunnar Artéus, Ulf Olsson, and Kerstin Stromberg-Back, "The Influence of the Armed Forces on the Transformation of Society in Sweden, 1600–1945," *Kungl. Krigsvetenskaps akademius Bihafte—Militarhistorisk Tidskrift* (1981), pp. 133–144; Klaus-Richard Böhme, "Schwedische Finanzbürokratie und Kriegsführung 1611 bis 1721," in Goran Rystad, ed., *Europe and Scandinavia: Aspects of the Process of Integration in the 17th Century* (Lund: Esselte Studium, 1983); Helga Hernes, "Scandinavian Citizenship," *Acta Sociologica* 31 (1988): 199–215; Eiko Ikegami and Charles Tilly, "State Formation and Contention in Japan and France," in James L. McClain, John M. Merriman, and Ugawa Kaoru, eds., *Edo and Paris: Urban Life and the State in the Early Modern Era* (Ithaca, NY: Cornell University Press, 1994), pp. 429–454; Jan Lindegren, "The Swedish 'Military State,' 1560–1720," *Scandinavian Journal of History* 10 (1985): 305–336; Sven Lundqvist, *Folkrörelserna i det svenska samhället, 1850–1920* (Stockholm: Almqvist & Wiksell, 1977); Sven A. Nilsson, "Imperial Sweden: Nation-Building, War, and Social Change," in Sven A. Nilsson et al., *The Age of New Sweden* (Stockholm: Livrustkammaren, 1988); Bo Öhngren, *Folk i rörelse: Samhállsutveckling, flyttningsmonster och folkrörelser i Eskilstuna, 1870–1900* (Uppsala: Almqvist & Wicksell, 1974. Studia Historica Upsaliensia, 55); Dietrich Rueschemeyer, Evelyne Huber Stephens, and John D. Stephens, *Capitalist Development and Democracy* (Chicago: University of Chicago Press, 1992); Charles Tilly, "The Long Run of European State Formation," in Wim Blockmans and Jean-Philippe Genet, eds., *Visions sur le développement des Etats européens: Théories et historiographies de l'Etat moderne* (Rome: Ecole Française de Rome, 1993), pp. 137–150. For Great Britain, see John Brewer, *The Sinews of Power: War, Money, and the English State, 1688–1783* (New York: Knopf,

1989); Norman Chester, *The English Administrative System, 1780–1870* (Oxford: Clarendon Press, 1981); Linda Colley, *Britons: Forging the Nation, 1707–1837* (New Haven, CT: Yale University Press, 1992); James E. Cronin, *The Politics of State Expansion: War, State, and Society in Twentieth-Century Britain* (London: Routledge, 1991); Eric J. Evans, *The Forging of the Modern State: Early Industrial Britain, 1783–1870* (London: Longman, 1983); Michael Mann, *States, War, and Capitalism* (Oxford: Blackwell, 1988); Peter Mathias and Patrick O'Brien, "Taxation in Britain and France, 1715–1810: A Comparison of the Social and Economic Incidence of Taxes Collected for the Central Governments," *Journal of European Economic History* 5 (1976): 601–650; Patrick K. O'Brien, "The Political Economy of British Taxation, 1660–1815," *Economic History Review* 41 (1988): 1–32; Patrick K. O'Brien, "Power with Profit: The State and the Economy, 1688–1815," inaugural lecture, University of London, 1991; Lawrence Stone, ed., *An Imperial State at War: Britain from 1689 to 1815* (London: Routledge, 1994).

5. For technical descriptions and other analyses of the evidence, see R. A. Schweitzer, "A Study of Contentious Gatherings in Early Nineteenth-Century Great Britain," *Historical Methods* 12 (1979): 1–4; R. A. Schweitzer and Steven C. Simmons, "Interactive, Direct-Entry Approaches to Contentious Gathering Event Files," *Social Science History* 5 (1981): 317–342; Charles Tilly, *Popular Contention in Great Britain, 1758–1834* (Cambridge, MA: Harvard University Press, 1995); Charles Tilly, "Contentious Repertoires in Great Britain, 1758–1834," in Mark Traugott, ed., *Repertoires and Cycles of Collective Action* (Durham, NC: Duke University Press, 1995), pp. 15–42.

6. For detail on quality controls, see appendices to Tilly, *Popular Contention in Great Britain,* and technical reports listed there.

7. For example, R. A. Schweitzer and Charles Tilly, "How London and Its Conflicts Changed Shape, 1758–1834," *Historical Methods* 5 (1982): 67–77; Charles Tilly, "Repertoires of Contention in America and Britain," in Mayer N. Zald and John D. McCarthy, eds., *The Dynamics of Social Movements* (Cambridge, MA: Winthrop, 1979); "Proletarianization and Rural Collective Action in East Anglia and Elsewhere, 1500–1900," *Peasant Studies* 10 (1982): 5–34; "Britain Creates the Social Movement," in James Cronin and Jonathan Schneer, eds., *Social Conflict and the Political Order in Modern Britain* (London: Croom Helm, 1982); "Les origines du répertoire de l'action collective contemporaine en France et en Grande Bretagne," *Vingtième Siècle* 4 (1984): 89–108; "Social Movements, Old and New," in Louis Kriesberg, Bronislaw Misztal, and Janusz Mucha, eds., *Social Movements as a Factor of Change in the Contemporary World,* Research in Social Movements, Conflicts, and Change, vol. 10 (Greenwich, CT: JAI Press, 1982); "Réclamer Viva Voce," *Cultures et Conflits* 5 (1992): 109–126; "Social Movements as Historically Specific Clusters of Political Performances," *Berkeley Journal of Sociology* 38 (1993–1994); 1–30.

8. Stanley Wasserman and Katherine Faust, *Social Network Analysis: Methods and Applications* (Cambridge: Cambridge University Press, 1994), chaps. 9–10.

9. For detailed argument and evidence, see Tilly, *Popular Contention in Great Britain,* which does not, however, report the analyses of parliamentarization in this paper.

· Part Four ·

POPULATION PROCESSES

POPULATION AND PEDAGOGY IN FRANCE

THE CONTRIBUTION OF PHILIPPE ARIÈS

Disguised as demographic analyst and historiographical innovator, Philippe Ariès launched his own clandestine attack on modernism in the middle of the twentieth century. As a demographic analyst, he carried on a series of perceptive interpretations of typical French populations and their evolution from the eighteenth century onward: Parisians, miners of the northeast, villagers of Touraine, Bretons, southerners, dwellers in the Alps all paraded past his eyepiece. As a historiographical innovator, he provided a way of inserting demographic material directly into history. In 1946, that was a daring thing to do. Ariès also showed how family portraits, wardrobes, textbooks, and other antiquarian paraphernalia, long condemned to supply the comic relief for serious history, could become evidence of the deepest, longest transformations of social life.

Ariès's accomplishments as demographic analyst and historiographical innovator are real and influential. The general message that emerges from his work is nevertheless a moral one. He portrays the disappearance of a communal world in which people were satisfied to stay in their places and the rise of an egoistic world in which people sacrifice one another for social mobility, as effective emotional life shrinks to the scale of the nuclear family. In his *History of French Populations,* integrated communities lose their coherence as a consequence of rampant differentiation.[1] In *Centuries of Childhood,* there grows a conception of the family as an entity distinct from society, opposed to society, and seeking its own interests at the expense of society.[2] A new and separate conception of childhood appears as a by-product of that change. The argument stands nineteenth-century sociologists on their heads, for it portrays the family as the antithesis—not the essence—of *Gemeinschaft.* This important qualification aside, Ariès's view

This chapter was first published as "Population and Pedagogy in France," *History of Education Quarterly* 13 (Summer 1973): 113–128. Reprinted with permission.

coincides with the nineteenth-century apprehensions that brought the discipline of sociology into being: different forms of egoism have destroyed a coherent way of life; perhaps a science of society can help restore the coherence.

Does this sound unlike the Ariès you remember? Well, listen to a fragment of the analysis of three mining villages in the Pas-de-Calais:

> So an industry succeeded in building up significant concentrations of people without resorting to immigration, thanks to its own natural development. There is an important requirement, however: that the population be strictly specialized in one occupation, one way of life, that a whole crowd of men, women and children commit themselves to the same tasks, the same schedules, the same joys and sorrows, the same climate. Only at that price is it possible to form a homogeneous setting which imposes its own traditions and holds individual wills in check. Then the collectivity behaves as an immovable block. Everyone accepts his condition resignedly without dreaming of leaving the area or the trade. Generations come one after another, resembling each other greatly, equally stable (absorbed, as they are, by the mine), equally fertile, unconscious of the opportunities available in the great outside world. That has probably been the situation of all industrial countries, at least at the beginning, so long as industrialization was rapid and massive, quickly dragging a considerable mass of workers into the same infernal round. That is what happened at the beginning of the industrial revolution. But the stability of the population and its fertility depend on the simplicity of the social group, and thence on its stability. If it becomes complicated, it loses its homogeneity, its fundamental unity; if external pressures disturb its equilibrium, it runs the risk of not maintaining itself. We are astonished by its fragility. Its human substance leaks through its cracks; the demographic balance changes. Or the escape occurs in space, and we have emigration, the break with the group and its geographic base; or the escape is from the occupation, and we have social climbing, *embourgeoisement,* occupational mobility.[3]

The closing words of *Centuries of Childhood* convey that same sad sense of history:

> Starting in the eighteenth century, people began defending themselves against a society whose constant intercourse had hitherto been a source of education, reputation and wealth. Henceforth a fundamental movement would destroy the old connections between masters and servants, great and small, friends or clients. It was a movement which was sometimes retarded by the inertia of geographical or social isolation. It would be quicker in Paris than in other towns, quicker in the middle classes

than in the lower classes. Everywhere it reinforced private life at the expense of neighborly relationships, friendships, and traditional contacts. The history of modern manners can be reduced in part to this long effort to break away from others, to escape from a society whose pressure had become unbearable. The house lost the public character which it had in certain cases in the seventeenth century, in favour of the club and the cafe, which in their turn have become less crowded. Professional and family life have stifled that other activity which once invaded the whole of life: the activity of social relations.[4]

Narrow interests, in other words, triumph over the common weal.

Neither the despair nor the conservatism of Ariès's general analyses, to be sure, disqualify them as scholarly contributions. Nevertheless, the implicit moral argument matters. It fits the conventional wisdom concerning the moral consequences of urbanization and industrialization. It adds to the persuasiveness of what would otherwise seem a risky and wrongheaded set of arguments.

EDUCATION, ARIÈS, AND SNYDERS

Before considering the evidence for Ariès's idea of a transformation of popular mentalities, and the alternatives to that idea, we might look at the educational side of the argument. Pedagogy does not figure prominently in the *History of French Populations.* The subject comes up in passing, in support of other arguments. It appears, for example, in the observation that "Rousseau's originality consists less in his system than in his application of the system to a tender age, a stage previously ignored by pedagogues who were only interested in the student, the grown-up student, and not the child."[5] In *Centuries of Childhood,* on the other hand, schools are one of the principal arenas for the action. There, pedagogical materials provide an important share of the evidence. There, as Georges Snyders says,

> Mr. Ariès attributes to the seventeenth century a very modern feeling about childhood, a delicate understanding of the youngest ages: the seventeenth-century family seems to him the focus of a "new affectivity" in which we recognize our own way of dealing with the child.[6]

Writings by educators and about education constitute an important part of the evidence Ariès offers in support of that idea. He does not, however, assign much *independent* significance to pedagogical arrangements. In his view, forms of teaching reflect the prevailing attitudes of the dominant classes.

There he parts company with someone like Snyders. Snyders argues that seventeenth-century education worked to isolate the child from a wicked, tempting world and to immerse the child in an artificial preservative of classical literature, rhetoric, and philosophy. Of course, Snyders also traces the pedagogical practice back to the spirit of the age. He portrays a shift in the predominant sentiments concerning the nature of society and the fate of the child: before, a sense of enveloping darkness from which heroic effort may save a few elite souls; after, a more inviting, manipulable world in which it is possible—at least for the bourgeoisie—to live and to acquire civic virtues.

The transformation of thought about schooling corresponds to this shift in general attitudes toward life and the child. Rousseau, then, provides a synthesis of the old and the new. Despite Snyders's emphasis on the ideological origins of pedagogical doctrine, he considers the practice itself to have had a significant impact on the lives of the students and teachers involved: "as if it were a role in the theater," Snyders says, "the child responds and plays out the part the others have begun to sketch for him."[7] With Rousseau, he therefore concludes that one could reshape social life by reforming education.

Hunt on Parenthood

Regardless of whether they consider pedagogical procedures to have some independent effect on the lives of children (and thence on the adults they become), most historians of French education and of French family life have attributed overriding importance to the Zeitgeist. Take David Hunt as one more example.[8] Hunt's main task is to check out the applicability of two rather different descriptive schemes—Ariès's and Erik Erikson's—to the realities of child care in the seventeenth century. He builds a fascinating structure out of fragile materials: a few journals, some memoirs, scattered literary sources. On the whole, he rules against Ariès's characterization of seventeenth-century elders as indifferent to the fates of very young children; he finds them anxious and demanding. On the whole, he rules for Erikson's developmental approach, despite significant reservations concerning the applicability of some of Erikson's stage formulations and concerning the generality of parental impulses to nurture their children. He does not make much effort to establish how much child care changed from the seventeenth century, or by what mechanisms. Toward the end of his analysis, in fact, he begins to suggest that the contemporary world is not only just as punishing to the young as it ever was, but that it is punishing in essentially the same ways, and for the same reasons.

Somewhere behind this durable condition is an enduring structure of power and repression. But in Hunt's own arguments, parents act as carriers of the general mentality of the time:

> Parents communicate with their newborn infants as carriers of a world view, almost as philosophers, who in handling the child instill in him some sense of the setting in which he is going to live, whether it is a good place or a bad one, whether he should hope for the best, or on the contrary adopt a stance of suspicion and mistrust. In the second phase, the parents speak as political animals, acting out of their sense that the community is (or is not) a just and well-ordered arena in which the individual is allowed to guard his integrity and self-respect. In the third phase, the relevant frame of reference is not the world (that is, the general milieu in which life unfolds), and not the community (a particular political, economic and social order), but is instead the household itself.[9]

Ariès had seen the whole society as shifting from a broad focus on the world to a narrow focus on the household. Hunt sees the individual child as making that transition. In rejecting Ariès, he denies that ontogeny recapitulates phylogeny.

Hunt's Eriksonian phases cover approximately the first seven years of life. In adopting the three-phase scheme, Hunt is mainly concerned to counter the notion of an undifferentiated childhood, sharply separate from adult life, likewise spanning those first seven years or so. Yet in order to make that point, he adopts (like other historians) a portrayal of parents as bearers of the Zeitgeist, as executors of the general will.

MENTALITIES

General wills, Zeitgeisten, and popular mentalities are always convenient explanations of social behavior, for they are practically irrefutable. They lend themselves readily to proof by definition. It is no doubt mean-spirited of me to suggest we look elsewhere for explanations of some of the phenomena with which Ariès, Snyders, and Hunt are dealing. The mean spirit will out. It tells me that Ariès began his work extremely well, but abandoned the demographic thread of the argument just as it was beginning to lead somewhere interesting.

At one point, Ariès almost reversed the relationship between mentalities and family organization. In an essay on the spread of contraceptive practices, he argued that

> The demographic importance of contraception only began with its adoption by the family, when it became an instrument of family policy. We must therefore seek its true explanation in the history of the family. The appearance in the sixteenth and seventeenth centuries of a Malthusian mentality coincided, after an understandable lag, with a profound transformation of family structure which prepared the arrival of the modern family in the eighteenth century.[10]

During this transformation, according to Ariès, parents began to worry about the impact of the child's fate on the fate of the whole family and to respond to that worry by searching for mobility opportunities, adopting an instrumental approach to schooling, restricting births, and concentrating the available capital on fewer offspring. To be sure, Ariès argues that a whole new way of looking at the family, at children, and at education developed from these circumstances; mentalities changed. Yet this version of the argument gives unaccustomed prominence to the opportunities and costs confronting the family, treats demographic changes as a possible response to changing opportunities and costs, and places considerable limits on the autonomous importance of mentalities themselves.

A Demographic Alternative

Instead of returning to the exegesis of Ariès or his successors, let me move at once to the demographic alternatives that Ariès's own discussion uncovers. Instead of analyzing popular mentalities, let us concentrate on family strategies. Let us imagine, for the sake of argument, that general attitudes toward children have not changed much, that the desire of parents to have offspring who will honor, sustain, and finally succeed them has endured for centuries, but that the conditions under which the desire can be satisfied have changed considerably.

To be more concrete, consider the possibility that European parents have for centuries tried to act so as to have at least one child who would, in the parents' declining years, be both somewhat better off than the parents were at that age and obliged to transfer to the parents some of the return from that relative well-being. If that were the case, changes in the cost of a child's social mobility would significantly affect parental behavior without any necessary change in attitudes. So would changes in the arrangements available for enforcing obligations. So would changes in the likelihood that any particular child would survive to adulthood.

The last possibility is the one I want to grasp right now: that the declining mortality of infants and children significantly affected the predominant strategies of European parents. I suggest that a major part of the change in orientation to children that others have attributed to the spread of a "modern" mentality occurred without any particular shift in mentality at all; it resulted from two tough realities of increasing life expectancy—first, that a high-fertility strategy stopped being a sensible way to assure a family's survival; second, that an investment of attention, love, and money in a young child began to have a reasonable chance of return for the parents and for the family as a whole.

The average seventeenth-century European didn't live very long. Over Western Europe as a whole, expectation of life at birth was then quite possibly less than thirty years. That compares with something over seventy years today. But remember what a large part the death rates of infants and children play in that statistic. In the model life table representing female life expectancy at birth of thirty, the average woman who has managed to survive to the age of twenty has another thirty-four years to live; for life expectancy at birth of forty, the figure for the twenty-year-old is thirty-nine; for seventy at birth, the figure at age twenty is still only fifty-three more years. When mortality declines, the great gains obviously come not after twenty, but in the first years of life.

Anyone who dips into Old Regime statistics of child mortality for the first time is likely to be appalled. In the village of Challain, between Angers and Nantes, from 1670 to 1700, François Lebrun calculates that 18 percent of the children born died in the first month, 35 percent in the first year, 53 percent before the age of twenty; those proportions correspond roughly to an expectation of life at birth of twenty-five. In all of seventeenth-century Anjou, the proportions of children dying within a year of birth generally ran from a quarter to a third.[11] In today's France, the comparable figure is around 2 percent.

With high mortality, if it is important for a particular nuclear family to have survivors, yet adoption of other people's children is difficult or unacceptable, a low-fertility strategy runs a serious risk of destroying the family; the worst a high-fertility strategy can do is to increase the pressure of poverty on a family with many survivors. In Europe, even that eventuality could be minimized by the widespread arrangement of sending youngsters out to work and feed in households that were short of labor. Under these conditions, couples have many children, but only a few survive to adulthood. A major part of the resources invested in a child's preparation for adult performance is therefore wasted; the advantageous strategy is to spread a portion of the success-producing resources over many children more or less equally, to hoard a portion of the available resources, then to concentrate them on a child who has survived the vulnerable years, who seems likely to survive through the parents' old age, and who shows signs of adult competence. As life expectancy increases, the advantageous strategy turns sour: it leaves the household with a labor surplus, depletes the family capital, and destroys the possibility of investing enough in any one child to assure the family's success. *For the same objectives,* a strategy of limiting births, beginning preparation for adulthood early, and concentrating the available resources on the chances of one or two heirs becomes increasingly attractive, more and more sensible.

E. A. Wrigley has done some valuable, if hypothetical, calculations concerning the impact of mortality on family strategies.[12] He considers the situation in which it is important for the family to have an heir of a particular sex surviving the death of the parent of the same sex; that was ordinarily the situation of landholding peasants and commonly the situation of artisans who had a good deal of capital invested in their craft. Considering a strategy pointing toward male heirs (and making some simplifying assumptions), Wrigley takes up three model populations: one in which each child has a one-third chance of surviving until the death of the father, another in which each child has one chance in two of surviving until the death of the father, and still another in which the chances are two out of three. The life expectancies corresponding to these three possibilities depend on the characteristic ages of parents when their children are born, which in turn depend on the characteristic ages at marriage; where the mean age of the father at the child's birth is twenty-five, the three possibilities correspond roughly to life expectancies of twenty, thirty, and forty-five years.

If the population remains about the same size and if families act so that 60 percent of them have at least one male heir at the death of the father, the median number of children ever born will be two or three in the low-mortality case, four in the medium-mortality case, and seven in the high-mortality case. Under conditions of high mortality, then, even a median of seven births per family will leave two-fifths of the families without male survivors. Whatever the prevailing combination of egoism, contraceptive knowledge, or familistic mentality, the pressure toward high fertility in such a system is very strong.

What I have called the low-mortality case is not really very low, since it implies infant mortality on the order of 15 percent. In that case, nevertheless, a seven-child strategy would be suicidal—or, better, familicidal. Somewhere around an expectation of life at birth of forty, Wrigley's hypothetical population crosses a threshold: below the threshold, strong pressures for fertility, high risk that an investment in any particular youngster will be lost; above the threshold, strong pressures against fertility, increasing chances of payoff from a concentrated investment in the success of one child. All this without any necessary change in the way people in general value family life or measure success.

FRENCH EXPERIENCE WITH DEATH

What was the actual course of mortality in France? Emanuel Etienne Duvillard's life table for eighteenth-century France yields a life expectancy of about twenty-eight.[13] Life expectancy crossed the threshold of forty around 1850, reached forty-five shortly before the end of the century, was up to sixty-six by 1950, is over seventy today. Unfortunately, Duvillard's table can't be trusted very far, not enough local and regional studies have been completed to fill in anything like a continuous national record for the seventeenth and eighteenth centuries, and, in any case, variation by region and by class was great enough to make national totals misleading. On the basis of rich but still fragmentary evidence, the current consensus among French demographic historians[14] has mortality declining somewhat during the eighteenth century, largely because of the diminishing impact of great crises of famine and disease, then declining more rapidly and irreversibly during the nineteenth century, especially after 1870.

If this calendar were to provide any understanding of the changes in family behavior and pedagogy described by Ariès and Snyders, we would have to do some shuffling of dates. The decisive decline in mortality comes rather late to have produced a general change in orientations toward children during the eighteenth century—unless, of course, the change only started in the eighteenth century and did not generalize until the nineteenth.

Edging even farther out on my limb, I suggest two related possibilities: (1) that whatever substantial changes in the treatment of children occurred before the nineteenth century took place within the bourgeoisie, which experienced the decline of mortality earlier than the rest of the population; (2) that the shift toward a small-family mobility strategy only generalized as life expectancy improved for the bulk of the population during the nineteenth century.

Unfortunately, this particular limb shakes when you put your weight on it. If the overall trends in fertility, family structure, child care, and pedagogy are uncertain before 1800, the *differentials* are almost guesswork. That is a pity, since in principle abundant evidence is available, at least on the demographic side of the question.

On the basis of such analyses as Louis Henry's demographic reconstruction of Genevan bourgeois families, one can reasonably argue that the complex of low mortality, birth control, and investment in education as a means to children's success spread through the bourgeoisie long before it affected the bulk of the population. Henry sees the bourgeoisie's change in demographic behavior as a fairly direct response to population pressure:

> it appears that the ruling class was under strong demographic pressure and that it therefore had a powerful incentive for the adoption of restraint. The strong pressure resulted from a seventeenth-century expansion which was much more rapid than that of Geneva as a whole; it produced a notable increase in emigration. At the same time, celibacy became more frequent and marriage later.[15]

The bourgeois of Geneva were, in fact, experiencing the consequences of declining mortality. Henry estimates life expectancy for fifty-year "generations" beginning in 1550 and ending in 1899 at roughly twenty-nine, thirty-two, thirty-six, forty-three, forty-eight, fifty-two, and sixty-three years.[16] By those calculations, life expectancy increased noticeably in every half century, and it more than doubled over 350 years.

The increase accelerated after 1650. The Genevan bourgeois crossed the hypothetical threshold of forty years not long after 1700. Henry finds his first indications of population control in the "generation" born from 1650 to 1699 and sees the following "generation" as the first one to be quite modern in its demographic behavior. These changes did, indeed, occur in the bourgeoisie well ahead of their appearance in the rest of the population. Working from genealogies alone, Henry can say nothing about child care or pedagogy. His analysis therefore provides some encouragement for the demographic portion of my speculation, but no evidence one way or another concerning the hypothetical links to the treatment of children.

SCHOOLING

Information about schooling likewise misses the precise mark, but runs in the right direction. Until early in the nineteenth century, schooling was nearly an elite monopoly in France. François de Dainville attributes the relatively high eighteenth-century enrollment of the secondary schools of

Chalons and Troyes to "the ambition of the inferior strata of the Third Estate to procure their children the Latin certificate which gave them access to minor public positions."[17] In most of France, the peasant majority remained outside the educational system. The northeastern corner of France, which was the most prosperous urban and industrial section of the country, also led in school enrollments, level of instruction, and literacy.

Although the French government began to encourage the founding of primary schools in the 1830s, it relied on the initiative of individual communes. Moreover, fully tax-supported schools were rare before the middle of the century and not general until the law of 1881. (Compulsory attendance arrived in 1882.) Primary school enrollments grew apace: around half a million at the end of the Revolution, near three million in 1840, rounding off at something over five million by the end of the century. The founding of boys' schools preceded the founding of girls' schools; female enrollments in primary schools only overtook male enrollments in the 1880s. As one might expect, the rural areas were the last to join the movement—and within the countryside, peasants held their children back longer than the petite bourgeoisie and artisans.[18] Although contemporaries were inclined to attribute that reluctance to peasant ignorance of the benefits of schooling, we should consider the possibility that they knew what they were doing. So long as there was room for their surviving offspring on the land, why *should* the peasants sacrifice the labor of their children to the school and take the chance that the children would leave the old folks stranded on the farm?

A VILLAGE

A good, old-fashioned antiquarian essay—Roger Thabault's *Mon village*[19]— offers a good deal of insight into the way the extension of schooling worked out on the ground. Thabault, himself a schoolteacher and then an educational official, simply traced the village of Mazières-en-Gâtine and its school through the nineteenth century. The demographic information he provides is simple, too simple to make possible any firm test of the link among declining mortality, changing family strategies, and pedagogy. At least the region is an appropriate one; according to Etienne van de Walle's calculations, life expectancy in the department of Deux-Sèvres began the nineteenth century at thirty-seven, crossed forty during the First Empire, hovered in the vicinity of forty-five until it began to rise again during the 1870s, reaching fifty-six in the first years of the twentieth century. The department's crude birthrate declined slowly from the beginning of the century until the 1850s, paused, then began an accelerated decline in the 1870s; the rate was not extraordinarily high—twenty-eight or twenty-nine—in 1800; it was a little under twenty-five at midcentury; by 1900, it had dropped to nineteen. In Mazières itself, if Thabault's raw figures are correct, the crude birthrate ran a little above the departmental average until the 1870s, when it plummeted: around thirty in the 1860s, fifteen in the 1880s, seven or eight at the turn of the twentieth century. To be sure, an important part of the drop was due to the departure of men and women of childbearing age. Nevertheless, the overall trends identify the 1870s as a crucial transition: crucial for the village, and crucial for the sort of argument I have been unfolding.

In the nineteenth century, Mazières-en-Gâtine had the usual traits of a bocage village: almost entirely devoted to agriculture, with much of the land owned by absentees. The labor force of 1841 consisted of 2 prosperous landowners, a doctor, a notary, a couple of clerks, a priest, a teacher, a tax collector, five gendarmes, twenty-two artisans, thirteen others in service trades and about 150 peasant households.[20] This peasant village responded to the new government policy by founding its first public school in 1833. Twenty years later, however, only 42 of the village's 174 eligible children were attending school. All but eight were boys, and those boys were drawn in tremendous disproportion from the families of tradesmen and artisans.

What is more, the farm boys ordinarily attended no more than a few months per year. Of this period, Thabault says:

> The respect for knowledge . . . . was not strong enough around 1850 to push the peasants to shake off their old habits, to give up the labor of their children, or to impose on them the necessary discipline, at the cost of paying constant attention to their performance.[21]

The school did not provide any useful skills beyond reading and writing. The one teacher led his pupils through rote memorization and recitation, and little else.

From 1850 to 1870, school enrollments moved up steadily from 40-odd to around 150. After 1870, and before the beginning of compulsory attendance, they shot up. At the same time, teaching shifted toward the preparation of written texts, severely corrected by the schoolmaster. Thabault explains the increased enrollments as the result of rising prosperity, greater geographic mobility, and increasing opportunity for the social mobility of ordinary people.

The only village youngsters to improve their condition in the decades before 1870 were those who had attended the school. Thabault suggests that their example, too, aroused interest in schooling. He relates the life of Pascal Chaignon, born to a poor peasant family in the 1860s. Pascal had gone to school, learned to read and write, worked a while as a hired hand, served in the army, gotten a job as mailman through the influence of a local landlord, married, and had one—just one—son. Pascal longed to send his son to secondary school so he could become a postal official. But that would require a scholarship. He approached the landlord, who might be able to influence the award. The landlord questioned whether an overeducated son "of the people" wouldn't simply become an idle failure. And Pascal Chaignon is supposed to have replied, "I don't know if I'll make a failure of him; but I sure hope to make him someone better than his father."[22]

One man and a half-remembered phrase don't add up to a social trend. The histories of Chaignon and Mazières-en-Gâtine do, however, illustrate the emergence of the complex of declining mortality, controlled fertility, orientation to schooling, and planning for social mobility. Thabault sums up his discussion of fertility control neatly:

> "Your 20-sous pieces have just become 10 sous," said an old peasant to his grandson at the birth of a second child. Because one was a landowner one sought to avoid breaking up the property. Because one believed in a better future for the family, one calculated; one increased the family's chances for social mobility by limiting the number of children. The families of average prosperity, without reserves of property or money, could send them to boarding school; they couldn't have done that if they had many children. Finally, customs having changed, the poorest were ashamed to hire out their children when they were very young; they sent the children to school up to thirteen years of age. And they hesitated to appropriate the children's wages, as had once been the usual arrangement.[23]

In Thabault's mind, new opportunities outside played the major part in wreaking this transformation. But it followed hard on the village's arrival at the point where natural increase, the surplus of births over deaths, began to swell the local population. Natural increase accelerated because the death rate fell much faster than the birthrate. The people of Mazières-en-Gâtine behaved more or less as they should have, if declining mortality builds up the pressure for a change in family strategy.

CONCLUSIONS AND POSSIBILITIES

To tell the truth, Thabault's marvelous portrait doesn't resolve our question; it complicates things. The experience of Mazières lends itself, not to two, but to four alternative interpretations. perhaps modern mentalities appeared first and the changes in family strategy and in pedagogy followed. Perhaps increasing life expectancy had the sort of autonomous effect I have suggested. Perhaps—and this is the new element suggested by Thabault—the alteration of the structure of opportunities for young people was the crucial element. Finally, perhaps mentalities, demographic conditions, and opportunities changed interdependently, jointly producing new ways of treating children.

Does that leave us in an impasse? Not quite. First, if we could look carefully at many places like Mazières, the relative timing of the different changes we have been reviewing would give us an idea of their role: do we consistently get evidence of changes in ideas about childhood before any substantial improvement in life expectancy occurs? Do school enrollments and the quality of pedagogy respond rapidly to outside changes in opportunity?

Second, we can make the differentials within the population work for us. Do class differences in actual treatment of children correspond to class differences in "modernism" as established by other evidence? What about differences by region, type of community, religious affiliation? [The study of male/female differences might be especially rewarding, since we have a reasonable chance of locating populations, within which the mobility opportunities for boys and girls are changing rapidly, but at different rates.] If the sex ratios of school enrollments shift in cadence with the changes in opportunities, for example, we will be inclined to assign autonomous importance to opportunity itself.

Both the study of fluctuations over time and the inspection of differentials, however, challenge out technical expertise. I see two great challenges.

1. the development of truly independent evidence concerning attitudes toward children, demographic change, shifts in opportunities, schooling and pedagogical practices;
2. establishing the connection between aggregate changes and changes in the experiences of individuals and particular families.

From the material I have reviewed here, it appears that getting reliable, independent evidence on any one of the several factors requires long, hard digging in stubborn soil. In the cases of demographic changes, shifts in opportunities, and extent of schooling, we have a good idea of the necessary materials and procedures. With respect to attitudes toward children and the actual form or content of pedagogy, we are not so fortunate. I have never been sure how to gather independent evidence on attitudes; we might at least try to systematize the sort of iconographic and textual analysis to which Ariès opened the way. I leave the professional historians of education to determine whether the documents and artifacts left behind by actual teaching (as opposed to treatises and obiter dicta thereon) are rich enough and evocative enough to make possible the detection of fine changes in practice. My ignorant guess is that it will turn out as it has in such matters as fertility and social mobility: the materials are there, but will only yield to a rare combination of imagination, technique, and *Sitzfleisch*.

The connection between the aggregate and the individual has troubled historians, sociologists, and economists for a long time. We have developed some standard ways of filling in the connection, none of them quite satisfactory, which I won't review here.[24] The study of population and pedagogy has an opportunity that, so far as I know, no one has pursued seriously. That is the possibility of collective psychohistory.

Collective history has had a great impact in the historical study of demographic change, social mobility, political behavior, and several related subjects. It consists of collecting standard information concerning considerable numbers of events, individuals, or social units selected according to some uniform criterion, then aggregating those individual observations into collective outcomes: changing birthrates, voting patterns, rises or falls of the gentry, and so on.[25] So far, pyschohistorians have preferred either to concentrate on single individuals or to refer to whole populations as if they were undergoing the same individual experience. They have eschewed collective history.

I'm not sure why. There is no obvious reason why one could not, for example, take up the ideas about the modern German experience recently sketched by Peter Loewenberg[26] and find out, birth cohort by birth cohort, how many individuals (and who) experienced the loss of their fathers during World War I, unemployment afterward, and then chose the Nazis over the Communists. No obvious reason except the fact that it would be hard work.

In the study of population and pedagogy, wouldn't it be possible to accumulate individual dossiers on the Pascal Chaignons of the world? Couldn't we mark off their lives into phases identified by birth, the arrival of other children, deaths of siblings and parents, entry into school, leaving school, travel, boarding out with other families, employment, marriage, parenthood, loss of children, placement of other children, retirement, death? Why not group that information into the very Eriksonian phases proposed by David Hunt? At the moment, historians of the family in Europe and America are edging in that direction.[27] Isn't the same thing possible with teachers and schools? With exposure to the materials of education themselves?

With the collective psychohistorical approach, some of the questions raised by Philippe Ariès, Georges Snyders, and David Hunt would remain unanswered. Ordinary life histories would not yield much direct information on changes in deeply held attitudes; life histories would only display their results. They would, however, set the limits within which attitudinal explanations would have to work.

That outcome would, I think, be an appropriate reply and tribute to the Philippe Ariès who began it all: a reply, because it would permit us to comment cogently on the idea that a decay of the old solidarity led to the limitation of births, a quest for privacy, a new conception of childhood, a demand for schooling; a tribute, because it was Ariès, after all, who showed us that the broad traits of civilization and the fine details of demography depend intimately on each other.

NOTES

I am grateful to Priscilla Cheever and Leila Al-Imad for research assistance, and to Joan Lind, Penni Snyder, and Louise Tilly for suggestions concerning the presentation of the argument. Different segments of the research beneath this paper received support from National Science Foundation grant GS-2674, from a Faculty Research grant of the Rackham School of Graduate Studies, University of Michigan, and from the Mathematical Social Science Board. I offer these comments as a sympathetic outsider's proposals for future inquiry. The text is essentially as given in February 1973 at the annual meeting of American Educational Research Association, New Orleans.

1. Philippe Ariès, *Histoire des populations françaises et de leurs attitudes devant la vie depuis le XVIIIᵉ siècle,* 2nd ed. (Paris: Le Seuil,1971).

2. Philippe Ariès, *Centuries of Childhood: A Social History of Family Life* (New York: Vintage, 1962).

3. Ariès, *Histoire des populations,* pp. 116–117.

4. Ariès, *Centuries of Childhood,* pp. 406–407.

5. Ariès, *Histoire des populations,* p. 323.

6. Georges Snyders, *La pedagogie en France aux XVIIIᵉ et XVIIIᵉ siècles* (Paris: Presses Universitaires de France, 1965), p. 9.

7. Ibid., p. 437.

8. David Hunt, *Parents and Children in History: The Psychology of Family Life in Early Modern France* (New York: Basic Books, 1970).

9. Ibid., pp. 193–194.

10. Philippe Ariès, "Interprétation pour une histoire des mentalités," in Hélène Bergues, ed., *La prévention des naissances dans la famille* (Paris: Presses Universitaires de France, 1960), pp. 311–327.

11. François Lebrun, *Les hommes et la mort en Anjou aux XVIIe et XVIIe siècles* (Paris: Mouton, 1971).

12. E. A. Wrigley, "Fertility Strategy for the Individual and the Group," in Charles Tilly, ed., *Historical Studies of Changing Fertility* (New Jersey: Princeton University Press, 1978). See also E. A. Wrigley, *Population and History* (New York: McGraw Hill, 1969).

13. Jean Bourgeois-Pichat, "Evolution générale de la population française depuis le XVIIIe siècle," *Population* 6 (1951): 635–663.

14. See Marcel Reinhard, André Armengaud, and Jacques Dupâquier, *Histoire générale de la population mondiale* (Paris: Montchrestien, 1968); P. Guillaume and J. P. Poussou, *Démographie historique* (Paris: Armand Colin, 1970).

15. Louis Henry, "L'Apport des témoignages et de la statistique," in Hélène Bergues, ed., *La prévention des naissances dans la famille* (Paris: Presses Universitaires de France, 1960), pp. 361–376.

16. Louis Henry, *Anciennes familles génévoises: Etude démographique, XVIe-XXe siecles* (Paris: Presses Universitaires de France, 1956), p. 156.

17. François de Dainville, "Effectifs des collèges et scolarité aux XVIIe et XVIIIe siècles dans le Nord-Est de la France," *Population* 11 (1957): 455–488.

18. Antoine Prost, *L'Enseignement en France, 1800–1967* (Paris: Armand Colin, 1968), p. 99.

19. Rogert Thabault, *L'ascension d'un peuple: Mon village, ses hommes, ses routes, son école, 1848–1914* (Paris: Delagrave, 1945).

20. Ibid., pp. 50–51.

21. Ibid., p. 84.

22. Ibid., p. 192.

23. Ibid., pp. 201–202.

24. See, for example, Mattei Dogan and Stein Rokkan, eds., *Quantitative Ecological Analysis in the Social Sciences* (Cambridge, MA: MIT Press, 1969), and Michael T. Hannan, *Problems of Aggregation and Disaggregation in Sociological Research,* Working Papers in Methodology no. 4. (Chapel Hill: University of North Carolina, Institute for Research in Social Science, 1970).

25. E. A. Wrigley, ed., *Identifying People of the Past* (London: Edward Arnold, 1973).

26. Peter Loewenberg, "The Psychohistorical Origins of the Nazi Youth Cohort," *American Historical Review* 76 (1971): 1457–1502.

27. Daniel Scott Smith, "The Dating of the American Sexual Revolution: Evidence and Interpretation," in Michael Gordon, ed., *The American Family in Socio-Historical Perspective* (New York: St. Martin's Press, 1973); and Daniel Scott Smith, "Parental Power and Marriage Patterns: An Analysis of Historical Trends in Hingham, Mass." *Journal of Marriage and the Family* (1973).

· 11 ·

MIGRATION IN MODERN EUROPEAN HISTORY

WHAT IS MIGRATION?

Some apparently crisp concepts owe their crispness to bureaucracy. After many centuries in which workers had now and then walked off the job to put pressure on the boss, only in the nineteenth century did firms, unions, and governments coerce one another into precise definitions of the strike. Thenceforth, the strike became routinized, and strike statistics based on standard definitions proliferated. Slowdowns, wildcats, demonstrations, tardiness, absenteeism, unauthorized holidays, sabotage, mass resignation came to seem distinct alternatives to the strike. Most of the organized parties came to consider these other forms of action less desirable than the strike because they were riskier and less routine. Yet in the eighteenth century, the boundaries among these ways of behaving had been unclear indeed. Bureaucracies, by defining the strike as a distinctive form of action, helped create the modern strike.

Other commonly employed and frequently statisticized concepts owe the same debt to bureaucracy: unemployment, employment, production, consumption, perhaps marriage and illegitimacy as well. Years ago, Oskar Morgenstern pointed out that fluttering definitions introduce significant errors into economic statistics. But Morgenstern thought the main problems were theoretical:

> There is often lack of definition or classification of the phenomenon to be measured or recorded, and in addition, there is the difficulty of applying correctly even a faultless system of classification. The theoretical characteristics of, say, an industry or simply of a "price" are less well established than those of a wave length. Almost everything turns around the question of classification. This is a well known difficulty and much

This chapter was first published as "Migration in Modern European History," in William McNeill and Ruth Adams, eds., *Human Migration: Patterns, Implications, Policies* (Bloomington: Indiana University Press, 1976), pp. 48–72. Reprinted with permission.

effort has been directed towards the establishment of uniform classifications, of employment categories and commodities in foreign trade. But
there are large fields where very little has been done and where deep
theoretical problems await solution before classification can be significantly improved. (Morgenstern 1963. 35)

Morgenstern shows appropriate indignation when faced with evidence that
organizations actually fabricate or manipulate definitions for their own purposes:

Perhaps equally important is the often arbitrary, willful, and frequently
politically determined procedure employed by customs officials. In spite
of a perfectly definite classification scheme, commodities are sometimes
put into a similar category carrying higher duties in order to impede their
import (or, as the case may be, into one that will make the import
cheaper). This plays havoc, of course, with statistical accuracy. (Ibid.:
37–38)

Here is a less testy, but more cynical, interpretation: bureaucracies first
produce definitions to serve their own purpose. Economists come along
later to rationalize the definitions.

The concept of migration faces the same difficulties. From the continuous locomotion of human beings, to pick out some moves as more definitive than others reflects the concern of bureaucrats to attach people to
domiciles where they can be registered, enumerated, taxed, drafted, and
watched. A vagrant—a person without a domicile—gives trouble not only
to the police, but also to definitions of migration. Are gypsies migrants?
The crisp definitions and statistics essential to an answer emerged with the
consolidation of national states and state bureaucracies.

With rare exceptions, both practical definitions and available evidence
concerning migration state the answers to some combination of these three
questions:

1. Who lives here *now?*
2. Where did they live *then?*
3. Who else lived *here* then?

A single enumeration of the population can produce answers to the first
two questions. The third question requires enumerations at more than one
point in time. But all three can be answered within a single administrative
unit. Only rarely do we find an answer to a fourth obvious question in the
series: where do they live *now?* That requires two difficult operations: look-

ing in several places, and tracing people forward in time. Counts of migration therefore consist mainly of comparisons, one place at a time, first between the answers to questions 1 and 2, then among the answers to questions 1, 2, and 3.

All the elements—who, where, when—are problematic. All are quite vulnerable to the administrative vagaries that vexed Oskar Morgenstern. "Who" may refer to heads of households, workers, citizens, legal residents, or everyone on hand. "Where" may mean in some particular dwelling, in some particular parish, or in some much larger administrative unit. "When" is the most elusive of all. For the innocent theorist, to live somewhere sometime implies a durable attachment to the place. For the actual collector of the information, however, physical presence on census day, or mere registry as an inhabitant, whether the person is physically present or not, is commonly all that matters. As a consequence, both our conceptions of migration and our evidence concerning it emphasize changes of legal domicile and crossings of administrative boundaries.

In order to make sense of the long-run changes in European migration patterns, we must therefore add social content to our measures and classifications. Whatever else migration is about, it is about moves that are relatively long and relatively definitive. Figure 11.1 presents a simple classification scheme based on length and definitiveness. It classifies moves of individuals, households, or other social units. Its first dimension is distance: we have the choice of simple geographic distance, time, expense, cultural distance, or some combination of them. Below some minimum distance, no move (however definitive) constitutes migration. Although any such minimum is arbitrary, we are unlikely ever to consider a move from one house to the house next door to qualify as migration.

The second dimension is the extent of the social unit's break with the area of origin. At the one extreme lie moves that entail no breaking of social ties; at the other, the complete rupture of ties at the move's place of origin. Below some minimum amount of rupture, no move (however distant) constitutes migration. Such a minimum requirement corresponds readily to our intuitive reluctance to consider a long round-the-world voyage as migration; to our intuitions, the maintenance of a household "back home" says that too few ties have been broken.

Given the two dimensions, most moves—a walk around the block, a vacation trip to London, the daily trip to the factory and back—involve too little distance and/or too little break with the place of origin to count as migration at all. The diagram labels those moves "mobility." It includes them to emphasize that the line between mobility and migration is arbitrary. The point may be obvious, but it is important. For example, histori-

Figure 11.1. Four Standard Migration Patterns

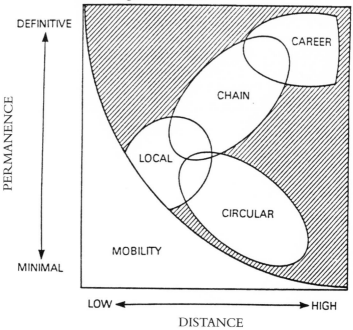

ans working with village population registers frequently encounter individuals who kept the same legal domicile for years while working in distant cities; before calculating migration rates and describing the characteristics of the village's "resident" population, historians must decide on which side of the curved line to put those vagrant individuals.

LOCAL, CIRCULAR, CHAIN, AND CAREER MIGRATION

The most interesting distinctions appear within the shaded migration area of figure 11.1. They depend on the social organization of the move in question. *Local migration* shifts an individual or a household within a geographically contiguous market—a labor market, a land market, or perhaps a marriage market. In local migration, the distance moved is small by definition; the extent of break with the place of origin is also likely to be small. On the whole, the migrant is already quite familiar with the destination before making the move; he or she therefore has relatively little learning of a new environment to do after the move.

Take Uppsala-Nås, an agricultural parish near Uppsala, Sweden, for an example. There, the continuous population registers make it possible to pinpoint different types of moves from 1881 to 1885. There were many moves. Calculated as rates per year per hundred persons who could have moved, the figures (Eriksson and Rogers 1973: 67) are:

moves into or out of the parish	35.2
moves within the parish	40.6
movers into or out of the parish	25.1
movers within the parish	26.9

In 1882, an ordinary year, in a parish the population of which remained a little under 500, 76 in-migrants arrived, 93 people left the parish, and 27 more moved within the parish. If the parish boundary is the line between "local mobility" and "migration," migrants were equal to about a third of the total population. In 1883, the figure went up to about two-fifths. Yet the occupational structure remained fairly constant, no devastating social change occurred, and the great bulk of the migrants moved to or from other parishes in the immediate vicinity. Although many migrants tried their hands in Uppsala or Stockholm at one time or another, Eriksson and Rogers suggest that the structure of local agriculture accounted for most of the movement:

> Large estates required hired labor, and a landless proletariat quickly developed, which in turn contributed to a higher rate of movement. Landless and almost entirely restricted to agricultural occupations, these groups had little chance for social advancement until the breakthrough of industry, bringing changes in society and new opportunities. (Ibid.: 79)

The local migration rates for this one well-studied Swedish parish were probably above average for Europe as a whole. Yet where hired labor and a landless proletariat prevailed, local migration rates on the same order seem to have been common.

Circular migration takes a social unit to a destination through a set of arrangements that returns it to the origin after a well-defined interval. Seasonal work on harvests, pastoral transhumance, the sending of young people into domestic service before they married, and the circuits of Alpine villagers who served long years in the lowlands as schoolteachers, soldiers, or craftspeople before their long-planned return to the mountains with the accumulated capital all represent variants of circular migration. Today, many Turks, Algerians, West Indians, Spaniards, and Portuguese are traveling in similar circles.

In Limousin in the nineteenth century, for example, there were a number of cantons in which a quarter, two-fifths, or even three-fifths of the adult males reported their occupations as "mason" (Corbin 1975: 197). That was possible only because each spring thousands of men who worked on Limousin farms during the winter months walked off to earn money in construction elsewhere, and each fall most of them returned with the bulk of their earnings hidden in their knapsacks. Taking all trades together, at midcentury some 50,000 Limousins joined each year's circular migration. In Paris, "mason" and "Limousin" were nearly synonymous.

Because of their migratory regularity, the Limousins bore the nickname "Swallows." Although the road from Limoges to Paris was close to 200 miles, before the railroad offered a cheap alternative, hundreds of village bands tramped most of it together each year. The famous mason-become-politico Martin Nadaud took his first trip in 1830, when he was fourteen. He, his father, and other masons from their village walked the roughly 150 miles of back roads and woods to Orleans in four days before boarding their hired coaches for the last leg to Paris. Once in Paris, the Limousin masons gathered for the construction season in cheap, dingy rooming houses run by their countrymen. During the great Parisian workers' insurrection of June 1848, 575 masons were among the roughly 11,600 people arrested and charged. Of those 575 masons, 246 were from northern Limousin. The great bulk of them lived in central-city lodging houses, especially in the narrow streets behind the Hotel de Ville.[1] The Limousin masons were at once countrymen, migrants, and active participants in Parisian life.

Chain migration is our third type. Chain migration moves sets of related individuals or households from one place to another via a set of social arrangements in which people at the destination provide aid, information, and encouragement to new migrants. Such arrangements tend to produce a considerable proportion of experimental moves and a large backflow to the place of origin. At the destination, they also tend to produce durable clusters of people linked by common origin. At the extreme, the migrants form urban villages. In medieval and Renaissance Europe, cities often permitted, or even required, these clusters of people to organize as "nations" sharing well-defined privileges and bearing collective responsibility for the policing and welfare of their members. In those cities, migrants of one nationality or another frequently established a quasi monopoly of some particular trade. In sixteenth-century Rome, for example, the most successful courtesans were Spanish. So well known was this fact that in 1592 other members of "the Spanish nation," no doubt wishing their reputation to rest on other accomplishments, formally petitioned Pope Clement VIII to banish Spanish courtesans from Rome (Delumeau 1957: I, 201). To this day, the old university of Uppsala is organized in nations representing the major provinces of Sweden. But most chain migrants have formed and reformed their communities without the benefit of such formal recognition of their common origin.

When the chain works well as a transmission belt, it continues to stretch from origin to destination until no members are left at the origin. In the 1950s and 1960s, for example, chain migration was emptying Tierra de Campos, a Castillian agricultural region of some 120,000 people in 178 small settlements. In one sample of out-migrants interrogated by Victor Perez Díaz, 60 percent of the migrants already knew someone at the destination before they left home. Once departed, the migrants sent back letters and remittances at an impressive rate: a reported average of forty letters and 8,000 pesetas per year (Perez Díaz 1971: 148–153). In general, the more distant and costly the migration, the more people rely on others at the destination to ease the way. The extreme—for the cace of Tierra de Campos and for the migration of poor Europeans in general—is overseas migration, where the great majority of moves belong to well-defined chains.

Career migration, finally, has persons or households making more or less definitive moves in response to opportunities to change position within or among large structures: organized trades, firms, governments, mercantile networks, armies, and the like. If there is a circuit, it is based not on the social bonds at the migrant's place of origin, but on the logic of the large structure itself. If people within the migrant mass help and encourage one another, they are generally colleagues, not neighbors or kin. The migrations of scientists, technicians, military officers, priests, and bureaucrats commonly fall into this type, rather than into local, circular, or chain migration.

Sixteenth-century migrants to Canterbury and other towns of Kent, according to Peter Clark, consisted mainly of two groups: poor people from the countryside who moved relatively long distances to take up unskilled urban work, and more comfortable people from other towns and the nearby countryside who entered crafts and other fairly skilled urban employment. Both of these groups probably consisted chiefly of chain migrants. But with the economic expansion of the sixteenth century, another category was becoming more important: itinerant professionals, craftspeople, and other specialists. As Clark puts it:

> If the itinerant craftsman or specialist had also been a medieval figure the expansion of this kind of professional migration in the sixteenth century in response to the needs of an increasingly sophisticated social and eco-

nomic order had a new, radical importance—both in numbers and impact. The growth of internal trade entailed a major increase in the
numbers of pedlars, chapmen and other itinerant retailers with their own
trade routes across countries. (Clark 1972: 146)

In the same general category were clergymen seeking new posts. None of
those people were undergoing the sorts of station-to-station transfers that
became the common experience of employees in big twentieth-century
organizations. Yet as compared with the other migrants to Kentish towns,
they were clearly migrating in response to career opportunities.

The types overlap. Sometimes they change from one to another. For
example, most systems of circular migration leave a residue of migrants at
the destination. The stayers include both successful people who make a
good thing of mediating between their mobile compatriots and the local
population, and failures who die before accumulating the capital to go back
home. A circular system with a rising residue eventually becomes a chain.
In migration from the high Alps, for example, the peddler-migrants who
made good tended to establish shops in lowland towns and to provide the
contacts for subsequent migrants from the uplands (Merlin et al. 1971: 34).

In another overlap, local migration systems sometimes provide the
basis for long-distance chain migration. One of the most spectacular examples is the local system of labor migration around seventeenth-century
Tourouvre-au-Perche: it extended into the long chain that through transatlantic migration, North American propagation, and subsequent migration
within Canada, gave ancestors to much of Quebec's contemporary population. Some 300 migrants from the small region of Tourouvre-au-Perche
left for Canada in the seventeenth century, especially toward 1650. Labor
recruiters encouraged the move to Quebec and drew a disproportionate
number of men in their twenties. Despite the unbalanced sex ratio, the
migrants married and bore children in exceptional numbers. Some migrated as families, some sent later for families already begun in France, some
returned to marry in the region of Tourouvre, and almost all the rest married in Canada soon after arrival (Charbonneau 1970).

Despite the overlap, the systems have some characteristic differences.
On the whole, circular migration is very sex selective: practically all-male
or all-female, depending on the occupation at the destination. Chain migration's sex selectivity tends to change over time. One typical arrangement
is for single males to make up the vanguard, with single females and then
whole families joining them later. Local and career migration, in contrast,
are not generally very selective by sex; either whole households migrate,
or the stream comprises both men and women.

The geographic pattern also varies from one type to another. Chain migration tends to link a particular origin with no more than a handful of possible destinations. But those destinations are often at a considerable distance. Circular migration may do the same thing, but it is somewhat more likely to disperse the available workers among a number of opportunities. Local migration involves many destinations within a circumscribed range. Career migration, finally, tends to spread people far and wide. The geographic differences suggest the following grouping of the migration patterns:

	Supply of Relevant Skills	
Cost of Information about Opportunities	*General*	*Special*
High	Chain	Circular
Low	Local	Career

Chain and circular migration are ways of combatting high costs of information about opportunities for employment, proprietorship, and other desired ends. Circular and career migration respond to situations in which the skills the migrants exercise are not generally available—because they are hard to learn, because the migrants have monopolized them, or because other people are unwilling to work at them. Thus as the cost of information about job opportunities declines, chain and circular migration give way to local and career migration. But to the extent that all job skills are unevenly distributed, circular and career migration tend to supplant chain and local migration.

The rough classification of migration into local, circular, chain, and career does not exhaust the significant distinctions one might make. For example, it catches quite imperfectly the important difference between individual and collective migration; although on the whole chain and circular migration involve single individuals less frequently than do local and career migration, there are individual and collective versions of all four types. The classification does not embody the distinction between forced and voluntary migration; it therefore deals awkwardly with the expulsion of the Huguenots from France and the flight of Jews from Eastern European pogroms. Since it concentrates on particular moves, it does not easily separate two rather different relationships between a major city and its hinterland: the rare pattern in which migrants come directly to the city from the distant countryside, and the common pattern in which country people move to nearby small towns, small-town people move to large towns, and so on, step by step to the metropolis. The classification into local, circular, chain, and career migrations separates some significantly different social arrangements from one another, but it does not make all the distinctions one might wish to employ.

The sorts of administratively produced evidence we have concerning European migration do not permit us to distinguish easily among local, circular, chain, and career migration. To do so, one needs life histories, detailed accounts of intentions and social relations at the time of moves, or both. Records of official changes of domicile yield the former with great difficulty, and the latter not at all. On the basis of the scattered evidence available, nevertheless, it seems safe to say that in the age of industrialization, the general character of European migration shifted from the lower left to the upper right of Figure 11.1: away from local and short-distance circular migration, toward longer-distance, more definitive chain and career migration. It also seems safe to say that the *pace* of migration changed much less than its *character*. The history of Europe shows us not so much periods of immobility and mobility as decisive shifts among types of mobility.

The Great Flows

William McNeill has portrayed the repeated sweeps of conquering bands across the Continent. He has also recounted the less dramatic, but no less momentous, flows of agricultural settlers into the Continent's emptier spaces. Before the last millennium, large-scale movements of armed men and tribute takers set the rhythm of European political history. Armed men and tribute takers have thrived into our own time, but on the whole, they have fixed themselves in space, reduced the scale and duration of their movements, and worked harder and harder at controlling the flows of people and goods into and out of their own fixed territories. Within Europe, long-distance flows of agricultural settlers continued, although their relative volume seems to have declined irregularly with the approach of our own time.

The last massive migration of agricultural workers within Europe was the medieval flow of German speakers into the east and south of the Continent. That flow continued past 1500. But by then, its volume had greatly diminished. By that time, German-speaking migrants consisted mainly of one variety or another of conqueror: officials, managers, merchants, and landlords. The seventeenth- and eighteenth-century expansion of the Prussian state formally incorporated a number of eastern German enclaves and took in a good deal of predominantly Slavic population. It did not, however, produce movements of population comparable to those of three or four centuries earlier. Despite Frederick the Great's strenuous efforts at settlement, for example, Silesia remained predominantly Polish-speaking. Further south, the Austrians also sought to settle German speakers to their east by such straightforward devices as dispossessing the Czech landlords of Moravia. Although such planned migrations were of the greatest political importance, the numbers involved were relatively small. Indeed, they bucked the long-range trend, which was for Slavic speakers, given weight by their generally higher levels of natural increase, to push westward into areas earlier occupied by Finns, Swedes, and Germans. On either side of the linguistic frontier, massive long-distance rural-to-rural migration became less prevalent after 1500.

Long-distance moves of workers into nonagricultural employment are a different matter. They accelerated some 200 years ago and have remained important since then. The migration of Poles into the mining areas of western Germany and eastern France and the rush of the Irish to Liverpool and London illustrate the importance of long-distance migration within industrial Europe. Contrary to first impressions, few of these long-distance migrants moved directly from farm to factory. For the most part, the farmers who moved to cities found low-level employment in services and commerce. The apparent exceptions were commonly small-town artisans or rural industrial workers, rather than peasants or farm laborers. Indeed, over the last two centuries, the most important single category of urban employment for rural-to-urban migrants within Europe has most likely been domestic service. Only an undue concentration on males and on manufacturing has obscured that fact.

During the period of swift natural increase from the mid-eighteenth century to the end of the nineteenth, Europe also sent millions of its residents to the agricultural and industrial areas of the Americas and of Oceania. The great flows of the nineteenth and twentieth centuries followed smaller, but still important, migratory movements that accompanied European colonial expansion during the three previous centuries. In this great overseas migration, millions of rural Europeans *did* migrate to farms. French migrants peopled rural Quebec as well as Quebec City and Montreal. Portuguese emigrants became Brazilian farmers as well as residents of São Paulo and Rio de Janeiro. Later, more than two million Germans and Scandinavians sailed to America. There, many of them settled on frontier farms.

Altogether, Europe's net migration from 1800 to World War I was on the order of 50 million persons. Given the frequent returns of chain migrants, a much larger number must have made the trip at one time or another. Since a return rate of 30 percent is plausible, the true number could easily be 65 million sometime emigrants. Over half of all European emigrants in that period went to the United States.

The British Isles—especially Ireland—were the champion exporters of humankind and the chief purveyors to America. About three-quarters of nineteenth-century emigrants from Britain went to North America. As a result, at least a third of all American immigrants in that century were native speakers of English. Nevertheless, Germany, Greece, Italy, and the Scandinavian countries all became major sources of overseas migrants at some time during the nineteenth century.

One of the best-documented cases is Denmark. With a total population in the range of 2 million, Denmark sent over 300,000 migrants overseas between 1840 and 1914 (Hvidt 1975. 9). Over 90 percent went to North America. Within that small country, rates of emigration differed dramatically from one district to another. On the whole, they were much higher in the southeast than elsewhere. More generally, urban areas sent migrants at a significantly higher pace than rural areas did. Yet where urban growth and industrialization were vigorous, relatively little emigration occurred.

The ideal origin for Danish emigrants seems to have been the stagnant town in which underemployed long-term migrants from nearby rural areas were accumulating. Landless laborers and servants were especially good prospects for emigration. Kristian Hvidt quotes a letter describing the situation on the high-migration island of Bornholm:

> The Bornholm farmers pay their small-holding laborers much too poorly in relation to the prices of necessities. But the huge number of immigrating Swedes rules out a rise in wages. An ordinary laborer who is not a craftsman has often only the choice between America or the poorhouse. (Ibid.: 129)

Chain migration was the predominant pattern among the 300,000 Danes who left Denmark. Toward the end of the nineteenth century, around a quarter of all Danish migrants to the United States came on steamship tickets prepaid by migrants already in America. (The comparable figures for Norway and Sweden run from 40 to 50 percent.) "Letters, money, and prepaid tickets came in a constant stream, the volume of which would quite likely surprise most people," writes Hvidt,

> since the emigrants were generally believed to have formed the poorest part of the population and to have been characterized by intellectual narrowness and insufficient education. Improved economic conditions in the United States combined with the emotional longings inherent in emigration furthered both letter writing and sending tickets home. These personal contacts with the Old Country may well be sufficient explana-

tion of why mass emigration accelerated whenever economic conditions permitted. (Ibid.: 194)

Indeed, it was partly *because* they were poor and uneducated that the Danish emigrants relied on their compatriots for aid, encouragement, and information in the long migration to America.

In the period after World War I, with declining European rates of natural increase and rising American resistance to immigration, the pace of European emigration diminished. Nevertheless, Canada, Argentina, Brazil, Australia, and New Zealand continued to receive large numbers of European migrants. In that period, as Table 11.1 shows, the British Isles regained the predominance they had lost to Italy during the period from 1891 to 1920. Poorer areas of the British Isles, such as the declining Welsh mining region, sent their surplus labor overseas in the company of a smaller number of highly educated people from all over Britain. Since the table deals only with the total number of overseas emigrants, it conceals an important countercurrent: while the poor areas of northwestern Europe continued to send migrants overseas, the more prosperous areas began to bring in migrants from elsewhere in Europe.

Since World War II, northwestern Europe has become an even more

Table 11.1. Percentage of All European Overseas Emigrants Leaving from Selected Countries, 1846–1963

Countries	Period			
	1846–90	1891–1920	1921–39	1946–63
British Isles	47.9	17.7	29.0	27.7
Germany	20.2	3.4	9.8	15.7
Sweden, Denmark, Norway	6.9	3.8	3.8	2.1
France, Switzerland, Netherlands	4.2	1.5	2.5	14.9
Italy	8.2	27.0	18.6	19.0
Austria, Hungary, Czechoslovakia	3.7	15.9	4.1	?
Russia, Poland, Lithuania, Estonia, Finland	2.1	13.0	12.0	?
Spain, Portugal	6.9	15.3	15.0	12.1
Total emigrants from Europe per year (× 1,000)	376	910	366	585

The figures describe gross migration, not net loss through migration. Boundaries as of the 1960s apply to all periods.

Source: Calculated from Kosiński 1970: 57.

active importer of migrants. Yugoslavia, Spain, Portugal, Italy, Ireland, and Turkey became major suppliers to the highly industrialized regions of Europe. This last shift has its ironies: we see the nations that peopled the rest of the Western world with their poor now drawing their unskilled labor from poor immigrants and fretting about the disruption such migrations may cause. Switzerland, which long disposed of its surplus men as mercenaries in European armies, now has a sixth of its population foreign born. Great Britain, which flooded America with English-speaking families, now debates the desirability of its 5 percent born elsewhere. According to Stephen Castles and Godula Kosack, France, West Germany, Switzerland, and Great Britain, among others, have come to rely almost entirely on foreigners to do their dirty work. Yet they have proved quite hostile to granting the newcomers a permanent stake in their host countries. Xenophobia is nothing new. But the backing it has received from West European states in recent years is unusual.

THE IMPACTS OF WAR AND POLITICS

The most dramatic twentieth-century change in European migration patterns was not the northwest's shift from export to import of migrants. It was the expanding role of political pressures and political controls. Politics impinged on migration in three distinct ways: through war, through deliberate relocation of ethnic minorities, and through stringent national controls over immigration and emigration.

During the twentieth century, in more senses than one, war became the prime mover. Earlier, such continental conflicts as the Thirty Years' War and the Napoleonic Wars had produced hordes of refugees. They also produced some long-term displacement of population away from the war zones. But World Wars I and II produced incomparably greater migratory currents in Europe. According to Eugene Kulischer's compilation (Kulischer 1948: 248–249), the largest flows within Europe and the adjacent sections of Asia from 1918 to 1939 were:

> 1.2 million Greeks to Greece from Turkey (1922–1923)
> 1.15 million Russians to Europe outside the Soviet Union (1918–1922)
> 1.1 million repatriated from Russia to Poland (1918–1925)
> 900,000 Poles from former Russian and Austrian Poland to former German Poland (1918–1921)
> 700,000 Germans from western Poland, Danzig, and Memel to Germany (1918–1925)

Only then do we arrive at migratory streams in which the war and the peace settlement did not play a large, direct part: the estimated 650,000 Italians who went from Italy to France over the twenty-one years from 1919 to 1939, and the estimated 450,000 Poles who made the move to France over the same period. (These are net figures; according to Polish statistics, for example, 622,000 Poles went to France from 1919 through 1939, but 200,000 returned to Poland, for a net of 422,000 migrants [Kosínski 1970: 79–80].)

These numbers are large. They are, however, modest compared to the figures for World War II and its aftermath. To take again the leaders in Kulischer's compilation (Kulischer 1948: 302–304):

6 million Reich Germans from New Poland to Germany (1944–1947)
5 million Jews from Germany to extermination camps in Poland and elsewhere (1940–1944)
4 million Reich Germans from the Soviet zone to the United States and British zones (1945–1946)
3 million Poles from Old Poland to New Poland (1945–1947)
2.7 million ethnic Germans from Czechoslovakia to Germany and Austria (1945–1946)
1.8 million Czechs and Slovaks from Inner Czechoslovakia to the former Sudetenland (1946–1947)
1 million ethnic Germans from Old Poland to Germany (1944–1945)

The list goes on. However approximate these figures are, and however much double counting they include, they portray World War II and—especially—the postwar settlement as one of the greatest demographic whirlwinds ever to sweep the earth.

Some of these migrants fled from war zones. Many more of them moved at the behest of governments. On the whole, the refugees contributed to the diversity of population at their destinations. When states deliberately relocated people, however, they tended to homogenize the language and culture of the people within any particular set of national boundaries. The net effect of the migrations surrounding the two world wars was therefore to homogenize nation-states and probably to increase their capacity for nationalism.

Heightened nationalism and the recurrent labor shortages of the richer European countries have combined to produce a contradictory situation. On the one hand, such countries as Switzerland, West Germany, and France have become sorely dependent on poorer countries for supplies of unskilled labor. On the other hand, those same countries and their neighbors have greatly increased their controls over immigration and emigration.

There is, to be sure, a sharp difference between Eastern and Western Europe in those regards. On the whole, the richer Western European countries have encouraged circular migration of low-wage workers from elsewhere, but have made it difficult for them to become long-time residents and, especially, to acquire citizenship. The Soviet Union and other communist states have simply made all forms of entry and exit difficult.

The last five centuries of European long-distance migration show us three major factors at work: (1) a changing geographic distribution of opportunities for employment; (2) alterations of regional differentials in natural increase; and (3) actions and policies of national states—notably, making war, controlling migration, and deliberately recruiting, expelling, or relocating specific ethnic and religious groups. The first two factors have shaped migration throughout the 500 years. To explain why and how they worked is to trace out the expansion of capitalism, the proletarianization of the European population as a whole, and the march of urbanization and industrialization. The third factor—actions and policies of national states—gained importance as the five centuries wore on. By the twentieth century, wars and their settlements rivaled the interplay of employment and natural increase as incentives to long-distance migration.

THE LOCAL FLOWS

No one has given us a comprehensive statistical atlas of long-distance migration within, from, and to the European continent. That would be a useful enterprise. But at least the existence and broad directions of the long-distance flows are well known. In the present state of our knowledge, local migration provides more puzzles.

Recent work on the historical demography of Europe has experienced a nice dialectic. The fastidious methods for reconstructing precensus demographic characteristics developed by such scholars as Louis Henry and E. A. Wrigley sometimes assume, and always apply more easily to, relatively immobile populations. Yet one of the most impressive and consistent findings of the historical demographers has been the high level of local mobility among preindustrial European people. In studies of eighteenth-century agricultural villages, it is not unusual to find over a tenth of the population making a significant change of residence each year. If the sheer frequency of moves (rather than the distance moved) is the criterion, it is not at all clear that industrialization produced a major increase in the European population's mobility.

The findings coming in jar our preconceptions concerning the settled peasant world that industrialization is supposed to have broken up. Still, the idea of a settled peasant world is not so much wrong as incomplete. Let us consider "peasants" to be members of households whose major activity is farming, households that produce a major share of the goods and services they consume, that exercise substantial control over the land they farm, and that supply the major part of their labor requirements from their own energies. If that is what we mean by peasants, a majority of the European population was probably peasant until late in the eighteenth century. The true peasant population was, so far as we know, relatively immobile.

But the extrapolation of peasant immobility to the European population as a whole errs in several ways. A substantial minority of the population was *not* peasant. From the later eighteenth century, the nonpeasants were probably a majority. Among the nonpeasants were significant groups of traders and artisans for whom movement was a way of life. Less obvious among them was a large, growing mass of landless laborers. (To take one of the extreme cases, Gregory King estimated for the England of 1688 that only 350,000 of the 1.2 million families in agriculture lived from their own land [Pollard and Crossley 1968: 154].)

The landless and land-poor moved frequently, sometimes seasonally, in response to the demand for wage labor. As Paul Slack points out, the seventeenth-century English local authorities regularly whipped the "vagrants" who were multiplying in the countryside and sent them back to their parishes of origin. But those vagrants were only a minority of the many landless laborers then on the roads. They were the ones who had failed to find work. As enclosures and populations growth swelled the numbers of people who had no place on the land in their home villages, many migrated in search of employment elsewhere. Local authorities treated them ambivalently: welcoming their labor if the parish needed it and could control it, but striving to make sure the wanderers gained no claims on parish welfare funds. Hence the whip.

Contrary to ideas linking high mobility to industrialization, however, the spread of rural industry seems to have helped the landless to settle down. It meant they could piece together starvation wages from industrial and agriculture work in their own villages. In his rich study of the Zurich uplands during early industrialization, Rudolf Braun shows us exactly this fixing of the proletarian population in place via cottage industry. Whereas the surplus hands of previous generations had walked off to military careers, domestic service, or another kind of unskilled work elsewhere, the villagers of the eighteenth century began to stay on the land, spinning and weaving. Take, for example, the Leicestershire village of Shepshed, where cottage industry grew considerably during the eighteenth century:

In pre-industrial Shepshed just 46% of the families entering the observation had been married in the parish whereas during protoindustrialization the proportion of parochial marriage rose so that after 1810 76.9% of all families had been married in the village church. (Levine 1977: 40)

As opportunities for industrial employment expanded in Shepshed, more people lived out their lives in the parish and saw their children do the same.

Some true peasant households were also quite mobile. It is doubtful that the majority of European peasant households owned the bulk of the land they farmed before some time in the nineteenth century. Most were tenants of one type or another. Tenancy meant turnover. Annual, quinquennial, or even nine-year leases brought the significant possibility of a move when the lease expired. The scattered studies in historical demography that have been able to make the essential distinctions with respect to control of land have found tenants migrating to and from villages in significant numbers. During the nineteenth- and twentieth-century "rural exodus," landless laborers were generally the first to leave the countryside, tenants next, and owners quite slow to depart.

DEMOGRAPHIC STIMULI TO MIGRATION

In addition to the effects of tenancy and employment, Old Regime demographic conditions provided their own spurs to migration. The best-known of those demographic conditions was the enormous death rate in cities. The rates were high enough that, before the nineteenth century, large cities could maintain their populations only through substantial in-migration and could grow only through massive recruitment of outsiders. For example, in the little North Sea port of Husum from 1765 to 1804, the crude birthrate was about 26.6 and the crude death rate about 28.9, for a natural *decrease* of about 2.3 persons per thousand per year. That was true despite an age structure favorable to low mortality. In the forty years after 1804, by contrast, the crude birthrate rose a trifle to 27.1, while the crude death rate declined to 24.8. That produced a natural *increase* of about 2.3 per thousand (computed from Momsen 1969: 58, 66). In actual numbers, the breakdown of Husum's growth in the two periods ran like this:

Period	Population Change	Births-Deaths	Net Migration
1769–1802	+ 165	− 345	+ 510
1803–1844	+ 245	+ 358	− 110

Thus, in the early nineteenth century, natural increase more than supplied Husum's need for new hands, and a surplus migrated elsewhere. But in the eighteenth century, the city had to bring in migrants simply to maintain its population.

Husum and other small cities generally drew the bulk of their migrants from their immediate hinterlands. In most cases, a small city's radius of intensive attraction was no more than 10 or 15 miles (see Patten 1973). Before the rising natural increase of the eighteenth and nineteenth centuries, the supply of migrants behaved a good deal like the supply of food: cities consumed more than they produced; they drew the hard-won surplus from many surrounding communities, and thus affected those communities deeply; they drew more specialized supplies from greater distances via other cities; when they grew fast, that growth generated a demand that reverberated through more and more of the hinterland.

Large cities drew on correspondingly larger areas of supply. In times of relatively rapid urban growth, such as significant parts of the sixteenth and eighteenth centuries, major cities drew their increments from vast hinterlands. London grew from about 400,000 in 1650 to about 650,000 a century later. That growth had a large impact on the food production of southern England. It also altered English migration systems, despite the fact that they were already centered in London. E. A. Wrigley speculates that in the high-growth century from 1650 to 1750, a sixth of the entire adult population of England spent some part of their lives in London (Wrigley 1967: 49). The high-mortality metropolis stuffed itself with an entire country's demographic surplus.

Urban natural decrease was not the only important demographic condition. In a time of high, fluctuating fertility and high, unstable mortality, households that had relatively inelastic labor requirements often found their supply and demand badly matched. Artisans with an expensive stock in trade and peasants with fixed allotments of land, for instance, tended to develop a well-defined household division of labor by age, sex, and marital status. They could absorb an extra hand or do without one of the standard household members only at great strain. Either the death of a mother or the survival of an extra child jostled a delicate equilibrium. In the short run, such households used migration to adjust the supply to the demand. Extra children migrated, temporarily or definitively, into domestic service, armies, peddling. The household made up shortages by bringing in servants and/or kinsfolk from elsewhere. A very high proportion of all individual migration before the twentieth century consisted of these transfers of labor among households.

In quantitative terms, however, marriage and the termination of marriage were probably the most significant demographic spurs to migration. Throughout the centuries, almost every European marriage has required at least one spouse to make a definitive change of residence. With some lags and exceptions due to coresidence with parents, the great majority have led to the formation of a new household in a new location. As nuptiality rose in the nineteenth century, the frequency of marriage-linked migration rose as well. The termination of marriages through divorce or death played a smaller part, but not a negligible one, in causing migration. To know whether its importance increased or decreased, we need not only to grasp the trends in the divorce rates, but also to balance off the migration-inducing effects of remarriages against the changing likelihood that a bereaved spouse will remain in the household she or he already occupies. We do not now have the necessary evidence. My speculation is that the termination of marriages became a less important occasion for migration in Europe after the eighteenth century.

QUALIFICATIONS AND CONCLUSIONS

Over the five centuries or so we have been reviewing, most migrants have moved short distances. Most moves have responded to demographic imbalances and changing employment opportunities. Both conditions remained true during the nineteenth century, with its massive overseas migration, and during the twentieth century, with its major displacements by war. Furthermore, local systems of migration often provided the bases of subsequent longer-range migration. That happened in circular migration systems that included cities; if opportunity rose in the city and declined in the countryside, the system started depositing a permanent residue of migrants in the city. It also happened in some essentially rural systems of labor migration to which an overseas destination became available: mobile agricultural workers in Denmark or Portugal found themselves working, in the company of their compatriots, in New York or Toronto. The long-run trend of European migration ran from local and circular migration to chain and career migration. The average distances moved and the definitiveness of breaks with the place of origin both increased. But the continuities between the older and newer forms of migration were impressive.

I have stressed the high mobility of European populations before the nineteenth century because it requires us to rethink the relationship between industrialization and mobility. If I have given the impression that nothing changed in the nineteenth and twentieth centuries, however, that is wrong. The average distances of migration rose dramatically with large-scale industrialization. The unprecedented concentration of opportunities for employment in large cities oriented migration to those cities as never before. The growing power of national states impinged on twentieth-century migration through war and through deliberate controls over entries and exits. Those are novelties of the modern world.

The high mobility of the preindustrial world also requires some qualification. In general, the distances involved in rural migration or in migration to small cities were small. The bulk of the migrants to any locality typically came from within 5 or 10 miles. Only larger cities regularly escaped from that rule. If we were to set a local labor market as the limit within which a move counts as "mobility" instead of "migration," we would eliminate many of the extremely high rates of migration now coming in from demographic studies of preindustrial European populations. The generalization would then read: before large-scale industrialization, rural labor markets were typically larger than a single village; they were often very active, especially where tenancy and/or wage labor prevailed; people moved frequently within those labor markets in response to demographic imbalances and shifting opportunities for livelihood.

We might speculate, in fact, that despite all the reverence for the village, the parish, or the commune that European historians have developed, the fundamental local unit was larger than any of them. The area served by a single market has turned out to be the basic building block of traditional China (Skinner 1964–1965). It defined the familiar world, the world of labor exchange, marriage, social mobility, local solidarity. Perhaps local market areas played a similar role in traditional Europe. The village, parish, or commune then may have acquired importance only when national states required mutually exclusive administrative units that they could hold collectively responsible for taxation, conscription, road labor, the provision of food, and the maintenance of public order.

To the degree that we expand the definition of local mobility and become more stringent in our definition of migration, the era of large-scale industrialization and massive expansion of national states separates from the previous era. Long-distance, definitive migration did increase with industrialization and state making. Gross and net flows of migrants from rural to urban areas came to dominate the migration map as never before. As urban mortality declined, large rural-urban flows increasingly meant rapid urban growth. As rural natural increase declined, large rural-urban flows increasingly meant a depletion of the rural population. As national states grew, wars, peace settlements, and national policies acted more and more powerfully as spurs and checks to migration. In the same era, local mobility did not increase significantly; in rural areas and small towns, it probably declined.

The study of migration, then, gets us into the homely adjustments ordinary Europeans made among their own life plans and the labor requirements of the various organizations that had claims on them, or on which they had claims. Organizational structure, life plans, demography: changes in any of these three large elements eventually affect the character of the other two. Every major change in European organizational structure, life plans, and demography has produced a durable transformation of European migration patterns. As time has gone on, national states have increasingly shaped and reshaped those patterns—by deliberately controlling the possibilities of migration, by intentionally relocating ethnic minorities, and by destructively making war. The history of European migration is the history of European social life.

Notes

I am grateful to Martha Guest for assistance in my search of the literature and to Louise Tilly for comments on earlier drafts. An early draft of this paper circulated as a Discussion Paper of the Center for Western European Studies, University of Michigan, under the title "Preliminary Notes on European Migration." The Horace Rackham School of Graduate Studies, University of Michigan, gave financial support to the research in European historical demography that underlies some parts of this paper. The National Science Foundation supported other parts of the work.
    1. Computed from dossiers in Archives Nationales (Paris), F^7 2586, and in Archives Historiques de L'Armée (Vincennes), series A.

References

Anderson, Grace. 1974. *Networks of Contact: The Portuguese and Toronto.* Waterloo, Ontario: Wilfred Laurier University Press.

Aymard, Maurice. 1974. "La Sicile, Terre d'Immigration." In M. Aymard et al., *Les migrations dans les pays méditerranéens au XVIIIe et au debut du XIXème.* Nice: Centre de la Méditerranée Moderne et Contemporaine.

Banks, J. A. 1968. "Population Change and the Victorian City." *Victorian Studies* 11: 277–289.

Beijer, G. 1963. *Rural Migrants in Urban Setting: An Analysis of the Literature on the Problem Consequent on the Internal Migration from Rural to Urban Places in European Countries* (1945–1961). The Hague: Nijhoff.

Blaschke, Karlheinz. 1967. *Bevölkerungsgeschichte von Sachsen bis zur industriellen Revolution.* Weimar: Böhlhaus.

Brandes, Stanley H. 1975. *Migration, Kinship, and Community: Tradition and Transition in a Spanish Village.* New York: Academic Press.

Braun, Rudolf. 1960. *Industrialisierung und Volksleben: Die Veränderung der Lebensformen in einem landlichen Industriegebiet vor 1800 (Züricher Oberland).* Zürich: Rentsch.

————. 1970. *Sozio-kulturelle Probleme der Eingliederung italienischer Arbeitskräfte in der Schweiz.* Zurich: Rentsch.

Buckatzsch, C. J. 1949–1950. "Places of Origin of a Group of Immigrants into Sheffield, 1624–1799." *Economic History Review,* 2nd ser., 2: 303–306.

————. 1951. "The Constancy of Local Populations and Migration in England before 1800." *Population Studies,* pp. 62–69.

Butcher, A. F. 1974. "The Origins of Romney Freeman, 1433–1523." *Economic History Review,* 2nd ser., 27: 16–27.

Castles, Stephen, and Godula Kosack. 1973. *Immigrant Workers and Class Structure in Western Europe.* London: Oxford University Press.

Chambers, J. D. 1965. "Three Essays on the Population and Economy of the Midlands." In D. V. Glass and D. E. C. Eversley, eds., *Population in History: Essays in Historical Demography.* Chicago: Aldine.

Charbonneau, Hubert. 1970. *Tourouvre-au-Perche aux XVIIe et XVIIIe siecles.* Paris: Presses Universitaires de France, Institut National d'Etudes Démographiques, Travaux et Documents, Cahier 55.

Chevalier, Louis. 1950. *La formation de la population parisienne au XIXe siècle.* Paris: Presses Universitaires de France.

Clark, Peter. 1972. "The Migrant in Kentish Towns, 1580–1640." In Peter Clark and Paul Slack eds., *Crisis and Order in English Towns, 1500–1700.* London: Routledge & Kegan Paul.

Corbin, Alain. 1975. *Archaisme et modernité en Limousin au XIXe siècle.* 2 vols. Paris: Marcel Rivière.

Cornwall, Julian. 1967. "Evidence of Population Mobility in the Seventeenth Century." *Bulletin of the Institute of Historical Research* 40: 143–152.

Delumeau, Jean. 1957. *Vie économique et sociale de Rome dans la second Vie moitié du XVIe siècle.* 2 vols. Paris: Boccard.

Eriksson, Ingrid, and John Rogers. 1973. "Mobility in an Agrarian Community: Practical and Methodological Considerations." In Kurt Ågren et al., *Aristocrats, Farmers, Proletarians: Essays in Swedish Demographic History*. Uppsala: Scandinavian University Books, Studia Historica Upsaliensa, 47.

Friedl, Ernestine. 1976. "Kinship, Class, and Selective Migration." In J. G. Peristiany, ed., *Mediterranean Family Structures*. Cambridge: Cambridge University Press.

Goreux, L. M. 1956. "Les migrations agricoles en France depuis un siècle et leur relation avec certains facteurs économiques." *Etudes et Conjoncture* 11: 327–376.

Hammer, Carol. 1976. "The Mobility of Skilled Labour in Late Medieval England: Some Oxford Evidence." *Vierteljahrschrift für Sozial und Wirtschaftsgeschichte* 63: 194–210.

Hannan, Damian. 1970. *Rural Exodus*. London: Geoffrey Chapman.

Henry, Louis. 1967. *Manuel de démographie historique*. Geneva and Paris: Droz.

————. 1972. *Démographie, analyse, et modèles*. Paris: Larousse.

Hesse, Sharlene. 1975. "Migrants as Actors: A Case Study of Life-Cycle and Geographical Mobility in Sweden." Doctoral dissertation, Department of Sociology, University of Michigan.

Hollingsworth, T. H. 1971. "Historical Studies of Migration." *Annales de Démographie Historique 1970*, pp. 87–96.

Hvidt, Kristian. 1975. *Flight to America: The Social Background of 300,000 Danish Emigrants*. New York: Academic Press.

Iatsunsky, V. K. 1971. "Le rôle des migrations et de l'accroissement naturel dans la colonisation des nouvelles régions de la Russie." *Annales de Démographie Historique 1970*, pp. 302–308.

Kasdan, Leonard. 1965. "Family Structure, Migration, and the Entrepreneur." *Comparative Studies in Society and History* 7: 345–357.

Kollmann, Wolfgang. 1959. "Industrialisierung, Binnenwanderung, und 'Soziale Frage.' " *Vierteljahrschrift für Sozial und Wirtschaftsgeschichte* 46: 45–70.

Kosínski, Leszek A. 1970. *The Population of Europe: A Geographic Perspective*. London: Longman.

Kulischer, Eugene M. 1948. *Europe on the Move: War and Population Changes, 1917–47*. New York: Columbia University Press.

Laslett, Peter. 1968. "Le brassage de la population en France et en Angleterre aux XVIIe et XVIIIe siècles." *Annales de Démographie Historique 1968*, pp. 99–109.

Levi, Giovanni. 1971. "Migrazioni e popolazione nella Francia del XVII e XVIII secolo." *Rivista Storica Italiana* 83: 95–123.

――――. 1974. "Sviluppo urbano e flussi migratori nel Piemonte nel 1600." In M. Aymard et al., *Les migrations dans les pays méditerranéens au XVII-Ième et au début du XIXème.* Nice: Centre de la Méditerranée Moderne et Contemporaine.

Levine, David. 1977. *Family Formation in an Age of Nascent Capitalism.* New York: Academic Press.

Liang, Hsi-Huey, 1970. "Lower-Class Immigrants in Wilhelmine Berlin." *Central European History* 3: 94–111.

Lopreato, Joseph. 1962. "Economic Development and Cultural Change: The Role of Emigration." *Human Organization* 21: 182–186.

MacDonald, John S., and Leatrice D. MacDonald. 1964. "Chain Migration, Ethnic Neighborhood Formation, and Social Networks." *Milbank Memorial Fund Quarterly* 42: 82–97.

McNeill, William H. 1963. *The Rise of the West: A History of the Human Community.* Chicago: University of Chicago Press.

Merlin, Pierre, et al. 1971. *L'exode rural, suivi de deux études sur les migrations.* Paris: Presses Universitaires de France, Institut National d'Etudes Demographiques, Travaux et Documents, Cahier 59.

Momsen, Ingwer Ernst. 1969. *Die Bevölkerung der Stadt Husum von 1769 bis 1860.* Kiel: Selbstverlag des Geographischen Instituts der Universität Keil.

Morgenstern, Oskar. 1963. *On the Accuracy of Economic Observations.* 2nd ed. Princeton, NJ: Princeton University Press.

Morrill, Richard L. 1965. *Migration and the Spread and Growth of Urban Settlement.* Lund Studies in Geography, ser. B, no. 26. Lund: Gleerup.

Norberg, Anders, and Sune Åkerman, 1973. "Migration and the Building of Families: Studies on the Rise of the Lumber Industry in Sweden." In Kurt Ågren et al., *Aristocrats, Farmers, Proletarians: Essays in Swedish Demographic History.* Uppsala: Scandinavian University Books, Studia Historica Upsaliensia, 47.

Öhngren, Bo. 1974. *Folk i rörelse: Samhallsutveckling, flyttningsmönster och folkrörelser i Eskilstuna, 1870–1900.* Uppsala: Almqvist and Wiksell, Studia Historica Upsaliensia, 55.

Pasigli, Stefano. 1969. *Emigrazione e compartamento politico.* Bologna: Il Mulino.

Patten, John. 1973. *Rural-Urban Migration in Pre-Industrial England.* Research Papers no. 6. Oxford: School of Geography.

————. 1976. "Patterns of Migration and Movement of Labour to three Pre-Industrial East Anglian Towns." *Journal of Historical Geography* 2 111–119.

Perez Díaz, Victor. 1971. *Emigración y cambio social: Procesos migratorios y vida rural en Castilla.* 2nd ed. Barcelona: Ariel.

Perrenoud, Alfred. 1971. "Les migrations en Suisse sous l'Ancien Régime: Quelques problèmes." *Annales de Démographie Historique 1970,* pp. 251–259.

Pitié, Jean. 1971. *Exode rural et migrations intérieures en France: L'exemple de la Vienne et du Poitou-Charentes.* Poitiers: Norois.

Pollard, Sidney, and David W. Crossley. 1968. *The Wealth of Britain.* London: Batsford.

Pourcher, Guy. 1964. *Le peuplement de Paris.* Paris: Presses Universitaires de France, Institut National d'Etudes Démographiques, Travaux et Documents, Cahier 43.

Poussou, Jean-Pierre. 1971. "Les mouvements migratoires en France et à partir de la France de la fin du XVe siècle au début de XIXe siècle: Approches pour une synthèse." *Annales de Démographie Historique 1970,* pp. 111–178.

————. 1974. "Introduction à l'étude des mouvements migratoires en Espagne, Italie, et France méditerranéenne au XVIIIe siècle." In M. Aymard et al., *Les migrations dans les pays méditerranéens au XVIIIème et au début du XIXème.* Nice: Centre de la Méditerranée Moderne et Comtemporaine.

Pred, Allen. 1961. *The External Relations of Cities during "Industrial Revolution."* Chicago: Department of Geography, University of Chicago.

Redford, Arthur. 1964. *Labor Migration in England, 1800–1850.* W. H. Chaloner, ed., 2nd ed. Manchester: Manchester University Press.

Reinhard, Marcel R., André Armengaud, and Jacques Dupâquier. 1968. *Histoire générale de la population mondiale.* Paris: Montchrestien.

Roof, Michael K., and Frederick A. Leedy. 1959. "Population Redistribution in the Soviet Union, 1939–1956." *Geographical Review* 49: 208–221.

Russell, J. C. 1959. "Medieval Midland and Northern Migration to London, 1100–1365." *Speculum* 34: 641–645.

Sabean, David. 1971. "Household Formation and Geographic Mobility: A Family Register Study in a Wurttemberg Village, 1760–1900." *Annales de Démographie Historique 1970,* pp. 275–294.

Saville, John. 1957. *Rural Depopulation in England and Wales, 1851–1951.* London: Routledge & Kegan Paul.

Schofield, R. S. 1971. "Age-Specific Mobility in an Eighteenth-Century Rural English Parish." *Annales de Démographie Historique 1970,* pp. 261–274.

Schon, Lennart. 1972. "Västernorrland in the Middle of the Nineteenth Century: A Study in the Transition from Small-Scale to Capitalistic Production." *Economy and History* 15: 83–111.

Shaw, R. Paul. 1975. *Migration Theory and Fact: A Review and Bibliography of Current Literature.* Bibliography Series no. 5. Philadelphia: Regional Science Research Institute.

Skinner, G. William. 1964–1965. "Marketing and Social Structure in Rural China," pts. 1, 2, and 3. *Journal of Asian Studies* 24: 3–43, 195–228, 363–399.

Slack, Paul A. 1974. "Vagrants and Vagrancy in England, 1598–1664." *Economic History Review,* 2nd ser., 27: 360–379.

Smith, C. T. 1968. *An Historical Geography of Western Europe before 1800.* London: Longmans.

Tauriaienen, Juhani, and Samuli Koivula. 1973. *The Conditions in and Problems of Rural Depopulation Areas.* Official Statistics of Finland, ser. 32, no. 33. Helsinki: Department for Social Research, Ministry of Social Affairs and Health.

Willcox, Walter F., ed., 1929–1931. *International Migrations.* 2 vols. Publications of the National Bureau of Economic Research, nos. 14 and 18. New York: National Bureau of Economic Research.

Wrigley, E. A. ed., 1966. *An Introduction to English Historical Demography.* London: Weidenfeld & Nicholson.

———. 1967. "A Simple Model of London's Importance in Changing English Society and Economy, 1650–1750." *Past and Present* 37: 44–70.

———. 1969. *Population and History.* New York: McGraw-Hill.

· 12 ·

DEMOGRAPHIC ORIGINS OF THE EUROPEAN PROLETARIAT

A PROLETARIAN WORLD

We live in a proletarian world. Depending on how we classify workers in various sorts of socialist states, either a majority or a fat majority of the world's labor force are people who work for wages, using means of production over the disposition of which they have little or no control. They are proletarians. In this broad but authentic sense of the word, almost all of us are proletarians. Yet quite recently—only a few hundred years ago—very few people anywhere worked for wages. Most people lived in households that exercised considerable control over their means of production, however meager those means. In the past few hundred years, the world has become proletarianized.

That proletarianization was arguably the most far-reaching change in the quality of everyday life to occur in the modern era. It had a more profound impact than did urbanization, secularization, bureaucratization, or any of the other "izations" that occurred in its company. The growth of wage labor at expropriated means of production transformed family life, altered the structure of local communities, created whole new varieties of politics, and overturned the conditions determining the life chances of individuals and households. What is more, the process of proletarianization is continuing in the already quite proletarian Western world and accelerating outside the West. A majority of the world's physicians, for example, now work for wages in large organizations, especially state-run organizations. Dreams and struggles over workers' control, over land reform, and over the growth of alienated labor under socialism all attest to the pressure of proletarianization today.

This chapter was first published as "Demographic Origins of the European Proletariat," in David Levine, ed., *Proletarianization and Family Life* (Orlando, FL: Academic Press, 1984), pp. 1–85. © 1984 by Academic Press, Inc. Reprinted with permission.

Given all this profound transformation, it is astounding to turn to so-cial-scientific writings on large-scale social change. For most of academic social science, proletarianization is a phantom. Amid the tons of writing on industrialization and on the growth of "modern" attitudes, we are lucky to find a few ounces on the emergence of the proletariat. And those rare discussions, for the most part, treat proletarianization as a special case or an incidental consequence. Of what? Of occupational differentiation, of industrialization, or of increase in the scale of production.

Recently, it is true, students of the labor process such as Harry Braver-man, Richard Edwards, and Michael Burawoy have opened up important inquiries into management's strategies of expropriation, and labor historians such as David Montgomery, Michael Hanagan, and Klaus Tenfelde have paid attention to the ways that artisans and skilled workers became increas-ingly subject to capitalist work discipline. Furthermore, European agricul-tural historians, as well as students of cottage industry and related forms of production, have for some time been enriching our understanding of expropriation and wage labor in the villages of Europe. My later discussion will draw extensively on their research. Yet these varied inquiries focus on the experiences of workers who were (or are) already essentially proletar-ian: dependent for survival on the sale of their labor power to capitalists of one sort or another. In any case, social scientists lack a general analysis of proletarianization to complement and modify their many analyses of industrialization or urbanization, whereas historians lack a general account of the processes by which the essentially nonproletarian population of a few hundred years ago turned into the largely proletarian population of today.

The lack is visible even in the one area in which we might have ex-pected a general historical account to fall into place: the growth of the European proletariat since 1500 or so. There, the increase of landless labor has stirred recurrent concern; the relevant evidence is abundant if scattered; and bitter scholarly controversies have borne on such questions as whether English enclosures created a rural proletariat.

Adam Smith addressed the question more than two centuries ago: "The demand for those who live by wages," wrote Smith in *The Wealth of Nations*, "naturally increases with the increase of national wealth, and can-not possibly increase without it."[1] "Those who live by wages" is a short definition of the proletariat. "The liberal reward of labor, therefore," said Smith later on, "as it is the effect of increasing wealth, so it is the cause of increasing population. To complain of it is to lament over the necessary effect and cause of the greatest public prosperity."[2] In Adam Smith's analy-sis, the increasing division of labor resulted from the rational disposition of the factors of production—land, labor, and capital—by those who controlled each of them. Since the increasing division of labor enhanced productivity, it increased the return to all factors of production, including labor. Indirectly, the rational disposition of resources led to the growth of that part of the population that lived from wages alone. It led to the growth of the proletariat.

But how did that growth occur? So far as I know, Adam Smith never analyzed the historical process in detail.[3] Perhaps it seemed too obvious: wage laborers multiplied because the demand for their labor increased. Parson Malthus's pessimistic gloss on Smith, after all, does little more than elaborate that basic relationship. Both Adam Smith and Thomas Robert Malthus lived in a world in which landless laborers were already numerous. In that world, it was common bourgeois practice to wring hands over the decline of independent craftsmen and yeomen and to deplore the reckless breeding of the poor—without doing anything substantial to reverse either one.[4] Smith's innovation was to treat the growth of the proletariat as an inevitable, perhaps even desirable, consequence of increasing wealth.

MARX VERSUS MALTHUS

Writing a century later, however, Karl Marx considered the historical process of proletarianization to be both fundamental and problematic. Chapters 25–32 of his *Capital* discuss at length the formation of the English proletariat. Marx denied emphatically that the smooth operation of demand accounted for the proletarianization of the English labor force. "The proletariat created by the breaking up of the bands of feudal retainers and by the forcible expropriation of the people from the soil," he wrote, "this 'free' proletariat could not possibly be absorbed by the nascent manufactures as fast as it was thrown upon the world."[5]

Note that Marx concentrated on rural, and especially agricultural, workers; only since his time has the term *proletarian* taken on its current connotation of large-shop manufacturing. Although Marx did present the factory wage slave as the extreme case of proletarianization, his own analysis of proletarianization dealt largely with rural workers.

In general, Marx portrayed proletarianization as the forcible wresting of control over the means of production from artisans and, especially, from peasants. "In the history of primitive accumulation," he declared at the end of chapter 26:

> All revolutions are epoch-making that act as levers for the capitalist class
> in course of formation; but, above all, those moments when great masses

of men are suddenly and forcibly torn from their means of subsistence, and hurled as free and "unattached" proletarians on the labor-market. The expropriation of the agricultural producer, of the peasant, from the soil, is the basis of the whole process.[6]

Thus the central fact was the creation of a rural proletariat, working mainly for wages in agriculture, but available at bargain rates for industrial production.

Insofar as he discussed the changing size of the proletariat at all, Marx described two contradictory processes. He followed the classical economists, including Adam Smith, in seeing a general association between capital accumulation and the growth of the proletariat. Although Marx did not specify the population process involved, a plausible reading of his text is that an increase in the total volume of wages permitted more children of existing proletarians to survive. In this reading, the death rate serves as the gatekeeper. It guards the gate both from and to the proletariat. When death relaxes its cold grip on the gate, the proletariat grows. At one point, however, Marx suggested that the substitution of child labor for adult labor encouraged the poor to marry young and to bear many children. If so, changes in the marriage and birthrates mattered as well.

Marx's main argument, in any case, ran in the other direction. Under capitalism, he argued, employers extracted surplus value from the labor power they hired, essentially by squeezing more value in production from workers than it cost to hire them. Then the capitalists reinvested their surplus in the means of production. As a result, the fixed capital represented by the means of production necessarily increased faster than did the variable capital directly committed to the employment of labor. Economies of scale alone would have produced that effect of capital accumulation. Both the centralization of capital in large firms and the imposition of more intensive labor discipline accelerated it. In consequence, according to Marx, the demand for labor power increased much more slowly than capital accumulated.

As workers became increasingly redundant, the famous Industrial Reserve Army—whose existence presumably guaranteed the holding near subsistence of the wages for those who worked—came into being. That was, to Marx's eyes, the central demographic process of capitalism. It was, he said, a cruel peculiarity of the system:

The laboring population therefore produces, along with the accumulation of capital produced by it, the means by which itself is made relatively superfluous, is turned into a relative surplus-population; and it does this to an always increasing extent. This is a law of population peculiar to the capitalist mode of production; and in fact every special historic mode of production has its own special laws of population, historically valid within its limits alone.[7]

Later in the same chapter, Marx briefly mentioned the declining rate of growth of the whole English population as if it supported his analysis. In general, however, Marx seems to have reasoned differently: first, the important increases in the number of proletarians occurred in bursts of expropriation such as the enclosures. Second, once people were proletarians, they more or less reproduced themselves: proletarians begat proletarians, in roughly constant numbers. If that is the case, the growth of the proletariat directly measures both the progress of expropriation and the current extent of exploitation.

In his notebooks of 1857 and 1858, the famous *Grundrisse*, Marx heaped scorn on Malthus. Malthus, Marx complained, had confused the specific conditions of capitalism with a general law of population growth:

It is Malthus who abstracts from these specific historic laws of the movement of population, which are indeed the history of the nature of humanity, the *natural* laws, but natural laws of humanity only at a specific historical development, with a development of the forces of production determined by humanity's own process of history.[8]

In his discussion, nevertheless, Marx appeared to accept a hedged version of Malthus's thesis: that under capitalism population did, indeed, tend to grow faster than the means of subsistence did and thus to encounter devastating positive checks. If so, Marx was admitting implicitly that natural increase played a significant part in the proletariat's growth.

In any case, Marx's main argument was that "overpopulation" was not an objective external condition that somehow weighed on the system of production, but a consequence of the social organization linking different sorts of people to the existing means of production. "Never a relation to a *non-existent* absolute mass of means of subsistence," he wrote in his notebook,

but rather relation to the conditions of production, of the production of these means, including likewise the *conditions of reproduction of human beings*, of the total population. This surplus purely relative: in no way related to the *means of subsistence* as such, but rather to the mode of producing them.[9]

Then he bent the discussion back to an analysis of the tendency of capitalism to separate increasing numbers of workers from the means of production. Thus Marx was clear enough about the structural conditions favoring the growth of a proletariat, but vague about the demographic processes involved.

A CHANCE FOR SYNTHESIS

Marx's analysis and his apparent indecision about the relevant demographic mechanisms provide a prime opportunity for complementary work by historians, demographers, and other social scientists. There is the opportunity to verify the main lines of Marx's analysis; for example, the idea of spurts of proletarianization as the consequence of massive expropriation. There is the opportunity to specify the different paths by which people moved from artisanal or peasant production into various forms of wage labor. There is the opportunity to assign relative weights to those paths: which ones bore the most traffic? There is the opportunity to integrate them into a general account of the flows of people by which the largely peasant and artisanal European population of 1500 or 1600 became the overwhelmingly proletarian European population of 1900 and later.

How and why did that great shift occur? Why in Europe rather than elsewhere? In the century since Marx's death, one version or another of that double question has dominated the agenda of modern European economic and social history. Some of the debate has pivoted on the facts: how many yeomen, for example, did the enclosures actually displace? Some of the debate has concerned the proper way to state the questions: Weber and Tawney differed over the appropriate *Problemstellung* as much as over the historical facts. And much of the debate has dealt with explanations: why did capitalism flourish earlier in Britain than in Prussia?

Since the questions are vast and compelling, fragments of the debate on proletarianization, including the debate on the population changes involved, appear in widely scattered literatures. Historians of industrialization (especially British industrialization), for example, have carried on a long discussion of labor supply in the industrial revolution. The discussion pivots on the demographic origins of the proletariat.[10]

Demographers who have looked to the European experience for guidance in understanding the transition from high to low fertility and morality throughout the world have repeatedly asked one another whether massive proletarianization was by-product, cause, or countercurrent of that transition in Europe.[11] Local and regional historians have edged into the demographic problem by discovering, in place after place, similar transformations of the labor force: the disproportionate increase of proletarian occupations and industries.[12] Students of poverty and of control over the poor have necessarily brushed against the problem of proletarianization but have not posed the demographic changes very directly or effectively.[13]

Analysts who have sought self-consciously to trace the process of proletarianization have commonly come from the ranks not of historians, but of economists and sociologists. They have focused, by and large, on the expropriating and disciplining of wage workers, rather than on the development of wage labor itself.[14] Finally, the builders and critics of Marxist schemata concerning the general development of capitalism have had to commit themselves to one view or another of the origins of the proletariat.[15] These many overlapping enterprises offer the student of proletarianization a rich, broad, vigorous literature. The literature's richness, breadth, and vigor, however, make the task of synthesis mindbreaking.

I do not claim to have surveyed all the relevant sources, much less to have synthesized them. In this chapter, I aim merely to tidy up a small but crucial corner of this vast space: the demographic corner. The chapter discusses where population processes fit into general accounts of Europe's proletarianization. It specifies which features of those population processes have to be explained and why they are problematic. It offers a limited review of existing knowledge concerning those processes and proposes some tentative explanations of the particular paths taken by European proletarianization. On its way, the chapter spends more time on concepts and techniques than any reader will enjoy; conceptual and technical questions, it turns out, comprise a significant obstacle to understanding how proletarianization occurred.

Nevertheless, the chapter's main point is to pursue into the demographic sphere two of Marx's central insights concerning proletarianization: that the basic population processes respond to the logic of capitalism instead of being somehow exogenous to it, and that the strategies of capitalists themselves determine the form and pace of proletarianization.

COMPONENTS OF GROWTH

A dull, routine sociological procedure promises to help the search for the origins of the European proletariat. It is to break the search into three parts: (1) analysis of components of growth, (2) explanation of individual components and their interactions, and (3) integration of those partial explanations into a general account of the process. Let me stress at once that these are logical subdivisions of the task, not distinct temporal stages. If we do not begin with a piece of the third part—with a tentative account of the entire process of proletarianization—we are quite likely to wander through the analysis of components and to stumble through the explanation of individual components and their interactions. The secret is to begin with a tentative account that is clearly verifiable, falsifiable, and correctible—or better yet, two or three competing accounts that are clearly verifiable, falsifiable, and correctible: accounts built, let us say, on the arguments of Adam Smith and Karl Marx.

Components of growth? At its simplest, the analysis consists of defining precisely the change being analyzed, preparing a logically exhaustive list of the components of that change, and estimating the contribution of each component to the change as a whole. In the case of European proletarianization, we must begin with working definitions of *Europe* and *proletarian*. That means deciding what to do with Iceland, Constantinople, Malta, the Azores, and so on. It also means deciding whether it is possible to be a little bit proletarian—for example, whether the independent weaver who hires himself out for the harvest qualifies as a proletarian, as one-quarter of a proletarian, or as no proletarian at all. What about his young children? Uninteresting decisions, these, except that they significantly affect the results of the analysis.

These tedious but crucial decisions made, we can begin to ask how the absolute number and the proportion of the European population in the category *proletarian* changed from, say, 1500 to 1900. We shall come back to guesses at the real numbers later. For now, the thing to notice is that we can break down those numbers into geographic, temporal, and, most important, logical components. We may ask *where* the transformation of nonproletarian populations into proletarian populations occurred. Did it happen mainly in areas of advanced capitalism? We may ask *when* the transformation occurred. Did the process accelerate greatly with the expansion of large-scale manufacturing after 1800? We may also ask *how* it happened. But the how, in this case, concerns the change's logical components.

If we turn to standard demographic accounting procedures, we shall find three logical possibilities. Each is, in turn, the result of two possible changes. The three logical possibilities are social mobility, natural increase, and net migration. Marx stressed *social mobility*: the movement of a particular social unit from one category to another as a consequence of an alteration in its own characteristics or relationships. If individuals are our social units, all persons who, in their own lifetimes, lose control over their means of production and move into wage labor add to the toll of proletarianization. In fact, the same individuals often oscillate between the two categories throughout their lifetimes. The net effect of all such moves across the boundary is the component of social mobility.

Natural increase is the result of births and deaths. If I read him aright, Marx implicitly assumed that natural increase was an unimportant component of the European proletariat's growth: the deaths more or less balanced out the births, and the net enlargements of the proletariat depended on new entries by people who began life as nonproletarians. This is where the components-of-growth analysis gets interesting, for several alternative possibilities exist. Given their vulnerability to infectious disease, starvation, and war, proletarians sometimes underwent a natural *decrease*: deaths exceed births. The question is: how often and how much? If natural decrease were the normal situation of proletarians, the proletarian population would be in something like the situation of most preindustrial cities: they would have to recruit substantial numbers of newcomers merely to maintain their current size. To grow, they would have to recruit very large numbers indeed.

The birthrates of proletarians could also normally have run above their death rates. In that case, the proletarian population could grow without any new recruitment of nonproletarians. If the proletarian rate of natural increase were higher than that of the rest of the population, the proletarian share of the total population would tend to rise—even in the absence of lifetime mobility from nonproletarian to proletarian. With additional permutations of fertility and mortality, still further alterations are quite possible. For example, the proletarian rate of natural increase could have risen over time.

The third component—*net migration*—likewise offers multiple possibilities. If we are considering the European population as a whole, the migration that matters consists of moves of proletarians into and out of the Continent. Because that component, too, sums up numerous losses and gains, its overall effect may have been nil, a substantial addition to the proletariat, a substantial subtraction from the proletariat, or something else. If we start considering migration into and out of the proletarian populations of different European regions, instead of reckoning for Europe as a whole, the problem becomes more complex and interesting.

To recapitulate: as in any population change, we can break down the increase of the European proletarian population from 1500 to 1900 (or for any other interval) in terms of a standard accounting equation:

$$P_2 = P_1 + (IC - OC) + (B - D) + (IM - OM) + e$$

where P_1 and P_2 are the population at the beginning and end of the interval; IC and OC are the numbers of persons who make lifetime moves into and out of the category; *B* and *D* are the births and deaths of members of the category; *IM* and *OM* are in-migration and out-migration; and *e* is the measurement error summed over all these observations.

THE IMPORTANCE OF GROWTH COMPONENTS

Why should anyone care about these hypothetical numbers? For more reasons than one. First, if we are to attempt any general account of Europe's proletarianization, we have no choice but to formulate hypotheses about the components of growth. The hypotheses may be implicit, and they may be very crude; they may consist, for example, of assigning an indefinitely large positive value to the net effect of lifetime moves and zero values to all the other components. That is the tone of Marx's analysis. Adam Smith, on the other hand, wrote as if natural increase were the only component differing significantly from zero. Thus in the absence of any exact numbers, simple knowledge of which components were positive or negative, large or small, would give us the means of judging whether Marx's formulation, Smith's formulation, or some modification of one or the other was more adequate.

The choice is not merely hypothetical. Although the problem has often been badly posed, how the proletariat grew figures somehow in every account of industrialization and every history of the working class. Speaking of Sweden from 1750 to 1850, Christopher Winberg points out that the peasantry increased by about 10 percent, whereas the landless classes of the countryside more than quadrupled. "The dominant interpretation of this development," he comments,

> can be summarized as follows: An important part is played by the "autonomous death-rate," i.e., a death-rate that remains relatively autonomous in relation to the economic development. Particularly from c. 1810 onwards, the decline of the death-rate was due to a series of exogenous factors, such as smallpox vaccination, the peace period from 1814 onwards and the cultivation of the potato. The result was a rapid increase in population that led to a subsequent proletarianization.[16]

"This interpretation," Winberg continues, "is not based on any coherent theory." He counters with an argument having five important elements:

1. On the whole, the landless population of the early eighteenth century did not constitute a distinct social class, since it consisted

largely of widowed old people and other nonproducers; the separate class formed mainly after 1750.

2. The peasant population of the eighteenth century generally maintained an implicit system of population control in which, for example, declines in mortality normally produced a visible narrowing of opportunities for employment, which in turn led young people to delay marriage and to have fewer children.

3. After 1750, widespread reorganization of rural estates by their landlords turned many peasants into landless laborers.

4. Peasant villages themselves became increasingly stratified, with many smallholders likewise becoming landless laborers.

5. In the process, the rural population as a whole broke out of the older, implicit system of population control and moved toward strategies of relatively early marriage and high fertility.

Winberg documents these generalizations by means of a close study of a sample of Swedish rural parishes. In those parishes, he finds a general tendency for the landless to marry later and have fewer children than do the full-fledged peasantry. He also finds a small movement from landless labor into landholding and a very large move in the opposite direction. The bulk of the rural proletariat's increase, in his analysis, resulted from the unequal balance between these flows. Thus Winberg ends up assigning central importance to social mobility. yet he by no means eliminates natural increase from the picture. Swedish villages, however, are not the whole of Europe. We must find out how generally Winberg's model of proletarianization applies elsewhere.

We have a second reason for concern about the three components of growth, as their relative weight and direction make a genuine difference to our understanding of the historical experience of proletarianization. To the extent that lifetime moves into the proletariat comprised the dominant process, we might expect a good deal of proletarian action to consist of efforts to retain or recapture individual control over the means of production. On the other hand, the same extensive recruitment through lifetime moves would make it more difficult to account for the persistence of an autonomous proletarian culture, enduring from one generation to the next.

To the extent that natural increase was the main source of growth in the proletariat, on the other hand, we would find it easy to understand autonomous, persistent proletarian culture, but hard to account for artisanal and peasant themes in that culture. To the extent, finally, that net migration was the primary source, we might expect the proletariat to be the locus not only of alienation, but also of aliens, and to be correspondingly resistant to unification. The contrasting portraits of proletarian experience that come to us from, say, E. P. Thompson and Louis Chevalier may result in part from their having studied populations differing significantly in these regards or from their having implicitly assumed differing configurations of social mobility, natural increase, and net migration.

Third, the *composition* of each of the three major components matters as well. Zero net migration over a long period may result from no moves in either direction, from large but exactly equal flows of definitive in-migrants and definitive out-migrants, from numerous circular migrants who spend some time at the destination and then return to their points of origin, and from a number of other equalizing migration patterns. These are very different social situations and have very different implications for social control, proletarian culture, class conflict, and the recruitment of an industrial labor force.

Positive or negative net migration may likewise result from a wide variety of migratory patterns, each affecting life at the destination in different ways. The same observation holds for the subcomponents of social mobility: temporary or definitive moves into the proletariat. Clearly it holds for births and deaths as well. Consider the difference between (1) slight natural increase due to high fertility almost balanced by high mortality and (2) slight natural increase due to low fertility matched with even lower mortality. That is the difference between the death-ridden experience of the sixteenth century and the long life of the twentieth. If we want to understand the quality of proletarian experience, we have to make that distinction very clearly.

Components of growth matter, finally, because their relative magnitudes bear directly on two continuing debates in European history. The two debates overlap. The first concerns the source of labor supply in the industrial revolution, the second the reasons for Europe's rapid population growth in the eighteenth and nineteenth centuries.[17] The debate about labor supply echoes the differences between Smith and Marx; it pits explanations in which the expropriation of peasants and artisans figures prominently against explanations in which population growth is a relatively smooth, automatic response to new opportunities for employment.

The debate on population growth begins with the fact that over Europe as a whole, natural increase accelerated markedly during the eighteenth century and continued rapidly into the nineteenth. The debate pivots on the extent to which declines in mortality due to life-saving technical improvements in medicine, sanitation, or nutrition (as opposed to more general improvements in the standard of living, temporary increases in fertility, or other alternatives) explain the acceleration of natural increase.

In both debates, the changes in places of mortality and fertility in the growth of landless labor are questions of central importance. If, for example, the growth of the proletariat was due mainly to decreasing mortality attributable to an improving standard of living, both the expropriation theory of labor supply and the fertility-increase interpretation of population growth become less credible. To make such distinctions, we do not need the precise numbers. But we do need to consider the full set of components of growth.

It is a good thing we do not need the precise numbers. If we did, the task would be impossible in our lifetimes. Although the methods of archeology, paleobotany, and historical demography may one day converge on fine estimating procedures for the European population, at present we have only a crude sense of the grand totals.

What is more, we have no large-scale estimates of the proletarian population. We face one of those recurrent historiographical ironies: the ideas of *labor force* and *employment* are at once essential to keeping the sorts of statistics we need and contingent on the very process we hope to trace, proletarianization. In the absence of capitalized firms and extensive wage labor, no one bothers to do the requisite bookkeeping. Generally speaking, we cannot look to the statistical reports of national states before the full bloom of nineteenth-century proletarianization. For earlier periods, we must combine analysis of trends in small areas that historians have studied intensively, with indirect inferences from evidence concerning other processes that are somehow connected with proletarianization.

Principles of Proletarianization

Before examining trends and making inferences, however, we had better get straight some definitions and principles. Let us seek definitions that are broad enough to permit solid comparisons across time and space, supple enough to capture matters of degree, and yet precise enough to call forth reliable measurement.

Whatever practical separation of proletarians from nonproletarians that we adopt, we must keep in mind that the process of proletarianization has two logically distinct components: (1) separation of workers from control of the means of production (*expropriation*, for short), and (2) increasing dependence of workers on the sale of their labor power (*wage work*, for short). To concretize these abstract components, we might imagine computing the following items for some specific population:

T: total hours per year spent in productive labor
L: hours per year spent in labor controlling the means of production
D: hours per year spent in dependent labor, defined as $T - L$
W: hours per year spent in labor for wages
e: level of expropriation, defined as D/T
w: wage dependence, defined as W/T
P: level of proletarianization, defined as $e \times w$
$\dot{P}$:   rate of proletarianization, defined as $\dot{e} + \dot{w}$

Thus an increase in either the proportion of all work time spent in dependent labor or the proportion of all work time spent in labor for wages raises, by definition, the level of proletarianization. Since the degree of control over the means of production actually forms a continuum rather than a simple either/or, in a practical application we would no doubt have to weight D—hours per year in dependent labor—for the extent of control exerted by workers.

Although expropriation and wage work have a strong historical connection—that is, after all, one of this chapter's premises—in some important circumstances they moved in different directions. The enserfment of European peasants, for example, certainly reduced their control of the land they tilled; they spent increasing shares of their total labor time in dependent labor. But enserfment did not ordinarily increase their dependence on wages for survival. Instead, landlords commonly assigned households to subsistence plots and forced each household to deliver some combination of monetary dues, agricultural products, and labor services. Expropriation increased, but wage work may well have declined.

In recent times, mine and factory workers who were already fully dependent on wages have often confronted bosses who were seeking to weaken the workers' control of the pace or quality of production by subdividing tasks, imposing time discipline, or applying piece rates. In these cases, dependent labor increased as a share of all labor; expropriation occurred without an increase in wage work.

The opposite case also occurred, although it was surely rarer: in nineteenth-century Europe, for instance, landlords frequently liquidated their rights to forced labor of villagers in the landlords' fields in favor of cash payments that they then used to hire labor in those same fields. Such a shift increases wage work without decreasing the workers' control over the means of production.

In principle, then, the two components of proletarianization—expropriation and wage work—vary in partial independence from each other. The extent and pace of proletarianization are, by definition, results of the two. Figure 12.1 lays out the definition schematically and also sketches four rough hypotheses concerning the extent and character of the two components' covariation under capitalism:

1. In general, expropriation and wage work increase together.
2. However, considerable expropriation sometimes occurs without changes in wage work.
3. Except at low levels of proletarianization, wage work rarely increases (or, for that matter, decreases) without corresponding changes in expropriation.
4. At the extreme, nevertheless, it is less likely—even under capitalism—that workers will be completely dislodged from control over the means of production than that they will become entirely dependent on wages.

My reasoning is simple: employers do not value wage work for its own sake. They impose it as a means of accomplishing expropriation, but not vice versa. To the extent that they can seize control of labor power without

Figure 12.1. The Components of Proletarianization and Their Likely Covariation

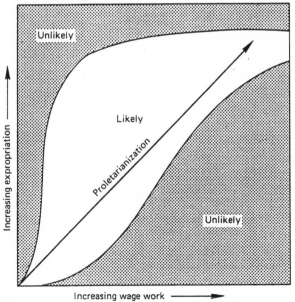

paying wages, they do so. The major exception to the rule comes at low levels of proletarianization, at which landlords and capitalists sometimes prefer the payment of a money wage to the provision of subsistence in kind; English farmers who had live-in hands, for example, tended to expel them from bed and board when food became expensive.[18]

The reasoning continues: employers seek to minimize the price they pay for labor power, as the standard Marxist analysis says, in order to maximize their return from the labor applied to production.[19] But they expropriate all factors of production, including labor power, in order to control the deployment of those factors in the service of increased return. Extensive proletarianization is therefore likely to occur only when the payment of wages is a relatively attractive means of expropriating labor power— because the need for labor is highly variable, because neither custom nor force will suffice, or for some other reason. At the extreme, however, the requirements of production themselves set greater limits on expropriation than they do on wage work: the costs of subdividing and degrading complex tasks eventually become prohibitive, and the worker whose skill and discretion make a difference to the quantity and quality of the product always has some vestige of bargaining power.[20]

Note how this approach works. Note especially how it does *not* work. It does not equate impoverishment or immiseration with proletarianization. So far as the definition is concerned, the rise or fall of real income is irrelevant to the extent of proletarianization. Nor does wealth as such figure in the definition of the proletariat; to the extent that household wealth consists of nonproductive goods—television sets, automobiles, and so on— many households are wealthy but proletarian. Nor do style of life, education, skill, or locus of employment, in themselves, become criteria of proletarianization. There is no requirement of consciousness: in principle, an expropriated wage worker might well think of himself or herself as a full-time member of the bourgeoisie.

In this approach, the idea of a *new working class* consisting of skilled technicians, professionals, and researchers in science-sector industries is no contradiction in terms. The concept does not require that proletarians be factory workers or even be producing commodities. Not that income, wealth, life style, education, skill, locus of employment, consciousness, or productive position are trivial matters; far from it. But the concepts adopted here make the relationships of these important aspects of social life to proletarianization into questions of fact rather than matters of definition.

The treatment of proletarianization as a result of expropriation and wage work neither assumes that the process continues indefinitely in one direction nor ties the proletariat, by definition, to capitalism. Both the continuity of the trend and the extent of its dependence on capitalism become questions for theory and for research. Worker-participation schemes, for example, do sometimes increase slightly the workers' control of production decisions and occasionally reduce the dependence of workers on wages.[21] To that small extent, they move the workforce's average position toward the lower left-hand corner of our diagram; they deproletarianize. But one could reasonably argue, on the other hand, that socialist regimes such as that of the Soviet Union have adopted capitalists' methods with a vengeance, using the full power of the state to accelerate expropriation and extend wage work in the name of the workers; they have been great proletarianizers.

Proletarianization within ostensibly noncapitalist states has led many observers to conclude that proletarianization has no special tie to capitalism but results inevitably from any form of industrialization. In my view, however,

1. Over the past few centuries, the association between the development of capitalism and the growth of proletarianization has been strong enough to indicate that in general, one causes the other.
2. The association between capital concentration and proletarianization in agriculture, as well as other forms of nonindustrial production, makes dubious the idea that *industrialization* is proletarianization's necessary condition.
3. On the whole, capitalists acquire a greater interest in expropriation and wage work than do other sorts of power holders.
4. When socialists push proletarianization, they do so in imitation of capitalists.

Fortunately for the pursuit of this chapter's purposes, only the first two propositions matter greatly to the search for the demographic origins of the European proletariat. During most of the European experience since 1500, capitalists have stood at the center of the proletarianizing process.

My approach, to be sure, rests on a guiding hypothesis: over the long run, expropriation and wage work were, and are, more fundamental than income, wealth, life style, and so on.

More fundamental? I mean that changes in expropriation and in dependence on wages have wider ramifications in everyday social life than do changes in income, wealth, etcetera. I also mean that to an important degree, changes in expropriation and wage dependence *cause* changes in income, wealth, life style, and so on. At this point, we move out of the simple, arbitrary world of concepts. We begin working with arguments that are open to empirical challenge, and to theoretical scrutiny as well.

EXPLAINING PROLETARIANIZATION

Remember the crude expression for the rate of proletarianization $\dot{P}$:

$$\dot{P} = \dot{w} + \dot{e},$$

where $\dot{w}$ is the rate of change of wage dependence and $\dot{e}$ is the rate of change of expropriation. If the sum of the two rates is positive, the population is proletarianizing. If it is negative, the population is deproletarianizing. If it stands at or near zero, the population's structure is remaining about the same. My general argument is elementary, perhaps obvious: the rate of proletarianization is a direct function of changes in each of the following variables: (1) the demand for goods and services; (2) the cost of establishing new units; (3) the concentration of capital; and (4) the coercive power of employers. The *mechanisms* by which these variables affect the increase of expropriation and wage dependence are mainly matters of the number, size, and internal organization of the producing units: concentration or deconcentration of control over production decisions within producing units, growth or decline in the average size of producing units, elimination or consolidation of the producing units that already exist, limits on the creation of new producing units, and increases or decreases in the amount of labor drawn from the average worker.

The most obvious illustrations of these mechanisms at work come from periods and places in which a small number of producers were expanding their scale of production at the expense of their neighbors. In his old but still useful analysis of the growth of a rural proletariat in England, William Hasbach gave center stage to *engrossing*: the building up of large farms by a few active landlords. Here is his summary of the background conditions for engrossing:

> They were, first, the more luxurious standard of life adopted by the landlord class, and their consequent need of a large income: secondly, the enclosures, for the most part results of that need; then the increased price of provisions, to which the enclosures contributed; next the system of the large farm, pioneered about this same period; and finally the new method of cultivation, which demanded men of a different class and larger capital. But besides these there were other forces at work. There

was the attraction which the great industry, then just developing, exercised on capacity, enterprise and capital. And there were the indirect taxes, imposed to pay the interest on the growing national debt rolled up by trade wars and colonial wars, which of course increased the cost of living.[22]

Under these conditions, according to Hasbach, those who had the power increased their holdings invested and reinvested their capital, and shifted to labor-efficient farming techniques. In the process, they squeezed smallholders, tenants, and squatters off the land into agricultural or industrial wage labor.

In our terms, then, engrossing directly and strongly reduced the number of nonproletarian positions in rural areas: the size of producing units increased, their number declined, production decisions concentrated, existing units disappeared, and the possibility of creating new units decreased. Behind these changes lay all the general conditions for proletarianization we have already reviewed: rising demand for goods and services, increasing cost of establishing new units, concentration of capital, and growing coercive power of employers.

We begin with the obvious part: changes in the demand for goods and services directly affect the rate at which new producing units come into being and the rate at which existing units change scale. Change in demand, however, likewise affect the rate of population growth, and thereby the rate of change in total labor supply. As a result, they have no necessary effects on the rate of proletarianization. Although economies of scale may well result from expanded demand, those economies have no reliable effects on the division of labor between proletarian and nonproletarian producers. All other things being equal, the system merely reproduces itself on a larger scale. In modern Europe, for example, household production proved itself enormously elastic in response to the demand for textiles, woodworking, metal crafting, and similar goods. Beyond some point of expansion, on the other hand, the cost of establishing new units often rises, since established producers squeeze the newcomers, the costs of materials and equipment rise, and/or the quality of available resources declines. The theorem of diminishing marginal returns in agriculture rests on just such an observation of the effects of bringing marginal land into cultivation.

From the perspective of proletarianization, however, the central process is the concentration of capital. When small producers become capitalists and when petty capitalists become big capitalists, they increase the share of all means of production they control and expand the amount of labor power they buy from others. Enclosing landlords, manufacturers who drive artisanal competitors out of business, local authorities who restrict the number of available farms, peasants who take on additional hired hands, masters who expand the numbers of their journeymen or apprentices, and merchants who build up networks of dependent domestic producers all are agents of proletarianization.

Broadly speaking, anyone who has an interest in buying labor power also has an interest in proletarianization. Buying is by no means the only way to control labor; coercing, bartering, and using kinship ties or patron-client networks also make labor available under some circumstances. Buying becomes attractive when those who control the means of production require large amounts of labor and when that requirement is discontinuous—for example, when the demand for agricultural labor swings importantly from season to season. The transformation of workers into proletarians serves the employer in several different ways: by expanding the employer's power to redirect the factors of production in search of maximum return, by increasing the employer's ability to capture the existing returns from labor, by externalizing some of the costs of maintaining the workforce, and by facilitating the employer's removal of unwanted labor power.

Each of these advantages to the employer, however, means disadvantages for other parties, especially the workers themselves. Workers have investments in their skills, and they therefore have the most to gain from allocations of production that differ from those that most favor the employer. Political authorities often have an interest in maintaining existing uses of land, labor, or commodities in order to ensure their revenues from taxation. Rentiers often have an interest in reliable rents from the very same land that capitalists want to commit to new uses. Workers have a direct interest in holding on to the returns from their labor. And the externalization of maintenance costs—supplying food, finding revenue in times of unemployment, caring for the ill, and so on—is likely to shift the burden to workers' households as well as to the community at large. Even if a giant neoclassical cost-benefit analysis gives the net advantage to proletarianization, therefore, the immediate interests of most of the parties directly involved dictate determined resistance. The employer's interest does not automatically prevail.

As Douglass North and Robert Thomas (who have, in fact, conducted something like a giant neoclassical cost-benefit analysis of capitalist property relations) suggest, one of the most important conditions promoting the growth of wage labor is the emergence of a state that supports the consolidation of property into disposable bundles and guarantees the owner a major part of the return from that property's use.[23] I am not so sure as

North and Thomas are that in the two leading examples, the Netherlands and England, the property-confirming state developed *before* capitalist property relations prevailed. Indeed, Alan Macfarlane has argued that a version of capitalist property was already quite visible in thirteenth-century England.[24] Yet the Dutch and English states surely did favor the consolidation of property into disposable bundles.

More generally, any conditions that augment the coercive power of employers favor proletarianization; and coincidence of economic and political power in the same capitalist hands, the outlawing of workers' organizations, the monopolization of food or land by employers, and the presence of surplus labor all make it easier to expropriate workers. But with this last item—the presence of surplus labor—we pass to the other side of the dependent/independent labor ratio and enter an area of intense controversy.

The question is: how and why does the total workforce increase? For practical purposes, we may concentrate on why the population as a whole increases. That simplification glides past several fascinating questions:

1. How does the changing age structure produced by alterations in fertility and mortality affect the proportion of the population in prime working ages?
2. Under what conditions do children and old people participate in productive labor?
3. What governs the extent of female labor force participation?
4. What part do household strategies play in the supply of different sorts of labor?
5. How do employers squeeze additional labor out of a given amount of labor power?[25]

However, the largest component by far of increase in the workforce—and the only one on which we can hope to assemble information for Europe as a whole—is growth in the base population from which the workforce comes. Let us think about that growth.

Many students of European history have treated population change as an essentially autonomous variable, a product of such "accidents" as plagues and crop failures. The rate of population growth figures as an exogenous variable—a very important one—in the North-Thomas account of European economic history. In his famous analysis of labor supply in the industrial revolution, J. D. Chambers proposed a general distinction between the period of slow growth before the mid-eighteenth century and the great acceleration thereafter. Chambers allowed for the possibility that after 1750

industrial employment encouraged earlier marriage, which in turn accelerated fertility. But on the whole his analysis treated the rate of population
growth as a powerful external determinant of labor supply. As Christer
Winberg points out, a similar argument has dominated historians' thinking
about changes in the Swedish labor force. Over Europe as a whole, most
historians have been willing to consider population growth a crucial but
exogenous variable in economic change.

Yet we have grounds for being skeptical: for doubting that the rate of
population increase was independent of the pace of proletarianization. The
most important ground for skepticism is the association, in region after
region of Europe, of rapid accelerations in population growth with visible
increases in landless labor; we shall review a number of cases later on.

Such an association could, of course, result from the application, over
and over again, of the rule that population pressure produces proletarians.
In fact, most such regions probably did begin their proletarianization with
a stock of underemployed, cheap labor; that made them attractive to entrepreneurs. But once the process had begun, rates of marriage, childbearing,
and migration all seem to have responded actively to employment opportunities. By that point, the growth of the workforce was at least partly dependent on the tempo of its proletarianization.

I suggest, then, that four major variables governed the rate of increase
in the total population:

1. changes in the demand for goods and services;
2. changes in the opportunity cost of childbearing;
3. previous proletarianization of the population, the effect of which
   operated with a lag corresponding to the average age at which children began productive labor; and
4. an exogenous component combining the effects of "natural" fluctuations of fertility and mortality due to alterations in disease, nutrition, disaster, and other factors external to the system.

I suggest, further, that as proletarianization proceeded, the first three variables—the demand for goods and services, the opportunity cost of childbearing, and previous proletarianization—became increasingly dominant.
Natural fluctuations declined in importance. The portmanteau "exogenous" component, to be sure, introduces a touch of magic into the analysis:
many irregularities will disappear into the portmanteau. The point of this
formulation, however, is not to provide a comprehensive explanation of
population growth, but merely to indicate that with proletarianization,

population growth responded increasingly to the economic situation of the proletarianized population.

Set down in tabular form and marked to indicate whether the general relationship is supposed to be positive ($+$), negative ($-$), or indeterminate ($\pm$), the variables I have proposed to explain the rate of proletarianization are shown in Table 12.1. Without specification of the effects of changing demand for goods and services, we have no reason to think that the growth or decline of demand will, in itself, affect the population's proletarianization; effects on the two sides are likely to cancel each other. But the lists say that everything else being equal, the following conditions will promote proletarianization:

1. increases in the cost of establishing new producing units;
2. concentration of capital;
3. increases in the coercive power of employers;
4. declines in the opportunity cost of childbearing; and
5. previous proletarianization.

As a model of the actual process, this is very crude. As a guide to searching through the historical experience of proletarianization, however, it will serve us well. We look for times and places in which capitalists are consolidating their power over production and in which the alternatives open to the local population are diminishing. That is, I think, a credible general description of the most common circumstances of proletarianization in Europe.

Table 12.1. Determinants of the Rate of Proletarianization

Determinants of increase in wage labor	Determinants of increase in potential workforce
Demand for goods and services ($+$)	Demand for goods and services ($+$)
Cost of establishing new production units ($+$)	Opportunity cost of childbearing ($-$)
Concentration of capital ($+$)	Existing level of proletarianization ($+$)
Coercive power of employers ($+$)	Natural fluctuations ($\pm$)

WHERE AND WHEN?

Concretely, where and when did these general conditions for proletarianization converge in modern Europe? Did they, in fact, reliably produce increases in expropriation and wage work? Despite innumerable fragments of the necessary evidence, we do not know. As a way of sorting out the evidence, we might try distinguishing some very different social settings:

Estate systems (example: East Prussia), in which large landlords produced grain for the market by means of servile labor, whose subsistence came mainly from small plots assigned in their households. The consolidation of landlord control ordinarily occurred at the expense of peasants who had been more or less independent producers; in those same areas, the nineteenth-century emancipation of servile laborers produced a temporary movement away from the proletariat, but the unfavorable conditions for access to the land pushed more and more of the freedmen into wage labor.[26]

Large-farm systems (example: East Anglia), in which large landlords or their tenants likewise produced grain for the market, but with wage labor. They grew variously from estate systems, from specialized farming, and from peasant farming. They expanded by adding more wage laborers. In most cases, however, small independent producers disappeared as the large farms grew.[27]

Specialized farming (example: coastal Flanders), in which peasants specialized in cash-crop production and nonproducing landlords were unimportant. It did not necessarily promote proletarianization. In the case of grain production, for instance, independent family units actually took up a larger share of the world market during the nineteenth and twentieth centuries.[28] Elsewhere, however, some specialists commonly expanded their holdings, accumulated capital, and hired their own wage laborers (e.g., the northern Netherlands).[29] In those cases, specialization also proletarianized the population.

Peasant farming (example: western France), in which landlords lived from rents and peasants lived from various combinations of owned, rented, and sharecropped land. Peasant farming, as such, tended to block proletarianization as long as it lasted. But peasant farming sometimes turned into specialized farming, as peasants took up more and more cash-crop production; sometimes gave way to large-farm or estate agriculture, as landlords seized their advantage; sometimes succumbed to the increasing subdivision of inheritances, which eventually became too small to support households; and sometimes—when the available labor was underemployed and markets for industrial products were more accessible than were markets for cash crops—hosted proletarianizing cottage industry.

Cottage industry (example: Lancashire), in which petty entrepreneurs parceled out industrial production among households that also devoted some of their labor to small-scale subsistence farming and/or seasonal wage labor in agriculture. Cottage industry always grew up on an agricultural base. It began as a complement to some sort of farming and as an alternative to less attractive and remunerative forms of labor, such as military and domestic service. But when cottage industry flourished, it tended to squeeze out other activities and to become an aggressive proletarianizer.[30]

Urban craft production (example: north Italian cities), in which masters of small shops controlled the labor of journeymen and apprentices lodged in their masters' households. Like peasant farming, urban craft production tended to resist proletarianization so long as it retained its pure form. But masters sometimes used the structure of the craft to expand the numbers of journeymen and, especially, apprentices under their control. When the masters succeeded, they helped create a proletarian large-shop and factory system.[31]

Large-shop and factory production (example: the Rhineland after 1850), in which capitalists assembled and coordinated the labor of many wage workers in the same place. This system has the reputation of being the great proletarianizer. In our time, it is no doubt the setting in which the workforce has come closest to being entirely expropriated and completely dependent on wages. Yet several features of large-shop/factory production qualify its claims to being the primary site of European proletarianization. First is its tardiness: prior to the twentieth century, large shops and factories were relatively rare; before then, most industrial expansion occurred through the proliferation of small shops and even of household production. Second, in skilled trades, the earlier grouping of workers in large shops often involved little change in the technology of production and in the relationship of the worker to the means of production, although it did eventually facilitate the owner's imposition of timing and work discipline. Third, in many industries the large-shop and factory workforce came largely from workers who were already involved in household or small-shop production within the same industry. All three of these features mitigate the historical impact of large shops and factories as the settings of European proletarianization. Nonetheless, when large shops and factories did grow fast, they had unparalleled power to proletarianize. Only mining (which came to share many organizational features with factory production) rivaled them.

The categories are neither tight nor exhaustive. On the one hand, the types overlap, and on the other, they leave out such important configurations as the smallholding cash-crop production that commonly appeared in Europe's winegrowing areas. Still, the typology suggests the sort of variation that any systematic analysis of proletarianization must take into account and identifies the chief settings in which European proletarianization actually did take place.

Given the general conditions for proletarianization enumerated earlier—increases in the cost of establishing new producing units, concentration of capital, increases in the coercive power of employers, declines in the opportunity cost of childbearing, and previous proletarianization—some of these settings stand out as prime candidates. The very creation of estate systems, large-farm systems, cottage industry, and large-shop/factory production entailed the creation or recruitment of local proletariats. Specialized farming, peasant farming, and urban craft production, in contrast, did not necessarily proletarianize. Which of the first four were the dominant settings for proletarianization changed over time. The two agricultural settings were probably the dominant sites of European proletarianization before the eighteenth century; cottage industry became increasingly important after 1700; and large-shop/factory production did not play the major role before the end of the nineteenth century.

In considering these alternative modes of production, let us flee from technological determinism. The seven settings did not differ in importance as precipitators of proletarianization because expropriated wage labor was technically essential to some of them and technically incompatible with others. The settings differed because of their varying association with the proletarianizing conditions we enumerated earlier: increasing costs of new productive units, concentration of capital, growing employer coercive power, declines in the opportunity cost of childbearing, and previous proletarianization. The expansion of cottage industry, for example, favored proletarianization, not because of any intrinsic affinity between expropriated wage labor and weaving or woodworking, but because (1) the concentration of capital in the hands of entrepreneurs and the domination of access to markets by those same entrepreneurs radically narrowed workers' room for maneuver, and (2) the opportunity cost of childbearing sank so dramatically—since young children could make significant contributions to household income, and older children became less expensive to "place" in adult positions—as to favor the production of more and more new proletarians. Ultimately, then, the search for general explanations of European proletarianization should concentrate less on such matters as the demand for textiles or wheat than on the conditions favoring the reorganization of relations of production. Perhaps we can gain insight into those conditions by breaking with the abstract, deductive approach to the problem that I have followed so far. Let us ask when, where, and in what quantities European proletarianization actually occurred.

How Many Proletarians?

Considering how much discussion has gone into the subject, we have amazingly little knowledge of the timing and loci of European proletarianization. For Britain, John Saville has ventured this general sketch:

1. the development of commercial farming during mediaeval times and the existence, by the beginning of the sixteenth century, of a class of capitalist farmers;
2. the slow disappearance of the peasantry as a substantial element in rural society over the three centuries from 1500 to 1800 . . .;
3. the presence in the countryside, from the sixteenth century onwards . . . of a class of landless labourers; their swelling numbers in the eighteenth century, in part the result of the former decline of the peasant class, in part the product of natural population growth;
4. the growth of the large farm . . .;
5. the growing concentration of land in the ownership of the landlord class from the middle of the seventeenth century onwards . . .;
6. accompanying the social changes in the agrarian structure went the technical transformation of learning methods.[32]

Saville's lucid distillation of a murky literature suggests that the timing of the major agrarian changes—hence the growth of an agricultural proletariat—is well known. It is not. Think, for example, about one of the easiest numbers to establish: the proportion of landless laborers in Britain's agricultural population. Table 12.2 presents commonly cited sources for estimates of the share of landless labor in the agricultural population as a whole at various times from about 1600 to 1851.

A glance at the table identifies two major difficulties: first, the numbers oscillate implausibly from one period to the next; second, the categories and base populations fluctuate almost as wildly. A comparison of Gregory King's high figure for 1688 with the Census of 1831 permitted J. H. Clapham to make his notorious "demonstration" that the scale of agricultural production had risen only modestly over the period of the enclosures and

Table 12.2. Estimates of the Percentage of the English, English and Welsh,
British, or British and Irish Agricultural Population Consisting of Laborers

Date	Percentage	Reference agricultural population	Author of estimate	Citation
c. 1600	25–33	Entire rural population, England and Wales	Alan Everitt	Everitt, 1967: 398
1688	66	English families[a]	Gregory King	Mathias, 1957: 45
1760	59	Families, England and Wales[b]	Joseph Massie	Mathias, 1957: 45
1803	62	Families, England and Wales[c]	Patrick Colquhoun	Colquhoun, 1806: 23
1812	49	Males in agriculture, Great Britain and Ireland	Patrick Colquhoun	Colquhoun, 1815: 124–125
1831	76	Males 20 and over in agriculture, Great Britain	1831 Census	Abstract: xiii
1841	76	All persons classified	1841 Census	Spackman, 1847: 143
1851	80	All persons classified[d]	1851 Census	Census, 1851: 148
1851	79	Total in agriculture[e]	1851 Census	Bellerby, 1958: 3
1911	64	Total in agriculture[e]	1911 Census	Bellerby, 1958: 3
1931	59	Total in agriculture[e]	1931 Census	Bellerby, 1958: 3
1951	54	Total in agriculture[e]	1951 Census	Bellerby, 1958: 3

[a]Includes nobility, gentry, freeholders, farmers, laboring people, outservants, cottagers, and paupers. I have taken "labouring people, outservants, cottagers and paupers" as laborers. From the total for those categories, I have subtracted my best estimate of the proportion of the total population of England and Wales in places of 20,000 or more—11.0 percent in 1688—to allow for the urban location of that share of general laborers.

[b]Reference population includes nobility, gentry, freeholders, farmers, husbandmen, and laborers. In this case, I have counted all "husbandmen and labourers" as agricultural laborers.

[c]Reference population includes nobility, gentry, freeholders, farmers, laborers in husbandry, pauper laborers, and pensioners who work. Here "labourers in husbandry, pauper labourers, and pensioners who work" count as agricultural laborers. I have, however, subtracted my best estimate of the proportion of the total population of England and Wales in places of 20,000 or more—17.4 percent in1803—from the total for pauper laborers and pensioners, to allow for the urban location of that share of general laborers.

[d]Excluding persons listed as wives, children, and relatives of farmers and graziers.

[e]Excluding "relatives occupied on the farm."

to conclude that enclosures could not have played a major part in the creation of the agricultural proletariat.

One reason that Joseph Massie's figures record an apparent drop in the proletarian share of the agricultural population between 1688 and 1760 is simply that in 1688, King saw no need to distinguish rural industrial workers from the rest of the laborers, whereas in 1760, Massie enumerated

100,000 families who were "Manufacturers of Wood, Iron, etc.," likewise in the country. Their inclusion in agricultural labor would bring Massie's proportion up to 66 percent: exactly the same as King's. But that correction would be risky; after all, the differences between Massie's estimates and King's could have registered a genuine increase in rural industry.

Again, Massie mentioned no "vagrants" in 1760; he was estimating the likely return from taxes on chocolate, and vagrants mattered little for that purpose. Gregory King, on the other hand, listed 30,000 vagrants for 1688, and Patrick Colquhoun counted a full 234,000 of them in 1803. Many "vagrants" were indubitably unemployed agricultural laborers on the road. Should they, too, be included in the agricultural proletariat? Judgments on such matters depend on knowledge of the very trends and processes one might have hoped to derive from the comparison of Alan Everitt, King, Massie, and Colquhoun.

We can, I fear, draw no more than a few tentative, meager conclusions from the series:

1. During most of the seventeenth and eighteenth centuries, a large share—most likely a majority—of Britain's agricultural labor force consisted of landless laborers.
2. Since the population of England and Wales may well have risen from 4 to 5 million people during the seventeenth century and from 5 to 9 million during the eighteenth, even a relatively constant proportion of proletarians implies a substantial increase in their absolute number.
3. During the early nineteenth century, both the absolute number and the proportion of agricultural laborers grew considerably.
4. After the middle of the nineteenth century, laborers left British agriculture so rapidly that the total agricultural labor force contracted, and the share of farmers rose significantly.

As Phyllis Deane and W. A. Cole put this last point:

Apart from a fall of about 8 1/2 percent in the 1870's, and a rise of about 13 percent between 1911 and 1921, the number of British farmers has shown remarkably little tendency to vary. Farmers (excluding relatives) thus accounted for about 15 per cent of the occupied population in agriculture in 1851, about 20 per cent in 1911 and about 27 per cent in 1951.[33]

Thus the century after 1851 witnessed a deproletarianization of British agriculture, at a time when the industrial labor force was proletarianizing rapidly. But when and how the earlier proletarianization of agriculture occurred does not leap out at us from the available national figures.

To locate any figures on proletarianization at a regional or national scale, we must cross over to the Continent. In his survey of changes in agrarian class structure at a number of locations across the continent, Slicher van Bath offers multiple examples of the disproportionate growth of small-holders, cottars, and laborers. (Slicher himself, I hasten to add, interprets the changes as illustrating "the influence that a rise in population had on the distribution of the various groups in rural society.")[34] In the Dutch province of Overijssel, he reports the pattern of increase among heads of household shown in Table 12.3. Two things were happening in Overijssel: first, a great expansion of cottage textile production was swelling the number of weavers and spinners in the countryside; second, the agricultural population itself was proletarianizing. The net effect of the two was a substantial proletarianization of Overijssel's population in the seventeenth and, especially, the eighteenth century.

We have already noticed the changes in Sweden's rural population—a full nine-tenths of the total population—between 1750 and 1850. There, the rural proletariat grew more than thirty times as fast as the peasantry did. (One consequence of that expansion was an overall decline in real wages for Swedish agricultural workers over the century after 1750.)[35] From about 30 percent of the rural population in 1750, the proletariat grew to about 60 percent in 1850. If we were to extrapolate that sort of change to the European scale, it would imply an increase from about 35 million rural proletarians in 1750 to about 90 million in 1850; the increase rate for the whole continent would be lower than that for Sweden, because in Europe as a whole, the rural population only increased by about a third, whereas in Sweden it doubled. Still, an increase of 55 million rural proletarians

Table 12.3. Growth Rates of Various Overijssel Populations, 1601–1795

Category	Base period	Annual rate of growth
Total population	1675–1795	0.7
Nonagricultural population	1675–1795	0.9
Agricultural population	1602–1795	0.3
Farmers on family-sized farms	1602–1795	0.1
Cottars on small holdings	1601–1795	0.2
Cottars and day laborers	1602–1795	0.4

Source: Computed from Slicher van Bath 1977:130.

would represent the great majority of the continent's total population increase (which was on the order of 85 million people) between 1750 and 1850.

Now, Sweden is most likely an extreme case because of its large rural population, its relative lack of rural manufacturing, and its fairly late industrialization. However, a similar computation based on one of Europe's old industrial areas, the Kingdom of Saxony, produces an estimate in the same general range: about 51 million of the total 85 million increase in population consisting of expansion in the continent's rural proletariat.[36]

Let us look more closely at Saxony, since it is the only large area of Europe for which we have reliable estimates of the proletarian population running back to the sixteenth century. For the years 1550, 1750, and 1843, Karlheinz Blaschke provides us with counts of the following categories of the Saxon population:

Urban	Rural
Bürger (full citizens)	*Bauern* (peasants)
Inwohner in Städten (dependent urban workers)	*Gärtner* and *Häusler* (gardeners, cottars)
Geistlichkeit (professionals, intellectuals, etc.)	*Grundherren* (noble landlords)

The classification into "urban" and "rural" is my own, but aside from the rural residence of a few parsons and professionals (*Geistlichkeit*) and the urban residence of a few noble landlords (*Grundherren*), it looks like a fairly accurate division. On the urban side, the *Inwohner*, or in-dwellers, were essentially proletarians: servants, journeymen, apprentices, and others. On the rural side, the *Gärtner* and *Häusler* (gardeners and cottars) join the *Inwohner* in the proletarian category. *Gärtner* had their own garden plots, *Häusler* nothing but their dwellings. *Gärtner* is sometimes also translated as "smallholder"—but in either translation designates a worker who had to sell a substantial part of his labor power to survive. Table 12.4 gives Blaschke's counts of the numbers of workers in each of these categories from 1550 to 1843.

Blaschke's figures tell an important story. Throughout the three centuries after 1550, according to this classification, the Saxon countryside was more proletarian than the cities were; even in 1550, gardeners, cottars, and village labor made up 25.6 percent of the rural workforce, and dependent workers comprised 15.5 percent of the urban total. Within both the urban and the rural sectors, the proletarian share rose dramatically. Both from

Table 12.4. Distribution of the Workforce of Saxony, 1550, 1750, and 1843

	Year		
Category	1550[a]	1750	1843
Urban			
Full citizens	82.0	54.0	47.5
Dependent workers	15.5	44.8	51.7
Professionals, etc.	2.5	1.2	0.7
	100.0	100.0	99.9
Number	141,500	370,500	631,000
Rural			
Peasants	73.5	38.6	20.4
Gardeners, cottars	6.8	47.9	70.9
Village labor	18.8	12.7	8.2
Noble landlords	0.8	0.8	0.5
	99.9	100.0	100.0
Number	292,400	647,500	1,225,000

[a]The 1550 figures omit the region of Oberlausitz.
Source: Blaschke 1967:1990–191.

1550 to 1750 and from 1750 to 1843, gardeners and cottars—the all-purpose wage workers of the countryside—grew the fastest. Translated into annual rates of increase, the comparison is shown in Table 12.5. The numbers of professionals and peasants hardly increased over three centuries, a fact that probably reflects the implicit fixing of quotas for each of them. Full-fledged burghers, regular village labor, and landlords did not increase

Table 12.5. Growth Rates of Various Saxon Populations, 1550–1843

Category	1550–1750	1750–1843
Full citizens	0.2	0.4
Dependent urban workers	1.0	0.7
Professionals, etc.	0.1	0.0
Peasants	0.1	0.0
Gardeners, cottars	1.4	1.1
Village labor	0.2	0.2
Noble landlords	0.4	0.1
Total	0.4	0.6

much faster. the dynamic categories were the proletarian ones. In terms of rates alone, those categories grew faster before 1750 than after. The fact that they made up an increasing share of the total, however, meant that their impact on total growth expanded later; as a result, the overall rate of growth in the workforce accelerated after 1750: 0.6 percent per year from 1750 to 1843, as opposed to 0.4 percent from 1550 to 1750.

We are not staring at the ripples of a backwater. The Kingdom of Saxony contained such major industrial centers as Leipzig and Dresden. With 46 percent of its labor force in manufacturing by 1849 and 53 percent in manufacturing by 1861, the Kingdom of Saxony moved at the leading edge of Germany industrialization.[37] The kingdom's "potential labor force" (the population fifteen and over, less housewives, dependent daughters, students, invalids, and certain other categories) grew by an average of 1.5 percent per year between 1822 and 1849 and by 1.2 percent per year between 1849 and 1864; those rates were higher than those elsewhere in Germany.[38] The kingdom was the only major region of Germany gaining from migration more or less continuously from 1817 to 1865.[39] In fact, Wolfgang Köllman offers the Kingdom of Saxony as a principal example of the overrunning of employment opportunities by population growth—in his view, the crucial process that depressed wages in the old crafts, drove workers out of those old crafts, and provided a labor force for expanding large-scale industry. We do not have to accept Köllmann's whole analysis of proletarianization to recognize Saxony as a good base for the analysis of European proletarianization as a whole.

Table 12.6 shows the results of imagining that the entire European population (except for Russia) behaved like Saxony. The procedure is simple: adopt Paul Bairoch's estimates of rural and urban population, interpolate values for 1550, 1750, and 1843, and then apply the percentages of proletarians that Blaschke finds in Saxony's rural and urban sectors to the whole European population. Although this approach multiplies suppositions by approximations, it suggests orders of magnitude for the growth of the European proletariat.

If Europe behaved like Saxony, both rural and urban proletarianization were massive. The totals show the proletarian population increasing more than eightfold, whereas the nonproletarian population increased by a mere 13 percent and the population as a whole rose from 71 million to 210 million people. The estimated absolute increase in the proletarian population from 1550 to 1843 was 131 million, nearly equivalent to the total increase in Europe's population; the computations suggest that the nonproletarian population hardly increased at all. Of the 131 million increase, furthermore, the estimates show 100 million as occurring within the rural

Table 12.6. Estimates of the European Proletarian Population, 1550, 1750, and 1843
(Based on Blaschke's figures for Saxony)[a]

Year and category	Total population	Proletarian population	Nonproletarians	Percentage proletarian
1550				
Rural	61,175	15,661	45,514	25.6
Urban	10,325	1,600	8,725	15.5
	71,500	17,261	54,239	24.3
1750				
Rural	113,100	68,539	44,561	60.6
Urban	18,150	8,131	10,019	44.8
	131,250	76,670	54,580	58.4
1843				
Rural	146,453	115,844	30,609	79.1
Urban	63,194	32,671	30,523	51.7
	209,647	148,515	61,132	70.8

[a]In thousands. I have changed Bairoch's estimate of total population for 1500 (85 million), which is implausibly high, to a more conventional 56 million. The adjustment diminishes the estimate of the proletarian population in 1550 from 24.5 to 24.3 percent.
Sources: Blaschke 1967:190–191; Bairoch 1977:42.

sector, only 31 million in the cities. That was especially true for the period before 1750, when only a small share of Europe's proletarianization *could* have occurred in the cities. After 1750 (and, in fact, especially after 1800), the balance shifted toward urban proletarianization: in short, a massive proletarianization of the population, occurring first and foremost in the countryside.

No one region can sum up the experience of the whole continent. Yet, in the absence of other series as ample in space and time, we have no reason to shrug off the experience of the region of Leipzig, Chemnitz, and Dresden as an inappropriate model for Europe. The orders of magnitude are likely to be correct, and if so, we can reasonably adopt three working hypotheses: (1) that the increase in Europe's proletarian population was on the order of its *total* population increase—the nonproletarian population barely increased; (2) that over the sixteenth to the mid-nineteenth centuries, most of Europe's proletarianization took place in village and country; and (3) that with the nineteenth century, cities became increasingly important as the sites of proletarianization. These hypotheses call for careful verification.

Given a broad definition of the proletariat, the second and third hypotheses become more plausible as we examine the temporal pattern of Europe's urbanization. Figure 12.2 graphs Bairoch's estimates of changes since 1500 in the European population by size of place. It reminds us that the great majority of the population lived in rural areas until quite recently. More important, it shows that Europe did not urbanize significantly between 1500 and 1800. Indeed (if you accept my reduction of Europe's total population in 1500 from 85 million to a more plausible 56 million), the estimates suggest that Europe as a whole *de*urbanized slightly over those three centuries. Here are the percentages: 1500, 16.1 percent; 1700, 13.0 percent; 1800, 14.4 percent; 1900, 41.3 percent; 1970, 62.4 percent. Only after 1800, according to these figures, did the frenzied urbanization with which we are familiar begin.

In absolute terms, the rural population never actually declined. But by the middle of the nineteenth century, with about 150 million people, it had come close to its limit. From that point on, almost the whole of the European population increase occurred in urban areas.

The site of proletarianization shifted as the locus of the population growth changed. Blaschke's figures simply show that shift to have occurred a bit earlier in relatively industrial Saxony than in Europe as a whole. My grafting of Blaschke's figures onto Bairoch's estimates for urban and rural population adjusts for the difference in timing. But both sets of figures indicate that the nineteenth century swung the active loci of European proletarianization toward the cities.

If we start our inquiry at 1500, we will be dealing with a total of about 56 million people. If we end it in 1900, we will arrive at a total of around 285 million people. That is an increase of some 230 million people in the four centuries. At the beginning (to extrapolate from the estimates we have squeezed from the combination of Blaschke with Bairoch), perhaps 17 million of the 56 million total were proletarians of one kind or another. By 1900, on the order of 200 million out of the 285 million total were proletarians. That gives us an increase of around 180 million proletarians to account for, and it also gives us a smaller increase—perhaps 45 million—of nonproletarians to explain. If those are the numbers, then we must ask when, where, and how the increase occurred.

The timing of population growth sets important limits on the possible timetable of proletarianization. Since the population of Europe (not including Russia and Turkey) rose from about 150 million to 285 million during the nineteenth century, a large part of the net increase in the proletariat must also have occurred in the nineteenth century. Nevertheless, given the significant eighteenth-century expansion of wage labor in such widely

Figure 12.2. Bairoch's Estimates of the European Population by Size of Place, 1500–1970

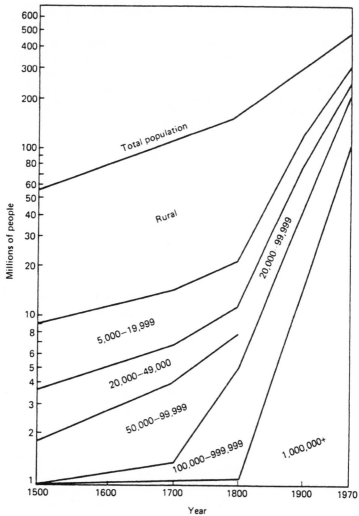

Note: Excludes Russia and Turkey.
Source: Bairoch 1977: 42.

scattered areas as England, Poland, and Spain, it is quite possible that by 1800 something like 100 million Europeans were already proletarian workers and members of their households. Notice again the implications of Bairoch's estimates for 1800: only 20 million or so Europeans then lived in urban areas. At least there-quarters of the proletariat must have lived in small towns, villages, and open countryside. In tracing the proletarianization of Europe before 1800, we have to give priority to farms and villages, but from the nineteenth century onward, cities start occupying our attention.

Let me sum up these speculations and approximations. We are thinking of components of growth within a population that broke down something like this (in millions):

	1500	1800	1900
Total population	56	150	285
Nonproletarians	39	50	85
Proletarians in cities	1	10	75
Rural proletarians	16	90	125

To avoid any misunderstanding, let me repeat: these numbers are no more than thoughtful guesses, orders of magnitude, and hypotheses to verify. Their revision stands high on the agenda of historical demography. If they hold up to further investigation, the numbers will have important implications. They suggest a seventy-five-fold increase in the proletarian population of European cities from 1500 to 1900, an eightfold increase of the rural proletariat during the same period. They concentrate the great bulk of European proletarianization in rural areas before 1800 and in cities after then. With these orders of magnitude in mind, let us return to the components of growth: social mobility, natural increase, and net migration.

SOCIAL MOBILITY

Speaking of the sixteenth- and seventeenth-century Netherlands, Jan de Vries distinguishes between two models of rural social organization: a peasant model and a specialization model. Peasants produce enough to survive at a conventional level of well-being and to meet their basic outside obligations. They work to insulate themselves from the market's volatility while avoiding as much as possible purchases of goods and services. They seek, in general, to maintain all their offspring on the land. With natural increase, that strategy produces a subdivision of holdings and intensified cultivation of the available land. the result is that per capita income almost never rises; it remains constant or declines.

Specialists, on the other hand, exploit the market by concentrating on profitable crops. They specialize in agricultural production and purchase those goods and services they cannot produce profitably. They accumulate capital and reinvest it in land and equipment. Such children as they cannot profitably employ on the land they place in other forms of enterprise. Over the long run, their per capita income tends to rise. Specialists are capitalists, peasants are noncapitalists. In fact, the peasants are often anticapitalists.

The two models identify two quite different exits from the peasantry. The peasant path leads eventually to wage labor in agriculture or industry. The specialization path leads to cash-crop farming. The peasant strategy proletarianizes, whereas the specialization strategy—if successful—capitalizes. The peasant strategy leads to wage labor for two reasons: first, because its internal logic results sooner or later in the overrunning of the household's capacity to support itself from the land it controls and, second, because in the meantime capitalists are expanding *their* control over the land and over other means of production. English enclosures and Polish "refeudalization" are variants of that second pattern.

Whether the new proletarians remained in agricultural wage labor, moved into manufacturing, or took up some combination of the two varied significantly as a function of the local labor requirements of agriculture and the market for local manufactures. In the Swiss mountain areas studied by Rudolf Braun, cottage textile manufacturing oriented toward Zurich displaced the subsistence agriculture of the highlands. In the Leicestershire agricultural villages studied by David Levine, cottage industry provided the context for proletarianization where the landlord tolerated it, but dairy farming produced a later, slower, and more subtle form of proletarianization where the landlord would not tolerate manufacturing. In the Flanders studied by Franklin Mendels, the proletarianizing populations of the coast moved into agricultural wage labor, whereas those of the interior moved into a mixture of agriculture and textile industry and shifted their weight from one to the other as a function of the available wage.

This last example serves as a reminder that the specialists' strategy also fostered a certain amount of proletarianization. Although those who succeeded in specializing became petty capitalists, those who failed moved into the proletariat. Moreover, the more successful cash-crop farmers became employers of wage laborers from among their skidding neighbors and from nearby regions of mixed agriculture and industry. Mendels has pointed out, in fact, that small-scale industrial production tended to expand especially in

regions having nearby sources of part-time and seasonal agricultural employment, which reduced the industrial employer's minimum maintenance
costs for labor. The interdependence of Flanders's coastal cash-crop areas
and internal cottage-industry areas illustrates the point very well.[40]

Parallel paths to those of peasants and specialists led away from the
world of artisans. Artisans slipped into the proletariat as cheaper production
processes reduced the demand for their wares and as entrepreneurs assumed
control over the means of production. But a few artisans climbed into the
bourgeoisie by becoming successful entrepreneurs. Herbert Kisch gives us
the contrast between Silesia and the Rhineland.[41] In both places, the
growth of rural textile production undercut the urban craft guilds. But in
Silesia, the process was one of almost pure proletarianization: a small number of chartered merchants worked with large landlords who were happy
to have the weaver serfs contributing to the incomes of their estates. In the
Rhineland, proletarianization was likewise the main trend, but a few master
craftsmen in Cologne, Barmen, Aachen, and elsewhere accumulated capital
and made themselves pivotal figures in textile production. Although Kisch
does not give us the details of labor-force recruitment, lifetime movement
from artisan to proletarian must have been a common experience in both
regions. In neither case, however, is it likely that social mobility was the
main component of the proletariat's growth. Natural increase and migration must have been important in both Silesia and the Rhineland.

NATURAL INCREASE

Natural increase or decrease is the net effect of births and deaths. the proletariat grows through natural increase when, in any given period, more
proletarians are born than die. Perhaps we should distinguish between the
proletarian children of nonproletarian parents and the proletarian children
of proletarians. In the first case, we stand midway between social mobility
and natural increase: if, at a given succession, a peasant holding fragments
into pieces too small to support the heirs, we may debate how much of
that family's move into the proletariat is due to natural increase. The same
is true of the "extra" child of a peasant family who spends his or her life as
a servant or day laborer. Yet at least some of the resulting expansion of the
proletariat is attributable to natural increase.

The least ambiguous and most important case is somehow the most
ignored. It is the natural increase of full-fledged proletarians. If, on the
average, the natural increase of wage laborers were greater than that of
peasants and artisans, that fact alone would suffice to produce a relative

growth of the proletariat without any skidding of peasants or artisans and without any in-migration of proletarians. I suggest that differential natural increase was the principal component in the relative growth of the European proletariat from 1500 to 1900. More precisely, I suggest that the principal component was a natural increase resulting from the difference between fairly high mortality and very high fertility.

To be even more exact (and at the risk of being ponderous), I propose the following hypothesis: on the average, proletarians responded to economic expansion with greater declines in mortality and greater increases in fertility than nonproletarians did and responded to economic contraction with greater increases in mortality but no greater declines in fertility than nonproletarians did. The consequence was a disproportionate natural increase of proletarians in good times, not completely compensated by the natural decrease of bad times. Since the period we are considering was, on the whole, an era of economic expansion, such a system would have produced a significant tendency for the proletariat to increase more rapidly than the rest of the population. My hypothesis is that it did.

In its main lines, the hypothesis generalizes to the entire proletarian population the model of demographic change that Mendels developed to deal with the "proto-industrialization" of Flanders and elsewhere.[42] The hypothesis does not mean that proletarians always had higher fertility than nonproletarians did. We have already seen that the opposite was true among the Swedish villagers studied by Winberg and can find similar evidence elsewhere. The hypothesis does mean that the demographic responses of proletarians and nonproletarians to economic expansion and contraction differed significantly. To put it schematically, nonproletarians responded to changing opportunities for the placement of their household capital, whereas proletarians responded to changing opportunities for wage labor.

In one muted form or another, the hypothesis has been around a long time. In his pioneering study of the Vale of Trent, Chambers noted the higher natural increase of parishes with rural industry between 1670 and 1800. Although they lack crucial evidence concerning the components of growth, Blaschke's analysis of Saxony, Klíma's discussion of Bohemia, and Braun's portrayal of the Zurich highlands all bring out a similar contrast between the slow-growing regions of peasant agriculture and the fast-growing regions of rural industry.[43] In his direct attack on the problem, Levine identifies a relationship between the rising natural increase and rural industrial growth in eighteenth-century Shepshed and between the rising natural increase and agricultural proletarianization in nineteenth-century Bottesford. Levine also provides a plausible interpretation of the demographic ups and downs of the famous village of Colyton, Devon, as a consequence of the rise and fall of rural industry.[44]

Following the same line of inquiry, Wrightson and Levine trace the population growth of Terling, Essex, to the proletarianizing effects of a large-farm system.[45] Kussmaul has made a good case for a sequence in which English farmers expelled live-in servants during periods of rising food prices; servants became day laborers; day laborers married younger and in greater numbers; and fertility rose.[46] Elsewhere, and with very fine evidence, Gaunt has argued for a similar tuning of natural increase to opportunity among Swedish rural proletarians.[47]

If such a relationship holds, it reverses conventional wisdom. We commonly think of rural proletarianization as a *consequence* of rapid population growth—too many people for the available land. But the possibility we see here is that proletarianization may induce rapid population growth. Of course, both may be true. Then a process of proletarianization initiated by some such action as enclosure will tend to perpetuate itself up—or, rather, down—to the limit set by starvation. At the limit and in this special case, Malthusian models begin to work fairly well. (Even in the case of widespread famine, however, the usual circumstance is not usually an absolute shortfall in available food per capita, but a maldistribution due to the lack of fit between needs and entitlements.)[48]

How and why would the natural increase of proletarians tend to exceed that of nonproletarians? The critical relationships link fertility, marriage, and the availability of employment. In a world in which most households control their own means of production, the chief opportunities for young adults are to inherit positions within their own households or to enter other households. In the world of European artisans and peasants, the capital of a household set stringent limits on the number of persons it could sustain; household capital thereby limited the number of children who could remain at home into adulthood, and especially into marriage and parenthood. The only way to enter another household as a full-fledged adult was to marry into it. Persons who entered as servants, apprentices, day laborers, and the like ordinarily acquired no control over the household means of production and no right to marry or to procreate. Opportunities to marry, to have children, and to place one's children in full-fledged adult positions thus depended on the rate at which senior positions in households were opening up. Mortality was the chief determinant of that rate. But sometimes out-migration or the putting of new land into cultivation also provided adult opportunities. To an important degree, the system regulated itself: nuptiality and fertility adapted to changing opportunity, and total population remained fairly constant over the medium run.[49] Under these circumstances, couples adjusted both their marriages and their childbearing to the probable availability of adult positions and to the probability that their newborn children would survive to adulthood. As a result, marriage and fertility surged after famine or pestilence wiped out many adults and slowed when mortality declined. Or so it seems. In the present state of our knowledge, any hypothesis implying widespread, deliberate fertility control before the nineteenth century and outside the Westernized industrial countries is controversial.[50]

The idea of deliberate fertility control of any great extent before the nineteenth century counters a set of ideas that demographers cherish:

1. that in general, human populations have lived under a regime of "natural" fertility, without imposing deliberate, self-conscious controls over conception;
2. that variations in the fertility of populations outside the wealthy nations of our own era have resulted from differences over which people did not exert deliberate control, at least not for the purpose of controlling conception, such as marriage customs, sexual taboos, breast-feeding practices, nutrition, illness, and so on;
3. that once the members of a population *do* begin to control births, they keep at it, with the consequence that a fertility decline begun in earnest leads unerringly to a stable low fertility; and
4. that such a decline requires a fundamental shift in attitudes away from ignorance, passivity, and short-run gratification.

Students of European population changes who subscribe to these views point to several different sorts of evidence. First, following Louis Henry, they commonly insist that deliberate fertility control will show up in the record as differential age-specific fertility: at a given age, women who have been married longer and/or who have had more children will bear children at a lower rate than will other women in the same population; solid evidence of those age-specific differentials is, in fact, quite rare for periods before the nineteenth century. Second, they draw attention to the fact that when strong evidence of deliberate fertility control does appear, it tends to increase irreversibly with time. Third, the broad similarity in the timing of fertility decline in different parts of Europe, despite drastic differences in levels of income, urbanization, and industrialization, couples with an apparent tendency of culturally homogeneous regions to behave as units within the fertility decline: some sort of diffusion and cultural change is suggested.

Yet there is evidence on the other side. First, there *are* well-documented "preindustrial" cases that meet the stringent tests of parity-dependence.[51] Second, there are many more cases in which the evidence is less direct and compelling, but in which differentials in nuptiality and fertility by class and time period correspond closely to variations in economic interest.[52] Third, Ronald Lee's exacting time-series analyses of the best national data available for the long run of English history display a significant tendency for both nuptiality and fertility to rise and fall as a function of real wages.[53]

The main relationships are hard to disentangle empirically from the contrary effects. It is likely, for example, that improvement in nutrition simultaneously boosted fertility and depressed mortality.[54] It is quite possible, as William Langer has suggested, that the expanding cultivation of American plants, such as the potato, significantly improved life expectancy and thus contributed to natural increase without any necessary rise in fertility. Yet the general hypothesis that people adjusted marriage and fertility to the availability of adult places in crafts and on the land is not absurd. In one form or another, it has been around since Malthus. And it is compatible with many forms of fertility control short of the self-conscious efficacy of twentieth-century contraception.

Proletarians faced a set of circumstances different from that for peasants and artisans. To the extent that the world around them was proletarian, they had both the incentive and the opportunity to marry and form their own households early. They could acquire at quite a young age the means of survival as adults. The characteristic organization of work and the characteristic lifetime curve of earnings—rising rapidly with adolescence, falling steadily from young adulthood—provided further encouragements to marriage and fertility.

On balance, these generalizations hold more clearly for employment in rural industry than for employment in agriculture. In agriculture, landlords' great control over the opportunities for wage labor, coupled with their characteristic political authority, gave them strong influence over the possibility that young people could settle, marry, and bring up children. The rise of wage labor in agriculture—as rural Sweden has already taught us—sometimes *diminished* opportunities for marriage. Industrial employment, mediated by small merchants, gave householders more independence. Indeed, it sometimes promoted marriage.

Especially in the many variants of domestic industry, the standard labor unit was not a single individual, but a household: for example, a weaver plus several spinners and tenders.[55] To work in these arrangements, it was almost essential to form a household. Speaking of the region of Charleroi (now in southern Belgium) during the eighteenth century, Hervé Hasquin declares, "Thus, in these working-class settings, *all* members of the family worked, since *all* wages were welcome. The women and girls made spun goods; at a very young age, the boys were pushed hard; they were not spared the most demanding work."[56] Hasquin shows that the birthrate rose in the towns in which industry was expanding—by now, a classic finding. He concludes that "having children resulted increasingly from deliberate intention."[57]

In his more general analysis of the Belgian fertility decline, Ron Lesthaege adopts a similar argument:

> With the accelerated growth of employment outside the family-related artisanal workshops or agricultural enterprises during the Industrial Revolution, an even larger section of the population became both economically independent and capable of establishing a household at an earlier age. The precariousness of the wage-earners' sustenance ceased to be related to their age, and they had no more grounds for postponing their marriages.[58]

So long as employment opportunities, however marginal, were expanding, a proletarian strategy of early marriage and high fertility made sense. At least it made sense in the short run.

The findings from Wrigley's and Schofield's reconstruction of English population dynamics from 1541 to 1871 deserve special attention. The English evidence shows clearly that well before the decisive nineteenth-century decline in fertility, rates of marriage and birth more than once had risen and fallen significantly. In general, nuptiality and fertility rose with real wages, at a lag of about forty years. That relationship grew stronger over time as the link between the aggregate population growth and food prices grew weaker. (Wrigley himself, I must admit, considers the nuptiality-wage link to have remained substantially uniform from the sixteenth to nineteenth centuries and regards the downturn in nuptiality after the downturn of real wages after about 1780 as "fatal" to the view that proletarianization promoted nuptiality.)[59]

In the medium and long runs, furthermore, death rates did not depend on real wages. The results strike a blow against a strict Malthusian interpretation of English experience, since the English seem to have avoided the positive check of heightened mortality in response to excessive population growth. The results also strike a blow against the notion of population pressure, since the rate of population growth apparently had little independent effect on mortality, fertility, or nuptiality. But these results are at least compatible with the emergence of a wage-driven demographic system. David Weir has shown that as a whole, similar dynamics operated in France from 1740 to 1829. Both countries give evidence of having turned marriage and childbirth to employment opportunities.

Net Migration

Migration figured in the formation of the European proletariat in two rather different ways. From the perspective of Europe as a whole from 1500 to 1900, migration's chief contribution was negative: the Continent shipped out many more migrants than it took in, and the bulk of the out-migrants were proletarian. Before 1750, the net outflows were small: colonists to the Americas, Slavs into continental Asia, trickles of settlers into other parts of the world. With the accelerating population growth of the later eighteenth century, out-migration speeded up as well. A plausible estimate for the period from 1800 to World War I is a net loss of 50 million Europeans to extracontinental migration. Before 1900, those out-migrants came disproportionately from the British Isles. From 1846 to 1890, for example, an estimated 48 percent of all European out-migrants came from England, Scotland, Wales, or Ireland.[60] The loss of migrants was equivalent to a fifth or a sixth of the Continent's entire nineteenth-century population growth.

Most of those millions were proletarians. A prototype of the transatlantic migration was the outflow from seventeenth-century Tourouvre-au-Perche.[61] The roughly 300 migrants from Tourouvre and vicinity and their numerous descendants played a major part in the settlement of Quebec. Labor recruiters intervened in a local but very active system of migration, in which wage laborers already predominated. The recruiters drew a high proportion of young men in their twenties, most of them apparently servants and day laborers. In Canada, to be sure, their grants of land transferred them out of the proletariat. In the European reckoning, nevertheless, they amounted to a loss of a few hundred proletarians.

Or take one of the best-documented flows after 1800: from Denmark to America.[62] Denmark's nineteenth-century population ran in the vicinity of 2 million people. That small country sent almost 300,000 migrants to North America between 1840 and 1914. The bulk of the migrants were servants, wage laborers, and other proletarians. The ideal candidates for emigration seem to have been young people who had already made the move from farms and villages to a nearby, slow-moving regional center. Many—probably the great majority—moved within chains of friends, neighbors, and kinspeople who kept information about American opportunities flowing back to Denmark and who helped the migrants find passage money, jobs, and housing. The chains also made it easier for those who disliked America to return home; almost 100,000 emigrants went back to Denmark. But their main effect was to facilitate the flow of emigrants from

Denmark. Their demographic consequence was a net loss of some 200,000 Danish proletarians.

Migration also influenced the growth of the proletariat indirectly through its effect on social mobility and natural increase. One of the most valuable by-products of recent European historical demography has been the accumulating evidence of high mobility levels before the period of large-scale industrialization. Contrary to the idea of an immobile preindustrial world, historians of many different parts of Europe turn up village after village with annual migration rates of 10 percent or more.[63] Americans of the last century considered themselves exceptionally mobile because in the average year, about 20 percent of the population changed residence—and a great many of them moved within the same community. Comparable levels of mobility are showing up in many parts of Europe before massive industrialization.

That high preindustrial mobility, however, requires several qualifications: first, that earlier Europe was not preindustrial in any strict sense of the term. Dispersed, small-scale manufacturing played an important part in rural and small-town life, occupying a significant share of the population at least part time. People working in small-scale industry were a relatively mobile segment of the population. They also comprised an important fraction of the European proletariat. Second, most of the moves were quite local, consisting largely of exchanges of labor among nearby villages and of a small city's recruitment of youngsters from its immediate hinterland. Third, the most active migrants were proletarians. Proletarianization itself produced migration, as when a household displaced by enclosures left the land or when an extra child of a peasant family trudged off to work as a mercenary soldier or domestic servant. In addition, the proletarian worker had the least to tie him to any particular locality and the greatest incentive to follow the scent of better wages into a new labor market. The local authorities of seventeenth-century England considered the ever-present wanderers as potential workers in good times, but as "vagrants" in bad times.[64] In good times or bad, they were quintessential proletarians.

Long-distance migration probably became an increasingly common context of proletarianization during the nineteenth century. The average distances moved increased, the definitiveness of the departure from home probably increased as well, and the growth in the scale of production diminished the likelihood that an expanding firm could draw its new workers from its region's existing proletarians. Furthermore, as Abel Châtelain has pointed out, the innumerable circuits of seasonal migration that permitted people to lead a nonproletarian existence at least part of the year finally began to disintegrate during the nineteenth century. Two opposite movements—short-distance commuting and definitive long-distance migration—began replacing them. Nevertheless, even during the nineteenth century, the new industrial labor force came largely from the small towns and rural areas in which small-scale industrial production was declining.[65] If so, small towns and rural areas continued to serve as important way stations on the road to the proletariat.

The pattern of proletarian geographic mobility affected the way that social mobility and natural increase performed as a component of the proletariat's growth. The existence of well-established flows of migrants probably facilitated the proletarianization of the population in two ways. First, it helped produce a whole series of intermediate positions between the full artisan or peasant and the full proletarian—the alpine peasant who walked off to be a peddler in the winter, the weaver who followed the harvest in the fall, and so on.[66] Temporary expedients imperceptibly became a proletarian life. Second, the existence of well-established migratory flows withdrew the proletarianizing populations from the communities in which they had rights and solidarity and placed them in communities in which they had neither.

If the choice had been sharper and more dramatic in either regard, one might suppose that the proletarians would have resisted their fate with greater determination and effectiveness. When the choice was sharp and the proletarianizing populations were still embedded in their communities, they did often fight back against expropriation, by attacking others who were seizing control of the means of production. They also fought by adopting family strategies that limited the strain on household resources: strategies of late marriage, low fertility, regrouped inheritance, and so on. That fight against proletarianization pervades eighteenth-century peasant struggles against the enclosures and alienation of common rights, nineteenth-century artisanal struggles against work discipline, and twentieth-century winegrowers' struggles against big producers. It was a losing battle, but passionately fought.

WEIGHING THE COMPONENTS

Anyone who has watched how the evidence has leaked into and out of this discussion will realize that I am in no position to build estimates of the components of proletarianization that will hold water. For the sake of refocusing the inquiry, however, we may as well speculate about the relative weights of social mobility, natural increase, and net migration. Remember first the approximations of the European proletariat's size. In millions, the numbers run:

	1500	1800	1900
Total population	56	150	285
Nonproletarians	39	50	85
Proletarians	17	100	200

Remember also that the likely effect of net migration on the proletarian population of the Continent was a small loss before 1800 and a large loss—on the order of 50 million—during the nineteenth century. If we set the loss from 1500 to 1800 at a modest 10 million (a mere 33,000 per year) and retain the estimate of 50 million for between 1800 and 1900, we arrive at guesses of the amounts of change attributable to the sum of social mobility and natural increase:

	1500–1800		1800–1900	
Total population	+ 104	(0.3)	+ 185	(0.8)
Nonproletarians	+ 11	(0.1)	+ 35	(0.5)
Proletarians	+ 93	(0.6)	+ 150	(0.9)

(The figures in parentheses represent the implied annual rates of growth.) For the three centuries from 1500 to 1800, the figures indicate a mild increase for the nonproletarian population and a significant increase for the proletarians. In the nineteenth century, they indicate substantial increases in both categories, with the proletariat growing almost twice as fast as the nonproletarian population did.

Imagine a nonproletarian population with zero natural increase: a population that simply reproduced itself over the four centuries under examination. That would be consistent with the models of peasant and artisanal demographic behavior reviewed earlier. With a zero natural increase in the nonproletarian population, the figures would imply that (1) the net increase of 11 million nonproletarians between 1500 and 1800 was entirely due to social mobility out of the proletariat, and (2) the European proletariat added 104 million via natural increase and lost 11 million of them to social mobility. Those implications are, to say the least, unconventional. For the nineteenth century, the same assumption of zero natural increase among nonproletarians would suggest an even more surprising pair of conclusions: that (3) from 1800 to 1900, the net effect of social mobility was not to create massive numbers of new proletarians, but to move 35 million people out of the proletariat into nonproletarian positions, and (4) that the natural increase of the proletarian population was on the order of 185 million people, about 1.1 percent per year over the century as a whole.

Note that we are imagining *net* effects. For example, a net gain of 11 million nonproletarians via social mobility could easily mean that 25 million proletarians moved into nonproletarian positions and 14 million nonproletarians moved into the proletariat. Likewise, the nineteenth century transfer from proletariat to nonproletariat could result from, say, 60 million moves out of the proletariat balanced by 25 million moves into the proletariat. From a technical point of view, there is nothing implausible about the levels of natural increase that the figures suggest; for example, an average crude birthrate of thirty-five coupled with an average crude death rate of twenty-four would produce the sort of natural increase indicated for proletarians in the nineteenth century.

For the sake of a contrasting argument, let us imagine equal rates of natural increase among proletarians and nonproletarians. The rates of natural increase are equal to the annual rates of growth of the total European population plus the migration rate: 0.4 percent per year from 1500 to 1800 and 0.8 percent per year from 1800 to 1900. Again, these figures are perfectly acceptable from a strictly technical point of view. Under the assumption of an equal natural increase, our general figures imply an accounting of the following order: (1) that between 1500 and 1800, nonproletarians had a natural increase of 72 million people, counterbalanced by social mobility into the proletariat of 61 million; (2) that in the same period, proletarians experienced a natural increase of 32 million people, received 61 million newcomers via social mobility, and lost 10 million through migration from Europe; (3) that during the nineteenth century, the nonproletarian population added 62 million people through natural increase and lost 27 million to social mobility; and (4) that during the same century, the proletariat augmented its 27-million-person gain from social mobility with a natural increase of 123 million people, but exported 50 million of its members overseas. (See Table 12.7.)

We have, then, two extreme models: one with zero natural increase for nonproletarians and the other with nonproletarians experiencing the same natural increase as proletarians did. The *zero increase* model suggests some departure of proletarians from the proletariat before 1800, a massive movement out of the proletariat during the nineteenth century. The *same increase* model suggests a huge transfer of nonproletarians into the proletariat before 1800 and a more modest transfer in the same direction from 1800 to 1900.

Table 12.7. Components of Growth in the Total, Nonproletarian, and
Proletarian Populations of Europe, under Alternative Assumptions, 1550–1900

Component	Total	Nonproletarian	Proletarian
Number in 1500	56	39	17
Number in 1800	150	50	100
Change, 1500–1800	+ 94	+ 11	+ 83
Estimate of net migration, 1500–1800	− 10	0	− 10
Estimated sum of social mobility and natural increase, 1500–1800	+ 104	+ 11	+ 93
Implied annual percentage increase	0.4	0.1	0.6
Natural increase under zero hypothesis	+ 104	0	+ 104
Social mobility under zero hypothesis	0	+ 11	− 11
Natural increase under equal hypothesis	+ 104	+ 72	+ 32
Social mobility under equal hypothesis	0	− 61	+ 61
Number in 1900	285	85	200
Change, 1800–1900	+ 135	+ 35	+ 100
Estimate of net migration, 1800–1900	− 50	0	− 50
Estimated sum of social mobility and natural increase, 1800–1900	+ 185	+ 35	+ 150
Implied annual percentage increase	0.8	0.5	0.9
Natural increase under zero hypothesis	+ 185	0	+ 185
Social mobility under zero hypothesis	0	+ 35	− 35
Natural increase under equal hypothesis	+ 185	+ 62	+ 123
Social mobility under equal hypothesis	0	− 27	+ 17

Note: In millions of people. *Zero hypothesis:* nonproletarians have zero natural increase (fertility is equal to mortality). *Equal hypothessis:* nonproletarians and proletarians have equal rates of natural increase (i.e., rate of increase of total population, net of migration).

Figure 12.3 locates the zero and equal hypotheses within the range of likely combinations of natural increase and social mobility. Using Figure 12.3, we can construct any number of other hypotheses. Yet the graph makes clear that if my assumptions about net migration and the magnitude of increase in the proletariat are correct, the plausible hypotheses all will lie within a fairly narrow range. The zero hypothesis, as the graph shows, marks an extreme; it requires exceptional rates of proletarian natural increase and of mobility out of the proletariat, especially after 1800. The equal hypothesis positions itself on more plausible terrain. Before 1800, however, it requires a very high rate of social mobility into the proletariat: about 0.5 percent per year. If we were willing to contemplate even higher rates of social mobility, the graph would show the possibility of a truly extreme hypothesis: that nonproletarian natural increase ran substantially ahead of proletarian natural increase.

Figure 12.3. Proletarian Rate of In-Mobility and Nonproletarian Rate of Natural Increase (NPNI), 1500–1900
(As a function of proletarian rate of natural increase for Europe as a whole)

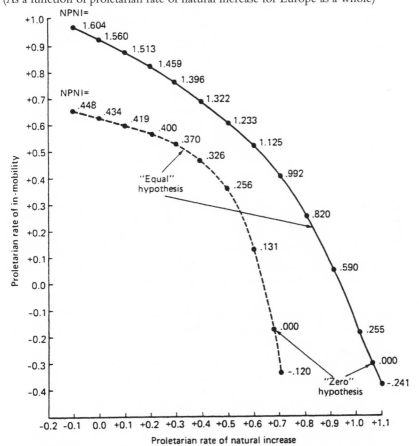

Note: Broken line = 1500–1800; solid line = 1800–1900. All rates in percentage change per year.

The reality and all useful models of it lie between the two extremes. We could, for example, reasonably argue that natural increase declined earlier among nonproletarians than among proletarians and that we should therefore shift from the same increase model toward the zero increase model as time moves on. That suggests, however, a zigzag: huge moves into the proletariat before 1800 and large moves out of the proletariat between 1800 and 1900. Unconventional? Yes. Absurd? Perhaps. Yet that very absurdity has its value, for it clears the way to the real challenge: to fashion these crude estimates and fragile models into genuine portrayals of the proletariat's growth.

If forced to sum up the arguments and evidence of this chapter (and allowed to rely on some strong guesses), I would sketch a model midway between the equal and zero hypotheses. That would imply something like the following levels:

Period	Nonproletarian Natural Increase	Proletarian Natural Increase	Mobility into Proletariat
1500–1800	0.25	0.50	0.40
1800–1900	0.60	0.90	0.10

These are plausible levels with interesting implications. They imply, for example, a marked slowing of individual mobility into the proletariat from the eighteenth to the nineteenth century—a circumstances that would be consistent with Marx's suggestion of a massive and early displacement of the rural population, although the pattern as a whole would still challenge his apparent assumption of a zero natural increase among proletarians. The hypothetical numbers provide a means of following up the implications of alternative theories and of weighing the significance of empirical observations concerning real European populations. Yet I must insist that the numbers come from nothing more than informed speculation.

Still, the speculative reasoning we have just gone through actually imposes serious constraints on those portrayals. For instance:

1. By any reasonable argument, natural increase must have played the major role in the growth of the European proletariat since 1500, and especially since 1800.
2. Well-grounded estimates of fertility, mortality, and their trends among specific European populations will set serious limits on the part that social mobility could have played in the proletarianization of those populations; to the extent that the patterns and trends are similar from one population to another, they will set limits on the possible role of social mobility in the growth of the whole European proletariat.
3. Earlier, I sketched the argument that nonproletarians tend to adjust their fertility to the availability of land and capital, whereas proletarians adjust their fertility to the availability of wages. That argument can be verified, modified, and refined through the examination of

local populations. To the extent that it applies in a similar fashion throughout Europe, it limits the assumptions we can plausibly make concerning the trends in natural increase among proletarian and nonproletarian populations from 1500 to 1900.

Thus, reasoning about the broad trends for Europe as a whole clarifies what sorts of conclusions we need to draw from the local studies of demographic processes that are now proliferating.

Let me stress that outcome. The numbers with which we have been working are temporary constructions, useful mainly as shelter while we catch our bearings. But in the long run, they will not withstand the historical wind. Two sorts of new building are essential. First, the broad estimates must be verified, revised, and refined. Even if the numbers I have proposed were precise and reliable, they would leave us far from the historical reality we are trying to understand. Most pressing is the need to specify the actual flows into and out of the proletariat that leave the net effects we have been discussing. How many people, for example, spent their lives straddling the line between proletarian and nonproletarian existence, by alternating between wage labor and independent production? How many proletarian emigrants actually realized the recurrent migrant dream: to accumulate capital at their destinations and then return home as peasants, artisans, rentiers, or capitalists?

Second, the sharp distinctions among migration, natural increase, and social mobility will eventually have to give way. We must examine their combinations and interactions. How often were the people who made the lifetime move from nonproletarian to proletarian households "extra" children of peasants and artisans, thus in some sense creatures of natural increase? How frequently did social mobility occur as a correlate or consequence of long-distance migration? Was the exclusion of squatters and tenants from common rights, and thus from the village, the potent proletarianizer it seems to have been? For such questions, more reliable estimates of the components of growth on a continental scale will be of little help. We need precise, textured local analyses.

CONCLUSIONS

In hacking out the contours of this massive problem, then, I have neglected all the graceful refinements that make the problems interesting. For example, the detailed timetable of proletarianization matters a good deal. Cottage industry and agricultural wage labor seem to have expanded much more rapidly in the seventeenth and, especially, the eighteenth century than before. Yet there was a good deal of population increase in Europe during the sixteenth century. Is it possible that during the sixteenth century, peasants, artisans, and other nonproletarians increased more rapidly than did the general population and that it was therefore a century of *de*proletarianization?

The geography of proletarianization likewise cries out for attention. At a minimum, we need contrasts among the legal enserfment of essentially landless laborers on the large estates of Eastern Europe, the creation of a legally free proletarian labor force in England, and the emergence of landowning peasants and cash-crop farmers in important parts of Western Europe.

Finally, a historically useful portrayal cannot stop with the tabulation of social mobility, natural increase, and net migration as separate components; it must specify their interplay. And all this requires a more refined analysis than I have provided here.

Qualifications, hesitations, and apologies duly registered, what provisional conclusions may we draw? From where did the European proletariat come? One answer recurs through the arguments and evidence of this chapter: *Cherchez le capitaliste.* The activity of capitalists, not the abstract mechanics of population growth, lay behind all the components of the proletariat's growth. On the side of social mobility, we have encountered the old processes of capitalist expropriation, although less frequently than the simplest Marxist accounts lead us to expect. More often, the piece-by-piece consolidation of land and capital by small producers gradually but inexorably edged their neighbors into the proletariat.

In migration, the capitalist's hand is gloved, but no less powerful: to the extent that capitalists accomplished expropriation and the imposition of control over labor by transferring capital from one work site to another, and thus attracted proletarianizing flows of migrants, they did the work more subtly and effectively.

The most surprising implication of this chapter's analysis, however, is the importance of capitalists to natural increase. Perhaps there was some "exogenous" decline in mortality due to climatic shifts, extinction of the natural carriers of the plague, and so on. But the alterations in nutrition that are the strongest candidates for explanations of involuntary long-term changes in fertility and mortality before the nineteenth century surely depended to an important degree on the activities of merchants and agricultural capitalists. And—most important—the pattern of proletarian natural increase in response to the availability of wage labor we have encountered depended entirely on the capitalists' provision of employment. Specialist farmers who offered work to day laborers and petty entrepreneurs who built cottage industry thereby incited the disproportionate natural increase of the proletariat. Not that they plotted to do so or ceased to condemn the heedless breeding of their workers: the power of a system like capitalism is that it does not require malevolent, or even self-conscious, agents to do its work.

For all its Marxist accent, to be sure, such an analysis revises an important element of Marx's own analysis and makes significant concessions to Malthus. Whereas Marx implicitly treated the lifetime mobility of workers and their households from nonproletarian to proletarian positions as the principal component of the proletariat's growth, my account gives far greater weight to the movement between generations and to differential natural increase. Expropriation and the extension of wage labor occurred widely, all right, but they happened to whole populations rather than to individuals. The stress on natural increase, with the fluctuations in fertility driven largely by fluctuations in marriage, has a Malthusian edge. Parson Malthus saw clearly enough that the poor English people of the later eighteenth century had strong incentives to marry and multiply and that the old system of enforced celibacy for large numbers of servants and laborers was disintegrating as wage labor expanded. His errors, then, were to inflate the particular circumstances of capitalist expropriation into general laws, to misunderstand the incentives to high fertility, and to neglect the importance of capitalist farmers, merchants, and manufacturers to the increase of the proletariat.

Back at the start of this long discussion, I said that there were three steps to the appropriate sociological procedure: the delineation of the components of growth, the separate explanation of each of the components, and the integration of those explanations into a comprehensive account of the whole process. We have not, by any means, completed that entire program. Yet the fragmentary observations we have made point to the utility of a modified Marxist account of European proletarianization. The most important modification consists of the large significance attributed to natural increase within the existing proletariat. Marx implicitly made lifetime entries of nonproletarians—that is, social mobility—the major component of the proletariat's increase. The modification fits nicely with that brand of Marxist analysis, typified by E. P. Thompson, that emphasizes the continuity of working-class culture from one generation to the next.

APPENDIX: THE RATE OF PROLETARIANIZATION, ITS COMPONENTS,
AND ITS LIKELY DETERMINANTS

T: total hours per year spent in productive labor
L: hours per year spent in labor controlling the means of production
D: hours per year spent in dependent labor $= T - L$
W: hours per year spent in labor for wages
e: level of expropriation $= D/T$; $\dot{e}$: rate of change in e
w: wage dependence $= W/T$; $\dot{w}$: rate of change in w
P: level of proletarianization $= e - w$
$\dot{P}$: rate of proletarianization $= \dot{e} + \dot{w}$

Determinants of Increase in Wage Labor	*Determinants of Increase in Potential Workforce*
Demand for goods and services (+)	Demand for goods and services (+)
Cost of establishing new production units (+)	Opportunity cost of childbearing (−)
Concentration of capital (+)	Existing level of proletarianization (+)
Coercive power of employers (+)	Natural fluctuations (±)

Proletarianization is likely to occur under these conditions:

1. increases in the cost of establishing new producing units,
2. concentration of capital,
3. increases in the coercive power of employers,
4. declines in the opportunity cost of childbearing, and
5. previous proletarianization.

NOTES

Previous versions of this chapter have taken shape as an address to the American Historical Association (1976) as "Sociology, History, and the Origins of the European Proletariat" (CRSO Working Paper 148, 1976) and as "Demographic Origins of the European Proletariat" (CRSO Working Paper 207, 1979; revised version CRSO Working Paper 286, 1983). The reactions of audiences at the University of Michigan, the University of Missouri, the University of Utah, Emory University, California Institute of Technology, and a number of other places have stimulated some of that incessant revision. Searching criticism, coupled with encouragement to keep on revising, have come from Ron Aminzade, Rod Aya, John Knodel,

David Levine, Franklin Mendels, Richard Tilly, Jan de Vries, and David Weir. I am especially grateful to Knodel for challenging my demographic thinking and to Mendels, de Vries, and Weir for saving me from technical blunders. A major part of the formalization derives from advice given me by Mendels; I have not, however, adopted his intriguing idea of incorporating the intensity of work directly into the definition of *proletarianization*, I owe thanks to Martha Guest, Cecilia Brown, Joan Skowronski, Dawn Hendricks, and Phil Soergel for help with the bibliography and to Rose Siri and Sheila Wilder for help in producing the paper. The Horace Rackham School of Graduate Studies (University of Michigan) and the National Science Foundation have supported the work on European social change that lies behind this chapter.

1. Smith 1910: bk. 1 chap. 8. Given the many editions of this work, I am citing by chapter for the convenience of readers.

2. Ibid.

3. For indirect confirmation, see A. W. Coats, "The Classical Economists and the Labourer," in E. L. Jones and G. E. Mingay, eds., *Land, Labour, and Population in the Industrial Revolution: Essays Presented to J. D. Chambers* (London: Arnold 1967); and J. J. Spengler, "Adam Smith on Population," Population Studies, 2d ser., 17 (1970): 377–388.

4. For a convenient review, see Carl Jantke, "Zur Deutung des Pauperismus," in Carl Jantke and Dietrich Hilger, eds., *Der deustche Pauperismus und die Emanzipationskrise in Darstellung der zeitgenossischen Literatur* (Munich: Karl Alber, 1965).

5. Marx 1970: chap. 26. Again, I am citing by chapter for the convenience of readers.

6. Ibid.

7. Ibid: chap. 25.

8. Karl Marx, *Grundrisse: Foundations of the Critique of Political Economy* (rough draft) (London: Allen Lane, 1973), p. 606.

9. Ibid.

10. For example, J. D. Chambers, "Enclosure and the Labour Supply in the Industrial Revolution," *Economic History Review*, 2d ser., 5 (1953): 319–343; Jon S. Cohen and Martin L. Weitzman, "Enclosures and Depopulation: A Marxian Analysis," in William N. Parker and Eric L. Jones, eds., *European Peasants and Their Markets* (Princeton, NJ: Princeton University Press, 1975); D. C. Coleman, "Labour in the English Economy of the Seventeenth Century," *Economic History Review*, 2d ser., 8 (1955–1956): 280–295; J. P. Cooper, "The Social Distribution of Land and Men in England, 1436–1700," *Economic History Review*, 2d ser., 20 (1967): 419–440; Ingrid Eriksson and John Rogers, *Rural Labor and Population Change* (Stockholm: Almqvist & Wiksell, 1978); H. J. Habakkuk, *Population Growth and Economic Development since 1750* (Leicester: Leicester University Press, 1971); Gerd Hohorst, *Wirtschaftswachstum und Bevölkerungsentwicklung in Preussen, 1816–1914* (New York: Arno Press, 1977); E. L. Jones, "The Agricultural Labour Market in England, 1793–1872," *Economic History Review*, 2d ser., 17 (1964): 322–338; Hermann Kellenbenz, *Agrarisches Nebengewerbe und Formen der Reagrarisierung im Spätmit-*

telalter und 19./20 Jahrhundert (Stuttgart: Gustav Fischer, 1975); William Lazonick, "Karl Marx and Enclosures in England," *Review of Radical Economics* 6 (1974): 1–59; Yves Lequin, *Les ouvriers de la région lyonnaise (1848–1914)*, 2 vols. (Lyon: Presses Universitaires de Lyon, 1977); Sture Martinius, *Befolkningsrörlighet under industrialismens inledningsskede i Sverige* (Gothenberg: Elanders, 1967); Horst Matzerath, "Industrialisierung, Mobilität und sozialen Wandel am Beispiel der Stadte Rheydt und Rheindalen," in Hartmut Kaelble et al., eds., *Probleme der Modernisierung in Deutschland* (Opladen: Westdeutschen Verlag, 1978); Alan S. Milward and S. B. Saul, *The Economic Development of Continental Europe, 1780–1870* (London: Allen & Unwin, 1973); John Saville, "Primitive Accumulation and Early Industrialization in Britain," *Socialist Register* (1969): 247–271; Lawrence Schofer, *The Formation of a Modern Labor Force: Upper Silesia, 1865–1914* (Berkeley and Los Angeles: University of California Press, 1975); Louise A. Tilly, "Urban Growth, Industrialization and Women's Employment in Milan, Italy, 1881–1911," *Journal of Urban History* 3 (1977): 467–484; Richard Tilly and Charles Tilly, "An Agenda for European Economic History in the 1970s," *Journal of Economic History* 31 (1971): 184–197; E. A. Wrigley, *Industrial Growth and Population Change* (Cambridge: Cambridge University Press, 1961).

11. For example, Lutz Berkner and Franklin F. Mendels, "Inheritance Systems, Family Structure, and Demographic Patterns in Western Europe, 1700–1900," in Charles Tilly, ed., *Historical Studies of Changing Fertility* (Princeton, NJ: Princeton University Press, 1978); David Gaunt, "Pre-Industrial Economy and Population Structure: The Elements of Variance in Early Modern Sweden," *Scandinavian Journal of History* 2 (1977): 183–210; Michael Haines, *Fertility and Occupation: Population Patterns in Industrialization* (New York: Academic Press, 1979); John Knodel and Etienne van de Walle, "Lessons from the Past: Policy Implications of Historical Fertility Studies," *Population and Development Review* 5 (1979): 217–245; Wolfgang Köllmann, "Zur Bevölkerungsentwicklung der Neuzeit," in Reinhart Koselleck, ed., *Studien zum Beginn der Modernen Welt* (Stuttgart: Klett-Cotta, 1977); Peter Kriedte, Hans Medick, and Jürgen Schlumbohm, *Industrialisierung vor der Industrialisierung: Gewerbliche Warenproduktion auf dem Land in der Formationsperiode des Kapitalismus* (Göttingen: Vandenhoeck & Ruprecht, 1977); Ron J. Lesthaege, *The Decline of Belgian Fertility, 1800–1970* (Princeton, NJ: Princeton University Press, 1977); Edward E. McKenna, "Marriage and Fertility in Postfamine Ireland: A Multivariate Analysis," *American Journal of Sociology* 80 (1974): 688–705.

12. For example, Kurt Ågren et al., *Aristocrats, Farmers, Proletarians: Essays in Swedish Demographic History* (Uppsala: Almqvist & Wiksell, 1973); Sune Åkerman, Hans Christian Johansen, and David Gaunt, eds., *Chance and Change: Social and Economic Studies in Historical Demography in the Baltic Area* (Odense: Scandinavian Universities Press, 1978); J. Bourget, "Prolétarisation d'une commune de l'agglomération parisienne: Colombes," *La Vie Urbaine. Urbanisme et Habitation*, n.s., nos. 3 and 4 (1954): 185–194; Rudolf Braun, *Industrialisierung und Volksleben* (Zurich: Rentsch, 1960); Rudolf Braun, *Sozialer und kultureller Wandel in einem ländlichen Industriegebiet* (Zurich: Rentsch, 1965); J. D. Chambers, *The Vale of Trent, 1670–*

1800: A Regional Study of Economic Change (Cambridge: Cambridge University Press, 1957); Alain Corbin, *Archaisme et modernité en Limousin au XIXe siècle*. 2 vols. (Paris: Marcel Rivière, 1975); Paul Deprez, "The Demographic Development of Flanders in the Eighteenth Century," in D. V. Glass and D. E. C. Eversley, eds., *Population in History* (Chicago: Aldine, 1965); John Foster, *Class Struggle and the Industrial Revolution: Early Industrial Capitalism in Three Towns* (London: Weidenfeld & Nicolson, 1974); David Gaunt, "Familj, Hushall och Arbetsintensitet," *Scandia* 42 (1976): 32–59; Franz Gschwind, *Bevölkerungsentwicklung und Wirtschaftsstruktur der Landschaft Basel im 18. Jahrhundert* (Liestal: Kantonal Drucksachen- und Materialzentrale, 1977); Hervé Hasquin, *Une mutation: Le "Pays de Charleroi" aux XVIIe et XVIIIe siècles* (Brussels: Editions de l'Institut de Sociologie, Université Libre de Bruxelles, 1971); Karlbernhard Jasper, *Der Urbanisierungsprozess dargestellt am Beispiel der Stadt Köln* (Cologne: Rheinisch-Westfälischen Wirtschaftsarchiv zu Köln, 1977); Herbert Kisch, *Die Hausindustriellen Textilgewerbe am Niederrhein von der industriellen Revolution: Von der ursprünglichen zur kapitalistischen Akkumulation* (Göttingen: Vandenhoeck & Ruprecht, 1981); Arnost Klíma, "The Role of Rural Domestic Industry in Bohemia in the Eighteenth Century," *Economic History Review* 27 (1974): 48–56; David Levine, *Family Formation in an Age of Nascent Capitalism* (New York: Academic Press, 1977); David Levine, "Proto-Industrialization and Demographic Upheaval," in David Levine et al., *Essays on the Family and Historical Change* (College Station, TX: A&M Press, 1983); Sven Lundqvist, *Folkröreiserna i det svenska samhallet, 1850–1920* (Stockholm: Almqvist & Wiksell, 1977); Bo Ohngren, *Folk i rörelse: Samhallsutveckling, flyttningsmonster och folkrürelser i Eskilstuna, 1870–1900* (Uppsala: Almqvist Wiksell, 1974); Jaroslav Purš, "Struktur und Dynamik der industriellen Entwicklung in Böhmen im letzten Viertel des 18. Jahrhunderts," *Jahrbuch für Wirtschaftsgeschichte* (1965): 160–196; Jaroslav Purš, "Die Aufhebung der Hörigkeit und die Grundentlastung in den böhmischen Ländern," *Second International Conference of Economic History: Aix-en-Provence 1962* (Paris: Mouton, 1965); Jane Schneider and Peter Schneider, *Culture and Political Economy in Western Sicily* (New York: Academic Press, 1976); Joan W. Scott, *The Glassmakers of Carmaux: French Craftsmen and Political Action in a Nineteenth Century City* (Cambridge, MA: Harvard University Press, 1974); Margaret Spufford, "Peasant Inheritance Customs and Land Distribution in Cambridgeshire from the Sixteenth to the Eighteenth Centuries," in Jack Goody, Joan Thirsk, and E. P. Thompson, eds., *Family and Inheritance: Rural Society in Western Europe, 1200–1800* (Cambridge: Cambridge University Press, 1976); Pierre Vilar, *La Catalogne dans l'Espagne moderne*, 3 vols. (Paris: SEVPEN, 1962); Jan de Vries, "Peasant Demand Patterns and Economic Development: Friesland, 1550–1750," in William N. Parker and Eric L. Jones, eds., *European Peasants and Their Markets* (Princeton, NJ: Princeton University Press, 1975); Keith Wrightson and David Levine, *Poverty and Piety in an English Village: Terling, 1525–1700* (New York: Academic Press, 1979).

13. For example, Wilhelm Abel, *Massenarmut und Hungerkrisen im vorindustriellen Europa* (Hamburg and Berlin: Paul Parey, 1974); A. W. Coats, "The Relief of Poverty, Attitudes to Labour and Economic Change in England, 1660–1782," *In-*

ternational *Review of Social History* 21 (1976): 98–115; Natalie Zemon Davis, "Poor Relief, Humanism, and Heresy: The Case of Lyon," *Studies in Medieval and Renaissance History* 5 (1968): 217–275; Pierre Deyon, "A propos du paupérisme au milieu du XVIIe siècle: Peinture et charité chrétienne," *Annales: Economies, Sociétés, Civilisations* 22 (1967): 137–153; Jean-Pierre Gutton, *La société et les pauvres en Europe, XVIe–XVIIIe siècles* (Paris: Presses Universitaires de France, 1974); Olwen Hufton, *The Poor of Eighteenth-Century France, 1750–1789* (Oxford: Clarendon Press); Jeffrey Kaplow, *The Names of Kings: The Parisian Laboring Poor in the Eighteenth Century* (New York: Basic Books, 1972); Catharina Lis and Hugo Soly, *Poverty and Capitalism in Pre-Industrial Europe* (Atlantic Highlands, NJ: Humanities Press, 1979); Jill Quadagno, *Aging in Early Industrial Society: Work, Family, and Social Policy in Nineteenth-Century England* (New York: Academic Press, 1982); Paul A. Slack, "Vagrants and Vagrancy in England, 1598–1664," *Economic History Review*, 2d ser., 27 (1974): 360–379.

14. For example, Stanley Aronowitz, "Marx, Braverman, and the Logic of Capital," *Insurgent Sociologist* 8 (1978): 126–146; Reinhard Bendix, *Work and Authority in Industry: Ideologies of Management in the Course of Industrialization* (New York: Wiley, 1956); Michael Burawoy, "Towards a Marxist Theory of the Labor Process: Braverman and Beyond," *Politics and Society* 8 (1979): 247–312; Michael Burawoy, *Manufacturing Consent: Changes in the Labor Process under Monopoly Capitalism* (Chicago: University of Chicago Press, 1979); Duncan Gallie, *In Search of the New Working Class: Automation and Social Integration within the Capitalist Enterprise* (Cambridge: Cambridge University Press, 1978); David Gartmen, "Marx and the Labor Process: An Interpretation," *Insurgent Sociologist* 8 (1978): 97–108; Herbert Gintis, "The Nature of Labor Exchange and the Theory of Capitalist Production," *Review of Radical Political Economy* 8 (1976): 36–54; Gerd H. Hardach, *Der soziale Status des Arbeiters in der Frühindustrialisierung* (Berlin: Duncker & Humblot, 1969); Stephen A. Marglin, "What Do Bosses Do? The Origins and Functions of Hierarchy in Capitalist Production," *Review of Radical Political Economics* 6 (1974): 60–112; David Montgomery, *Workers' Control in America* (Cambridge: Cambridge University Press, 1979); Wilbert E. Moore and Arnold S. Feldman, eds., *Labor Commitment and Social Change in Developing Areas* (New York: Social Science Research Council, 1960); Bernard Mottez, *Systèmes de salaire et politiques patronales* (Paris: Centre National de la Recherche Scientifique, 1966); Luciano Pellicani, "La rivoluzione industriale e il fenomeno della proletarizzazione," *Rassegna Italiana di Sociologia* 14 (1973): 63–84; François Perroux, *Aliénation et société industrielle* (Paris: Gallimard, 1970); Katherine Stone, "The Origins of Job Structures in the Steel Industry," *Review of Radical Political Economics* 6 (1974): 113–173; E. P. Thompson, "Time, Work-Discipline, and Industrial Capitalism," *Past and Present* 38 (1967): 56–97; Michael Vester, *Die Entstehung des Proletariats als Lernprozess: Die Entstehung antikapitalistischer Theorie und Praxis in England, 1792–1848* (Frankfurt am Main: Europäische Verlaganstalt, 1970); Hartmut Zwahr, "Zur Konstituierung des Proletariats als Klasse: Strukturuntersuchung über das leipziger Proletariat während der industriellen Revolution," in Horst Bartel and Ernst Engelberg, eds., *Die grosspreussischmilitarische Reichsgründung 1871*, vol. 1 (Berlin: Akademie Verlag, 1971).

15. For example, Perry Anderson, *Lineages of the Absolutist State* (London: NLB, 1974); Fernand Braudel, *Civilisation matérielle, économie et capitalisme, XVe–XVIIIe siècles*, 3 vols. (Paris: Colin, 1979); Robert Brenner, "Agrarian Class Structure and Economic Development in Pre-Industrial Europe," *Past and Present* 70 (1976): 30–75; Robert Brenner, "The Origins of Capitalist Development: A Critique of Neo-Smithian Marxism," *New Left Review* 104 (1977): 25–92; Pierre Chaunu, *La civilisation de l'Europe classique* (Paris: Arthaud, 1970); Patricia Croot and David Parker, "Agrarian Class Structure and Economic Development," *Past and Present* 78 (1978): 37–46; Maurice Dobb, *Studies in the Development of Capitalism* (London: Routledge & Kegan Paul, 1963); Hermann Kellenbenz, *The Rise of the European Economy: An Economic History of Continental Europe from the Fifteenth to the Eighteenth Century* (London: Weidenfeld & Nicolson, 1976); David S. Landes, *The Unbound Prometheus: Technological Change and Industrial Development in Western Europe from 1750 to the Present* (Cambridge: Cambridge University Press, 1969); Emmanuel Le Roy Ladurie, "Pour un modèle de l'économie rurale française au XVIIIe siècle," *Cahiers d'Histoire* 29 (1974): 5–27; Barrington Moore Jr., *Social Origins of Dictatorship and Democracy: Lord and Peasant in the Making of the Modern World* (Boston: Beacon Press, 1966); Frits Redlich and Herman Freudenberger, "The Industrial Development of Europe: Reality, Symbols, Images," *Kyklos* 17 (1964): 372–401; Emilio Sereni, *Il capitalismo nelle campagne (1860–1900)* (Turin: Einaudi, 1948); Gabriel Tortella Cesares, *Los origines del capitalismo en España: Banca, industria y ferocarria en el siglo XIX* (Madrid: Editorial Jernos, 1973); Jan de Vries, *The Economy of Europe in an Age of Crisis, 1600–1750* (Cambridge: Cambridge University Press, 1976); Immanuel Wallerstein, *The Modern World System*, 2 vols. (New York: Academic Press, 1974 and 1980); E. A. Wrigley, "The Process of Modernization and the Industrial Revolution in England," *Journal of Interdisciplinary History* 3 (1972): 225–259.

16. Christer Winberg, *Folkökning och proletarisering kring den sociala strukturomvandlingen på Sveriges landsbygd under den agrara revolutionen* (Gothenberg: Historiska Institutionen i Göteborg, 1975), 331; see Gustaf Utterstrom, *Jordbrukets arbetare*, vol. 1 (Stockholm: Tidens Forlag, 1957), 68.

17. For summaries of the debates, see H. J. Habakkuk, *Population Growth and Economic Development since 1750* (Leicester: Leicester University Press, 1971); and Thomas McKeown, *The Modern Rise of Population* (New York: Academic Press, 1976).

18. Ann Kussmaul, *Servants in Husbandry in Early Modern England* (Cambridge: Cambridge University Press, 1981), 97–119.

19. Gartman, op. cit.; Gintis, op. cit.

20. See Stanley Aronowitz, "Marx, Braverman, and the Logic of Capital," *Insurgent Sociologist* 8 (1978): 126–146.

21. See Juan G. Espinosa and Andrew S. Zimbalist, *Economic Democracy: Workers' Participation in Chilean Industry, 1970–1973* (New York: Academic Press, 1978); Walter Korpi, *The Working Class in Welfare Capitalism: Work, Unions, and Politics in Scandinavia* (London: Routledge & Kegan Paul, 1978); Evelyne Huber Stephens, *The Politics of Workers' Participation* (New York: Academic Press, 1980).

354   *Chapter 12*

22. William Hasbach, *A History of the English Agricultural Labourer* (London: P. S. King, 1920), 103–104.

23. Douglass C. North and Robert Paul Thomas, *The Rise of the Western World: A New Economic History* (Cambridge: Cambridge University Press, 1973).

24. Alan Macfarlane, *The Origins of English Individualism* (Cambridge: Cambridge University Press, 1978).

25. On these issues, see John D. Durand, *The Labor Force in Economic Development: A Comparison of International Census Data, 1946–1966.* (Princeton, NJ: Princeton University Press, 1975); Richard Edwards, "Social Relations of Production at the Point of Production," *Insurgent Sociologist* 8 (1978): 109–125; Louise A. Tilly and Joan W. Scott, *Women, Work, and Family* (New York: Holt, Rinehart & Winston, 1978).

26. Jerome Blum, *The End of the Old Order in Rural Europe* (Princeton, NJ: Princeton University Press, 1978).

27. See for example, Habakkuk, op. cit.

28. Harriet Friedmann, "World Market, State, and Family Farm: Social Bases of Household Production in the Era of Wage Labor," *Comparative Studies in Society and History* 20 (1978): 545–586.

29. Jan de Vries, *The Dutch Rural Economy in the Golden Age, 1500–1700* (New Haven, CT: Yale University Press, 1974).

30. For example, Rudolf Braun, "Early Industrialization and Demographic Change in the Canton of Zurich," in Charles Tilly, ed., *Historical Studies of Changing Fertility* (Princeton, NJ: Princeton University Press, 1978).

31. For example, Kisch, op. cit.

32. John Saville, "Primitive Accumulation and Early Industrialization in Britain," *Socialist Register* (1969): 251–252.

33. Phyllis Deane and W. A. Cole, *British Economic Growth, 1688–1959: Trends and Structure* (Cambridge: Cambridge University Press, 1967), 143–144.

34. B. H. Slicher van Bath, "Agriculture in the Vital Revolution," in E. E. Rich and C. H. Wilson, eds., *Cambridge Economic History of Europe V: The Economic Organization of Early Modern Europe* (Cambridge: Cambridge University Press, 1977), 127.

35. Lennart Jorberg, "The Development of Real Wages for Agricultural Workers in Sweden during the 18th and 19th Centuries," *Economy and History* (1972): 41–57.

36. Computed from Karlheinz Blaschke, *Bevölkerungsgeschichte von Sachsen bis zur industriellen Revolution* (Weimar: Böhlhaus, 1967), 190–191; Paul Bairoch, *Taille des villes, conditions de vie et développement économique* (Paris: Ecoles des Hautes Etudes en Sciences Sociales, 1977), 42.

37. Wolfgang Köllmann, *Bevölkerung in der industriellen Revolution* (Göttingen: Vandenhoeck & Ruprecht, 1974), 88–90.

38. Ibid., 74.

39. Ibid., 70.

40. Franklin L. Mendels, "Aux origines de la proto-industrialisation," *Bulletin du Centre d'Histoire Economique et Sociale de la Région Lyonnaise,* no. 2 (1978): 1–25.

41. Kisch, op. cit.

42. For an extensive review of the evidence on protoindustrial demography, see Kriedte, Medick, and Schlumbohm, op. cit., especially pp. 155–193; for an empirical challenge, see Gerd Hohorst, op. cit., especially pp. 208–227; and Gerd Hohorst, "Protoindustrialisierung im Übergang zum industriellen Kapitalismus: Die demoökonomische Entwicklung im Kreis Hagen 1817 bis 1863," in Pierre Deyon and Franklin L. Mendels, eds., *Protoindustrialisation: Théorie et réalité* (Lille: Université des Arts, Lettres, et Sciences Humaines, 1982).

43. Blaschke, op. cit.; Klima, op. cit.; Braun, op. cit.; 1978.

44. Levine, op. cit., pp. 103–115; for a skeptical commentary, see E. A. Wrigley, "The Changing Occupational Structure of Colyton over Two Centuries," *Local Population Studies* 18 (1977): 9–21.

45. Wrightson and Levine, op. cit.

46. Kussmaul, op. cit.

47. Gaunt, op. cit., 1977.

48. See Amartya Sen, *Poverty and Famines: An Essay on Entitlement and Deprivation* (Oxford: Clarendon Press, 1981).

49. See Ronald Lee, "Models of Pre-Industrial Population Dynamics, with Application to England," in Charles Tilly, ed., *Historical Studies of Changing Fertility* (Princeton, NJ: Princeton University Press, 1978).

50. See John C. Caldwell, "Towards a Restatement of Demographic Transition Theory," *Population and Development Review* 2 (1976): 321–366; John C. Caldwell, *Theory of Fertility Decline* (New York: Academic Press, 1982); John Knodel, "Natural Fertility in Pre-Industrial Germany," *Population Studies* 32 (1978): 481–510; Knodel and van de Walle, op. cit.

51. Rudolf Andorka, "Family Reconstitution and Types of Household Structure," in Jan Sundin and Eric Soderlund, eds., *Time, Space, and Man* (Stockholm: Almqvist & Wiksell International, 1979); Gaunt, op. cit., 1977; Levine, op. cit., 1977; E. A. Wrigley, "Family Limitation in Pre-Industrial England" *Economic History Review*, n.s., 19 (1966): 82–109.

52. For a review of many such cases, see Charles Tilly, "The Historical Study of Vital Processes," in Charles Tilly, ed., *Historical Studies of Changing Fertility* (Princeton, NJ: Princeton University Press, 1978).

53. Ronald Lee, "An Historical Perspective on Economic Aspects of the Population Explosion: The Case of Pre-Industrial England," unpublished paper, National Bureau of Economic Research; Ronald Lee, op. cit., 1978; E. A. Wrigley and R. S. Schofield, *The Population History of England, 1541–1871: A Reconstruction* (London: Arnold, 1981).

54. McKeown, op. cit.; Lee, op. cit., 1978.

55. L. Tilly and J. Scott, op. cit., chap. 2.

56. Hasquin, op. cit., pp. 292–293.

57. Ibid., 292.

58. Lesthaege, op. cit., p. 69, citing Hofstee as the argument's source.

59. E. A. Wrigley, "The Growth of Population in Eighteenth-Century England: A Conundrum Resolved," *Past and Present* 98 (1983): 121–150.

60. Leszek A. Kosinski, *The Population of Europe: A Geographical Perspective* (London: Longmans, 1970), 57.

61. Hubert Charbonneau, *Tourouvre-au-Perche aux XVIIe et XVIIIe siècles* (Paris: Presses Universitaires de France, 1974).

62. Kristian Hvidt, *Flight to America: The Social Background of 300,000 Danish Emigrants* (New York: Academic Press, 1975).

63. For example, C. J. Bukatsch, "The Constancy of Local Population and Migration in England before 1800," *Population Studies* 5 (1951): 62–69; Julian Cornwall, "Evidence of Population Mobility in the Seventeenth Century," *Bulletin of the Institute of Historical Research* 40 (1967): 143–152; Eriksson and Rogers, op. cit.; Carl Hammer, "The Mobility of Skilled Labour in Late Medieval England: Some Oxford Evidence," *Vierteljahrschrift für Sozial- und Wirtschaftsgeschichte* 63 (1976): 194–210; T. H. Holingsworth, "Historical Studies of Migration," *Annales de Démographie Historique 1970* pp. 87–96; Martinius, op. cit., John Patten, *Rural-Urban Migration in Pre-Industrial England* (Oxford: School of Geography, 1973); Jean-Pierre Poussou, "Introduction à l'étude des mouvements migratoires en Espagne, Italie et France méditerranéenne au XVIIIe siècle," in M. Aymard et al., eds., *Les migrations dans les pays méditerranéens au XVIIIème au début du XIXème* (Nice: Centre de la Méditerranée Moderne et Contemporaine, 1974); David Sabean, "Household Formation and Geographic Mobility: A Family Register Study in a Wurttemburg Village, 1760–1900," *Zeitschrift für Agrargeschichte und Agrarsoziologie* 14 (1971): 137–175.

64. Slack, op. cit.

65. Abel Châtelain, *Les migrants temporaires en France de 1800 à 1914: Histoire économique et sociale des migrants temporaires des campagnes françaises du XIXe siècle au début du XXe siècle,* 2 vols. (Lille: Publications de l'Université de Lille, 1976). See also Braun, op. cit., 1965; Kellenbenz, op. cit., 1975; Lequin, op. cit.; L. Tilly, op. cit., 1977.

66. See Châtelain, op. cit., for numerous examples.

BIBLIOGRAPHY

In addition to each item cited in the text, I have included a number of historical surveys that shed light on the creation of the European proletariat, a few relevant theoretical essays, and a great many local or regional studies that contain evidence on one aspect of proletarianization or another. For syntheses and bibliographies of major literatures on which the paper draws, see especially Blum 1978; Braverman 1974; Cipolla 1976; Goody, Thirsk, and Thompson 1976; Kellenbenz 1976; Kriedte, Medick, and Schlumbohm 1977; Landes 1969; Lis and Soly 1979; McKeown 1976; Milward and Saul 1973; Slicher van Bath 1977; C. Tilly 1975, 1978a, 1978b, 1979, 1982; L. Tilly and J. Scott 1978; R. Tilly and C. Tilly 1971; and de Vries 1976.

Wilhelm Abel. 1974. *Massenarmut und Hungerkrisen im Vorindustriellen Europa.* Hamburg and Berlin: Paul Parey.

Gerhard Adelmann. 1979. "Die ländlichen Textilgewerbe des Rheinlandes vor der Industrialisierung." *Rheinische Vierteljahrsblätter* 43: 260–288.

Kurt Ågren, Sune Åkerman, Ingrid Erikson, David Gaunt, Andres Norberg, and John Rogers. 1973. *Aristocrats, Farmers, Proletarians, Essays in Swedish Demographic History.* Uppsala: Almqvist & Wiksell. Studia Historica Upsaliensia, 47.

Sune Åkerman, Hans Christian Johansen, and David Gaunt, eds. 1978. *Chance and Change: Social and Economic Studies in Historical Demography in the Baltic Area.* Odense: Scandinavian Universities Press.

Eric L. Almqvist. 1979. "Pre-Famine Ireland and the Theory of European Proto-industrialization: Evidence from the 1841 Census." *Journal of Economic History* 39: 399–718.

Perry Anderson. 1974. *Lineages of the Absolutist State.* London: NLB.

Rudolf Andorka. 1979. "Family Reconstitution and Types of Household Structure. In Jan Sundin and Eric Soderlund, eds., *Time, Space, and Man.* Stockholm: Almqvist & Wiksell International.

Stanley Aronowitz. 1978. "Marx, Braverman, and the Logic of Capital." *Insurgent Sociologist* 8: 126–146.

Lothar Baar. 1968. "Probleme der industriellen Revolution in grosstädtischen Industriezentren: Das Berliner Beispiel." In Wolfram Fischer, ed., *Wirtschafts- und sozialgeschichtliche Probleme der frühen Industrialisierung.* Berlin: Colloquium Verlag.

Klaus J. Bade. 1982. "Transnationale Migration und Arbeitsmarkt im Kaiserreich.: Vom Agrarstaat mit stärker Industrie zum Industriestaat mit stärker agrarischen Basis." In Toni Pierenkemper and Richard Tilly, eds., *Historische Arbeitsmarktforschung: Enstehung, Entwicklung, and Probleme der Vermarktung von Arbeitskraft.* Göttingen: Vandenhoeck & Ruprecht.

Paul Bairoch. 1977. *Taille des villes, conditions de vie et développement économique.* Paris: Ecole des Hautes Etudes en Sciences Sociales.

Paul Bairoch and J. M. Limbor. 1968. "Changes in the Industrial Distribution of the World Labour Force, by Region, 1880–1960." *International Labor Review* 98: 311–336.

A. L. Beier. 1978. "Social Problems in Elizabethan London." *Journal of Interdisciplinary History* 9: 203–221.

J. R. Bellerby. 1958. "The Distribution of Manpower in Agriculture and Industry, 1851–1951." *Farm Economist* 9: 1–11.

Reinhard Bendix. 1956. *Work and Authority in Industry: Ideologies of Management in the Course of Industrialization.* New York: Wiley.

Lutz Berkner. 1977. "Peasant Household Organization and Demographic Change in Lower Saxony (1689–1766)." In Ronald Lee, ed., *Population Patterns in the Past.* New York: Academic Press.

Lutz Berkner and Franklin F. Mendels. 1978. "Inheritance Systems, Family Structure, and Demographic Patterns in Western Europe, 1700–1900." In Charles Tilly, ed., *Historical Studies of Changing Fertility.* Princeton, NJ: Princeton University Press.

Karlheinz Blaschke. 1967. *Bevölkerungsgeschichte von Sachsen bis zur industriellen Revolution.* Weimar: Böhlhaus.

Grethe Authén Blom, ed. 1977. *Industrialiseringens første fase.* Olso: Universitetsforlaget. Urbaniseringsprosessen i Norden, 3.

Jerome Blum. 1978. *The End of the Old Order in Rural Europe.* Princeton, NJ: Princeton University Press.

Willi A. Boelcke. 1967. "Wändlungen der dorflichen Sozialstruktur während Mittelalter und Neuzeit." In Heinz Haushofer and Willi A. Boelcke, eds., *Wege und Forschungen der Agrargeschichte.* Frankfurt am Main: DLG Verlag.

Ingomar Bog. 1975. "Über Arme und Armenfürsorge in Oberdeutschland in der Eidgenossenschaft im 15. und 16. Jahrhundert." *Jahrbuch für fränkische Landesforschung* 34–35: 983–1001.

Douglas E. Booth. 1978. "Karl Marx on State Regulation of the Labor Process: The English Factory Acts." *Review of Social Economy* 36: 137–158.

Peter Borscheid. 1978. *Textilarbeiterschaft in der Industrialisierung: Soziale Lage und Mobilität in Württemberg (19. Jahrhundert).* Stuttgart: Klett-Cotta.

J. Bourget. 1954. "Prolétarisation d'une commune de l'agglomération parisienne: Colombes." *La Vie Urbaine: Urbanisme et Habitation*, n.s., nos. 3 and 4: 185–194.

Samuel Bowles and Herbert Gintis. 1975. "Class Power and Alienated Labor." *Monthly Review* 26: 9–25.

Robert Boyer. 1979. "Wage Formation in Historical Perspective: The French Experience." *Cambridge Journal of Economics* 3: 99–118.

Fernand Braudel. 1979. *Civilisation matérielle, économie, et capitalisme, XVe–XVIIIe siècles.* 3 vols. Paris: Colin.

Rudolf Braun. 1960. *Industrialisierung und Volksleben.* Zurich: Rentsch.

———. 1965. *Sozialer und Kultureller Wandel in einem ländlichen Industriegebiet.* Zurich: Rentsch.

———. 1978. "Early Industrialization and Demographic Change in the Canton of Zurich." In Charles Tilly, ed., *Historical Studies in Changing Fertility.* Princeton, NJ: Princeton University Press.

Harry Braverman. 1974. *Labor and Monopoly Capital: The Degradation of Work in the Twentieth Century.* New York: Wiley.

Robert Brenner. 1976. "Agrarian Class Structure and Economic Development in Pre-Industrial Europe." *Past and Present* 70: 30–75.

———. 1977. "The Origins of Capitalist Development: A Critique of Neo-Smithian Marxism." *New Left Review* 104: 25–92.

John D. Buissink. 1971. "Regional Differences in Marital Fertility in the Netherlands in the Second Half of the Nineteenth Century." *Population Studies* 25: 353–374.

C. J. Bukatsch. 1951. "The Constancy of Local Population and Migration in England before 1800." *Population Studies* 5: 62–69.

Larry L. Bumpass. 1969. "Age at Marriage as a Variable in Socio-economic Differentials in Fertility." *Demography* 6: 45–54.

Michael Burawoy. 1979a. *Manufacturing Consent. Change in the Labor Process under Monopoly Capitalism.* Chicago: University of Chicago Press.

———. 1979b. "Towards a Marxist Theory of the Labor Process: Braverman and Beyond." *Politics and Society* 8(3–4): 247–312.

John C. Caldwell. 1976. "Towards a Restatement of Demographic Transition Theory." *Population and Development Review* 2: 321–366.

———. 1981. "The Mechanisms of Demographic Change in Historical Perspective." *Population Studies* 35: 5–27.

———. 1982. *Theory of Fertility Decline.* New York: Academic Press.

Gösta Carlsson. 1970. "Nineteenth Century Fertility Oscillations." *Population Studies* 24: 413–422.

N. Caulier-Mathy. 1963–1964. "La composition d'un prolétariat industriel: Les cas de l'entreprise Cockerill." *Revue d'Histoire de la Sidérurgie* 4: 207–222.

Pierre Cayez. 1981. "Une proto-industrialisation décalée: la ruralisation de la soierie lyonnaise dans la première moitié du XIXème siècle." *Revue du Nord* 63: 95–104.

J. D. Chambers. 1953. "Enclosure and the Labour Supply in the Industrial Revolution." *Economic History Review*, 2nd ser., 5: 319–343.

———. 1957. *The Vale of Trent, 1670–1800: A Regional Study of Economic*

Change. Cambridge: Cambridge University Press. *Economic History Review Supplements*, 3.

————. 1965. "Three Essays on the Population and Economy of the Midlands." In D. V. Glass and D. E. C. Eversley, eds., *Population in History*. Chicago: Aldine.

J. D. Chambers and G. E. Mingay. 1966. *The Agricultural Revolution, 1750–1800*. London: Batsford.

Hubert Charbonneau. 1974. *Tourouvre-au-Perche aux XVIIe et XVIIIe siècles*. Paris: Presses Universitaires de France. Institut National d'Etudes Demographiques, Travaux et Documents, Cahier 55.

Serge Chassagne. 1981. "Aspects des phénomènes d'industrialisation et de désindustrialisation dans les campagnes françaises au XIXème siècle." *Revue du Nord* 63: 35–58.

Abel Châtelain. 1976. *Les migrants temporaires en France de 1800 à 1914: Histoire économique et sociale des migrants temporaires des campagnes françaises du XIXe siècle au début du XXE siècle*. 2 vols. Lille: Publications de l'Université de Lille.

Pierre Chaunu. 1970. *La civilisation de l'Europe classique*. Paris: Arthaud.

A. V. Chayanov. 1966. *The Theory of Peasant Economy*. Homewood, IL: Richard D. Irwin.

Louis Chevalier. 1958. *Classes laborieuses et classes dangéreuses*. Paris: Plon.

Helena Chojnacka. 1976. "Nuptiality Patterns in an Agrarian Society." *Population Studies* 30: 203–226.

Carlo Cipolla. 1976. *Before the Industrial Revolution: European Society and Economy, 1000–1700*. New York: Norton.

J. H. Clapham. 1923. "The Growth of an Agrarian Proletariat, 1688–1832. A Statistical Note." *Cambridge Historical Journal* 1: 92–95.

L. A. Clarkson. 1971. *The Pre-Industrial Economy in England, 1500–1750*. London: Batsford.

Hugh D. Clout. 1977. "Industrial Development in the Eighteenth and Nineteenth Centuries." In Hugh D. Clout, ed., *Themes in the Historical Geography of France*. New York: Academic Press.

Ansley Coale. 1969. "The Decline of Fertility in Europe from the French Revolution to World War II." In S. J. Behrman, ed., *Fertility and Family Planning*. Ann Arbor: University of Michigan Press.

————. 1983. "Recent Trends in Fertility in Less Developed Countries." *Science* 221: 828–832.

A. W. Coats. 1967. "The Classical Economists and the Labourer." In E. L.

Jones and G. E. Mingay, eds., *Lands, Labour, and Population in the Industrial Revolution: Essays Presented to J. D. Chambers.* London: Arnold.

————. 1976. "The Relief of Poverty, Attitudes to Labour, and Economic Change in England, 1660–1782." *International Review of Social History* 21: 98–115.

Jon S. Cohen and Martin L. Weitzman. 1975. "Enclosures and Depopulation: A Marxian Analysis." In William N. Parker and Eric L. Jones, eds., *European Peasants and Their Markets.* Princeton, NJ: Princeton University Press.

D. C. Coleman. 1955–1956. "Labour in the English Economy of the Seventeenth Century." *Economic History Review*, 2nd ser., 8: 280–295.

E. J. T. Collins. 1969. "Labour Supply and Demand in European Agriculture, 1800–1880." In E. L. Jones and S. J. Woolf, eds., *Agrarian Change and Economic Development: The Historical Problems.* London: Methuen.

Patrick Colquhoun. 1806. *A Treatise on Indigence.* London: J. Hatchard.

————. 1815. *Treatise on the Wealth, Power, and Response of the British Empire.* London: Joseph Mawman.

J. P. Cooper. 1967. "The Social Distribution of Land and Men in England, 1436–1700." *Economic History Review*, 2nd ser., 20: 419–440.

Alain Corbin. 1975. *Archaisme et modernité en Limousin au XIXe siècle.* 2 vols. Paris: Marcel Rivière.

Julian Cornwall. 1967. "Evidence of Population Mobility in the Seventeenth Century." *Bulletin of the Institute of Historical Research* 40: 143–152.

Marcel Couturier. 1969. *Recherches sur les structures sociales de Châteaudun.* Paris: SEVPEN.

Patricia Croot and David Parker. 1978. "Agrarian Class Structure and Economic Development." *Past and Present* 78: 37–46.

Herman E. Daly. 1971. "A Marxian-Malthusian View of Poverty and Development." *Population Studies* 25: 25–37.

Mike Davis. 1975. "The Stop Watch and the Wooden Shoe: Scientific Management and Industrial Workers of the World." *Radical America* 9: 69–85.

Natalie Zemon Davis. 1968. "Poor Relief, Humanism and Heresy: The Case of Lyon." *Studies in Medieval and Renaissance History* 5: 217–275.

Alan Dawley. 1976. *Class and Community: The Industrial Revolution in Lynn.* Cambridge, MA: Harvard University Press.

Phyllis Deane and W. A. Cole. 1967. *British Economic Growth, 1688–1959: Trends and Structure.* Cambridge: Cambridge University Press.

Paul Deprez. 1965. "The Demographic Development of Flanders in the Eighteenth Century." In D. V. Glass and D. E. C. Eversley, eds., *Population in History*. Chicago: Aldine.

Bernard Desrouet. 1980. "Une démographie différentielle: Clés pour un système autorégulateur des populations rurales d'Ancien Régime." *Annales: Economies, Sociétiés, Civilisations* 35: 3–41.

Pierre Deyon. 1967a. *Amiens capitale provinciale: Etude sur la société urbaine au 17e siècle*. Paris: Mouton.

————. 1967b. "A propos du paupérisme au milieu du XVIIe siècle: Peinture et Charité chrétienne." *Annales: Economies, Sociétés, Civilisations* 22: 137–153.

————. 1979a. "L'Enjeu des discussions autour du concept de 'protoindustrialisation.' " *Revue du Nord* 61: 9–15.

————. 1979b. "La diffusion rurale des industries textiles en Flandre française à la fin de l'Ancien Régime et au début du XIXe siècle." *Revue du Nord* 61: 83–95.

————. 1981. "Un modèle à l'épreuve, le développement industriel de Roubaix de 1762 à la fin du XIXème siècle." *Revue du Nord* 61: 59–66.

H. van Dijk. 1980. *Wealth and Property in the Netherlands in Modern Times*. Rotterdam: Centrum voor Maatschappijgeschiedenis.

Maurice Dobb. 1963. *Studies in the Development of Capitalism*. Rev. ed. London: Routledge & Kegan Paul.

Folke Dovring. 1969. "Eighteenth-Century Changes in European Agriculture: A Comment." *Agricultural History* 43: 181–186.

Michael Drake. 1969. *Population and Society in Norway, 1735–1865*. Cambridge: Cambridge University Press.

Robert S. DuPlessis and Martha C. Howell. 1982. "Reconsidering Early Modern Urban Economy: The Cases of Leiden and Lille." *Past and Present* 94: 49–84.

John D. Durand. 1975. *The Labor Force in Economic Development: A Comparison of International Census Data, 1946–1966*. Princeton, NJ: Princeton University Press.

Stale Dyrvik. 1972. "Historical Demography in Norway, 1660–1801: A Short Survey." *Scandinavian Economic History Review* 20: 27–44.

Richard A. Easterlin. 1978. "The Economics and Sociology of Fertility: A Synthesis." In Charles Tilly, ed., *Historical Studies of Changing Fertility*. Princeton, NJ: Princeton University Press.

Richard Edwards. 1978. "Social Relations of Production at the Point of Production." *Insurgent Sociologist* 8: 109–125.

Mohamed El Kordi. 1970. *Bayeux aux XVIIe et XVIIIe siècles.* Paris: Mouton.

Rudolf Endres. 1975. "Das Armenproblem im Zeitalter des Absolutismus." *Jahrbuch für Fränkische Landesforschung* 34–35: 1003–1020.

Ingrid Eriksson and John Rogers. 1978. *Rural Labor and Population Change: Social and Demographic Development in East-Central Sweden during the Nineteenth Century.* Stockholm: Almqvist & Wiksell. Studia Historica Upsaliensia, 100.

Juan G. Espinosa and Andrew S. Zimbalist. 1978. *Economic Democracy: Workers' Participation in Chilean Industry, 1970–1973.* New York: Academic Press.

Alan Everitt. 1967. "Farm Labourers." In H. P. R. Finberg, ed., *The Agrarian History of England and Wales IV, 1500–1640.* Cambridge: Cambridge University Press.

J. A. Faber, H. K. Roessingh, B. H. Slicher van Bath, A. M. van der Woude, and H. J. van Xanten. 1965. "Population Changes and Economic Developments in the Netherlands: A Historical Survey." *A.A.G. Bijdragen* 12: 47–114.

Wolfram Fischer. 1963. "Soziale Unterschichten im Zeitalter der Frühindustrialisierung." *International Review of Social History* 8: 415–435.

Michael W. Flinn. 1970. *British Population Growth, 1700–1850.* London: Macmillan.

———. 1981. *The European Demographic System, 1500–1820.* Baltimore, MD: Johns Hopkins University Press.

Michael Fores. 1981. "The Myth of a British Industrial Revolution." *History* 66: 181–198.

John Foster. 1974. *Class Struggle and the Industrial Revolution: Early Industrial Capitalism in Three Towns.* London: Weidenfeld & Nicolson.

Etienne François. 1975. "Unterschichten und Armut in rheinischen Residenzstädten des 18. Jahrhunderts." *Vierteljahrschrift für Sozial- und Wirtschaftsgeschichte* 62: 433–464.

Gunther Franz. 1970. *Geschichte des deutscher Bauernständes vom frühen Mittelalter bis zum 19. Jahrhundert,* ed. Gunther Franz. Vol. 4. Stuttgart: Ulmer. Deutsche Agrargeschichte.

Rainer Fremdling and Richard Tilly, eds. 1979. *Industrialisierung und Raum: Studien zur regionalen Differenzierung im Deutschland des 19. Jahrhunderts.* Stuttgart: Klett-Cotta.

Herman Freudenberger. 1960. "Industrialization in Bohemia and Moravia in the Eighteenth Century." *Journal of Central European Affairs* 19: 347–356.

———. 1968. "Die Struktur der frühindustriellen Fabrik im Umriss (mit besonderer Berüksichtigung Böhmens)." In Wolfram Fischer, ed., *Wirtschafts- und sozialgeschichtliche Probleme der frühen Industrialisierung*. Berlin: Colloquium Verlag.

Gunnar Fridlizius. 1975. "Some New Aspects of Swedish Population Growth." *Economy and History* 18: 3–33, 126–154.

Dov Friedlander. 1973. "Demographic Patterns and Socioeconomic Characteristics of the Coal-Mining Population in England and Wales in the Nineteenth Century." *Economic Development and Cultural Change* 22: 39–51.

Harriet Friedmann. 1978. "World Market, State, and Family Farm: Social Bases of Household Production in the Era of Wage Labor." *Comparative Studies in Society and History* 20: 545–586.

Fridolin Fürger. 1927. *Zum Verlagssystem als Organisationsform des Frühkapitalismus im Textilgewerbe*. Beihefte zur Vierteljahrschrifte für Sozial- und Wirtschaftsgeschichte. Vol. 11. Stuttgart: W. Köhlhammer.

Giorgio Gagliani. 1981. "How Many Working Classes?" *American Journal of Sociology* 87: 259–285.

D. Gallie. 1978. *In Search of the New Working Class: Automation and Social Integration within the Capitalist Enterprise*. Cambridge: Cambridge University Press.

Maurice Garden. 1970. *Lyon et les Lyonnais au XVIIIe siècle*. Paris: Les Belles Lettres.

David Gartman. 1978. "Marx and the Labor Process: An Interpretation." *Insurgent Sociologist* 8: 97–108.

David Gaunt. 1976. Familj, Hushall och arbetsintensitet." *Scandia* 42: 32–59.

———. 1977. "Pre-Industrial Economy and Population Structure: The Elements of Variance in Early Modern Sweden." *Scandinavian Journal of History* 2: 183–210.

B. Geremek. 1968. "La popolazione marginale tra il medioeve e l'era moderne." *Studi Storici* 9: 623–640.

Herbert Gintis. 1976. "The Nature of Labor Exchange and the Theory of Capitalist Production." *Review of Radical Political Economy* 8: 36–54.

Jack Goody. 1973. "Strategies of Heirship." *Comparative Studies in Society and History* 15: 3–20.

Jack Goody, Joan Thirsk, and E. P. Thompson, eds. 1976. *Family and Inheritance: Rural Society in Western Europe, 1200–1800*. Cambridge: Cambridge University Press.

David M. Gordon, Richard Edwards, and Michael Reich. 1982. *Segmented Work, Divided Workers: The Historical Transformation of Labor in the United States*. Cambridge; Cambridge University Press.

Pierre Goubert. 1968. *Cent mille provinciaux au XVIIe siècle: Beauvais et le Beauvaisis de 1600 à 1730*. Paris: Flammarion.

———. 1969. *L'Ancien Régime. I. La Société*. Paris: Colin.

Franz Gschwind. 1977. *Bevölkerungsentwicklung und Wirtschaftsstruktur der Landschaft Basel im 18. Jahrhundert*. Liestal: Kantonal Drücksachen- und Materialzentrale.

Philippe Guignet. 1979. "Adaptations, mutations et survivances proto-industrielles dans le textile du Cambrésis et du Valenciennois du XVII-Ième au début du XXème siècle." *Revue du Nord* 61: 27–59.

Gay L. Gullickson. 1981. "The Sexual Division of Labor in Cottage Industry and Agriculture in the Pays de Caux: Auffay, 1750–1850." *French Historical Studies* 12: 177–199.

———. 1982. "Proto-industrialization, Demographic Behavior, and the Sexual Division of Labor in Auffay, France, 1750–1850." *Peasant Studies* 9: 106–118.

Myron P. Gutmann and René Leboutte. 1979. "Early Industrialization and Population Change: Rethinking Protoindustrialization and the Family." Austin: Texas Population Research Center, Papers.

Jean-Pierre Gutton. 1974. *La société et les pauvres en Europe, XVIe–XVIIIe siècles*. Paris: Presses Universitaires de France.

H. J. Habakkuk. 1955. "Family Structure and Economic Change in Nineteenth-Century Europe." *Journal of Economic History* 15: 1–12.

———. 1965. "La disparition du paysan anglais." *Annales: Economies, Sociétés, Civilisations* 20: 649–663.

———. 1971. *Population Growth and Economic Development since 1750*. Leicester: Leicester University Press.

Michael Haines. 1979. *Fertility and Occupation: Population Patterns in Industrialization*. New York: Academic Press.

John Hajnal. 1982. "Two Kinds of Preindustrial Household Formation System." *Population and Development Review* 8: 449–494.

Carl Hammer. 1976. "The Mobility of Skilled Labour in Late Medieval England: Some Oxford Evidence." *Vierteljahrschrift für Sozial- und Wirtschaftsgeschichte* 63: 194–210.

Michael Hanagan. 1980. *The Logic of Solidarity: Artisans and Industrial Workers in Three French Towns, 1871–1914.* Urbana: University of Illinois Press.

Gerhard Hanke. 1969. "Zur Sozialstruktur der ländlichen Siedlungen Altbayerns im 17. and 18. Jahrhundert." In *Gesellschaft und Herrschaft. Forschungen zur sozial- und landgeschichtlichen Problemen vornehmlich in Bayern.* Munich: C. H. Beck.

Gerd H. Hardach. 1969. *Der Soziale Status des Arbeiters in der Frühindustrialisierung.* Berlin: Duncker & Humblot.

Hartmut Harnisch. 1975. "Bevölkerung und Wirtschaft: Uber Zusammenhänge zwischen sozialökonomischen Struktur und demographischer Entwicklung im Spätfeudalismus." *Jahrbuch für Wirtschaftsgeschichte* 2: 57–87.

———. 1978. "Produktivkräfte und Produktionsverhältnisse in der Landwirtschaft der Magdeburger Börde von der Mitte des 18. Jh. bis zum Beginn der Zuckerüberanbaus in der Mitte de dreissiger Jahre des. 19. Jh." In Hans-Jürgen Rach and Bernhard Weissel, eds., *Landwirtschaft und Kapitalismus.* Berlin: Akademie Verlag.

William Hasbach. 1920. *A History of the English Agricultural Labourer.* London: P. S. King.

Hervé Hasquin. 1971. *Une mutation: Le "Pays de Charleroi" aux XVIIe et XVIIIe siècles.* Brussels: Editions de l'Institut de Sociologie, Université Libre de Bruxelles.

Friedrich-Wilhelm Henning. 1977. "Der Beginn der modernen Welt im agrarischen Bereich." In Reinhart Koselleck, ed., *Studien zum Beginn der modernen Welt.* Stuttgart: Klett-Cotta.

———. 1978. "Humanisierung und Technisierung der Arbeitswelt: Über den Einfluss der Industrialisierung auf die Arbeitsbedingungen im 19. Jahrhundert." In Jürgen Reulecke and Wolfhard Weber, eds., *Fabrik, Familie, Feierabend.* Wuppertal: Peter Hammer.

David G. Hey. 1969. "A Dual Economy in South Yorkshire." *Agricultural History Review* 17: 108–119.

Christopher Hill. 1952. "Puritans and the Poor." *Past and Present* 2: 32–50.

———. 1967. "Pottage for Freeborn Englishmen: Attitudes to Wage Labour in the Sixteenth and Seventeenth Centuries." In C. H. Feinstein, ed., *Socialism, Capitalism, and Economic Growth: Essays Presented to Maurice Dobb.* Cambridge: Cambridge University Press.

R. H. Hilton. 1957. *The English Peasantry in the Later Middle Ages.* Oxford: Oxford University Press.

Kurt Hinze. 1963. *Die Arbeiterfrage zu Beginn des modernen Kapitalismus in Brandenburg-Preussen, 1685–1806*. 2nd ed. Berlin: Walter de Gruyter.

E. J. Hobsbawm. 1980. "Scottish Reformers of the Eighteenth Century and Capitalist Agriculture." In E. J. Hobsbawm et al., *Peasants in History: Essays in Honour of Daniel Thorner*. Calcutta: Oxford University Press.

E. W. Hofstee. 1968. "Population Increase in the Netherlands." *Acta Historiae Neerlandica* 3: 43–125.

Erland Hofsten and Hans Lundstrom. 1976. *Swedish Population History: Main Trends from 1750 to 1970*. Stockholm: Statistika Centralbyran Urval, no. 8.

Gerd Hohorest. 1977. *Wirtschaftwachstum und Bevölkerungsentwicklung in Preussen, 1816–1914*. New York: Arno Press.

———. 1982. "Protoindustrialisierung im Übergang zum industriellen Kapitalismus: Die demoökonomische Entwicklung im Kreis Hagen 1817 bis 1863." In Pierre Deyon and Franklin Mendels, eds., *Protoindustrialisation: Theorie et réalité*. Lille: Université des Arts, Lettres, et Sciences Humaines.

B. A. Holderness. 1972. " 'Open' and 'Close' Parishes in England in the Eighteenth and Nineteenth Centuries." *Agricultural History Review* 22: 126–138.

T. H. Hollingsworth. 1971. "Historical Studies of Migration." *Annales de Démographie Historique 1970*, pp. 87–96.

David W. Howell. 1978. *Land and People in Nineteenth-Century Wales*. London: Routledge & Kegan Paul.

Olwen H. Hufton. 1974. *The Poor of Eighteenth-Century France, 1750–1789*. Oxford: Clarendon Press.

Volker Hunecke. 1978. *Arbeiterschaft und Industrielle Revolution in Mailand, 1859–1892*. Göttingen: Vandenhoeck & Ruprecht.

James P. Huzel. 1980. "The Demographic Impact of the Old Poor Law: More Reflexions on Malthus." *Economic History Reveiw*, n.s., 33: 367–381.

Kristian Hvidt. 1975. *Flight to America: The Social Background of 300,000 Danish Emigrants*. New York: Academic Press.

V. K. Iatsunsky. 1965. "Formation en Russie de la grande industrie textile sur la base de la production rurale." *Second International Conference of Economic History: Aix-en-Provence 1962*. Vol. 2: 365–376. Paris: Mouton.

————. 1971. "Le rôle des migrations et de l'accroissement naturel dans la colonisation des nouvelles régions de la Russie." *Annales de Démographie Historique* 1970: 302–312.

Arthur Erwin Imhof. 1976. *Aspekte der Bevölkerungsentwicklung in den nordischen Ländern, 1720–1750.* 2 vols. Bern: Francke Verlag.

Maths Isacson. 1979. *Ekonomisk tillvaxt och social differentiering, 1680–1860: Bondeklassen i By Socken, Kopparbergs Lan.* Stockholm: Almqvist & Wiksell International.

Carl Jantke. 1965. "Zur Deutung des Pauperismus." In Carl Jantke and Dietrich Hilger, eds., *Die Eigentumslösen: Der deutsche Pauperismus und die Emanzipationskrise in Darstellung der zeitgenossischen Literatur.* Munich: Karl Alber.

Karlbernhard Jasper. 1965. *Der Urbanisierungsprozess dargestellt am Beispiel der Stadt Köln.* Cologne: Rheinisch-Westfälischen Wirtschaftsarchiv zu Köln. Schriften zur Rheinisch–Westfälischen Wirtschaftsgeschichte, 30.

Hans Christian Johansen. 1975. *Befolkningsudvikling og familie Struktur: Det 18. arhundrede.* Odense: Odense University Press.

Arthur Henry Johnson. 1909. *The Disappearance of the Small Landowner.* Oxford: Clarendon Press.

Robert Eugene Johnson. 1979. *Peasant and Proletarian: The Working Class of Moscow in the Late Nineteenth Century.* New Brunswick, NJ: Rutgers University Press.

E. L. Jones. 1964. "The Agricultural Labour Market in England, 1793–1872." *Economic History Review* 17: 322–338.

————. 1969. "The Agricultural Origins of Industry." *Past and Present* 40: 58–71.

Lennart Jorberg. 1972a. "The Development of Real Wages for Agricultural Workers in Sweden during the 18th and 19th Centuries." *Economy and History* 15: 41–57.

————. 1972b. *A History of Prices in Sweden, 1732–1914.* 2 vols. Lund: Gleerup.

Etienne Juillard, ed. 1976. *Apogée et crise de la civilisation paysanne.* Vol. 3 of *Histoire de la France rurale,* ed. Georges Duby and Armand Wallon. Paris: Seuil.

Eino Jutikkala. 1975. "Large-Scale Farming in Scandinavia in the Seventeenth Century." *Scandinavian Economic History Review* 23: 159–166.

Ann-Sofie Kalvemark. 1977. "The Country That Kept Track of Its Population." *Scandinavian Journal of History* 2: 211–230.

Jeffrey Kaplow. 1972. *The Names of Kings: The Parisian Laboring Poor in the Eighteenth Century.* New York: Basic Books.

Hermann Kellenbenz. 1965. "Ländliches Gewerbe und bauerliches Unternehmertum in Westeuropa von Spätmittelalter bis ins XVIII. Jahrhundert." *Second International Conference of Economic History. Aix-en-Provence 1962.* Vol. 2: 377–428. Paris: Mouton.

―――. 1975. *Agrarisches Nebengewerbe und Formen du reagrarisierung im Spätmittelalter und 19./20 Jahrhundert.* Stuttgart: Gustav Fischer. *Forschungen zur Sozial- und Wirtschaftsgeschichte,* 21.

―――. 1976. *The Rise of the European Economy: An Economic History of Continental Europe from the Fifteenth to the Eighteenth Century.* London: Weidenfeld & Nicolson.

J. Thomas Kelly. 1977. *Thorns on the Tudor Rose: Monks, Rogues, Vagabonds, and Sturdy Beggars.* Jackson: University Press of Mississippi.

Hubert Kiesewetter. 1980. "Bevölkerung, Erwerbstätige und Landwirtschaft im Königreich Sachsen, 1815–1871." In Sidney Pollard, ed., *Region und Industrialisierung: Studien zur Rolle der Region in der Wirtschaftsgeschichte der letzten zwei Jahrhunderte.* Göttingen: Vandenoheck & Ruprecht.

Gregory King. [1696] 1936. "Naturall and Politicall Observations and Conclusions upon the State and Condition of England." In G. E. Barnett, ed., *Two Tracts by Gregory King.* Baltimore, MD: Johns Hopkins University Press.

Bernard Kirchgassner. 1974. "Der Verlag im Spannungsfeld von Stadt und Umland." In Eric Maschke and Jurgen Sydow, eds., *Stadt und Umland: Protokoll der X. Arbeitstagung des Arbeitskreises für sudwestdeutsche Stadtgeschichtsforschung.* Stuttgart: Köhlhammer. Veröffentlichungen der Kommission für Geschichtliche Landeskunde in Baden-Württemberg, Reihe B, 82. Pp. 72–128.

Herbert Kisch. 1981. *Die Hausindustriellen Textilgewerbe am Niederrhein vor der industriellen Revolution: Von der ursprünglichen zur kapitalistischen Akkumulation.* Göttingen: Vandenhoeck & Ruprecht.

Arnost Klíma. 1965. "The Domestic Industry and the Putting-out System (Verlags-System) in the Period of Transition from Feudalism to Capitalism." *Second International Conference of Economic History: Aix-en-Provence 1962.* Vol. 2: 477–482. Paris: Mouton.

―――1968. Die Entstehung der Arbeiterklasse und die Anfänge der Arbeiterbewegung in Böhmen." In Wolfram Fischer, ed., *Wirtschafts- und sozialgeschichtliche Probleme der frühen Industrialisierung.* Berlin: Colloquium Verlag.

————. 1974. "The Role of Rural Domestic Industry in Bohemia in the Eighteenth Century." *Economic History Review* 27: 48–56.

John Knodel. 1977. "Family Limitation and the Fertility Transition: Evidence from the Age Patterns of Fertility in Europe and Asia." *Population Studies* 3: 481–521.

————. 1978. "Natural Fertility in Pre-Industrial Germany." *Population Studies* 32: 481–510.

————. 1982. "Demographic Transitions in German Villages." Research Reports, Population Studies Center, University of Michigan.

John Knodel and Etienne van de Walle. 1979. "Lessons from the Past: Policy Implications of Historical Fertility Studies." *Population and Development Review* 5: 217–245.

John Knodel and C. Wilson. 1981. "The Secular Increase in Fecundity in German Village Populations: An Analysis of Reproductive Histories of Couples Married, 1750–1899." *Population Studies* 35: 53–84.

Wolfgang Köllmann. 1974. *Bevölkerung in der industriellen Revolution.* Göttingen: Vandenhoeck & Ruprecht. *Kritsche Studien zur Geschichtswissenschaft,* 12.

————. 1977. "Zur Bevölkerungsentwicklung der Neuzeit." In Reinhart Koselleck, ed., *Studien zum Beginn der Modernen Welt.* Stuttgart: Klett-Cotta.

Walter Korpi. 1978. *The Working Class in Welfare Capitalism: Work, Unions, and Politics in Scandinavia.* London: Routledge & Kegan Paul.

Leszek A. Kosínski. 1970. *The Population of Europe: A Geographical Perspective.* London: Longman.

J. T. Krause. 1967. "Some Aspects of Population Change, 1690–1790." In E. L. Jones and G. E. Mingay, eds., *Land, Labour, and Population in the Industrial Revolution.* London: Arnold.

Peter Kriedte. 1982. "Die Stadt im Prozess der europäischen Proto-Industrialisierung." In Pierre Deyon and Franklin Mendels, eds., *Proto-industrialisation: Théorie et réalité.* Lille: Université des Arts, Lettres, et Sciences Humaines.

Peter Kriedte, Hans Medick, and Jürgen Schlumbohm. 1977. *Industrialisierung vor der Industrialisierung: Gewerbliche Warenproduktion auf dem Land in der Formationsperiode des Kapitalismus.* Göttingen: Vandenhoeck & Ruprecht.

Jürgen Kuczynski. 1965. "Industrieller Kapitalismus und Arbeiterklasse." *Second International Conference of Economic History: Aix-en-Provence 1962.* Vol. 2: 25–29. Paris: Mouton.

Witold Kula. 1980. "Money and the Serfs in Eighteenth Century Poland." In E. J. Hobsbawm et al., *Peasants in History: Essays in Honour of Daniel Thorner.* Calcutta: Oxford University Press.

Ann Kussmaul. 1981. *Servants in Husbandry in Early Modern England.* Cambridge: Cambridge University Press.

David S. Landes. 1969. *The Unbound Prometheus: Technological Change and Industrial Development in Western Europe from 1750 to the Present.* Cambridge: Cambridge University Press.

William Langer. 1972. "Checks on Population Growth, 1750–1850." *Scientific American* (February): 93–99.

Peter Laslett. 1968. "Le brassage de la population en France et en Angleterre aux XVIIe et XVIIIe siècles." *Annales de Démographie Historique 1968,* pp. 99–109.

V. M. Lavrosvkii. 1940. *Parlamentskaia Ogorozhivaniia obschinn'ix Zemel' v Anglii kontsa xvii-nachala xix vv.* Moscow: Izdatel'stvo Akademii Nauk SSSR.

William Lazonick. 1974. "Karl Marx and Enclosures in England." *Review of Radical Political Economy* 6: 1–59.

François Lebrun. 1971. *Les hommes et la mort en Anjou aux 17e et 18e siècles.* Paris: Mouton.

Robert Lee. 1972. "Introduction: Population Growth, Economic Development, and Social Change in Europe, 1750–1970." In W. R. Lee, ed., *European Demography and Economic Growth.* London: Croom Helm.

Ronald Lee. 1976. "An Historical Perspective on Economic Aspects of the Population Explosion: The Case of Pre-Industrial England." Unpublished paper, National Bureau of Economic Research.

———. 1977. "Methods and Models for Analyzing Historical Series of Births, Deaths, and Marriages." In Ronald Lee, ed., *Population Patterns in the Past.* New York: Academic Press.

———. 1978. "Models of Pre-Industrial Population Dynamics, with Application to England." In Charles Tilly, ed., *Historical Studies of Changing Fertility.* Princeton, NJ: Princeton University Press.

Pierre Léon, François Crouzet, and Raymond Gascon, eds. 1972. *L'Industrialisation en Europe au XIXe siècle: Cartographie et Typologie.* Paris: Editions du Centre National de la Recherche Scientifique.

Yves Lequin. 1977. *Les ouvriers de la région lyonnaise (1848–1914).* 2 vols. Lyon: Presses Universitaires de Lyon.

Emmanuel Le Roy Ladurie. 1966. *Les payans de Languedoc.* 2 vols. Paris: SEVPEN.

———. 1974. "Pour un modèle de l'économie rurale française au XVIIIe siècle." *Cahiers d'histoire* 29: 5–27.

———. 1977. "Les masses profondes: La paysannerie." In Fernand Braudel and Ernest Labrousse, eds., *Histoire économique et sociale de la France. 1, 2: De 1450 à 1660. Paysannerie et Croissance.* Paris: Presses Universitaires de la France.

Emmanuel Le Roy Ladurie, ed. 1975. *L'âge classique des paysans, 1340–1789.* Vol. 2 of *Histoire de la France rurale*, ed. Georges Duby and Armand Wallon. Paris: Seuil.

Ron J. Lesthaege. 1977. *The Decline of Belgian Fertility, 1800–1970.* Princeton, NJ: Princeton University Press.

Giovanni Levi. 1971. "Mobilità della popolazione e immigrazione a Torino nella prima metà del settecento." *Quaderni storici* 17: 510–554.

———. 1974. "Sviluppo urbano e flussi migratori nel Piemonte nel 1600." In M. Aymard, ed., *Les Migrations dans les pays méditerranéens au XVIIIème et au début du XIXème.* Nice: Centre de la Méditerranée Moderne et Contemporaine.

David Levine. 1977. *Family Formation in an Age of Nascent Capitalism.* New York: Academic Press.

———. 1983. "Proto-Industrialization and Demographic Upheaval." In David Levine, Leslie Page Moch, Louise A. Tilly, John Modell, and Elizabeth Pleck, *Essays on the Family and Historical Change.* College Station: Texas A&M Press.

Ulrich Linse. 1972. "Arbeiterschaft und Gebürtenentwicklung im Deutschen Kaiserreich von 1871." *Archiv für Sozialgeschichte* 12: 205–272.

Catharina Lis. 1976. "Sociale politiek in Antwerpen (1779): Het controleren van de relatieve overbevolking en het reguleren van de arbeidsmarkt." *Tijdschrift voor Sociale Geschiedenis* 5: 146–166.

Catharina Lis and Hugo Soly. 1979. *Poverty and Capitalism in Pre-Industrial Europe.* Atlantic Highlands, NJ: Humanities Press.

Orvar Lofgren. 1978. "The Potato People: Household Economy and Family Patterns among the Rural Proletariat in Nineteenth Century Sweden." In Sune Åkerman, ed., *Chance and Change: Social and Economic Studies in Historical Demography in the Baltic Area.* Odense: Odense University Press.

Sven Lundqvist. 1977. *Folkrörelserna i det svenska samhallet, 1850–1920.* Stockholm: Almqvist & Wiksell International.

Alan Macfarlane. 1978. *The Origins of English Individualism.* Cambridge: Cambridge University Press.

Stephen A. Marglin. 1974. "What Do Bosses Do? The Origins and Functions of Hierarchy in Capitalist Production." *Review of Radical Political Economics* 6: 60–112.

Sture Martinius. 1967. *Befölkningsrörlighet under industrialismens inledningsskede i Sverige.* Göteborg: Elanders. Meddelanden fran Economisk-Historiska Institutionen vid Göteborgs Universitet, 8.

———. 1977. *Peasant Destinies: The History of 552 Swedes Born 1810–1812.* Stockholm: Almqvist & Wiksell International.

Karl Marx. 1970. *Capital: A Critique of Political Economy.* 3 vols. London: Lawrence & Wishart.

———. 1973. *Grundrisse: Foundations of the Critique of Political Economy* (rough draft). London: Allen Lane.

Peter Mathias. 1957. "The Social Structure in the Eighteenth Century: A Calculation by Joseph Massie." *Economic History Review* 10: 30–45.

Albert Mathiez. 1930. "Notes sur l'importance du prolétariat en France à la veille de la Révolution." *Annales Historiques de la Révolution Française* 7: 487–524.

P. C. Matthiessen. 1970. *Some Aspects of the Demographic Transition in Denmark.* Copenhagen: Kobenhavns Universitets Fond til Tilvejebringelse af Laeremidler.

Horst Matzerath. 1978. "Industrialisierung, Mobilität, und sozialen Wandel am Beispiel der Städte Rheydt und Rheindalen." In Hartmut Kaelble, ed., *Probleme der Modernisierung in Deutschland.* Opladen: Westdeutscher Verlag.

Edward E. McKenna. 1974. "Marriage and Fertility in Postfamine Ireland: A Multivariate Analysis." *American Journal of Sociology* 80: 688–705.

Thomas McKeown. 1976. *The Modern Rise of Population.* New York: Academic Press.

Franklin Mendels. 1972. "Proto-industrialization: The First Phase of the Industrialization Process." *Journal of Economic History* 32: 241–261.

———. 1975. "Agriculture and Peasant Industry in Eighteenth-Century Flanders." In William N. Parker and Eric L. Jones, eds., *European Peasants and Their Markets.* Princeton, NJ: Princeton University Press.

———. 1978. "Aux origines de la proto-industrialisation." *Bulletin du Centre d'Histoire Economique et Sociale de la Région Lyonnaise,* no. 2: 1–25.

―――. 1981a. "Les temps de l'industrie et les temps de l'agriculture: Logique d'une analyse régionale de la proto-industrialisation." *Revue du Nord* 63: 21–33.

―――. 1981b. *Industrialization and Population Pressure in Eighteenth-Century Flanders.* New York: Arno Press.

―――. 1982. "Faut-il modifier le modèle flamand?" In Pierre Deyon and Franklin Mendels, eds., *Proto-industrialisation: Théorie et realité.* Lille: Université des Arts, Lettres, et Sciences Humaines.

Andrea Menzione. 1971. "Storia sociale quantitativa: Alcuni problemi della ricerca per i Secoli XVI–XVIII." *Studi Storici* 12 (July–September): 585–596.

Pierre Merlin, ed. 1971. *L'Exode rural, suivi de deux études sur les migrations.* Paris: Presses Universitaires de France. Institut National d'Etudes Demographiques, Travaux et Documents, Cahier 59.

John Merrington. 1975. "Town and Country in the Transition to Capitalism." *New Left Review* 93: 71–92.

Dennis Mills. 1976. "A Social and Demographic Study of Melbourn, Cambridgeshire c. 1840." *Archives* 12: 115–120.

Alan S. Milward and S. B. Saul. 1973. *The Economic Development of Continental Europe, 1780–1870.* London: Allen & Unwin.

Sidney W. Mintz. 1974. "The Rural Proletariat and the Problem of Rural Proletarian Consciousness." *Journal of Peasant Studies* 1: 291–325.

Joel Mokyr. 1976. *Industrialization in the Low Countries, 1795–1850.* New Haven, CT: Yale University Press.

David Montgomery. 1976. "Workers' Control of Machine Production in the Nineteenth Century." *Labor History Review* 17: 485–509.

―――. 1979. *Workers' Control in America.* Cambridge: Cambridge University Press.

Barrington Moore Jr. 1966. *Social Origins of Dictatorship and Democracy: Lord and Peasant in the Making of the Modern World.* Boston: Beacon Press.

Wilbert E. Moore and Arnold S. Feldman, eds. 1960. *Labor Commitment and Social Change in Developing Areas.* New York: Social Science Research Council.

R. B. Morrow. 1978. "Family Limitation in Pre-Industrial England: A Reappraisal." *Economic History Review* 31: 419–428.

Bernard Mottez. 1966. *Systèmes de salaire et politiques patronales.* Paris: Centre National de la Recherche Scientifique.

L. L. Murav'eva. 1971. *Derevensckaia prom'ishlennost' tsentral'noi Rossii vtoroi polovin'i xvii v.* Moscow: Izdatel'stvo Nauka.

A. E. Musson. 1978. *The Growth of British Industry.* New York: Holmes & Meier.

Douglass C. North and Robert Paul Thomas. 1973. *The Rise of the Western World: A New Economic History.* Cambridge: Cambridge University Press.

P. K. O'Brien, D. Heath, and C. Keyder. 1977. "Agricultural Efficiency in Britain and France, 1815–1914." *Journal of European Economic History* 6: 339–391.

Bo Öhngren. 1974. *Folk i rörelse. Samhallsutveckling, flyttningsmonster och folk-röresler i Eskilstuna, 1870–1900.* Uppsala: Almquist & Wiksell. Studia Historica Upsaliensia, 55.

Martha Paas. 1981. *Population, Labor Supply, and Agriculture in Augsburg, 1480–1618: A Study of Early Demographic-Economic Interaction.* New York: Arno Press.

John Patten. 1973. *Rural-Urban Migration in Pre-Industrial England.* Oxford: School of Geography. Research Papers, no. 6.

Luciano Pellicani. 1973. "La rivoluzione industriale e il fenomeno della proletarizzazione." *Rassegna Italiana di Sociologia* 14: 63–84.

Alfred Perrenoud. 1970. "Les migrations en Suisse sous l'Ancien Régime: Quelques problèmes." *Annales de Démographie Historique 1970,* pp. 251–259.

François Perroux. 1970. *Aliénation et société industrielle.* Paris: Gallimard.

Jan Peters. 1967. "Ostelbische Landarmut: Sozialökonomisches [*sic*] über landlöse und landärme Agrarproduzenten im Spätfeudalismus." *Jahrbuch für Wirtschaftsgeschichte* 3–4: 255–302.

Jean Pitié. 1971. *Exode rural et migrations intérieures en France: L'exemple de la Vienne et du Poitou-Charentes.* Poitiers: Norois.

Carlo Poni. 1982. "Protoindustrializzazione: Un commento." *Studi Storici* 51: 1103–1112.

Jean-Pierre Poussou. 1971. "Les mouvements migratoires en France et à partir de la France de la fin du XVe siècle au début de XIXe siècle. Approches pour une synthèse." *Annales de Démographie Historique 1970,* pp. 11–78.

———. 1974. "Introduction à l'étude des mouvements migratoires en Espagne, Italie et France méditerranéenne au XVIIIe siècle." In M. Aymard, ed., *Les migrations dans les pays méditerranéens au XVIIIème et au début de XIXème.* Nice: Centre de la Méditerranée Moderne et Contemporaine.

Walter Prochaska. 1956. "Die wirtschaftliche und kulturelle Entwicklung auf dem Eichsfelde von 1648 bis 1848." In Walter Prochaska, ed., *Eichsfelder Heimatsbuch*. Heiligenstadt: Rat des Kreises Heiligenstadt.

Adam Przeworski. 1977. "Proletariat into a Class: The Process of Class Formation from Karl Kautsky's The Class Struggle to Recent Controversies." *Politics and Society* 7: 343–401.

Jaroslav Purš. 1965a. "Struktur und Dynamik der industriellen Entwicklung in Böhmen im letzten Viertel des 18. Jahrhunderts." *Jahrbuch für Wirtschaftsgeschichte*, pp. 160–196.

———. 1965b. "Die Aufhebung der Hörigkeit und die Grundentlastung in den böhmischen Ländern." *Second International Conference of Economic History: Aix-en-Provence 1962*. Paris: Mouton.

Jill Quadagno. 1982. *Aging in Early Industrial Society. Work, Family, and Social Policy in Nineteenth-Century England*. New York: Academic Press.

Hans-Jürgen Rach and Bernhard Weissel, eds. 1978. *Landwirtschaft und Kapitalismus: Zur Entwicklung der ökonomischen und sozialen Verhältnisse in der Magdeburger Börde vom Ausgang des 18. Jahrhunderts bis zum Ende des ersten Weltkrieges. 1. Halbband*. Berlin: Akademie Verlag.

Arthur Redford. 1964. *Labour Migration in England, 1800–1850*. 2nd. ed. Manchester: Manchester University Press.

Fritz Redlich and Herman Freudenberger. 1964. "The Industrial Development of Europe: Reality, Symbols, Images." *Kyklos* 17: 372–401.

Alan R. Richards. 1979. "The Political Economy of Commercial Estate Labor Systems: A Comparative Analysis of Prussia, Egypt, and Chile." *Comparative Studies in Society and History* 21: 483–518.

Toni Richards. 1977. "Fertility Decline in Germany: An Econometric Appraisal." *Population Studies* 31: 537–553.

H. K. Roessingh. 1970. "Village and Hamlet in a Sandy Region of the Netherlands in the Middle of the 18th Century: An Application of the Guttman Scalogram Technique to Socio-historical Research." *Acta Historiae Neerlandica* 4: 105–129.

———. 1979. "Tobacco Growing in Holland in the Seventeenth and Eighteenth Centuries: A Case Study of the Innovative Spirit of Dutch Peasants." *Acta Historiae Neerlandica* 11: 18–54.

John Rogers, ed. 1980. *Family Building and Family Planning in Pre-Industrial Societies*. Uppsala: Family History Group, University of Uppsala.

Harald Runblom and Hans Norman, eds. 1976. *From Sweden to America: A History of the Migration*. Minneapolis: University of Minnesota Press.

Diedrich Saalfeld. 1966. "Die Produktion und Intensität der Landwirtschaft in Deutschland und angrenzenden Gebieten um 1800." *Zeitschrift für Agrageschichte und Agrarsoziologie* 14: 137–175.

David Sabean. 1971. "Household Formation and Geographic Mobility: A Family Register Study in a Wurttemburg Village, 1760–1900." *Annales de Démographie Historique 1978*, pp. 275–294.

———. 1976. "Aspects of Kinship Behavior and Property in Rural Western Europe before 1800." In Jack Goody, Joan Thirsk, and E. P. Thompson, eds., *Family and Inheritance: Rural Society in Western Europe, 1200–1800*. Cambridge: Cambridge University Press.

Osamu Saito. 1981. "Labour Supply Behaviour of the Poor in the English Industrial Revolution." *Journal of European Economic History* 10: 633–652.

John Saville. 1957. *Rural Development in England and Wales, 1851–1951*. London: Routledge & Kegan Paul.

———. 1969. "Primitive Accumulation and Early Industrialization in Britain." *Socialist Register* 1969: 247–271.

Jane Schneider and Peter Schneider. 1976. *The Formation of a Modern Labor Force: Upper Silesia, 1865–1914*. Berkeley and Los Angeles: University of California Press.

Lawrence Schofer. 1957. *The Formation of a Modern Labor Force: Upper Silesia, 1865–1914*. Berkeley and Los Angeles: University of California Press.

Lennart Schon. 1972. "Västernorrland in the Middle of the Nineteenth Century: A Study in the Transition from Small-Scale to Capitalistic Production." *Economy and History* 15: 83–111.

Bernd Schöne. 1977. *Kultur und Lebensweise Lausitzer Bandweber (1750–1850)*. Berlin: Akademie Verlag.

Joan W. Scott. 1974. *The Glassworkers of Carmaux: French Craftsmen and Political Action in a Nineteenth Century City*. Cambirdge, MA: Harvard University Press.

Wally Seccombe. 1983. "Marxism and Demography." *New Left Review* 137: 22–47.

Domenico Sella. 1975. "Les deux faces de l'économie Lombarde au XVIIe siècle." In Paul M. Hohenberg and Frederick Krantz, eds., *Transition du féodalisme à la société industrielle: L'echec de l'Italie de la Renaissance et des Pays Bas du XVIIe siècle*. Montreal: Centre Interuniversitaire d'Etudes Européennes.

————. 1979. *Crisis and Continuity: The Economy of Spanish Lombardy in the Seventeenth Century.* Cambridge, MA: Harvard University Press.

Amartya Sen. 1981. *Poverty and Famines: An Essay on Entitlement and Deprivation.* Oxford: Clarendon Press.

Emilio Sereni. 1948. *Il capitalismo nelle campagne (1860–1900).* Turin: Einaudi.

Alan Sharlin. 1978. "Natural Decrease in Early Modern Cities: A Reconsideration." *Past and Present* 79: 126–138.

June A. Sheppard. 1961. "East Yorkshire's Agricultural Labour Force in the Mid-Nineteenth Century." *Agricultural History Review* 9: 43–54.

Paul A Slack. 1974. "Vagrants and Vagrancy in England, 1598–1664." *Economic History Review,* 2nd. ser., 27: 360–379.

B. H. Slicher van Bath. 1969. "Eighteenth-Century Agriculture on the Continent of Europe: Evolution or Revolution?" *Agricultural History* 43: 169–180.

————. 1977. "Agriculture in the Vital Revolution." In E. E. Rich and C. H. Wilson, eds., *Cambridge Economic History of Europe V: The Economic Organization of Early Modern Europe.* Cambridge: Cambridge University Press.

Adam Smith. [1776] 1910. *The Wealth of Nations.* 2 vols. London: J. M. Dent.

Daniel Scott Smith. 1977. "A Homeostatic Demographic Regime: Patterns in West European Family Reconstitution Studies." In Ronald Lee, ed., *Population Patterns in the Past.* New York: Academic Press.

Richard Smith. 1981. "Fertility, Economy, and Household Formation in England over Three Centuries." *Population and Development Review* 7: 595–622.

————. 1983. "On Putting the Child before the Marriage: Reply to Birdsall." *Population and Development Review* 9: 124–136.

K. D. M. Snell. 1981. "Agricultural Seasonal Unemployment, the Standard of Living, and Women's Work in the South and East, 1690–1860." *Economic History Review,* 2nd. ser., 34: 407–437.

Johan Söderberg. 1982. "Causes of Poverty in Sweden in the Nineteenth Century." *Journal of European Economic History* 11: 369–402.

Hugo Soly. 1975. "Economische ontwikkeling en sociale politiek in Europa tijdens de overgang van middeleeuwen naar nieuwe tijden." *Tijdschrift voor Geschiedenis* 88: 584–597.

Werner Sombart. 1909–1911. "Verlagssystem (Hausindustrie)." *Handwörterbuch der Staatswissenschaften* 8: 233–261.

William Frederick Spackman. 1847. *An Analysis of the Occupations of the People . . .* London: The Author.

J. J. Spengler. 1945. "Malthus's Total Population Theory: A Restatement and Reappraisal." *Canadian Journal of Economics and Political Science* 11: 83–110, 234–264.

———. 1970. "Adam Smith on Population." *Population Studies*, 2nd ser., 17: 377–388.

Margaret Spufford. 1976. "Peasant Inheritance Customs and Land Distribution in Cambridgeshire from the Sixteenth to the Eighteenth Centuries." In Jack Goody, Joan Thirsk, and E. P. Thompson, eds., *Family and Inheritance: Rural Society in Western Europe, 1200–1800.* Cambridge: Cambridge University Press.

David Stark. 1980. "Class Struggle and the Transformation of the Labor Process: A Relational Approach." *Theory and Society* 9: 89–130.

Evelyne Huber Stephens. 1980. *The Politics of Workers' Participation.* New York: Academic Press.

Katherine Stone. 1974. "The Origins of Job Structures in the Steel Industry." *Review of Radical Political Economics* 6 (Summer): 113–173.

Albrecht Ströbel. 1972. *Agrarverfassung im Übergang: Studien zur Agrargeschichte des badischen Breisgaus vom Beginn des 16. bis zum Ausgang des 18. Jahrhunderts.* Freiburg: Albers.

W. Stys. 1957. "The Influence of Economic Conditions on the Fertility of Peasant Women." *Population Studies* 11–12: 136–148.

Albert Tanner. 1982. *Spulen—Weben—Sticken: Die Industrialisierung in Appenzell Ausserrhoden.* Zurich: Juris Druck.

R. H. Tawney. 1967. *The Agrarian Problem in the Sixteenth Century.* New York: Harper Torchbooks.

Arthur J. Taylor, ed. 1975. *The Standard of Living in Britain in the Industrial Revolution.* London: Methuen.

Klaus Tenfelde. 1977. *Sozialgeschichte der Bergarbeiterschaft an der Ruhr im 19. Jahrhundert.* Bonn/Bad Godesberg: Neue Gesellschaft.

Didier Terrier and Philippe Toutain. 1979. "Pression démographique et marché du travail à Comines au XVIIIème siècle." *Revue du Nord* 61: 19–25.

Joan Thirsk. 1961. "Industries in the Countryside." In F. J. Fisher, ed., *Essays in the Economic and Social History of Tudor and Stuart England in Honor of R. H. Tawney.* Cambridge: Cambridge University Press.

———. 1970. "Seventeenth-Century Agriculture and Social Change." *Agricultural History Review* 18 (Supplement): 148–177.

Malcolm I. Thomis. 1974. *The Town Labourer and the Industrial Revolution.* London: Batsford.

E. P. Thompson. 1963. *The Making of the English Working Class.* London: Gollancz.

———. 1967. "Time, Work-Discipline, and Industrial Capitalism." *Past and Present* 38: 56–97.

———. 1978. "Eighteenth-Century English Society: Class Struggle without Class?" *Social History* 3: 133–165.

Francis M. L. Thompson. 1966. "The Social Distribution of Landed Property in England since the Sixteenth Century." *Economic History Review,* 2nd ser., 19: 505–517.

———. 1969. "Landownership and Economic Growth in England in the Eighteenth Century." In E. L. Jones and S. J. Woolf, eds., *Agrarian Change and Economic Development: The Historical Problems.* London: Methuen.

Charles Tilly. 1975. "Food Supply and Public Order in Modern Europe." In Charles Tilly, ed., *The Formation of National States in Western Europe.* Princeton, NJ: Princeton University Press.

———. 1978a. "The Historical Study of Vital Processes." In Charles Tilly, ed., *Historical Studies of Changing Fertility.* Princeton, NJ: Princeton University Press.

———. 1978b. "Migration in Modern European History. "In William H. McNeill, ed., *Human Migration: Patterns, Implications, Policies.* Bloomington: Indiana University Press.

———. 1979. "Did the Cake of Custom Break?" In John Merriman, ed., *Consciousness and Class Experience in Nineteenth Century Europe.* New York: Holmes & Meier.

———. 1982. "Proletarianization and Rural Collective Action in East Anglia and Elsewhere, 1500–1900." *Peasant Studies* 10: 5–34.

———. 1983. "Flows of Capital and Forms of Industry in Europe, 1500–1900." *Theory and Society* 12: 123–143.

Louise A. Tilly. 1977. "Urban Growth, Industrialization, and Women's Employment in Milan, Italy, 1881–1911." *Journal of Urban History* 3: 467–484.

Louise A. Tilly and Joan W. Scott. 1978. *Women, Work, and Family.* New York: Holt, Rinehart & Winston.

Richard Tilly and Charles Tilly. 1971. "An Agenda for European Economic History in the 1970s." *Journal of Economic History* 31: 184–197.

Gabriel Tortella Cesares. 1973. *Les origines del capitalismo en España: Banca, industria y ferrocarria en el siglo XIX.* Madrid: Editorial Ternos.

G. N. von Tunzelmann. 1978. *Steam Power and British Industrialization to 1860.* Oxford: Clarendon Press.

Gustaf Utterström. 1957. *Jordbrukets arbetare.* 2 vols. Stockholm: Tidens Forlag.

Christiaan Vandenbroeke. 1981. "Mutations économiques et sociales en Flandre au cours de la phase proto-industrielle, 1650–1850." *Revue du Nord* 63: 73–94.

———. 1982. "Analyse critique de la phase proto-industrielle en Flandre: Evolution sociale et comportement démographique aux XVIIème-XIXème siècles." In Pierre Deyon and Franklin Mendels, eds., *Proto-industrialisation: Théorie et réalité.* Lille: Université des Arts, Lettres, et Sciences Humaines.

Etienne Van de Walle. 1974. *The Female Population of France in the Nineteenth Century: A Reconstruction of 82 Departments.* Princeton, NJ: Princeton University Press.

Herman Van der Wee. 1975. "Structural Changes and Specialization in the Industry of the Southern Netherlands, 1100–1600." *Economic History Review* 28: 203–221.

Herman Van der Wee and Eddy van Cauwenberghe, eds. 1978. *Productivity of Land and Agricultural Innovation in the Low Countries (1250–1800).* Louvain: Louvain University Press.

Benoit Verhaegen. 1961. *Contribution à l'histoire économique des Flandres.* 2 vols. Louvain: Nauwelaerts.

Michael Vester. 1970. *Die Enstehung des Proletariats als Lernprozess: Die Enstehung antikapitalistischer Theorie und Praxis in England, 1792–1848.* Frankfurt am Main: Europaïsche Verlaganstalt.

Jaime Vicens Vives. 1969. *An Economic History of Spain.* Princeton, NJ: Princeton University Press.

Pierre Vilar. 1962. *La Catalogne dans l'Espagne moderne.* 3 vols. Paris: SEVPEN.

Ia. E. Vodarskii. 1972. Prom'ishlienn'ie seleniia tsentral'noi Rossii v period genezisa i razvitiia kapitalizma. Moscow: Izdatel'stvo Nauka.

———. 1973. *Naselienie Rossii za 400 let (xvi–nachala xx v.v.).* Moscow: "Prosveschchenie."

———. 1977. "Naselenie Rossii v. kontsee xvii-nachalie xviii veka (problem'i, metodika issledovaniia, rezul'tat'i)." In R. N. Pullat, ed., *Prob-*

lem'i istoricheskoidemograffi SSSR. Tallinn: Institute of History, Academy of Sciences.

Günter Vogler. 1965. *Zur Geschichte der Weber und Spinner von Nowaes, 1751–1785*. Potsdam: Bezirksheimatmuseum.

Jan de Vries. 1974. *The Dutch Rural Economy in the Golden Age, 1500–1700*. New Haven, CT: Yale University Press.

————. 1975. "Peasant Demand Patterns and Economic Development: Friesland, 1550–1750." In William N. Parker and Eric L. Jones, eds., *European Peasants and Their Markets*. Princeton, NJ: Princeton University Press.

————. 1976. *The Economy of Europe in an Age of Crisis, 1600–1750*. Cambridge: Cambridge University Press.

————. 1981. "Patterns of Urbanization in Pre-Industrial Europe, 1500–1800." In H. Schmal, ed., *Patterns of European Urbanisation since 1500*. London: Croom Helm.

————. 1982. "Hierarchy Formation in the European Urban System, 1500–1800." Paper presented to the Social Science History Association, Bloomington, Indiana.

Immanuel Wallerstein. 1974. *The Modern World-System: Capitalist Agriculture and the Origins of the European World-Economy in the Sixteenth Century*. New York: Academic Press.

————. 1980. *The Modern World System. Vol. II: Mercantilism and the Consolidation of the European World-Economy, 1600–1750*. New York: Academic Press.

Susan Cott Watkins. 1981. "Regional Patterns of Nuptiality in Europe, 1870–1960." *Population Studies* 35: 199–215.

Max Weber. [1927] 1950. *General Economic History*. Glencoe, IL: Free Press.

————. [1921] 1972. *Wirtschaft und Gesellschaft*. 5th ed. Tübingen: Mohr.

David Weir. 1982. "Fertility Transition in Rural France, 1740–1829." Doctoral dissertation, Stanford University.

Christer Winberg. 1975. *Folkökning och proletarisering kring den sociala struckturomvandlingen på Sveriges landsbygd under den agrara revolutionen*. Gothenburg: Historiska Institutionen i Göteborg.

————. 1978. "Population Growth and Proletarianization: The Transformation of Social Structures in Rural Sweden During the Agrarian Revolution." In Sune Åkerman, ed., *Chance and Change: Social and Economic Studies in Historical Demography in the Baltic Area*. Odense: Odense University Press.

Nils Richard Wohlin. 1909. *Den Jordbruksidkande befolkningen i Sverige, 1751–1900: Statistik-demografisk studie på Grundval af de svenska yrkesrakningarna.* Stockholm: Emigrationsutredningen, Bil. IX.

Hermann Wopfner. 1938. "Guterteilung und Obervölkerung tirolischer Landbezirk im 16., 17. und 18. Jahrhundert. *Südostdeutsche Forschungen* 3: 202–232.

Keith Wrightson and David Levine. 1979. *Poverty and Piety in an English Village: Terling, 1525–1700.* New York: Academic Press.

E. A. Wrigley. 1961. *Industrial Growth and Population Change.* Cambridge: Cambridge University Press.

———. 1966. "Family Limitation in Pre-Industrial England." *Economic History Review* 19: 82–109.

———. 1967. "A Simple Model of London's Importance in Changing English Society and Economy." *Past and Present* 37: 44–70.

———. 1972. "The Process of Modernization and the Industrial Revolution in England." *Journal of Interdisciplinary History* 3: 225–259.

———. 1977. "The Changing Occupational Structure of Colyton over Two Centuries." *Local Population Studies* 18: 9–21.

———. 1978. "Fertility Strategy for the Individual and the Group." In Charles Tilly, ed., *Historical Studies of Changing Fertility.* Princeton, NJ: Princeton University Press.

———. 1981. "Marriage, Fertility, and Population Growth in Eighteenth-Century England." In R. B. Outhwaite, ed., *Marriage and Society: Studies in the Social History of Marriage.* London: Europa.

———. 1983. "The Growth of Population in Eighteenth-Century England: A Conundrum Resolved." *Past and Present* 98: 121–150.

E. A. Wrigley and R. S. Schofield. 1981. *The Population History of England, 1541–1871: A Reconstruction.* London: Arnold.

Hartmut Zwahr. 1971. "Zur Konstituierung des Proletariats als Klasse: Strukturuntersuchung über das Leipziger Proletariat während der industriellen Revolution." In Horst Bartel and Ernst Engelberg, eds., *Die grosspreussisch-militarische Reichsgründung 1871, Band I.* Berlin: Akademie Verlag.

Review Essay

· 13 ·

TILLY ON THE PAST AS A SEQUENCE OF FUTURES

Arthur L. Stinchcombe

In "Invisible Elbow," chapter 3 herein, Charles Tilly says, "Smart people correct their many errors fast and well." The mistake in this statement is that, since Tilly is a smart person who will have already corrected his errors well, there is no reason for me to be here at the end of his book. Yet he asked me. My argument is that there is a good reason, that smart *social structures* arrange things so that other smart people correct the few errors smart people missed. Science and scholarship is such a smart social structure. For example, Tilly correcting the mistakes of his juniors on ontology and epistemology, when at least some of them must be his and my betters, is the way that structure is supposed to be.

People are intentional and calculating animals, who build history out of their pictures of the future. This is Tilly's key proposition about history here, as well as the problem of useful social science. There is no sense in being rational about anything but the future, because one can't do anything about the past. But people's pictures of the future are always wrong. There would otherwise be no need for historians to tell us how the monarchy ended, even though Louis the XIV tried to make it different, and even though Louis XIV was smart especially in hiring and trusting Colbert to act on his behalf. Colbert was necessary for Louis XIV's kingship as a social structure to be smart. The presumption of scholarship as a social structure is that, on the average if not this time, someone like me makes someone like Tilly smarter. (I can testify that he makes me smarter.)

We all know this social basis of intelligence about the future in our subconscious. When the invisible elbow misses the door it is closing and the groceries end up all over the floor, we shout to whoever is in the house, "You could have unlocked the damn door." A social structure with two considerate people is even smarter than the 90 percent success rate Tilly claims for his own invisible elbow.

In particular, the central concept in most of Tilly's analysis, power, is a view of the future: "What will happen to me (or us) if we do this, or that, or the other?" "What will happen" is, of course, a social construction, but it has different degrees of "reality." People in France under Louis Napoleon evidently became convinced that if they came out on the street in protest, the army would shoot them, as Tilly mentions. And we are convinced that they were convinced because the army would indeed shoot them. But it is a deep confounding of the problem of power to take the high probabilities attached to getting shot by Louis Napoleon if one organized a collective protest as the normal exercise of power. Politics, like other more or less rational action, is about the future, and in particular, the exercise of government power is about "what will happen to me (or us) if we . . ." It is, then, the attachment of probabilities to various versions of personal futures, contingent on our and others' action in the present.

Others' power is especially how far they control the chances of my or our punishment and reward, so that they can make them contingent on our behavior. Our power is how far we control the probabilities of rewards and punishments of others and how much it costs us to administer and pay for them. The most powerful position is to control others' fates with someone else paying for the administration and finance of the relevant rewards and punishments, without either the others or the administrators controlling yours in return. Marx's theory of bourgeois democracy (but not Tilly's) was that the bourgeoisie had pulled it off.

Power in politics is different from the power of money in a reasonably stable economy, in that the probabilities of what will happen if one spends money for a house, or for an automobile, or for a unit share in a mutual fund all are moderately certain. They are a good deal more certain than what will happen if one organizes a Nazi demonstration in Skokie, or a sit-in in the General Motors plant in Flint, or a set of revolutionary councils in Sicily in a time of weakness of the Bourbon monarchy. But political as well as economic power goes on into the future, supported by institutions that also go on into the future, shaping the futures that people can construct to motivate their own lives.

A CENTRAL MECHANISM IN TILLY'S REASONING

In the above essay "Parliamentarization of Popular Contention in Great Britain," Tilly says:

> In two distinct senses of the word, parliamentarization entailed a profound alteration in contention's timing. First, ordinary people moved

away from forms of action that often accomplished their objectives in the very course of claim making toward other forms of action having peculiar properties:

1. they could almost never, even in principle, accomplish their proclaimed objectives in the short run;

2. they depended for effectiveness on extensive anticipation, cumulation, and coordination of efforts by multiple actors, often substantially removed from one another in time and space.

That is, the social transformation Tilly is looking at here has some of its most profound effects by changing the nature of the future that people *are working on* during their protests. Of course, Parliament itself, with its writing up of bills, hearings and debates, newspaper coverage, taught its own participants to consider the future as a long series of coordinated actions removed from one another in time and space. One of the reasons the English Crown could borrow money so easily as compared with most of its competing empires was that a promise from Parliament that general or specific tax money would be voted to pay the debt and interest was more believable than the king's promise that he or she would come up with the money somehow (Carruthers 1996; the Dutch had used a different set of arrangements to get the rich to agree to pay off the national debt earlier than the British ['t Hart 1994]). In short, the passing of laws is one way to construct a long-run future, with moderately concrete coordinated social activities already laid out in that future.

In "Democracy Is a Lake" above, Tilly makes two observations related to each other and to this mechanism. The first is borrowed from Robert Dahl: "much depends on the readiness of political actors who lose in the current round of struggle to believe that they will get another reasonably fair chance to win later on." Similarly, he argues that "protection from arbitrary state action depends on . . . subordination of the military to civilian control." "Subordination" is clearly a summary concept for a prediction that the military and their leaders are not expected to threaten the right of a civilian government to rule or to grant military services to some of the contending parties in a civilian contention for power. (I will come back to the "subordination" part below, because I think the implicit image quite often points us to the wrong things.) Both of these arguments imply that only a long-run, quite highly detailed (and historically quite unusual) view of what the future is likely to hold is a solid foundation for democracy.

Clearly, the building of the centralized autocratic state (e.g., by Louis XIV as a social structure) was an attempt to transform the future relations between the citizenry and the state, so that citizens could be relied on to provide taxes and conscripts when the state decided, rather than when the state had successfully negotiated with local nobles and notables.[1] Colbert scurrying around, dealing, compromising, and improvising to succeed in that construction looks like moment-to-moment adaptation. But its object was to leave behind an efficient mobilizing apparatus that extended into the localities but was controlled "by the state." In construction of buildings as well, people have to scurry and improvise to build a permanent structure.

Of course, the institution building was controlled by a sort of a state of continuing compromise between the Crown and the localities before Louis XIV. But what Louis XIV created was a particular believable future in which the policies of the national state would result in a straightforward way in the mobilization of resources to carry them out.

Finally, let me make a bit of a stretch to argue that in Tilly's paper on migration in modern European history (chapter 11) above, the dimension from the lower left (local and circular change of residence) to the upper right (chain migration and career migration) in Figure 11.1 has to do with creation of longer-term futures in the new residence. Futures in the new country can reach back to shape the anticipations of people who still might migrate from their places of origin. Chain migration creates, in both the sending and the receiving population, a relatively detailed view of how a migrant might make a long-term adjustment in the new place. Tilly's example of career migration is a stranger migrating as priest to a parish in southeast England. Ordination as a Church of England priest makes a move to a village in Kent a piece of a life in an understandable future environment in the church hierarchy, though that life may not all be in that village in Kent.

Local and circular migrations that do not involve creating a believable future in a distant place may, however, involve a detailed view of the future institutional environment after the move. But since that future environment is approximately the same in the new location as in the old, it does not require special social supports before and after the move to connect the future there to the place of origin.

It seems to me that in all these cases, there are five features of the mechanism Tilly is using to explain variations:

1. There is a lengthening of the time into the future that people can take account of in planning, because they "know" some of its main features. A dimension of migration decisions, for example, is from temporary to "definitive," the latter meaning that people are planning on and committed to a future in the place of destination.

2. There is an increase in the complexity of people's knowledge of

the future. In democratic politics, the probability that one could win in a fair process within the next twenty years or so is such a complexity.

3. Some parts of the anticipated future are "responsive" to future conditions, in the sense that they involve future coordinated action that will be different under different future conditions.

4. An important part of the structures that give reality to the future are social guarantees of various kinds: laws, contracts, offers of help from previous migrants, corporate existence of the Church of England, Parliament having already been around for several generations.

5. Knowledge of such futures are discussed with people close to one, that one can trust, or discussed in public in such a way that one believes one can trust them (in Parliament, in a fair trial, in the Council of Bishops).

WHY TILLY STUDIES INSTITUTIONS AND NETWORKS SIMULTANEOUSLY

In the next two sections, I will argue two main points about Tilly's mechanism. The first is that the social structures and processes that make parts of the future solid enough to plan on are, ordinarily, what we usually call *institutions*, and the process of creating solidity to the future is what we usually call *institutionalization*. Thus I will be arguing, in the light of point 4 above, that laws are a crucial part of building solidity in the future and that, therefore, legalization is central to institutions and institutionalization. Sociology adopted the word *institutions* from legal and quasi-legal ecclesiastical discourse, where the Latin *institutum* meant "purpose, design, plan, ordinance, instruction, precept" (*Oxford English Dictionary*, at "institute sb.").

This is quite obvious with the institutionalization of democracy, or of Parliament as the object of most petitions and protests in England. But it is useful to think of what makes chain migration possible as the building of institutions linking the place of destination with the place of origin in such a way that a future in the place of destination is reasonably predictable. The chains of chain migration are institutions in effect, if not in the manner of construction.

The second is that the communication of the solidity of institutional futures to individuals is normally a network phenomenon, in which trusted people familiar with how institutions build the relevant parts of the future originate communication to others (in electoral meetings, for example, or on trips of organizers of ethnic institutions in the place of destination going back to the place of origin) about how to build one's personal future using the futures being solidified by institutions. Or more briefly, institutions have their macrosocial effects by chains of social relations of trust between the cosmopolitan macroscopic environments where the solidity of the future is being created, to local environments where particular lives are connected to such futures.

The two arguments add up to an explanation and defense of two peculiarities of Tilly's method of analysis in these essays. The first peculiarity is that Tilly virtually always uses some sort of network analysis, but he does not sound like any other network analyst. That is because he cares what it is that flows over the links between people. Arcane structural properties of chain migration networks, of the sort that might be studied by Harrison White (e.g., White, Boorman, and Breiger 1976) or Ronald Burt (1992), are not so important as the fact that they carry to a little town in Italy information about what sort of future one might have in, say, Paterson, New Jersey.

Similarly, the link from a parish meeting to Parliament is crucial because it was Parliament that controlled what policy, for example, the navy would have toward the slave trade. As White and Burt would argue, the network positions of MP and parishioner-constituent had the same structure that connected the constituent indirectly to participation in a debate between the MP and other members of Parliament, so MPs had similar network positions to one another (as did their local constituents). The links then put the MP in a position to gain prestige and power by "representation" or "brokering." But this is a background fact for Tilly, because such links have the causal role for Tilly of providing the view of the solidity of the future that connects the past to the future in the minds of constituents and their communities. It is the fact that the future of the slave trade is in the hands of Parliament, rather than the fact that the only way most people's communications get into Parliament is through their MP, that is crucial for Tilly. That determines what flows on the links between parish and MP.

Second, Tilly always embeds his network analysis in a deep analysis of the historical context, and even in the wonderful network analysis of the parliamentarization of popular contention he makes the historical transformation of networks a major historical mover. Rather than looking for the laws of network structure, detached from place and time, Tilly wants to know what was distinctive in the network that Louis XIV and Colbert built linking the national government to localities as compared with that that came to link popular protest with Parliament a century or so later in

England. I argue that what makes this part of this analysis into sociology (as well as narrative) is that contexts are institutions, in the sense that I defined institutions above. And what matters about institutions for the significance of the context of networks is that they make bits of the future solid enough to plan on.

It is, then, particular aspects of what we usually consider institutions that have major macrosociological effects. These are the aspects that *bind parts of the future*, to some degree or other, for lots of people. That binding parts of the future is central to macrosociological effects makes the institutional context crucial. That binding of the future has to be real to people in their lives to have an effect. And that makes networks embedded in the institutions crucial for their macrosociological effects.

So when Louis XIV and Colbert scurry and improvise to abolish bargaining over the extraction of resources in localities, they bind the future in such a way that when the king made war he did not have to bargain for resources from the localities. A later king was therefore free to wage expensive wars on behalf of American colonists that brought little benefit to France. It was not, perhaps, wise for the king to have been so free of local bargaining, since if Theda Skocpol is right, Louis XVI lost his head because he took advantage of that freedom (1979: 54, 60–64). But then, in turn, the networks have to connect cosmopolitan causes to the localities, through, for example, the penetration of royal bureaucrats and tax farmers into tax collection, for these institutionalized arrangements to have their macrosocial effects. (Compared to the previous system, tax farmers under Louis XIV and after worked more through royal bureaucrats, there were fewer of them, and they advanced money more on commercial taxes as compared to rural taxes). It was creating that extension of the network without intervening notables that required scurrying and ad hoc innovation on the part of Colbert.

INSTITUTIONS, THE FUTURE, AND HISTORICAL CONTEXT

Tilly quite often objects to too much emphasis on ideology. But obviously, "subordination of the military" to civilian government, and "the probability that a party could win in a fair process another time" are ideological constructs. And clearly, the fact that the English Parliament embodies a different ideology of government than the duo of Louis XIV and Colbert is central to his analysis. It seems to me that Tilly's objection is not to the strong impact of ideology, but to any allegation that making a speech is as important as building an institution.[2] There is a usage in sociology of *ideol-*

ogy, quite different from that of Karl Mannheim in *Ideology and Utopia* ([1929] 1936: 109–123, 192–204, especially as a contrast to 229–239), that seems to mean the most airy and empty of speech. I want to distinguish ideology or other values that bind the future, that enable people and organizations and protesting mobs to orient to the long run, from ideology or values unconnected with futures and unconnected through networks to the people or organizations that might plan on the basis of the bound future.

Louis XIV and Colbert were trying to "institute" their values by making them a reliable part of the future: by changing laws and privileges, by changing bargaining and representation procedures for taxation and conscription, by connecting them to localities through a network the agents which were under the royal thumb, rather than through independent local notables and nobles. In the original meaning of the verb *to institute,* from which *institution* is derived, Louis XIV and Colbert were *instituting,* establishing continuing features of the future, so that they would monopolize the terms of the protection game that was statehood in those days. If they succeeded in so binding the future (which they did, at least for a while), then we would call it an *institution.* The bureaucratic autocratic national state became an institution during the reign of Louis XIV (and continued becoming for a century or so afterward), but not by speeches alone.

Ideologies, in the modern sense of worldviews in speeches, differ from what Mannheim called ideologies in not being instituted, not being "the ways things are done around here." They differ, in particular, in not being tied through networks along which real resources, help, responsiveness, threats of coercion, and pronouncements of law flow. Mannheim talked of the disintegrated intellectual structure of previously instituted modes of action. A coherent utopia did not, he argued, justify all the laws, customs, bureaucratic routines, tax assessment rolls, and the like that constituted the way things are. Conservatives whose sense of certainty about the future and their place in it rests on knowing the way things are, and who are satisfied with that future, then tend to have an ideology of why things ought to be the way they are that has an intellectually disintegrated, non-utopian, character.

Thus when we contrast the Great Reform Bill of 1832 in England with the proclamation of the Estates General making itself a Constituent Assembly in 1789 in France, we see the end result (as I understand Tilly's argument about parliamentarization) of different ways of centralizing the bargains with local notables and nobles. In England, those bargains were carried out in some measure through Parliament from before the mid-eighteenth century, where Tilly starts. The Reform Bill was the outcome of a long development of Parliament as the focus of that negotiation about the extraction of resources. What Parliament was supposed to do was to regularize those deals about extraction, so that when Parliament endorsed going to war, they also endorsed the taxes and conscription. Thus a money bill for war was a whole organized set of local deals about extraction of resources, so that the king could be sure he could pay for the war with the American colonies (for example) because Parliament had so promised. Louis XIV and Colbert set off on another path, of destroying rather than regularizing the dealing over extraction, leaving themselves free to extract. So the French king, too, could promise to pay for the war, unsuccessful or not, if only he could keep his head.

The Great Reform Bill then was, on the one side, an outcome of a large number of dispersed protests about the electoral standing of very many interest groups in very many constituencies, and so the outcome of the parliamentarization of popular contention. But it was also a continuation of the institution of making the dealing with constituencies about extraction through acts of Parliament, so that holders of Treasury bonds in London would know they would be paid because Parliament had agreed to the extraction. Those laws made uniform the deals between local notables and the state, by assembling the notables in Parliament and making them specify the terms of the deals, though not always so specifying to the Crown's liking. The Parliament's "power of the purse" was the outcome of the standardization of the contract of extraction, rather than the destruction of the power of the local notables as had happened in France.

But that standardized power then called into question the enormous variety of the historically existing deals between the state and local notables: rotten boroughs, personal representation of some notables in the House of Lords, varying suffrage criteria, and the like. It made sense to popular protesters to orient their demands for a fair share of the power of dealing to Parliament, because that was where things were regularized if they were to be regularized. Thus the future had solidity, a solidity it did not have in the collection of the *cahiers de doléances* in France just before the Revolution. Englishmen knew the deal would be worked out in Parliament. That, in turn, meant that the Reform Bill was the sort of thing that localities and their MPs had a detailed opinion on, *and had a way to get instituted by popular contention.*

Thus what flowed on the links between localities and the king through Parliament in England was an estimate of what terms of extraction, for what foreign military adventures and other protection racket operations, would be tolerable in the localities. This, in turn, determined what sorts of wars were possible and wise. That measure of willingness did not flow to the same degree upward from the local *élection* through the bureaucracy to the king in France. In the end, the *cahiers de doléances* were not embedded in an institutionalized network that made them an effective expression of how much extraction localities would tolerate. It did not generate, as it did in England, a return flow of commitment of the localities to whatever deal their representatives in Parliament had worked out. The English Parliament guaranteed that the government would keep its half of the deal, which generated that commitment.

So the Reform Bill was a regulation of the network of representation in much the way that Louis XIV's and Colbert's bureaucratization of tax collection and conscription in the localities was a regularization of the network of authoritative extraction. They both erased, to a considerable degree, the ancient "feudal" variety in the constitution of the contract between the state and localities. These, in turn, were new institutions. One could rely on them in future planning. And they had networks to affect people's and communities' vision of the future in the localities. They were both intended to be "future binding" pieces of ideology. But obviously, they embodied different ideas about how the future would be regulated, who would have the power to adapt coordinated action to contingencies in the future, and the like.

Whether or not my story of the contrast between the Great Reform Bill in England in 1832 and the constitution of the Constituent Assembly in 1789 in France would be endorsed by Tilly, my point here is that a network leading from the action of the Crown to extraction from the localities existed in both places. In both places, the extraction was considered generally inevitable, a bound part of the future. But they look very different because the institutions are different. And they are not only different because people make different speeches about democracy in them. They differ because the value premises, power arrangements, regulations, and general principles of operation are all instituted differently. Context matters, then, because networks with roughly the same structure carry different ideological and other materials at different times and places in history. It is what passes over the networks, as shaped by the institutions, that shapes people's view of what is a dependable feature of the future. The causes, then, are not so much in the network structure as on what flows over the links. And that is determined by the institutional context.

Tilly's plea for looking at the context sounds like the plea of humanities scholars to read more books and speeches to catch the spirit of the times, so that one can decipher the varieties of texts as understood in different times and places. But it is actually quite a different strategy. It is objection to this intellectual history view of ideology that makes Tilly foolishly rail against ideology as a cause. It is instituted ideology that is a big cause—

speech-making ideology usually is not. One tests which kind one has got by tracing out the networks over which a speech travels to get to the acting person. If one cannot find the network (or at least one growing), then don't pay much attention to the ideology.

NETWORKS

Tilly's originality in the analysis of networks can perhaps best be analyzed by contrasting the relevant parts of his theory with Mark Granovetter's analysis of "embedding" of economic action in networks (1985) and with Neil Smelser's analysis of the process of building institutions out of social movements (1962; also the historical work that lay at the foundation of that theoretical book, 1959). I will argue that Granovetter usually presumes that the causes that flow over the links of a network are what is "naturally" there in the kind of social relation it is. Tilly studies the flows of causes along networks that are determined by larger institutional forces.

Smelser tends to study the development (or failures of development) of social movements into functioning institutions by analyzing how the functions that the institution "needs" come to be fulfilled. The "need" for a function somehow "naturally" causes either the growth of the institution or its relapse into collective behavior. Tilly instead studies the same process by analyzing how people transform the nodes and links of a network to achieve their objectives. Thus Tilly regards neither the links in networks nor the needs of the institution as naturally existing causes, but instead as things brought into existence by human action on the links and nodes that are important for institutions.

To put it another way, networks are significant for Tilly not as causes themselves, but instead as channels that deliver causes to particular places in the social system. What causes they deliver depends not only on what causes started out (e.g., a general wish by Louis XIV and Colbert to be able to mobilize taxes and conscripts for internal or external warfare whenever they chose), but how the causes transformed, and were transformed by, the people and organizations through which they flowed.

For example, the wish to mobilize for warfare was transformed in different ways in England and France, after their two respective parliaments got the power of the purse and approved (or disapproved) taxes to pay for a war, and after Colbert turned the system of negotiation through estates in the various provinces into a centralized system of bureaucrats and centralized authority reaching into the localities. The "needs" of the kings were quite similar. The mobilization was through embedded networks reaching from the Crown and the needs of the armed forces into the purses and manpower of the localities in both countries. But the causes of the kings' needs were transformed differently before delivery in the localities, because of the different history of network formation by political institutions.

Ultimately, to mobilize for a war or other national good, universalistic claims of statecraft have to be turned into particularistic causes demanding specific sums from specific people, and enforcing particular young men's going off to war as conscripts or impressed seamen (Heimer 1992). Conversely, in order for an individual's trouble to become a collective grievance addressed to Parliament, it must undergo a transformation into a universalistically defined problem, be attached to some reform Parliament might conceivably carry out, and be adopted as a subject of protest by some social group.

In this book Tilly's paper above on the parliamentarization of popular protest in England is the core exemplar of network analysis in an institutional context.[3] Tilly is eminently aware that Parliament was a different thing by the mid-nineteenth century because the network structure of popular contention in which it was embedded was different from the structure in which the links originating in a protesting group stayed local, especially because, in particular, Parliament was much more central in that network as the object addressed by much of the protest. But Tilly thinks that the cause of that transformation was in part a transformation of Parliament, that it became more powerful in the government of England, and that it listened more to popular forces. Being the kind of node that listens makes one more central, and that effect is multiplied if it matters that one listens. The causes were not "naturally" in the network, as conveyed by Granovetter's use of *embedded* as carrying the rest of society into business relations. Instead, they were being transformed by historical forces and, in particular, by the development of Parliament as an institution.

Much of what Smelser argues about the functions of various things that are added to collective behavior, with its utopian ideologies, to make it into a functioning institution can be thought of as the stretching of the planning horizon of collective behavior. I have argued that this is also central to Tilly, especially in his paper on parliamentarization. We could summarize the implication of Tilly's paper for Smelser as: by knowing where power to implement remedies for grievances lies, and by addressing popular contention toward that place, collective behavior started, already in its grassroots parts, to be more an "institution" in the mid-1800s than in the mid-1700s. Popular protest was more ready to be implemented and to bind the future. But Tilly does not believe that these institutionalizing devices of protest to Parliament "naturally" come into existence in England, partly because he knows they did not naturally come into existence in France.

Smelser's analysis of the ideology of collective behavior can be summarized roughly as, "When people do not know how to build an institution to remedy their problems, they have funny ideas about how to remedy their grievances" (particularly in Smelser 1962). In particular, they tend to make speeches, rather than to build institutions. Part of Tilly's observation about the impact of parliamentarization on protesters' long-run thinking is to say that their ideas about building institutions were not as funny, not as ineffective in producing long-run remedies, by 1830 as they had been in 1750. Smelser was looking at collective behavior in the early nineteenth century by a public used to building institutions and a society that knew where to channel that construction.

Thus it seems to me that Tilly and Smelser are describing much the same variable (though the vague tone in Smelser that suggests that people who don't build institutions as they should are pretty neurotic is blessedly absent in Tilly; Tilly is more likely to think the House of Lords is pretty neurotic because they want to build the same old institutions). That variable is the degree of elaboration, especially in the elongation of the planning horizon and its accompanying predictions of solid features of the future. A high value of that variable makes contention part of a future course of action that is likely to bring about a solid institution. It had not been contention as a beginning of institution building, which Smelser thought natural, a century earlier.

Perhaps the most obvious network phenomenon studied by Tilly in these essays is chain migration. People go from Limousin to Paris to work as masons in the spring, come back for the winter, and bring information to other farmers and to possible young masons in Limousin. This is toward the low end of commitment to Paris, to which chain migration takes place, because they come back "home" every year. But since being a mason in Paris is a career for most of them, it is more like transhumance, migration in which people come to have two homes. In winter in Limousin, one can talk a good deal about what Paris is like, how one makes money, how to keep one's money from getting stolen, whether there are "girls" there, how much of the time you can expect to work, where you live, what you do with other masons there, who cooks the food, how it feels to be away from home, what kind of teasing you have to put up with, and so on.

Many of these pieces of information have no larger structural significance. But the implicit labor market information embedded in it is a report on what working-class institutions in Paris will mean to you, and the information on "girls" bears on what relation sex in Paris has to masons' family institutions.

Longer-term chain migration may involve people going back to the old country to retire, to look for a wife, or to look for someone promising to work in their restaurant at below-standard wages. The key is that a personal translation of a destination environment into a future to be lived in the destination takes place, by communication backward to someone now in the old country. And some of the institutional problems of the migration, such as a ship or airplane ticket, advise about what you have to tell the consular official about your job to get a visa, and what job actually awaits you regardless of what you told the consul, are dealt with. That is, the problems of migration are translated into concrete problem-solving episodes in the immigrant's future. That is what a network does, *given* that the future in the new place is predictable enough to tell about it.

Passing a resolution to be sent to the MP in a parish meeting may seem like quite a different thing to do. But some confidence that one will be heard is the purpose of speaking on political matters. One's own MP is known to (or known not to) listen to resolutions of parish meetings. He has been coming down to the constituency to be elected periodically, and one can listen and talk in election rallies to get a notion of that to which he (in those days essentially always he, though a woman might have a link to him) would listen. In the course of that conversation, he might tell you who your enemies in Parliament were and what institutional solutions to problems of various kinds might be.

In short, the constituent-MP relationship, in which the future of a course of political action would become part of a real future, had existed for some time. The institutional underpinnings for the relationship's continued existence were in the system of constituencies. In that continued institutional existence of a constituency-MP link, there was also a chance to build other institutions that would also carry pieces of the structure of contention on into the future. One would, for example, still know who one's enemies were next term because they, too, had learned what to do from their MP.

The difficulty of building such structures by solid *organizations* is that one may rigidify parts one wants to be responsive. For example, one had to know around 1800–1810 whether or not the British Navy was actually patrolling off Africa or in the Caribbean to know whether one needed to keep on petitioning for abolition (of the slave trade). If the patrol was effective, one could turn to the question of the abolition of slavery itself in the English colonies. The complexity of the future meant that one needed a continuing flexible and responsive link to Parliament that would change content as the nature of the problem of abolishing slavery changed. Ultimately, one wants to deliver one's grievance through the MP so that it will be a cause governing the behavior of a particular official. But which official that is changes with the change in the historical course of the contention.

So one does not want a solid organization linking a Wesleyan constituency to the navy, when the problem later is to send out salaried judges to Jamaica to replace ex–slave owners as justices of the peace trying the disobedient ex-slaves of their neighbors. Networks through Parliament reach where they need to reach; they channel causes to variable destinations over the course of history.

Let me now take the three elements of Tilly's reasoning that I have identified to try to show that one can do better with Tilly's apparatus than Tilly did when he adopted a conventional analysis of one of his problems. He argues that a prerequisite of democracy is the "subordination" of the military to civilian control. I will try to show that by applying Tilly's approach to the analysis of the lengthening and shortening of the duration of time into the future to which that behavior is oriented, by analyzing the institutional context, and by focusing on networks as a system of delivery of causes, one can do better than believe in the force of constitutional requirements. It was, after all, an ex-general, Andrew Jackson, who responded to a constitutional judgment of the Supreme Court with, "Let them enforce it." Why would an ex-general be cautious about using military power to protect a national treaty with a Native American tribe? And what does that mean for "subordination" of the military to the president?

"Subordination" of the Military to Civilian Control

The military precondition of democracy is that the military not intervene decisively in the political contest and that this low probability of intervention is widely known. It is thus a condition in the cultural construction of the future. In particular, the military should not routinely invade the security of citizens in order to destroy their capacity to participate in politics. *One* of the ways of securing that condition is the "subordination" of the military to civilian rule that Tilly mentions as a precondition. I will argue that there are other ways of meeting the precondition.

When one speaks of the subordination of the military to civilian rule, one is always speaking of a "rule of law." Law is one of the primary future-binding aspects of social organization and culture. But not all peaceful resolution of political disputes is by law. People bargain, use ritual tests of strength, vote, make donations of public goods if they like the government (Veyne [1976] 1990 has an excellent analysis of such a system in ancient Greek city-states), call on outside third parties (other countries or the United Nations or a king from a foreign royal lineage, for example) to mediate or arbitrate disputes, and so on. My argument is that deals with the military that protect democracy are not all effected by writing constitutions or passing laws. Constitutional provisions about the military have a bad effectiveness record. I will first argue that if we understand the legal problems of military action, we will not be surprised that law is often a precarious control, and so "subordination" is often not socially sufficient to produce military nonintervention.

Subordination of the military to the law consists in a specialized law, virtually always constitutional law, of exceptions to the law. The law governs who has authority to make and bring an end to those exceptions from the law that constitute martial law, a state of war, reading the riot act, and so on (compare Stinchcombe 1995). War, civil war, riot, frontiers that cannot be well guarded, genocide and incarceration of enemy ethnic groups, and natural disasters all are states in which acts normally illegal are tolerated for *raisons d'état*. Ordinarily, the military and various sorts of secret service are given special authority, especially to kill and to take territory and property, with the understanding that when a treaty is signed, the law of exception will come to an end. "Subordination" of the military means that the decision to declare war, riot, or genocide, and then of what treaties to accept and when to bring the war or civil war or genocide to an end, is specifically given to civilian authority, not to the secret service or the military.

Such constitutional arrangements are precarious even in quite stable democracies. There was, for example, some doubt whether the conservatives, in coordination with the military, would accept the 1926 treaty granting the whole island of Ireland independence, and such considerations may have entered into the decision to partition Protestant from Catholic Ireland. The fact that there was something of a general strike going on at the time made the conservatives and the military more antsy about democracy, and more unwilling to lose the reliably conservative Protestant vote in Northern Ireland. There were similar doubts about military obedience in France at the time of the independence of Algeria. And some difficulty with the subordination of the Southern military to the Union government was encountered between 1861 and 1865 in the United States, though the government of the South was also a civilian government with a subordinated, and in fact federalist, military system.

Let me try to describe in particular one condition: dispersal of military power. Dispersal seems to me often to satisfy the precondition for democracy and, in the long run, to sometimes lead to democracy, often after a period of essentially one-party national politics with federalist compromises about the jurisdiction of national government. Dispersal of military power takes two main forms. First, military power may be dispersed in rural areas, with feudal lords or caciques having military bands that may be federated into regional forces from time to time. Early in modernization, this may be combined with a more or less effective urban government controlled by an urban elite, sometimes organized into a "political party," to control what national government there is. I'd say that Mexico during the Institutional Revolutionary Party (PRI) government from about 1920 to 1950, and the Uruguayan government during the *Colorado* monopoly of national power from about 1880 to 1990 (Filgueira 1996) were quite clear cases. India under the first Congress Party government may have been another.

The sort of national democracy this creates is often in the short run not of the competitive parties form, though it may develop in that direction. It is more often an oligarchy, organized by internal bargaining of interest groups, that rules the country as a whole only as far as the coalitions of rural areas (also sometimes organized as parties and sometimes running in elections) consent. It is a sort of multiparty system with "ineffective" elections (though formal elections were carried out in all the cases mentioned). The latent function of elections is often to bargain out the boundaries of national power, with votes as a convenient measure of bargaining power.

The second variety is federalism, perhaps best exemplified by the Dutch Republic in the seventeenth and eighteenth centuries, the United States from the Articles of Confederation through the election of 1860, and the modern United Nations. A key exemplification of this structure is George Washington having to ask the states for the help of their militias to put down the Whiskey Rebellion; a key later one was that winning the election of 1860 did not in fact carry with it civilian control over the military forces of the Southern states.

The Dutch navy, the primary military force of the Dutch Republic of the seventeenth and eighteenth centuries, was created and financed by the customs tolls of the Dutch cities, and its government was more nearly a coalition of cities than a national government. The UN likewise begs for money and troops to carry out its missions, and the United States, for example, very often sends neither. The UN's military is not about to take over the UN or, in particular, to impose UN rule on the great powers, at least until the world's 1860.

In some ways, federalism is an institutionalized version of the informal dispersion of military power to feudal lords and caciques. And this suggests that the degree of institutionalization of the dispersal of military power is a variable that runs from low (in Mexico in the 1920s, say) to high (in the United Nations in the 1990s), with the United States, in, say, 1830, in the middle.

The history of the central government of the United States from the

Constitution to the 1850s could be called a succession of one-party regimes (Federalists, Jeffersonians, Jacksonians), with minor oppositions, that each looks a good deal like the Mexican PRI from 1920 to 1950, or the *Colorado* regime in Uruguay in the late nineteenth century. Except in the 1860s, the transitions between regimes were fairly peaceful, partly because the central government meant very roughly as much to American government as a whole as the UN and related organizations do to government of the world as a whole today. Beneath this level, the federal regime left each state pretty much to itself, except in war or when new states had to be admitted as either slave or free.

Except for the Civil War, then, the succession of one-party regimes without much power of oppression (if not much power against oppression either) seems to have been a pretty adequate background so that, after about 1876, competitive party democracy in which the minority party did not disappear could come into being. It seems to me that the federalist legitimation of the stalemate between state militias was more crucial to the stability of "partisan democracy" than the constitutional provisions, because when that stalemate was breached in the 1860s, the constitutional provisions about the military did not do much good.

My point is that military intervention, like warfare and civil war more generally, tends to be legitimated by the laws of exceptions. And who gets to declare exceptions to the law is inherently uncertain. The Supreme Court in the United States has always gone very far in legitimating military exceptionalism, and so have state governments in their riot acts and similar legislation. This means that stable laws are, in general, not very good predictors of what will happen in a "crisis." The same is true of federal provision of welfare payments in times of disaster (Landis 1997). The general tradition that the federal government did not give welfare directly to the inhabitants of the separate states was overruled regularly in the face of disaster. The social security legislation of the 1930s was legitimated in part as disaster relief, as a "law of exceptions." Constitutions are weak instruments in the face of crises, and military intervention is almost always legitimated by a declaration of crisis.

But the cognitive certainty about the low probability of military intervention—necessary to trust the effectiveness of civilian bargains within the government, to trust elections as a way of legitimating regimes and, even occasionally, changing regimes—may be backed by a continuing central-local military stalemate, sometimes institutionalized by federalist legal provisions.

INSTITUTIONS, STALEMATES, AND LONG-TERM PLANNING

A careful examination of the above argument will show that the central mechanism in the analysis of danger from military intervention is the reverse of that I have alleged is central to Tilly's analysis. Crises such as war, civil war, forced emigration, genocide, or natural disaster have in common that the most basic institutionalized features of the long-term future become radically uncertain. Doom is on every side. In crisis, rumors can create the "Great Fear," because nothing anchors the future; there is nothing sensible to do next to preserve the long-term future. It is precisely the institutional supports of planning for the future, such as laws or traditions of nonintervention by the military, that stop making sense. Having two governments, the dual power that Tilly takes as central to revolutions, is the most conspicuous form of institutional confusion that makes the shape of the future in the medium or long term radically uncertain.

It is because elsewhere and at other times than this emergency the law will continue to govern that "subordination" of the military to civilian government and its laws is a basis for democratic passing of laws. The exceptions to the law can remain exceptional because they are not doom. Even in an emergency, it makes sense for the English to address petitions to Parliament, in the faith that the emergency will pass. In the midst of the Irish civil war, it did not make much sense for the Irish revolutionaries to address their concerns to Parliament, because Parliament might well not be in their future.

From one point of view, then, a crisis is defined by the fact that anything is possible, including doom and millennium. But that does not mean that therefore "anything" can be planned. Planning is only possible when some substantial part of the future is "known," in the sense of fairly likely for the future up to, say, twenty years. In the United States between, say, the Whiskey Rebellion and the Kansas-Nebraska Act, planning was possible because one knew that the North (as the "national government") was not going to send troops into the South, and because if it did, the South might well win.

That confidence had become thoroughly unraveled by the election of 1860. Again by 1876, the terms of "invasion" of Southern states' labor relations by the national government was "settled," though with a great deal of residual bitterness. From 1861 to 1865, the country was clearly in crisis, specifically on the question of military intervention in the politics of federalism. In 1865, with the military uncertainty much reduced, almost everything seemed possible to the radical reconstructionist Republicans, though it was still difficult to plan anything because enforcement in the South (and the backing of the North for it) was problematic.

By 1876, both military subordination (including that of the South) and a new federalist compromise were fairly solidly in place, and one could develop new institutions on a fairly solid basis. Enough of the future was settled so that railroads in both sections and across the West, for example, made political and corporate economic sense.

The point of this account is that the constitutional provisions and legal conventions involved in military subordination did not change very much and were quite similar in the South and the North. But the institutions of government changed so radically that the military as well as the institutional future became unpredictable, and doom, disintegration, or Reconstruction became the alternatives. After 1876, constitutional subordination, rather than subordination combined with stalemate, became the only protection of the polity from the military, and by then, it was enough. One could start passing laws again the way a spottily democratic federal republic does that.

Coda

I have tried to show that much of Tilly's work here can be conceived as rebuilding the microfoundations of the theory of political rationality. It challenges the simpleminded rational-choice models by showing that people became more politically rational, more able in particular to take the long view as institutions facilitate that.[4] The key to that rebuilding is to realize that macrosociology, and therefore political rationality, has to be a sociology of the long pull. A century is perhaps enough to parliamentarize popular protest in England, *if the process goes on for a century.* Similarly, the centralization and deprovincialization of the civil service and military power in France was well started by Louis XIV and his prime ministers after the defeat of the Fronde and could perhaps be said to have come to an end with the establishment of the École Polytechnique as a source of reliable and skilled higher civil and military servants under Napoleon—a duration of about a century and a half. The nationalization of government in the United States took its first big steps in the 1780s and could be said to be stably established by 1876—about a century. To understand processes of this kind, one has to think of things built to last by people who think things can last and about the conditions under which they think they can last.

The timescale of proletarianization, thought of as transforming careers from the accumulation of property characteristic of personal success in agriculture to occupational commitments characteristic of urban economies, is similar. It can start with people taking jobs in a small textile factory in the foothill reaches of highland streams, but eventually involves people making their lives, in the longest term they can think of upon marriage, planning to live from wages and perhaps promotions. Similarly, the growth of the U.S. Catholic and Jewish populations involves some people building whole new lives in a new place.

Tilly has developed an eye for the details that make up these macroscopic processes. My argument is that this eye is a theoretical innovation, often implicit, about what has to be true of the larger structure *as it bears on small groups and individuals* for people to make long-term plans that change in the social structure.

The modern a priori prejudice is that law or lawlike regulation is the main way to guarantee the future enough so that rational planning, political or personal or economic, makes sense. And it is true that the exquisitely exact equilibria that we get in the stock market reflect not only the expected value of a future stream of real balances of firms, but also a complex filigree of contractual and regulatory law. But the equilibria of barter, or of gold bullion in goldsmith shops and in treasuries of nations, were shaped by the same real balances, and they responded in modern ways to bad harvests or gold found in Peru and Mexico.

I have argued that the military balance between rural caciques and urban governments in Mexico after the revolution of the teens and twenties, or between rural *Blancos* and urban *Colorado* controllers of the Uruguayan national state in the late nineteenth century, or between slave-state militias and the national army in the United States between the adoption of the Constitution and the Civil War, is stable in the same sense as legalized institutions. I have argued further that *in times of crisis* institutions tend to fall apart and that coups d'état mostly happen in times of crisis. So military balances are better than constitutional provisions exactly when nonintervention is most needed.

I believe that my minor emendation to a careless sentence in one of Tilly's essays comes from my following his own strategy where he forgot to do so. Thus it is an argument in favor of this book, rather than against it. And even if I am wrong about all that, imitate the paper on parliamentarization of popular contention if you can. It's a great paper.

Notes

1. A wonderful place to get a feel for what the extraction of conscripts by using local notables in rural villages is like is Tolstoy's short novel *Polikúshka* ([1863] 1965).

2. The best analysis I know of on the difference between speech-making ideology and institutionalized social action is Neil Smelser's *Theory of Collective Behavior* (1962). This is an attempt to describe what sort of thing building values into networks is, which I have left theoretically hermetic here. We have taken E. P. Thompson's (1963) brilliant critique of Smelser's earlier work on the English industrial revolution (Smelser 1959) to mean that the institutionalizing phenomena Smelser was trying to identify and explain were not there. To put it mildly, Thompson falls short of showing that. He does not demonstrate that the phenomena Smelser identified are adequately explained by his processes of making the English working class, perhaps because he did not try.

3. This is one of Tilly's masterpieces. One always learns more about that integration of theory and research that constitutes methodology by analyzing how people brought off their masterpieces than by picking holes in their ordinary contributions to knowledge. The "refereeing" of scientific papers tends to focus on the nitpicking kind of methodology that points to the remaining uncertainties after the evidence is analyzed, rather than on the kind that tells how the uncertainty reduction that is the accomplishment of a masterpiece was brought off. Refereeing is thus bad training for methodological and theoretical thinking, however necessary for selecting papers for a journal. At any rate, Kuhn (1962) taught us to study science by studying its exemplars, to find out what the paradigm really looked like. It is still good advice. The notion that there is really nothing to the exemplars except that they are imitated, which seems to be the coming thing in the sociology of science, is a further corruption of Kuhn's observation. Tilly's piece is an exemplar that deserves to be imitated, because it tells us a lot about why England and the English colonies are different from the rest of the world.

4. To put it in the traditional language, people's discount rates for investment in long-run objectives were lowered drastically by the parliamentarization of popular protest, by the development of chain migration, by the lessening of the probability of military coups d'état, and so on. This, in turn, meant that they thought more, were "more rational," about their long-run futures.

References

Burt, Ronald. 1992. *Structural Holes: The Social Structure of Competition.* Cambridge MA: Harvard University Press.

Carruthers, Bruce. 1996. *City of Capital.* Princeton, NJ: Princeton University Press.

Filgueira, Fernando. 1996. "Explaining Democratic Success and Failure: Elite Parties and Soldiers in Argentina and Uruguay, 1890–1930." Unpublished manuscript. Evanston, IL: Northwestern University.

Granovetter, Mark. 1985. "Economic Action and Social Structure: The

Problem of Embeddedness." *American Journal of Sociology* 91, no. 3 (November): 481–510.

't Hart, Marjolein. 1994. "Intercity Rivalries and the Making of the Dutch State." In Charles Tilly and Wim P. Blockmans, eds., *Cities and the Rise of States in Europe, A.D. 1000 to 1800*. Boulder CO: Westview Press, pp. 196–217.

Heimer, Carol A. 1992. "Universalism and Particularism." In Nitin Nohria and Robert G. Eccles, eds., *Networks and Organizations: Structure, Form, and Action*. Boston: Harvard School of Business Press, pp. 143–164.

Kuhn, Thomas S. 1962. *The Structure of Scientific Revolutions*. Chicago: University of Chicago Press.

Landis, Michele. 1997. "Next Time Let ME Be 'Tried by Fire': Natural Disaster Relief and the Origins of the American Welfare State, 1789–1874." *Northwestern University Law Review* (forthcoming).

Mannheim, Karl. [1929] 1936. *Ideology and Utopia: An Introduction to the Sociology of Knowledge*. New York: Harvest Books/Harcourt Brace.

Skocpol, Theda. 1979. *States and Social Revolutions: A Comparative Analysis of France, Russia, and China*. New York: Cambridge University Press.

Smelser, Neil J. 1959. *Social Change in the Industrial Revolution: An Application of Theory to the British Cotton Industry*. Chicago: University of Chicago Press.

———. 1962. *Theory of Collective Behavior*. New York: Free Press.

Stinchcombe, Arthur L. 1995. "Lustration as a Problem of the Social Basis of Constitutionalism." *Law and Social Inquiry* 20, no. 1 (Winter): 245–273.

Thompson, E. P. 1963. *The Making of the English Working Class*. New York: Vintage Books.

Tolstoy, Leo. [1863] 1965. "Polikúshka." In Earnest J. Simmons, ed., *Leo Tolstoy: Short Novels*, trans. Louise and Aylmer Maude. New York: Modern Library, pp. 214–278.

Veyne, Paul. [1976] 1990. *Bread and Circuses: Historical Sociology and Political Pluralism*. London: A. Lane, Penguin Press, and Paris: Éditions du Seuil.

White, Harrison C., Scott Boorman, and Ronald L. Breiger. 1976. "Social Structure from Multiple Networks, I: Blockmodels of Roles and Positions." *American Journal of Sociology* 81: 730–780.

Selected Scholarly Publications by Charles Tilly, 1959–1996

1959 "Civil Constitution and Counter-Revolution in Southern Anjou." *French Historical Studies* 1: 172–199.

1960 (with Arnold S. Feldman). "The Interaction of Social and Physical Space." *American Sociological Review* 25: 877–884.

1961 "Occupational Rank and Grade of Residence in a Metropolis." *American Journal of Sociology* 67: 323–330.

"Local Conflicts in the Vendée before the Rebellion of 1793." *French Historical Studies* 2: 209–231.

"Some Problems in the History of the Vendée." *American Historical Review* 67: 19–33.

1962 *Recent Changes in Delaware's Population.* Newark: Delaware Agricultural Experiment Station, DAES Bulletin No. 347.

"Rivalités de bourgs et conflits de partis dans les Mauges." *Revue du Bas-Poitou et des Provinces de l'Ouest*, no. 4 (July–August): 3–15.

1963 "The Analysis of a Counter-Revolution." *History and Theory* 3: 30–58.

1964 *The Vendée.* Cambridge, MA: Harvard University Press.

"Reflections on the Revolutions of Paris." *Social Problems* 12: 99–121.

1965 *Migration to an American City.* Newark: Division of Urban Affairs and School of Agriculture, University of Delaware.

(with Wagner Jackson and Barry Kay). *Race and Residence in Wilmington.* New York: Teachers College Press.

(with James Rule). *Measuring Political Upheaval.* Princeton, NJ: Center of International Studies, Princeton University.

"Metropolitan Boston's Social Structure." In Richard Bolan, ed., *Social Structures and Human Problems in the Boston Metropolitan Area.* Cambridge, MA: Joint Center for Urban Studies.

1966   "In Defence of Jargon." *Canadian Historical Association Record*, pp. 178–186.

1967   "Anthropology on the Town." *Habitat* 10: 20–25.

(with C. Harold Brown). "On Uprooting, Kinship, and the Auspices of Migration." *International Journal of Comparative Sociology* 8: 139–164.

"The State of Urbanization." *Comparative Studies in Society and History* 10: 100–113.

1968   "Race and Migration to the American City." In James Q. Wilson, ed., *The Metropolitan Enigma*. Cambridge, MA: Harvard University Press.

1969   "The Forms of Urbanization." In Talcott Parsons, ed., *American Sociology*. New York: Basic Books.

"Methods for the Study of Collective Violence." In Ralph W. Conant and Molly Apple Levin, eds., *Problems in Research on Community Violence*. New York: Praeger.

"Collective Violence in European Perspective." In Hugh D. Graham and Ted R. Gurr, eds., *Violence in America: Vol. 1*. Washington, DC: Government Printing Office.

1970   "Migration to American Cities." In Daniel P. Moynihan, ed., *Toward a National Urban Policy*. New York: Harper.

"Clio and Minerva." In John C. McKinney and Edward A. Tiryakian, eds., *Theoretical Sociology: Perspectives and Developments*. New York: Appleton-Century-Crofts.

"The Changing Place of Collective Violence." In Melvin Richter, ed., *Essays in Theory and History*. Cambridge, MA: Harvard University Press.

(with Joe Feagin). "Boston's Experiment with Rent Subsidies." *Journal of the American Institute of Planners* 36: 323–329.

1971   (with Edward Shorter). "The Shape of Strikes in France, 1830–1960." *Comparative Studies in Society and History* 13: 60–86.

(with David Landes, ed. and co-author). *History as Social Science*. Englewood Cliffs, NJ: Prentice-Hall.

(with Richard Tilly). "Agenda for European Economic History in the 1970s." *Journal of Economic History* 31: 184–198.

(with Edward Shorter). "Le déclin de la grève violente en France de 1890 à 1935." *Le Mouvement Social* 76: 95–118.

1972   (with James Rule). "1830 and the Un-Natural History of Revolution." *Journal of Social Issues* 28: 49–76.

(with David Snyder). "Hardship and Collective Violence in France." *American Sociological Review* 37: 520–532.

(with Joe Feagin and Constance Williams). *Subsidizing the Poor: Boston's Experiment with Rent Subsidies.* Lexington, MA: D. C. Heath.

"Quantification in History, as Seen from France." In Val Lorwin and Jacob Price, eds., *The Dimensions of the Past.* New Haven, CT: Yale University Press.

"How Protest Modernized in France, 1845 to 1855." In William Aydelotte, Allan Bogue, and Robert Fogel, eds., *The Dimensions of Quantitative Research in History.* Princeton, NJ: Princeton University Press.

"The Modernization of Political Conflict in France." In Edward B. Harvey, ed., *Perspectives on Modernization: Essays in Memory of Ian Weinberg.* Toronto: University of Toronto Press.

1973　"Does Modernization Breed Revolution?" *Comparative Politics* 5: 425–447.

"Population and Pedagogy in France." *History of Education Quarterly* 13: 113–128.

(with A. Q. Lodhi). "Urbanization, Criminality, and Collective Violence in Nineteenth-Century France." *American Journal of Sociology* 79: 296–318.

(with Edward Shorter). "Les vagues de grèves en France." *Annales: Economies, Sociétés, Civilisations* 28: 857–887.

"The Chaos of the Living City." In Herbert Hirsch and David Perry, eds., *Violence as Politics.* New York: Harper & Row.

"Do Communities Act?" *Sociological Inquiry* 43: 209–240.

"Computers in Historical Research." *Computers and the Humanities* 7: 323–335.

1974　*An Urban World.* Boston: Little, Brown.

(with Edward Shorter). *Strikes in France, 1830–1968.* Cambridge and New York: Cambridge University Press.

"Town and Country in Revolution." In John W. Lewis, ed., *Peasant Rebellion and Communist Revolution in Asia.* Stanford, CA: Stanford University Press.

(with Lynn Lees). "Le peuple de juin 1848." *Annales: Economies, Sociétés, Civilisations* 29: 1061–1091.

1975　"Revolutions and Collective Violence." In Fred I. Greenstein and Nelson Polsby, eds., *Handbook of Political Science. Vol. 3.* Reading, MA: Addison-Wesley.

"Reflections on the History of European Statemaking," "Food Supply and Public Order in Modern Europe," and "Postscript: European Statemaking and Theories of Political Transformation." Charles Tilly, ed., *The Formation of National States in Western Europe* (chaps. 1, 6, and 9). Princeton, NJ: Princeton University Press.

(with Louise A. Tilly and Richard Tilly). *The Rebellious Century, 1830–1930.* Cambridge, MA: Harvard University Press.

1976   "Rural Collective Action in Modern Europe." In Joseph Spielberg and Scott Whiteford, eds., *Forging Nations.* East Lansing: Michigan State University Press.

"Peeping through the Windows of the Wealthy." *Journal of Urban History* 2: 131–134.

"Major Forms of Collective Action in Modern Europe." Theory and Society 3: 365–375.

1977   "Getting It Together in Burgundy, 1675–1975." *Theory and Society* 4: 479–504.

"Talking Modern." *Peasant Studies* 6: 66–68.

"Collective Action in England and America, 1765–1775." In Richard Maxwell Brown and Don Fehrenbacher, eds., *Tradition, Conflict, and Modernization: Perspectives on the American Revolution.* New York: Academic Press.

1978   "Migration in Modern European History." In William McNeill and Ruth Adams, eds., *Human Migration: Patterns, Implications, Policies.* Bloomington: Indiana University Press.

From Mobilization to Revolution. Reading, MA: Addison-Wesley.

"The Historical Study of Vital Processes," and "Questions and Conclusions." In Charles Tilly, ed., *Historical Studies of Changing Fertility.* Princeton, NJ: Princeton University Press.

"Peasants against Capitalism and the State." *Agricultural History* 52: 407–416.

1979   "Repertoires of Contention in America and Britain." In Mayer N. Zald and John D. McCarthy, eds., *The Dynamics of Social Movements.* Cambridge, MA: Winthrop.

"Did the Cake of Custom Break?" In John Merriman, ed., *Consciousness and Class Experience in Nineteenth-Century Europe.* New York: Holmes & Meier.

1980   "Historical Sociology." In Scott G. McNall and Gary N. Howe, eds., *Current Perspectives in Social Theory: Vol. 1.* Greenwich, CT: JAI Press.

"Les Manchester du Nouveau Monde." *Urbi* 3: 102–105.

"Two Callings of Social History." *Theory and Society* 9: 679–681.

(with Louise A. Tilly). "Stalking the Bourgeois Family." *Social Science History* 4: 251–260.

1981   "Introduction," and "The Web of Contention in Eighteenth-Century Cities." In Louise A. Tilly and Charles Tilly, eds., *Class Conflict and Collective Action*. Beverly Hills, CA: Sage.

"Sinews of War." In Per Torsvik, ed., *Mobilization, Center-Periphery Structures, and Nation-Building*. Bergen: Universitetsforlaget.

As Sociology Meets History. New York: Academic Press.

1982   "Britain Creates the Social Movement." In James Cronin and Jonathan Schneer, eds., *Social Conflict and the Political Order in Modern Britain*. London: Croom Helm.

"Charivaris, Repertoires, and Urban Politics." In John Merriman, ed., *French Cities in the Nineteenth Century*. London: Hutchinson.

(with R. A. Schweitzer). "How London and Its Conflicts Changed Shape, 1758–1834." *Historical Methods* 5: 67–77.

"Vecchio e nuovo nella storia sociale." *Passato e Presente* 1: 31–54.

"Routine Conflicts and Peasant Rebellions in Seventeenth-Century France." In Robert P. Weller and Scott E. Guggenheim, eds., *Power and Protest in the Countryside: Studies of Rural Unrest in Asia, Europe, and Latin America*. Durham, NC: Duke University Press.

"Proletarianization and Rural Collective Action in East Anglia and Elsewhere, 1500–1900." *Peasant Studies* 10: 5–34.

1983   "Où va l'histoire?" (Contribution to symposium.) *Le Débat* (January): 182–187.

"Violenza e azione collettiva in Europa: Riflessioni storico-comparate." In Donatella della Porta and Gianfranco Pasquino, eds., *Terrorismo e violenza politica. Tre casi a confronto: Stati Uniti, Germania e Giappone*. Bologna: Il Mulino.

"Flows of Capital and Forms of Industry in Europe, 1500–1900." *Theory and Society* 12: 123–143.

(with Roberto Franzosi). "A British View of American Strikes." *Industrial Relations Law Journal* 5: 426–439.

"Karl Marx, Historian." *Michigan Quarterly Review* 22: 633–642.

"Speaking Your Mind without Elections, Surveys, or Social Movements." *Public Opinion Quarterly* 47: 461–478.

1984   "The Old New Social History and the New Old Social History." *Review* 7: 363–406.

"History: Notes on Urban Images of Historians." In Lloyd Rodwin and

Robert M. Hollister, eds., *Cities of the Mind: Images and Themes of the City in the Social Sciences*. New York: Plenum.

"Social Movements and National Politics." In Charles Bright and Susan Harding, eds., *Statemaking and Social Movements: Essays in History and Theory*. Ann Arbor: University of Michigan Press.

"Les origines du répertoire de l'action collective contemporaine en France et en Grande Bretagne." *Vingtième Siècle* 4: 89–108.

"Demographic Origins of the European Proletariat." In David Levine, ed., *Proletarianization and Family Life*. Orlando, FL: Academic Press.

1985   *Big Structures, Large Processes, Huge Comparisons*. New York: Russell Sage Foundation. "War and the Power of Warmakers in Western Europe and Elsewhere." In Peter Wallensteen, Johan Galtung, and Carlos Portales, eds., *Global Militarization*. Boulder, CO: Westview Press.

"De Londres (1768) à Paris (1788)." In Jean Nicolas, ed., *Mouvements populaires et conscience sociale, XVIe–XIXe siècles*. Paris: Maloine.

"Retrieving European Lives." In Olivier Zunz, ed., *Reliving the Past: The Worlds of Social History*. Chapel Hill: University of North Carolina Press.

"War Making and State Making as Organized Crime." In Peter Evans, Dietrich Rueschemeyer, and Theda Skocpol, eds., *Bringing the State Back In*. Cambridge: Cambridge University Press.

"Connecting Domestic and International Conflicts, Past and Present." In Urs Luterbacher and Michael D. Ward, eds., *Dynamic Models of International Conflict*. Boulder, CO: Lynne Rienner Publishers.

"Neat Analyses of Untidy Processes." *International Labor and Working Class History* 27: 4–19.

"Models and Realities of Popular Collective Action." *Social Research* 52: 717–747.

1986   "The Tyranny of Here and Now." *Sociological Forum* 1: 179–188.

The Contentious French. Cambridge, MA: Belknap Press of Harvard University Press.

"European Violence and Collective Action since 1700." *Social Research* 53: 159–184.

"Since Gilgamesh." *Social Research* 53: 391–410.

"Writing Wrongs in Sociology." *Sociological Forum* 1: 543–552.

"Space for Capital, Space for States." *Theory and Society* 15: 301–309.

1987   "Scioperi e conflitti sociali in Europa." (Contribution to symposium.) *Passato e Presente* 12: 12–17.

"The Analysis of Popular Collective Action." *European Journal of Operational Research* 30: 223–229.

"GBS + GCL = ?" *Connections* 10: 94–105.

"Family History, Social History, and Social Change." *Journal of Family History* 12: 319–330.

"Shrugging Off the Nineteenth-Century Incubus." In Jan Berting and Wim Blockmans, eds., *Beyond Progress and Development.* Aldershot: Avebury.

"Formalization and Quantification in Historical Analysis." In Konrad H. Jarausch and Wilhelm Schröder, eds., *Quantitative History of Society and Economy: Some International Studies.* St. Katharinen: Scripts Mercaturae Verlag.

1988   "Misreading, Then Re-Reading, Nineteenth-Century Social Change." In Barry Wellman and S. D. Berkowitz, eds., *Social Structures: A Network Approach.* Cambridge: Cambridge University Press.

"Social Movements, Old and New." In Louis Kriesberg, Bronislaw Misztal, and Janusz Mucha, eds., *Social Movements as a Factor of Change in the Contemporary World.* Research in Social Movements, Conflicts, and Change, vol. 10. Greenwich, CT: JAI Press.

(with Mark Granovetter). "Inequality and Labor Processes." In Neil J. Smelser, ed., *Handbook of Sociology.* Newbury Park, CA: Sage.

"Solidary Logics: Conclusions." *Theory and Society* 17: 451–458.

"Future History." *Theory and Society* 17: 703–712.

1989   "State and Counterrevolution in France." *Social Research* 56: 71–97.

"The Geography of European Statemaking and Capitalism since 1500." In Eugene Genovese and Leonard Hochberg, eds., *Geographic Perspectives in History.* Oxford: Blackwell.

"Gerarchie spaziali, mutamento economico, formazione degli Stati." In Franco Andreucci and Alessandra Pescarolo, eds., *Gli spazi del potere.* Forence: Istituto Ernesto Ragionieri.

"Theories and Realities," and "Introduction [to Part IV]." In Leopold Haimson and Charles Tilly, eds., *Strikes, Wars, and Revolutions in an International Perspective: Strike Waves in the Late Nineteenth and Early Twentieth Centuries.* Cambridge: Cambridge University Press.

"Collective Violence in European Perspective." In Ted Robert Gurr, ed., *Violence in America. Volume 2: Protest, Rebellion, Reform.* Newbury Park, CA: Sage.

"History, Sociology, and Dutch Collective Action." *Tijdschrift voor Sociale Geschiedenis* 15: 142–157.

"Tkacze, Kopacze i Egzegeci w Historii Spolecznej." *Historyka* 19: 33–45.

"Cities and States in Europe." *Theory and Society* 18: 563–584.

1990   *Coercion, Capital, and European States, A.D. 990–1990.* Oxford: Blackwell Publishers.

"Transplanted Networks." In Virginia Yans-McLaughlin, ed., *Immigration Reconsidered: History, Sociology, and Politics.* New York: Oxford University Press.

"How (and What) Are Historians Doing?" *American Behavioral Scientist* 33: 685–711.

"George Caspar Homans and the Rest of Us." *Theory and Society* 19: 261–268.

1991   "Changing Forms of Revolution." In E. E. Rice, ed., *Revolution and Counter-Revolution.* Oxford: Basil Blackwell.

"War and State Power." *Middle East Report* 21, no. 171 (July–August): 38–40.

"Domination, Resistance, Compliance . . . Discourse." *Sociological Forum* 6: 593–602.

"Ethnic Conflict in the Soviet Union." *Theory and Society* 20: 569–580.

"Police, Etat, contestation." *Cahiers de la Sécurité Intérieure* 7: 13–18.

1992   "Where Do Rights Come From?" In Lars Mjøset, ed., *Contributions to the Comparative Study of Development.* Oslo: Institute for Social Research.

"War in History." *Sociological Forum* 7: 187–197.

"Réclamer Viva Voce." *Cultures et Conflits* 5: 109–126.

"Conclusions." In Leopold Haimson and Giulio Sapelli, eds., *Strikes, Social Conflict, and the First World War: An International Perspective.* Milan: Feltrinelli. Fondazione Giangiacomo Feltrinelli, *Annali* 1990–1991.

"Prisoners of the State." *International Social Science Journal* 44: 329–342.

(with Louise A. Tilly and Richard Tilly). "European Economic and Social History in the 1990s." *Journal of European Economic History* 20: 645–672.

"The Europe of Columbus and Bayazid." *Middle East Report* 22, no. 178 (September–October): 2–5.

"L'Amérique en Théorie." In Christine Fauré and Tom Bishop, eds., *L'Amérique des Français.* Paris: François Bourin.

"K cemu je dobra historie mesta?" *Sociologicky casopis* (Prague) 28: 437–450.

"Cities, Bourgeois, and Revolution in France." In M'hammed Sabour, ed., *Liberté, Égalité, Fraternité: Bicentenaire de la Grande Révolution Française.*

University of Joensuu Publications in Social Sciences, 14. Joensu, Finland: Joensuun Yliopisto.

"Stein Rokkans begrepsmessige kart over Europa." In Bernt Hagtvet, ed., *Politikk mellom økonomi og kultur: Stein Rokkan som politisk sosiolog og forskningsinspirator.* Oslo: Ad Notam Gylendal.

"Futures of European States." *Social Research* 59: 705–717.

"Conflitto sociale." *Enciclopedia della Scienze Sociali* 2: 259–270.

1993   "The Bourgeois Gentilshommes of Revolutionary Theory." *Contention* 2: 153–158.

European Revolutions, 1492–1992. Oxford: Blackwell Publishers.

"Contentious Repertoires in Great Britain, 1758–1834." *Social Science History* 17: 253–280.

"Cambio social y revolución en Europa: 1492–1992." *Historia Social* 15: 71–100.

"National Self-Determination as a Problem for All of Us." *Daedalus* 122: 29–36.

"Blanding In." *Sociological Forum* 8: 497–506.

"Changing States, Changing Struggles." *South African Sociological Review* 5: 1–13.

"The Long Run of European State Formation." In Wim Blockmans and Jean-Philippe Genet, eds., *Visions sur le développement des Etats européens: Théories et historiographies de l'Etat moderne* (pp. 137–150). Rome: Ecole Française de Rome.

1994   "Stratification and Inequality." In Peter N. Stearns, ed., *Encyclopedia of Social History* (pp. 723–728). New York: Garland.

"States and Nationalism in Europe, 1492–1992." *Theory and Society* 23: 131–146.

"Collective Violence in Early Modern Europe." In Giorgio Chittolini, ed., *Two Thousand Years of Warfare.* Danbury, CT: Grolier.

"History and Sociological Imagining." *Tocqueville Review* 15: 57–74.

(with Chris Tilly). "Capitalist Work and Labor Markets." In Neil J. Smelser and Richard Swedberg, eds., *Handbook of Economic Sociology* New York: Russell Sage Foundation, and Princeton, NJ: Princeton University Press.

"Social Movements as Historically Specific Clusters of Political Performances." *Berkeley Journal of Sociology* 38 (1993–1994): 1–30.

"The Time of States." *Social Research* 61: 269–295.

"Entanglements of European Cities and States." In Charles Tilly and Wim

Blockmans, eds., *Cities and the Rise of States in Europe, A.D. 1000–1800.* Boulder, CO: Westview Press.

(with Eiko Ikegami). "State Formation and Contention in Japan and France." In James L. McClain, John M. Merriman, and Ugawa Kaoru, eds., *Edo and Paris: Urban Life and the State in the Early Modern Era.* Ithaca, NY: Cornell University Press.

"Afterword: Political Memories in Space and Time." In Jonathan Boyarin, ed., *Remapping Memory: The Politics of TimeSpace.* Minneapolis: University of Minnesota Press.

"In Search of Revolution." *Theory and Society* 23: 799–803.

"Softcore Solipsism." *Labour/Le Travail* 34: 259–268.

1995   "Globalization Threatens Labor's Rights." *International Labor and Working Class History* 47: 1–23.

"Stein Rokkan et les Identités Politiques." *Revue Internationale de Politique Comparée* 2: 27–45.

"To Explain Political Processes." *American Journal of Sociology* 100: 1594–1610.

"State-Incited Violence, 1900–1999." *Political Power and Social Theory* 9: 161–179.

Popular Contention in Great Britain, 1758–1834. Cambridge, MA: Harvard University Press.

"Democracy Is a Lake." In George Reid Andrews and Herrick Chapman, eds., *The Social Construction of Democracy.* New York: New York University Press, and Basingstoke: Macmillan.

"Macrosociology Past and Future." *Newsletter of the Comparative & Historical Section,* American Sociological Association, 8: 1, 3, 4.

"Citizenship, Identity and Social History," and "The Emergence of Citizenship in France and Elsewhere." In Charles Tilly, ed., *Citizenship, Identity, and Social History.* International Review of Social History Supplement 3. Cambridge: Cambridge University Press.

1996   "Contention and the Urban Poor in Latin America." In Silvia Arrom and Servando Ortoll, eds., *Riots in the Cities: Popular Politics and the Urban Poor in Latin America, 1765–1910.* New York: Scholarly Resources.

(with Doug McAdam and Sidney Tarrow). "To Map Contentious Politics." *Mobilization* 1: 17–34.

"Rich Göran's Almanac." *Arkiv för Studier i Arbetarrörelsens Historia* 66: 55–57.

"What Good Is Urban History?" *Journal of Urban History* 22: 702–719.

"Why Birth Rates Fell." *Population and Development Review* 22: 557–562.

"The State of Nationalism." *Critical Review* 10: 299–306.

"Invisible Elbow." *Sociological Forum* 11: 589–601.

"Donald Levine, Henry Petroski, and Boutros Boutros-Ghali." *Sociological Forum* 11: 669–673.

Index

Acker, Joan, 27–28
agendas for inquiry, 23
alternatives: to narrative, 22–25; need for, 18–19. *See also* possibilities
Americas: migration to, 275–77, 337. *See also* United States
Anderson, Barbara Gallatin, 76
Anderson, Perry, 133
Anderson, Robert T., 76
Ariès, Philippe, 247–49, 250–52, 262
Aristotle, 200–201
armies. *See* military forces
Aron, Raymond, 59, 64
associational life: industrialization and, 75; parliamentarization and, 226–27, 235–36, 238–41; social change and, 74–77, 91, 92; violence and, 91, 92
Auster, Paul, 43
avoidance, of social interaction, 1

Bairoch, Paul, 327
balanced-development theory, 114–19
Balzac, Honoré de, 73
banditry: revolutions and, 127–28; state makers' use of, 169–70
Bean, Richard, 174–75
birth rates, 301–2, 335–36. *See also* fertility rates
Blanqui, Auguste, 62
Blaschke, Karlheinz, 323, 327
Borges, Jorge Luis, 17
bottom-up hierarchies. *See* indirect rule
bottom-up models, of democratization, 193, 195

bourgeois: as capitalists, 135; children and, 255–56; the French Revolution as revolution of, 134, 150, 154–55
Bower, Gordon, 20–21
British Isles: migration from, 276, 277, 337. *See also* Great Britain; England
bureaucracies, 149, 179; definitions produced by, 265–66; futures and, 394, 395–96

capital, 135–36, 137
capital accumulation: parliamentarization and, 222, 237; proletarianization and, 296, 310–15, 318, 348; state making shaped by, 168–69. *See also* war making, financing of
capitalism, 135, 210; proletarianization and, 296–97, 307–9, 330, 346–47; stages of, 173–74
capitalists, 134; definition of, 135. *See also* bourgeois
career migration, 271–73, 390
causal reasoning, 23
causes, search for, 24, 32
chain migration, 270–73, 275, 276, 391, 399–400
Chartism, 207, 208, 240
children: demographics of, 247–62; family strategies and, 252–56; life expectancy and, 253–56; mortality rates of, 253–55, 256; pedagogy and, 249–50, 256–61; popular mentalities and, 251–52, 253, 260; proletarian-

About the Authors

After teaching at Delaware, Harvard, Toronto, Michigan, and the New School for Social Research, **Charles Tilly** is now Joseph L. Buttenwieser Professor of Social Science at Columbia University. His recent books include *Durable Inequality* (Univeristy of California Press) and, with his son Chris Tilly, *Work Under Capitalism* (Westview Press). True to his belief that you should say things clearly the first time, none of his books has had a subtitle.

Arthur L. Stinchcombe has retired. He holds part-time and honorary appointments at Northwestern University and the American Bar Foundation. Besides Northwestern, he has worked at Johns Hopkins, University of California at Berkeley, Essex University, University of Chicago, University of Arizona, and University of Bergen.